Re-forming Britain

Re-forming Britain considers the nature and practice of architectural modernism in inter-war Britain in a new light. Bringing hitherto little-considered protagonists and projects to the fore, it argues that rather than being an imported idiom, the new architecture in Britain formed part of an ongoing attempt to make a modern nation.

Spanning the period 1925–42, the book focuses on the key sites from and through which architectural modernism emerged in the UK. Part one considers the main arena in which a will to modernize Britain developed in the 1920s. In parts two and three the author documents, contextualizes and explains how this modernizing will was given modernist form, discussing the work of architects such as Wells Coates, Maxwell Fry, and Connell and Ward, and their allied ventures with like-minded reformers in other fields. These collaborations produced 'narratives of modernity': buildings, projects, exhibitions and books, through which, the book argues, modernist reformers were able to persuade politicians, and those with influence upon them, that modernism was the means to re-form the nation.

Re-forming Britain offers the first in-depth analysis of well-known modernist schemes such as Kensal House and the Pioneer Health Centre but also brings previously little-studied or unknown activities to light. This important work invites a new understanding of the nature of architectural modernism in inter-war Britain and the ways in which it ultimately gave form to post-war Britain.

Elizabeth Darling trained as an art and architectural historian at University College London. Since then she has taught, researched and published in the history of nineteenth- and twentieth-century architecture. She is now a Senior Lecturer in the Department of History of Art at Oxford Brookes University.

Re-forming Britain

Narratives of modernity before reconstruction

Elizabeth Darling

Routledge
Taylor & Francis Group

LONDON AND NEW YORK

First published 2007 by Routledge
2 Park Square, Milton Park, Abingdon, OX14 4RN

Simultaneously published in the USA and Canada
by Routledge
270 Madison Avenue, New York, NY10016

Routledge is an imprint of the Taylor & Francis Group, an informa business

Typeset in Univers by Bookcraft Ltd, Stroud, Gloucestershire
Printed and bound in Great Britain by TJ International Ltd, Padstow, Cornwall

British Library Cataloguing in Publication Data
A catalogue record for this book is available from the British Library

Library of Congress Cataloging in Publication Data
Darling, Elizabeth
Re-forming Britain: narratives of modernity before reconstruction / Elizabeth Darling.
  p. cm.
  Includes bibliographical references and index.
  1. Modern movement (Architecture)—Great Britain. 2. Architecture and society—
  Great Britain—History—20th century. I. Title.
NA968.5M64D37 2007
720.941'0904—dc22   2006022257

ISBN10: 0-415-33407-1 (hbk)
ISBN10: 0-415-33408-X (pbk)
ISBN10: 0-203-41462-4 (ebk)

ISBN13: 978-0-415-33407-5 (hbk)
ISBN13: 978-0-415-33408-2 (pbk)
ISBN13: 978-0-203-41462-0 (ebk)

For Anthony and Morag Darling

Contents

Illustration credits

Every effort has been made to contact and acknowledge copyright owners, but the editor and publishers would be pleased to have any errors or omissions brought to their attention so that corrections may be published at a later printing.

The Architect & Building News: 2.7, 2.10, 4.6, 4.7.
Ascot Gas Water Heaters Ltd, *Flats Municipal and Private Enterprise Ltd.*: 5.2, 5.6, 5.7, 5.8, 5.9, 5.10.
City of London and London Metropolitan Archive: 3.1, 4.1, 4.2.
Crown Copyright: 5.12, 5.17.
© Elizabeth Darling: 3.6, 4.8.
Design & Industries Association Publication: *Design for Today*, November 1934: 4.3, 4.4, 4.5.
With permission of Edinburgh University Library, Special Collections Department: 6.1, 6.2.
Estate of Abram Games: 6.7 (and cover).
E. O. Hoppé © Curatorial Assistance, Inc. Los Angeles: 2.5, 2.6.
E. Lanchester, *'Charles Laughton & I'*, London: Faber & Faber, 1938 (photog. Joan Woolcombe):1.3
David Lawrence, © davidlawrenceeverything.com: 3.2.
National Grid PLC: 5.11, 5.13, 5.14, 5.15, 5.16.
Origin Housing Group: 1.1.
Reproduced with permission of the Trustees of the Mass-Observation Archive, Copyright © The Trustees of the Mass-Observation Archive: 6.3, 6.4, 6.5, 6.6.
RIBA Library Drawings Collection: 2.1, 2.2, 6.3.
Dell & Wainwright/RIBA Library Photographs Collection: 1.4.
RIBA Library Photographs Collection: 2.3, 2.4, 2.8, 2.9, 2.11, 2.12, 3.4, 3.5, 5.1, 5.3, 5.4, 5.5, 5.18.
Richard St John Harrison: 3.3.
The Harry Simpson Memorial Library Trust: 1.2.

Acknowledgements

This book has been a long time in the making; its completion reflects the support of a great many people.

Much of this book was researched and written while I was a member of staff at the University of Brighton and I wish to thank the Faculty Research Support Fund of the Faculty of Arts and Architecture and my former Head of School, Anne Boddington, for their support of my research.

I am immensely grateful to the Canadian Centre for Architecture for making me a Research Associate and facilitating my access to the Wells Coates archive. I would also like to acknowledge the support of the Society of Architectural Historians of Great Britain, and the School of Arts and Humanities' Research Fund, Oxford Brookes University, for grants which covered some of the costs of the book's illustrations, as well as thank those archivists and librarians who were kind enough to waive permissions costs. At Routledge, my thanks are due to Caroline Mallinder, Hannah Tylee and Georgina Johnson, and at Bookcraft, Matthew Brown.

The often painful process of completing the manuscript, and the more enjoyable task of researching and thinking about it, was made considerably easier by the help, friendship and insights of the following, to whom I express my thanks and appreciation: Kathryn Ager, Iain Boyd Whyte, Marjorie Cleaver, Genevieve Dalpé, Luis Diaz, Josephine Dixon, Stuart Durant, Alice Friedman, Adrian Forty, Eleanor Gawne, Hilde Heynen, Claire Hoskin, Trevor Keeble, Andrea Kuchembuck, Phyllis Lambert, Glenn Longden Thurgood, Helen Potkin, Alan Powers, Mary Smith, Alexis Sornin, Dawn Whitaker, and the staff at the British Architectural Library. I wish to acknowledge especially the support and friendship of Alex Buchanan, David Lawrence, John McKean, Helen Richards, Andrea Tanner and Lesley Whitworth who read drafts of the manuscript, talked through particularly knotty themes and ideas with me, and otherwise put up with an increasingly distracted friend. All errors, blunders and oversights remain, of course, my own.

Ultimately, it has been my family who have made it possible for me to bring this project to fruition and, indeed, to have even contemplated embarking on it in the first place. My sister Marion Wood, my brother-in-law Kenneth Wood, and nephews Thomas Wood and Harry Wood, have, through a thousand acts of kindness, done more than they know to keep me sane when this project was in its most difficult stages. Above all, it is to my parents, Anthony and Morag Darling, that I owe the deepest and most heartfelt thanks, and it is as a small act of gratitude for a lifetime of support that I dedicate to them this book.

Abbreviations

AA	The Architectural Association
AAJ	*Architectural Association Journal*
ABN	*The Architect and Building News*
AD	*Architectural Design*
AIA	Artists' International Association
AJ	*The Architects' Journal*
AR	*The Architectural Review*
ARIBA	Associate of the Royal Institute of British Architects
BAL	British Architectural Library
BBC	British Broadcasting Corporation
BCGA	British Commercial Gas Association
BTE	Building Trades Exhibition
BUD	Building Uses Department (of Venesta Plywood Manufacturers)
CAI	Council for Art and Industry
CCA	Canadian Centre for Architecture
CIAM	Congrès Internationaux d'Architecture Moderne
CIRPAC	Comité International pour la Réalisation des Problèmes d'Architecture Contemporaine
CL	*Country Life*
CPGB	Communist Party of Great Britain
CPRE	Council for the Protection of Rural England
DIA	The Design and Industries Association
DMIHE	*Daily Mail* Ideal Home Exhibition
EPIC	Exhibition for Planned Industrial Construction
GCTPA	Garden Cities and Town Planning Association
GLCC	Gas, Light and Coke Company
HCT	Housing Centre Trust
HFL	House Furnishing Ltd
KHT	Kensington Housing Association and Trust
LCC	London County Council
LMA	London Metropolitan Archive
MARS Group	The Modern Architectural Research Group
NA	National Archive

NSA	Nursery School Association
NHFO	New Homes for Old Exhibitions
NSPG	North St Pancras Group of the Saint Pancras House Improvement Society
PEP	Political and Economic Planning
PHT	Pioneer Housing Trust
RIBA	The Royal Institute of British Architects
SPHIS	Saint Pancras House Improvement Society
SPRND	School for Planning and Research for National Development
TCG	Twentieth Century Group
UFC	Under Forty Club
V&A	Victoria & Albert Museum

Introduction

In 1956, the Arts Council held an exhibition, '45–'55, Ten Years of British Architecture'. Including sections on housing, school building and the South Bank Exhibition of 1951, in its coverage of both building type and style, the exhibition demonstrated that a remarkable transformation had taken place across Britain: socially and architecturally it was now a modernist nation. John Summerson, in his introduction to the accompanying catalogue, summarized the shift:

> In 1945, for the first time in Britain's history, building effort was canalized into great national schemes … designed for the welfare of the country at large. The contrast with 1938, with its lavish cinemas, its luxury flats, office blocks, town halls, and civic centres was complete: the war interval had constituted the most dramatic full stop in the history of building of Britain.[1]

It is the contrast between the lavish cinemas of 1938 and the great national schemes of 1945 that forms the starting point for this book. Its concern is to address the question, implicit in Summerson's observation, of how an approach to architecture which had been entirely marginal before the war achieved such hegemony so soon after hostilities ceased? Furthermore, how could it subsequently have gone on to exert a dominance over architectural and planning education and practice which has only begun to diminish significantly in the last twenty years? With the exception of the work of Andrew Saint and Nicholas Bullock, this has not been an issue which architectural historians have considered.[2] The fact remains, as Saint has observed that, 'as yet we have only the haziest of historical notions about how these ideas entered architectural currency in Britain during the early 1930s and '40s'.[3]

Problematic

We may as yet have little idea about how modernism was absorbed into architectural discourse in inter-war and wartime Britain; nevertheless there has been a considerable

1

amount of scholarship that has documented the modernist work which was produced, and a recognizable 'story' of its origins and nature has been constructed. Typically, this contrasts the vibrant development of modernism in continental Europe in the late 1910s and 1920s with a Britain content to lapse quietly into the historicism into which the pre-war Arts and Crafts movement had evolved. And it argues that since none of the preconditions which had generated modernism elsewhere existed – Cubism, progressive clients or talent, for example – modernism could not be generated from within and therefore had to be imported.[4] This importation happened variously. The reporting of European work in the pages of the architectural press, and the translation into English in 1927 of Le Corbusier's *Vers une Architecture* are often cited as important turning points in awakening those receptive enough to realize its potential. Modernism's arrival is, however, most often attributed 'to the work of outsiders'.[5] First came the colonial sons, uninhibited by native prejudices, such as Amyas Connell and Basil Ward (both New Zealanders) or Wells Coates (a Canadian born in Japan). This group 'started' (although it is rarely specified how) a movement in the late 1920s which was then shown how to do modernism properly by the émigré architects who arrived from Nazi Germany from around 1933.

For most historians, the history of British architectural modernism is therefore primarily a phenomenon of the 1930s. A chronology which is conveniently bookended by the house 'High and Over', designed by Connell for Professor Bernard Ashmole and built at Amersham in 1929–30 (the 'first' modernist building in Britain), and finishing, a decade later, with the Finsbury Health Centre by Tecton (1938), and Erno Goldfinger's terrace of three houses at Willow Road, Hampstead (1939). This story is then interspersed with other pioneer moments such as the founding of the Modern Architectural Research (MARS) Group in 1933 as the British chapter of CIAM, publications such as F. R. S. Yorke's *The Modern House* (1934) and other buildings such as Tecton's Penguin Pool (1934), Coates' Isokon Flats (1934) or Elizabeth Denby and Maxwell Fry's Kensal House (1937). Stylistic analysis usually revolves around observations about the clear European influence on the forms of British modernism, while historians go strangely silent when it comes to tracing a link between pre-war pioneering and post-war hegemony.[6]

Such an interpretation has its origins in the same decade as British architectural modernism is said to have developed, and Nikolaus Pevsner's assertion in 1936 that 'England's activity in the preparation of the Modern Movement came to an end during less than ten years after Morris's death'.[7] Deploying the trope of importation for the first time, he argued that it was only in the late 1920s that the 'forms of the Modern Movement began to penetrate into England, the forms which, between 1910 and 1925, had been developed by German, French and American architects'.[8] As this book will show, such a view is not without foundation or validity, but it offers only a partial view of the emergence and nature of architectural modernism in Britain, something which reflects the methodological prejudices of Pevsner and his heirs.

These prejudices might be listed as followed. First is a tendency to see architectural history as comprised solely by a series of 'actual monuments', and hence to analyse monuments primarily with reference to others, rather than relating them to the broader contexts within which architecture is embedded.[9] This is paralleled by the tendency to therefore see architecture as something produced solely by architects and to focus on them as protagonists of change. There are, for example, few accounts which have considered the role of clients as having played a role in the demand for new forms in this period of British architectural history. Likewise, a preoccupation with architecture as a primarily formal discipline has meant considerations of the significance of the building types in which British modernism was expressed are rare, yet these might have a great deal to tell us about its evolution.

While the Pevsnerian approach might be deemed adequate insofar as it has provided us with a basic chronology of British architectural modernism and, on occasion, produced fine monographs of some, although by no means all, of its key practitioners, they nevertheless leave much unexplained.[10] Remarkably, few historians have sought to explain why modernism might have emerged in Britain at the particular historical moment of the mid-to-late 1920s. For many it seems to have been enough to point to a set of buildings which prove that, as elsewhere, the British did, indeed, have a modern movement before the war. More generally its emergence is painted as an inevitable response to the *Zeitgeist* or the will of an individual practitioner rather than a response to a particular confluence of circumstances which created a demand for a new form of language and space. In sum, most have failed to consider modernism historically. And, in their focus on individuals – buildings or architects – they have rarely considered how a response to such demand coalesced, or was forged into, a critical mass – a British movement – which would by 1945, if not before, have secured for modernism its post-war cultural hegemony.

It is to the task of offering an historical account of architectural modernism that *Re-forming Britain* addresses itself. In embarking on such a project, it works from a number of premises and observations, not all of which are necessarily contradictory to the scholarship of the German and his heirs. This book will not challenge the notion that modernism can be distinguished as a phase in the history of British architecture, nor that it emerged at some time during the inter-war period, although precisely when and how is where this author and the Pevsnerian tradition begin to differ. Likewise, the significant role played by non-native architects in the emergence of the British movement is not doubted, although the significance of the émigrés is. But these are points on which it is quite easy to agree or disagree. The differences begin to emerge when we try to seek an understanding of the 'how' and 'why' of British architectural modernism.

If we follow the standard account, one which focuses on architects and buildings alone, then modernism has to be a phenomenon of the 1930s, as already noted. Given this, is it then conceivable that such a recently imported practice could have gained such a hold over policy makers so quickly, especially in a discipline as demand-led as architecture? Such a command can only be explained if we expand our view of what constituted architectural modernism in this period beyond 'actual monuments', and locate it within the wider contexts – social, political, economic, technological – in which it, like any other cultural practice, was and is embedded.

The contention therefore is that the emergence, development, and ultimate hegemony of modernism in Britain can only be understood if we see it as one of a range of attempts in the inter-war decades to engage with the problems of modernity through radical approaches to social and cultural reform. In other words, just as a generation of progressive reformers sought to re-think health care, design, fine art or planning, *inter alia*, at this time, so too the men and women of the British movement worked to re-think the nature of architectural and spatial culture at a time of national crisis.[11] Working sometimes as a purely architectural cohort, and sometimes in league with other like-minded reformers, they sought to convert governments to the merits of modernism as a solution to contemporary problems. To achieve this goal, their tools of persuasion were what are called here 'narratives of modernity'. These were projects, realized and unrealized, which were produced in, and reiterated through, media which encompassed the building, the exhibition, films, radio broadcasts and texts (journal articles, books, pamphlets). The process of reiteration was key. It allowed radical ideas to become first familiar and subsequently acceptable to politicians and their advisers. In this way, prototypical and hypothetical schemes and ideas were thereby rendered narratives of reform, ready to be adopted when the moment for change finally came.

By demonstrating how architectural modernism emerged as part of a wider project to modernize Britain, and its identification of modernism as more than monuments, *Re-forming Britain*, therefore provides an alternative geography for, and much earlier genealogy of, its emergence from that which historians have usually proposed. It was, then, not in the ateliers of Paris or the design studios of Weimar Germany that British architectural modernism was forged, although its practitioners were undoubtedly influenced by what they saw of continental European work. Nor was it suddenly introduced by an influx of émigrés in the early 1930s. In many respects, it was already here, and it would be through conscious effort and a carefully plotted campaign to exploit prevailing tendencies to the modern that a landscape for a modernist Britain would be created.

Structure

The book is organized to simulate what are proposed as the three main phases through which modernism emerged, developed and worked towards hegemony. This leads, on occasion, to some overlapping of chronology and protagonists between Parts 1 and 2 of the text, but it is hoped that this structuring allows the construction of a clearer picture of particular moments in the campaign. It also hints at the complexity of the process through which modernism came into being in Britain.

Part 1 seeks to locate the earliest manifestations of a modernist sensibility in Britain and it focuses, therefore, on the period often disregarded in histories of the British movement, the 1920s. Here discussion considers a number of sites where reformers in disciplines related to architecture first grappled with a second phase of modernization in Britain. One, in Berman's terms, which saw new forms of industrialization, new forms of corporate power and class conflict, and new systems of mass communication emerge in a country still struggling to come to terms with the psychological and economic impact of the Great War.[12]

These were sites such as the Design and Industries Association, a new wave of philanthropic housing associations, the architectural press and the artistic and political avant-gardes of Bohemian London. Through their occupation of and interaction with these sites, those who would go on to form the British movement would gain a will to modernize, a client base, and subsequently move towards the development of a new language of form and space. By 1933–4 this will had crystallized into a self-conscious movement, culminating in the formation of the MARS Group, and a growing number of buildings, from interiors to blocks of flats.

If Part 1 considers how modernists found and defined themselves into a movement, Part 2's focus is on how this movement sought to effect hegemony. This phase is labelled here Rhetorical Modernism, when our protagonists, realizing that their opportunities to build 'actual monuments' were always going to be limited, sought instead to build modernism through 'narratives of modernity'. Books, films, exhibitions, all became part of the armoury of modernist propaganda and those buildings which were constructed likewise, their difference of form serving as an ideal rhetorical tool.

The suggestion here is that members of the British movement worked very carefully to infiltrate their ideology into fields which were at the forefront of contemporary concerns, health and housing in particular. By forging alliances with other radicals who were similarly concerned to effect change, they created projects to re-form Britain and its people.

In the realm of housing, discussion focuses on the work of the modernist team of housing consultant and architect Elizabeth Denby and Max Fry and their schemes for R. E. Sassoon House and Kensal House. The collaboration among Wells Coates, Molly and Jack Pritchard on the Isokon projects is discussed, as is that between the Saint Pancras House Improvement Society and Connell and Ward which produced a block of flats (Kent House) and a town planning scheme for the local borough. In health, the collaboration between health reformers and architects in Peckham – the work of doctors Innes Pearse and George Scott Williamson and Owen Williams – and in Finsbury between Tecton and the borough councillors is considered. This is complemented by analysis of the many debates, texts and other media through which these prototypes and ideals became narratives for promulgation.

An emphasis on the contribution of individual pioneers is not a particular concern of this book. There is a desire to eschew what Michael Freeden has called the individualistic fallacy which 'overstresses the function of a particular individual as a creator of a system' and instead pay attention to the way individuals interacted to effect change.[13] Nevertheless, in its avoidance of the usual tropes of modernist architectural history, the book allows a set of actors who are not often included in accounts of the movement to take on a new significance. Clients such as the Pritchards and the Peckham doctors are seen to have made substantial contributions to the re-thinking of what architecture might be in this period, while the role played in the early years of the movement by Coates and Fry, the latter in particular, receives the attention it is long overdue. This approach also avoids the tendency to over-emphasize the contribution of the émigrés. Berthold Lubetkin, in this account, ceases to be a sole pioneer but one of a set of important figures. While the evidence suggests that visitors such as Walter Gropius and Marcel Breuer provided a confidence boost to the natives, but not a great deal more.[14]

The Britishness of the British movement is further explored in Part 3. This proposes the onset of a new phase in the movement's evolution which saw a younger generation of activists enter the campaign. It resulted in a move away from rhetorical modernism towards the formulation of the principles and practices which would underpin the modernism that would create the landscape of the post-war New Jerusalem. This process is explored through a discussion of the group of students at London's Architectural Association who formed part of a country-wide impetus to reform architecture from its roots upwards with a particular emphasis on transforming architectural education. With their tutors, they developed new modes of practice which emphasized teamwork and was research-led and sociologically driven, and heralded a new conception of the persona of the architect. It gave rise to a number of prophetic projects such as Unit 12's 'A Plan for a Town for 50,000 Inhabitants for 1950' (1936–7), and Unit 11's slum clearance scheme for Ocean Street, Stepney (1939) which drew on a survey conducted into what those due to be rehoused wanted from their new homes.

Re-forming Britain argues therefore that, by 1939, modernism was well established in Britain. Its principles and practices had been associated with the resolution of some of the most significant social problems of the day and links had thereby been made with policy makers and those with influence upon them. The education system was undergoing reform to ensure a future supply of modernists into the ranks. All that was needed were the great national schemes to give form to this desire to make of Britain a modernist nation. It is to a discussion of the first steps taken towards this goal that Part 1 now turns.

Part 1

A new spirit

Part 1

Introduction

In 1931, signs that something was afoot in the normally peaceable world of British architecture began to be seen in the pages of the architectural press. In March, *The Architect and Building News* reported the careful defence of the 'new architecture' which had been presented by Frederick Etchells at a debate entitled 'Tradition in Relation to Modern Architecture'.[1] Acknowledging that this was an 'admittedly immature movement', he nevertheless noted that a growing number of architects saw in it 'a new hope for their art'. Concluding, he rejected the claims of his fellow speakers that this new architecture, in its adherence to function, was therefore 'purely utilitarian engineering', and merely a 'stunt', and declared his conviction that

> There could be no doubt that there was growing up, through a thousand crude and doubtful forms, through a thousand immature experiments, a common state of mind in architecture, and this was the birth of a style, and therefore of a living tradition.

A few months later, his theme was echoed in even more vehement tones in the pages of *The Architects' Journal*. In his introduction to a special issue devoted to 'The New Materials', Wells Coates wrote of 'the new forces' which, he stated, 'the properties of steel, steel-concrete and glass' had unleashed.[2] These forces, he believed, had brought British architects and architecture to a turning point. He wrote:

> It is for architects to realize the possibilities of our lives now, in an age of Science, when life *could almost immediately become free*, that is to say, ordered, and refined, for all classes. Imprisonment (with torture) in the strait-jacket of old forms, a pretence to beauty at second hand? Or liberation (with refinement and delight) into movement, balance, harmony, *order from in outwards*?

That is the choice; the use of the new resources of materials as the prisoners – the slaves – of old habits, old social prejudices, old *visual* prejudices; or as the means to new forms, new habits of life, a new vision. The time has arrived for architects to reflect and to create.

In the final pages of the same issue, Coates' call to arms was reiterated. A transcript of a speech given by his contemporary and friend Serge Chermayeff, in this too was made a connection among new materials, new sciences and the need for an appropriate expression of the contemporary spirit. Likewise it noted a shift in architects' sensibilities, opening with the proclamation: 'Out of the twentieth century – our times and their own particular conditions – there is growing a new spirit and idealism.'[3]

The words of Etchells, Coates and Chermayeff demonstrate how at least some architects in Britain were thinking as the 1930s began, but the idea that a new movement was under way, and giving birth to a new style or tradition, was still relatively novel to British ears. It would not be too long before this tendency formed a coherent and manifest architectural presence, as the later chapters in this book will show, but at the time that these men were writing it was as yet glimpsed only fleetingly and in certain arenas. It is, therefore, with this particular phase in British architectural history that Part 1 of *Re-forming Britain* is concerned. It seeks to show how Etchells' 'thousand immature experiments' first emerged, and how they subsequently coalesced into the British movement.

In charting this process, the concern of Part 1 is to expand and revise the traditional 'story' of modernism's entry into the British architectural scene, and to elaborate the contention made in the Introduction that rather than 'coming' to England, modernism was, in many respects, already here. The chapter's focus, therefore, is on the work of those who had been attempting since the early 1920s, in fields relative to architecture, to create, or agitate for, the modern forms and spaces which would better meet the demands and conditions of the post-war age. Two locations are proposed as having been of particular significance in this process. The first is what might be characterized as 'sites of campaign', and the discussion commences with a consideration of the Design and Industries Association, and continues with a consideration of the new breed of voluntary housing associations formed in London in the 1920s, and the pages of the architectural press. Attention then turns to 'sites of encounter', the moments when the major protagonists of the British movement first met, and the clubs and sitting rooms of Bohemian London and Cambridge in which they socialized.

It would be through their encounters with the narratives of modernity formulated by those who occupied or created these sites, that members of what would become the British movement would be educated in new ways of thinking and practising. From these lessons and liaisons, Coates, Max Fry and others would forge first a modernist sensibility, and then a modernist identity.

Chapter 1

The conditions for an architecture for to-day

It must be conceded that, measured in actual achievement, the twenties were a barren period in British architecture; they should be judged rather by the study and planning which bore fruit in the thirties.[1]

Noel Carrington (1976)

A central premise on which this book rests is that the ultimate hegemony of British modernism can only have been achieved because it was rooted in existing attempts to work out the place and role of architecture in a country experiencing profound change. The processes through which, as Wells Coates put it, 'the conditions for an architecture for to-day' were formed, are therefore the subject of this chapter.[2] Such a discussion requires first, however, a consideration of the new Britain to which both the British movement, and those on whose shoulders its members stood, were trying to adapt.

Modernizing Britain

While there is not space here to enter into a detailed analysis of the Britain that some, at least, were trying to modernize in this period, it is important to outline the most significant economic, societal and political shifts which inaugurated this will to create new forms.[3] Central to this, was the fact that although Britain had won the Great War, the euphoria of victory could not mask the reality of its declining presence on the world stage. The overwhelming impression of Britain in the 1920s is, therefore, of a nation trying to make sense of itself as it was overwhelmed by profound structural changes.

The industrial growth which had made Britain the pre-eminent world power in the nineteenth century was, even before war broke out in 1914, being eclipsed by competitors in continental Europe, Japan and, in particular, the United States. So while Britain's share of world trade had been a third in 1870, by 1914 it was one-seventh, and its economic growth in the period between 1900 and 1913 was just over half what it had been before 1900.[4] The war complicated its position even further. Although the war effort sustained Britain's main industries, and also stimulated the development of newer ones, the fact that this 'progress' was paid for by loans from the US meant that Britain entered the post-war era a debtor nation, tied to the fortunes of its former colony. War also led to a decline in Britain's export trade as it lost its markets to neutral powers.

Britain's eclipse became all the more palpable in the 1920s. An economic boom inaugurated by the Armistice collapsed in 1920. By June 1921, nearly two million people were unemployed and the country entered a period of stasis and 'sitting tight'.[5] Conservative methods to control the economy, such as returning to the gold standard in 1925, were counter-productive. They increased the value of the pound abroad and made British industries even less competitive globally. This had a particular impact on the industries on which the economy had been founded: steel, shipbuilding, coal and textiles. With higher costs exacerbated by greater competition in the export market, these foundations were fatally undermined.

Yet at the same time as the Britain of heavy industry and empire was ebbing away, there were signs that a rather different country was emerging and that, in some places, a journey towards a new phase of modernity was being embarked upon. Under-pinned by the advances in technology occasioned by the Great War, new forms of manufacturing were developed: car making, pharmaceuticals, light industries. By the thirties, new methods of manufacturing would also have been introduced, informed by the Fordist techniques developed in the US. These industries, however, were located not in the traditional manufacturing areas of Britain but in the Midlands and south-east of England, and their emergence gave rise to an increasingly geographically and economically segregated nation. This saw the areas which heavy industry had domi-nated such as South Wales, Yorkshire, the north-east of England and Clydeside sink into despair and distress, while the south of England began to prosper. It is no coincidence that the majority of the projects discussed in this book are located in or around London, for that was where the money was.

If new forms of industrialization were one manifestation of a new phase in Britain's modernity there were others too. Chief among these was the emergence of a mass democracy. In 1918, all men over 21, and women over 30, were enfranchised, the latter's voting age subsequently lowered to 21 a decade later. This had two signifi-cant ramifications. First, it created a generation which required education in the rights and responsibilities of citizenship if democracy were to flourish, and the revolution and social disarray seen on the continent avoided in Britain. Second, since it brought political empowerment to the working class as a whole for the first time, it meant that the demands and needs of 'the workers' would henceforth be less easy to ignore. In this respect, the concomitant political maturation of the Labour Party, which became the official opposition in 1922, would, in the longer term, bring their voice to the heart of government.

Alongside its acquisition of the vote, this 'mass' also began to acquire another power: spending. While this was necessarily governed by geographies of prog-ress and decline, the majority of the population experienced a growth in net income in the inter-war period.[6] This, in turn, spawned the beginnings of a mass market in Britain for consumer goods such as household equipment and furniture. It also provided the money to pay for new technologies of fuel and lighting. Although this market would not develop fully until after the Second World War, more people bought more things in the inter-war decades than they had previously: expenditure on consumer durables rose from £169.6 million in 1910–14 to £332.2 million in 1929–34.[7] A further significant acquisition for many Britons in the same period was access to new forms of information and entertainment. In addition to the popular press, the inter-war decades saw the growth of cinema, women's magazines, the paperback novel and, above all, radio which brought information to a mass audience as never before; by the late 1930s eight million radio licences would have been issued.[8]

Such a modernity, as Marshall Berman has shown, required, indeed necessitated, a response and an expression.[9] In inter-war Britain, it would occasion reactions both positive and negative, and ones which changed over time. Politically, the late 1910s and 1920s, the period with which Part 1 of this book is principally concerned, can be characterized as a time when successive governments did their best to keep such change at bay, mitigating it only when absolutely necessary. Otherwise, as Paul Addison has noted, there prevailed 'a consensus to prevent anything unusual from happening'.[10] This approach reflected the ideology of a Conservative government, under Stanley Baldwin, reluctant to move too far away from a policy of laissez-faire, and a Labour government, under Ramsay MacDonald (which was in minority power in 1924), more concerned to demonstrate the party's eligibility for governance than enact radical legislation.[11] By the 1930s, as the discussion in Part 2 will show, this stasis would begin to shift. Fuelled by economic recovery, a more constructive attitude would emerge across the political spectrum.

In the meantime, the consensus against the unusual did not go unchallenged. There were those who saw in these unsettling shifts the beginnings of a better Britain. These people, who are the subjects of this book, were not paralysed by the prospect of a new age. Rather they sought accommodation with it, celebrated it, and, in so doing, anticipated the formation of a nation which could, once again, lead the world.

The attempts of the first generation to harness technology, the democratic spirit, and innovative means of communication in order to push the process of modernization along are documented in this chapter. These men and women spent the 1920s taking the first tentative steps towards the development of the new types of form and space which would accommodate emerging modes of modern life. At the same time, they also began to develop novel modes of operating, creating institutions and formulating media through which the unusual would be made acceptable. In Berman's terminology, such people are to be understood as 'pastoral modernists', those in pursuit of 'infinite human progress' in all fields: industry, politics and culture.[12] For them, progress was to be achieved through a process of assimilation: bringing together the worker, the artist, the industrialist and the politician in pursuit of a mutually beneficial goal.

The term 'pastoral modernism', while it conveys well the motivation and modus operandi of the protagonists under discussion, nevertheless sits slightly uncomfortably with the forms and spaces which they would produce. Here, therefore, they will, more simply, be called, 'moderns', in order to make clear the contrast between them and the generation of men and women – the British movement – which followed. It would be the latter who were able to achieve a complete expression – social, spatial, technological and formal – of the new age. We might understand them, therefore, as 'programmatic modernists' or, again more simply, modernists. For them, 'modernity' was a project, something inherently 'new'.[13] Their concern was to liberate and emancipate, something which could only be achieved through fundamental changes to space and form.

It is, then, with this transition from the modern to the modernist, and the locations in which it took place, that the rest of this chapter is concerned. Through a rather whistle-stop journey we will see how in sites of campaign and encounter, British proto-modernists studied and planned their way into an identifiable architectural avant-garde. This process culminated in the formation of the Modern Architectural Research (MARS) Group in February 1933, a move which inaugurated a new phase in the British movement.

Sites of campaign I: the Design and Industries Association

Although the Design and Industries Association (DIA) has been more or less disregarded in histories of the British movement, that it was an early gathering point for many of its members is evident from surviving membership lists.[14] Raymond McGrath, Mansfield Forbes, Wells Coates, Max Fry and Jack Pritchard all joined the DIA in the late 1920s, the latter three serving on its Council in the 1930s.[15] Both Pritchard and Fry would subsequently insist on its influence in their memoirs, Fry according it a central role in his evolution into a modernist.[16]

Yet this was an organization which, as its name suggests, was not concerned primarily with architecture. It had been formed in 1915 by those in the Arts and Crafts movement who had sought to marry its formal and social principles with its erstwhile nemesis, the machine: an assimilation which resulted in the design credo of 'fitness for purpose'.[17] The DIA's members believed that through the instigation of a campaign to persuade consumers, manufacturers and government of the merits of this credo, and the consequent re-formation of British products, manufacturers could recapture lost markets, and the national economy progress.[18]

It was this very engagement with the possibilities of technology and the machine, and the desire to assimilate them into something new through the cultural device of design, which is one reason why the DIA should have played a formative role in the evolution of the British movement. The object of its reforming zeal is therefore less important than the fact that this was an inherently modern group. It was the first in Britain whose members self-consciously set themselves the task of grappling with the role of design in a re-industrializing world, and of developing the formal language to express it. So when, a decade later, a classically trained architect like Fry found himself in search of 'authentic signals' in a London whose new buildings he labelled 'withering, falsely grafted, etiolating', the DIA offered just such signs. As he recalled:

> It was the best available cutting edge to be had at the time … Besides bringing me into close communion with the only architects who could see beyond their noses … it directed my gaze to the continent where I found what astonished me, being no less than the proposition of an architecture in its own right … It could be, and was, the first signal of release.[19]

If its very existence offered a precedent on which proto-modernists could build, another influential aspect of the DIA's modernity was its highly developed command of the techniques of communication and persuasion or, as they would have called it, propaganda. This command enabled them to endow their activities, which were enacted on a small scale by an organization whose membership never rose into the thousands, with a significance and weight which, quantitatively, they did not have. Through the mediation, and reiteration, of an approved example of good design in an exhibition, a lecture or an illustration in one of its numerous yearbooks and periodicals, the DIA was able to translate the unusual into the familiar. Such things were thereby rendered narratives of modernity: prototypes ready to be taken off the shelf when the moment for change finally came.[20] For the DIA, such iterative processes also served another purpose. They elucidated what was otherwise an immensely vague definition of what constituted good design. Since 'fitness for purpose' was a theory, it had no inevitable stylistic expression and, if it were to be interpreted 'correctly', that is in terms of the DIA's own aesthetic prejudices, then images were crucial in showing consumer, manufacturer or government, what it actually meant.[21]

Fry and his contemporaries came to the DIA at a moment when some of its members had begun to interrogate the prejudices with which they had first addressed the expression of 'fitness for purpose'. However 'modern' its founders' intentions had been, in its early years the DIA had tended to favour goods which connoted this through a simplicity of form allied to natural materials, rather than through an evident engagement with new technologies of production or new materials. By 1923–4, however, even the most Arts and Crafts-oriented of its members were recognizing that such a bias was unlikely to offer a permanent way forward.

The recognition stemmed from influences both internal and external. The *Exposition des Arts Décoratifs*, held in Paris in 1925, although the Association hardly approved of its predominantly decorative style, nevertheless focused attention on advances in design outside Britain and made the DIA 'discontented with progress'.[22] Similarly, the volatile economic situation at home was a constant reminder of the need for British industry to produce goods which could compete in an international market. Here it should be noted that the period of the DIA's renovation coincided with a period of slump, and the unimaginative attempts by government to ameliorate it through such techniques as the return to the gold standard. These factors were complemented by changes in the Council of the DIA as younger members like Wenman Basset-Lowke, Joseph Thorp, Robert Best and William Crittall begin to take over policy making. At the same time, one of its founders, Harold Stabler, argued that it was 'time we aimed at bigger things and realised what is being done abroad'.[23] He called therefore for an influx of new members, recruiting a young publisher and family friend, Noel Carrington, to set the DIA on a more organized basis. Around this time John Gloag also joined.

Under the leadership of these men, the DIA initiated a much more strategic campaign to persuade government that the union of design and industry might be the means to revivify British manufacturing. Ultimately it would be successful. In January 1934, the government ministry of the Board of Trade established the Council for Art and Industry and charged it to 'address questions affecting the relations between Art and Industry'.[24]

The factor which was, perhaps, of most significance in effecting this shift in state policy, was that the backgrounds of these men were not in the Arts and Crafts movement but in disciplines born of the twentieth, or very late nineteenth, century – light industry,

architectural journalism and advertising – and whose products had no particular precedents which might get in the way of a preference for new forms. Basset-Lowke's
Northamptonshire firm made metal toys and models. Best was a partner in the Birmingham-
based lighting manufacturers Best and Lloyd. Crittall was the scion of the Essex family firm
which made metal windows, and Read was a designer for the London firm of Troughton
and Young which, like Best and Lloyd, made electrical light fittings. They were joined by
Joseph Thorp, who had been a salesman for WH Smith and director of the private
Ashendene press, before he became an adviser on printing to the advertising industry.

These men were joined two by new recruits in Gloag and Carrington. At the
time Gloag joined the DIA, in around 1923, he was a writer for the periodical *The
Cabinet Maker*, of which he ultimately became editor. He subsequently joined the
advertising firm of Wood, Pritchard and Partners in 1928.[25] Carrington's background
was in publishing and he had spent time in India working for the Oxford University
Press. In 1923 or 1924 he joined the book production department of *Country Life*,
where his Oxford friend and contemporary Christopher Hussey worked, and joined the
DIA not long after.[26] The link with journalism, and advertising in particular, brought a
range of new reference points and sources to the DIA. As Carrington observed, what
was so significant about advertising was that in the inter-war years it became 'conscious of itself as a serious and highly progressive profession … [and it] attracted the
brightest young men in business'.[27]

In combination, this group of men shared a much better understanding of
mass production, the demands of the emerging mass market, and of how to communi-
cate with it, than their Arts and Crafts predecessors could ever have had. They were also
united in 'a powerful surge of idealism and hope' after the sacrifice of the Great War and
shared a 'new outlook on architecture and design. One cannot call it revolutionary: it
was more a readiness to take a fresh look at the physical structure of civilisation.'[28]

The 'fresh look' resulted in a concerted effort to confront modern conditions
head-on. It was manifested in a plan of action that laid down a programme of research
into the role of design in a mass society. This would be conducted under three head-
ings: Design in Individual Life (housing and equipment); Design in Collective Life (town,
transport, recreation); and Design in Production and Commerce (factories, offices and
shops).[29] The more detached terminology used to denote these categories is significant, indicative of the move from a crafts-based attitude to one more factory-oriented. A
more obvious reminder of this group's modernity, however, is the very idea of having a
plan. Perhaps the term most over-used by reformers in the inter-war years, planning, or
as Gloag defined it in 1927, 'clear thinking', was now seized on as the only way to
achieve progress, thereby escaping the chaos into which society had descended since
the laissez-faire days of the nineteenth century.[30] So to the DIA's ongoing concern to
demonstrate models of a design credo, this group added the new task of conveying the
necessity of the plan. Research would bring to light exemplary practices of planning
which, on the Association's well established model, would then be communicated
through various media to the membership.

The more modern mindset demonstrated in this group's adherence to
research, and to the concept of the plan, was augmented by Stabler's call for the DIA as
a whole to look to European example. This was the crucial step, for it offered the way out

of the impasse which linked modern design with an Arts and Crafts fondness for natural materials. Yet, through the continued insistence that European models should adhere to the credo of 'fitness for purpose', possible because it was a prescriptive not a descriptive criterion, the reformers in the DIA could not be accused of deviating from its guiding principle. The final challenge was to ensure that these new ideas reached members and the wider public, to which end another part of the plan was set in motion: the creation of a new journal with Carrington at its helm.

It can be imagined that it was in the pages of the *DIA Quarterly Journal*, as well as at DIA meetings, that Fry found the authentic signals which 'put an end to all vacillation and set me finally on course'.[31] Published between September 1927 and January 1932, its pages provide a fascinating documentation of a growing awareness among British reformers of continental European practice. This was evident in the series of well illustrated articles which documented the Association's regular trips abroad. In March 1928, for example, there was a report of a weekend visit to Amsterdam and Hilversum (where their guide was its architect, Willem Dudok), and in July a trip to Zurich was recorded. Much attention was given a year later to a cruise to the 'Northern Capitals' when these intrepid travellers went to Stockholm, Copenhagen and Hamburg.[32]

Individual members also reported on their journeying. Basset-Lowke was a frequent correspondent, his particular interest being Germany. He would write two significant articles about his visits to the Weissenhof Siedlung (December 1927) and to the centres of modernism at Cologne and Frankfurt (December 1928). His observations demonstrate the discerning eye that DIA moderns brought to such experiments. So while he was generally positive about the German work, several of his comments make it clear that his judgements were always set against the benchmark of what would work in Britain and what would not. At the Weissenhof he reported the lack of 'homely experience' in Corbusier's houses and contrasted this with Taut's 'most homely and efficient' dwelling. He seems to have been particularly impressed by Mies van der Rohe's apartment block which, he declared, 'shows how attractive a really plain building can be made'.[33] Of the work he saw at Ernst May's *Neue Frankfurt* he was less sure, writing, 'wholehearted advocate of modern design as I am, I must confess to being a little appalled by the standardization of the new housing at Frankfurt'. He conceded, nevertheless, that it exhibited, and therein lay the problem, 'a vitality and an adaptability to modern conditions which is bringing Germany to the forefront again as an industrial nation'.[34]

As well as instructing its readers in the lessons to be derived from exemplary buildings, under Carrington's lead the *DIA Quarterly Journal* was also concerned to provide them, through recommendation and additions to the DIA's library, with the literature with which they could deepen their understanding of continental ideas. The very first issue, for example, alerted readers to Frederick Etchells' translation of *Vers une Architecture*, while the next noted that a copy of this had been donated to the library. In the same issue, books 'of DIA interest' included Ludwig Hilbersheimer's *Internationale Baukunst* and Adolf Behne's *Neues Bauen – Neues Wohnen* which was described as 'a real DIA tract'.[35] In July 1929, it was suggested that readers subscribe to the French periodical *Art et Décoration* and to *The Architectural Review*, while approving nods were made to recent changes to *The Studio*. The next issue added *Die Form* to the list of recommended reading. In April 1930, Bruno Taut's *Modern Architecture*, which was published by *The Studio*, was given an approving review and *Decorative Art*, another *Studio* publication, was recommended for devoting itself to Le Corbusier and containing an article by 'that provocative pioneer'.[36]

Such articles and recommendations, and the attitudes they embodied, made the DIA by the late 1920s, as Fry recalled, 'the best available cutting edge' in Britain. Yet, just as it might have built on the momentum gained since Crittall and his co-modernizers had begun their plan in 1923–4, a faction within the Association elected to divert its campaigning energies towards another cause, the preservation of the English landscape against untrammelled suburban development.[37] This 'unscheduled excursion' would prove to be a turning point, not just in the DIA's evolution, but also for the future members of the British movement who had joined the DIA because of its very radicalism.[38] It would, however, take some years for this shift to manifest itself. The discussion of the part that this third phase in the DIA's history played in the evolution of a British architectural modernism is therefore better considered at the end of this chapter, consequent as it was to a number of other influences and factors.

Sites of campaign II: London's voluntary housing associations

Like the DIA, the voluntary housing associations which were formed in the 1920s to campaign for the resolution of a slum problem then largely overlooked by central government, have been more or less disregarded in accounts of the movement's genesis. This is a considerable oversight.[39] It would be from their encounters with London associations such as the Saint Pancras House Improvement Society (SPHIS) and the Kensington Housing Association and Trust (KHT), that architects like Fry and Coates would acquire an understanding of the moral purpose of reform, a particular philosophy of housing practice, and further 'training' in methods of propaganda. This progressive philosophy would play a central role in the development of the theory of British architectural modernism.

The origins of associations such as the SPHIS and the KHT, and the influence they would have over the British movement, lay in the immense housing problem which the country faced in 1918. At its root was the housing shortage which had been inherited from the period before the Great War, and which had been exacerbated a great deal by it; those four years, understandably, had seen minimal building activity. By 1919 it was estimated that there was an actual shortage of one million houses: a figure that did not include the 100,000 dwellings which were required to be built annually in order to take account of population growth and the deterioration of existing property.[40] The problem was made worse by the introduction of rent control during the War and its subsequent continuation in response to the high cost of building materials and increase in interest rates in the economic boom that followed the Armistice.

Over the next decade, various attempts would be made to resolve this problem. They would result in fundamental shifts in the nature of Britain's housing economy. The first, and most significant of these, was the assumption by the state of partial responsibility for the provision of working-class housing for rent. This, as Mark Swenarton has shown, was precipitated by the extraordinary stasis in the construction of new housing, and the realization by politicians that many of the soldiers who had fought in the Great War were returning to live in slums: poor recompense for their sacrifice.[41] Politicians were fearful of revolution in response to this neglect, and were also mindful of a growing belief in the entitlement of the poor to a basic standard of living.[42] The result was an unprecedented act of state intervention in the provision of housing when, in 1919, the Liberals introduced a new Housing Act to provide 'Homes fit for Heroes'. Through a direct subsidy from central government to local authorities, a programme of house building for rental by the working classes was commenced. This was never intended as anything other than a one-off subsidy and, when introduced, it was anticipated that as soon as circumstances got back to normal, private enterprise would resume its 'rightful' role as the chief supplier of workers' housing. However, the continuation of rent control in the face of ongoing housing shortage, and the fluctuating post-war economy, meant that normality never did return, and what had been intended as a stop-gap measure became a permanent part of successive inter-war governments' social welfare policy. Although the nature of the subsidy would change, and the type of housing it supported also, henceforth the state would now become the landlord of at least some Britons. Throughout the inter-war decades, therefore, housing would remain an issue high on the political agenda.

The New Philanthropy

The idea that the state might become landlord to its workers would become such a commonplace of mid-twentieth-century British welfare ideology that it is easy to forget that in 1919 such a role was quite extraordinary. The fact that it happened at all reflected, as noted, a particular set of circumstances; its perpetuation likewise. That it was even contemplated, however, is evidence of a more fundamental shift in concepts of what the relationship between state and individual and, indeed, private enterprise, should be. It would have a significant impact on the way the reformers discussed throughout this book conducted their campaigns.

Whereas in the nineteenth century the prevailing doctrine of laissez-faire had, for the most part, characterized state, individual and industry as discrete entities, as anxiety about Britain's standing in the world economy grew during the period which preceded the Great War, a more interventionist approach began to be taken. In particular, this saw the state involve itself in areas of social policy which had an impact on the health and well-being of the nation's workers. In so doing, the philanthropic voluntary organizations which had historically provided welfare for them began to be displaced.[43] By the late 1910s, a mixed economy of welfare had emerged, what the contemporary social theorist Elizabeth Macadam called the 'New Philanthropy ... the system of combined statutory and voluntary social service'.[44]

In the immediate post-war period, this mixed economy, as will be seen in Chapter 2, was most evident in fields of welfare provision which related to health, many voluntary sector organizations acting as agents of the state in this arena. In the field of housing provision, the relationship between the state and the voluntary sector was more complex. Social housing had been among the chief concerns of the sector since the 1840s, and the great trusts, like the Peabody Trust founded in 1862, built large estates of model dwellings across Britain.[45] It had only been in the 1890s that legislation had been passed to grant local authorities the discretionary right to clear slums and build new housing themselves. This, however, was to be done with no subsidy or financial support from central government, and it was motivated by fears for public health.

Since the post-war Housing Acts of 1919, 1923 and 1924 were intended to mitigate social unrest, not prevent urban pestilence, they required centralized control of housing provision, and state-authorized designs.[46] They produced, therefore, accommodation very different from the flatted dwellings in which the pre-war trusts had specialized. The vast majority of social housing constructed in the 1920s was targeted at better-off workers, those in regular employment and earning a weekly wage, for whom were built cottage estates sited on the peripheries of existing towns. Drawing on the garden-city planning techniques pioneered by Barry Parker and Raymond Unwin before 1914, these estates comprised two-storey houses built to generous space standards at the low densities of 12 per acre, either in semi-detached pairs or short terraces, with a varying provision of amenity alongside them.[47]

Although this effort would have seen the construction of 1,860,000 dwellings in England and Wales by 1932, a substantial number of the working-class population remained living in overcrowded and slum conditions.[48] Such people could not afford the rents charged for the new Homes fit for Heroes, nor the additional costs of travel to their work from the edges of a town or city. Successive governments hoped their housing needs would be addressed through the process of 'filtering up': moving in to the dwellings vacated by their better-off brethren who were rehoused in the cottage estates. But this rarely happened, and the slum problem, bad before the war, grew worse.[49] Indeed, it would become such an immense problem that rather than face it, governments elected to overlook it almost completely throughout the 1920s.[50] Its immensity was also such that it could not be tackled by the pre-war trusts alone.

It was in this context that a new breed of voluntary housing associations emerged.[51] Unlike their predecessors, which had not sought to influence state (in)action to any significant degree, the primary concern of the new groups was to campaign that public authorities address the issue of overcrowding and slum housing as a matter of absolute priority. Indeed, many were founded solely as campaign groups and only came to build new accommodation when governments continued to turn a deaf ear to their protests. Such building then came to form another part of their campaign. This was to persuade legislators that when a slum clearance policy was finally enacted, it should be the voluntary sector which was charged with its delivery. The sector's blocks of model flats, their programmes and designs carefully tailored to address the specific problem of rehousing former slum-dwellers, were built proof of their eligibility for this task.

In pursuing such exemplary and campaigning activity, groups like the SPHIS and KHT fulfilled other aspects of the New Philanthropy as defined by Macadam. For her, the fact that the sector had, in many areas, lost its leading role in welfare provision to the state, formed not a moment for its retreat, but the opportunity for its reinvention. Reconfigured as a vanguard, its challenge was to create new roles for itself, and develop new strategies to address the needs of a society undergoing rapid change. Hence, she argued, '[t]he propagation of ideas, which have not yet been accepted as part of the currency of thought [became] ... another of the most enduring possibilities for voluntary action'. This was where the sector had an advantage over the state, she believed, because the development of 'sound propaganda' depended on research and experimentation, something it was often impossible for governments to pursue because 'private action can penetrate where the state dare not venture'. She concluded, therefore, that 'the spread of ideas based on the result of careful research and experiment ... is the necessary precursor of all reform'.[52]

So like the DIA, the voluntary housing sector was an institution concerned with assimilating the mass (slum-dwellers rather than consumers in this instance) with something undergoing modernization. The fact that the object of its reforming eye was the dwelling was of particular importance. The 'research and experimentation' the volunteers conducted in pursuit of a better form of housing, and the techniques of propaganda they deployed to promote it, would provide the nascent British movement with a set of principles and practices from which they would, in time, develop their own campaign for modern housing.

The SPHIS and the KHT

The SPHIS and the KHT were typical of the new post-war voluntary housing associations. Both operated in areas where overcrowded and slum housing was rife, locations made all the more ironic given their juxtaposition with areas of great wealth. Formed in late 1924, the SPHIS was based in Somers Town, the pocket of land between Euston and King's Cross stations in the north London Borough of St Pancras, just north of the squares and terraces of affluent Bloomsbury. The KHT, formed in 1925, conducted its activities in north Kensington, the area beyond Notting Hill Gate and the other very prosperous parts of what was a royal borough. Both Somers Town and north Kensington were populated by those of the working-class poor who were 'trapped' in bad accommodation by their need to be close to their places of employment (the railways, gasworks, domestic service) and their inability to pay both rent and fares if they moved to the cottage estates. Both were also areas in which their local councils refused to confront the housing problems within their boundaries. So although the slums in north Kensington meant that the borough as a whole had some of the worst overcrowding and poverty statistics in London, its Municipal Reform (Conservative) council would build only 317 dwellings to meet this need between 1920 and 1927.[53]

The founders of the SPHIS and KHT were also typical of the rather curious blend of people who formed the inter-war voluntary sector: pre-war 'old' philanthropists and 'new philanthropists', younger, paid workers often with academic qualifications in social work or related fields. The guiding force of the SPHIS was Father Basil Jellicoe, who ran the Magdalen College mission in Somers Town. He worked alongside Edith Neville, secretary of the Saint Pancras Council of Social Service, and Norah Hill, a voluntary social worker in the area. They were subsequently joined by Irene Barclay and Eileen Perry, the first two women to qualify as chartered surveyors in Britain, who would act as estate managers and surveyors to the Society once its work was underway.[54] The KHT was founded by Rachel Alexander, a local Quaker philanthropist, long active as a social worker in north Kensington, and the politician Lord Balfour of Burleigh.[55] Like the SPHIS, the KHT would employ a paid professional, the better to conduct its work, appointing the social-work trained Elizabeth Denby as its Organizing Secretary in 1925.[56]

Neither organization had been started with the intention to build new housing. The SPHIS, as its nomenclature suggests, was founded to improve the existing housing – multiple-occupied Georgian terraces – in which locals lived. The KHT was initially founded as a lobby group, the Kensington Housing Association. Both turned to a policy of new building very quickly. The Society because it discovered that most of the dwellings it would acquire were too dilapidated and infested to be rebuilt. The KHT because one of the slum landlords against whom it was campaigning suggested that it might like to take over the lease and improve the housing itself.

New building created problems and opportunities. It was an expensive process and required the raising of significant funds.[57] More positively, it meant that the groups could now develop the very particular model of housing which they believed would best resolve, and resolve permanently, the slum problem. To achieve both aims, concerted propaganda campaigns were necessary and it was in evolving these that the SPHIS and the KHT excelled and innovated. Their purpose was to shame, embarrass and persuade donors, policy makers and politicians to action.

Much of this propaganda work, like that of the DIA, was founded on the provision of information, and the magnification of small-scale activities by their reiteration in assorted media. It ranged from the dissemination of basic statistical information about slum conditions to more spectacular headline grabbing events. Barclay and Perry produced a series of surveys of London housing conditions which offered sound evidence of the appalling accommodation in which so many of London's working classes dwelt.[58] From 1928 much of this information was promulgated through a magazine, *Housing Happenings*, sent to all subscribers to the Society. The KHT would issue *Annual Reports* and in the 1930s would likewise publish a journal, *The Phoenix*. Dropped through a concerned citizen's letterbox, or posted to local councillors, they served as regular reminders of the need to contribute, financially and politically, to the housing campaign.

The SPHIS propaganda machine specialized, however, in more flamboyant schemes and the use of the most up-to-the-minute media of propaganda. Acutely aware of the value of an image, from its inception, the Society was meticulous in its documentation of the process of constructing new accommodation through still photography and film; pioneering the latter's use as a vehicle for social reform.[59] Each stage of building would be marked with special events and recorded. Prior to demolition, future tenants would parade to the site carrying gigantic models of the bugs which infested the soon-to-be-toppled dwellings. These would then be burnt along with the first debris of the destruction. The films made of this activity would then be shown around the country by what the Society called its 'Flying Squad', a team of speakers who gave talks on its work to voluntary groups and other community organizations.

The KHT's methods were rather less flamboyant, its favoured technique that of embarrassment. Housing Sundays, when local clergymen were asked to raise awareness of Kensington's housing problems from the pulpits of churches located in wealthy parishes, were much used to elicit funds from a mortified congregation. The Trust again used films to bring the message home to the well-to-do. These were often shown at meetings held in the drawing rooms of socially concerned citizens. Few could remain unmoved by the contrast between a comfortable Kensington town house and the images of insect, and rat-infested one-room dwellings, or the scene of a man making a child's coffin, shown in the 1929 film 'Kensington Calling'.

The very accommodation the organizations built was also part of the propaganda war, featuring prominently in campaigners' publications and films as a shorthand for progress. Continuing the tradition of 'model dwellings' so associated with voluntary housing practice, their new blocks of flats served equally as models of an economy of building (rehousing as what Barclay called a 'practical business proposition'), and of a distinct philosophy about what form housing for former slum-dwellers should take.[60] This model was derived from the theory of welfare which had underpinned the practices of the voluntary sector since the late nineteenth century. It originated in the particular notions of the purpose of welfare and the discourse of citizenship which had been developed by British Idealist philosophers such as T. H. Green and Bernard Bosanquet in the 1860s and 1870s.

In the context of social distress, and fears about national decay, Green and Bosanquet had begun to argue against the free market and reconceptualize the relationship between the state and the individual, arguing that 'the purpose of the state is to promote the good life of its citizens and to develop the moral nature of man'.[61] Such a conceptualization was significant. Although there would be much debate about what constituted this 'good life' – for some it had a primarily economic dimension, while for others the political and social were foregrounded – these men had established a core precept and measure of twentieth-century welfare theory and practice. This was that 'the perfection and moral condition of a state is dependent upon the degree of citizenship in its members'.[62]

For the Idealists, and their inter-war heirs who are the focus of discussion here, citizenship was at once an economic, political and social condition, a triad they distilled into the concept of active citizenship. This posited a reciprocal relationship between citizen and state in which in return for the implementation of reform measures, whether social (such as improved housing) or political (the vote), and the particular nature of those reforms, citizens would be enabled to participate fully (and willingly) in corporate life. Only in this way could society progress. In the context of social reform, this Idealist concept was significant because it demanded action. Incumbent upon those who were already rational citizens was the duty to participate in civic life and to enable the less fortunate to realize their potential. That this was a realizable goal lay in the Idealists' belief that 'all human beings, however destitute were fundamentally rational'.[63]

Such attitudes gave rise to two main approaches to social work and reform from the 1870s. The first focused on work with the individual and was typified in the activities of the Charity Organization Society (of which the SPHIS's Neville was a stalwart). Its aim was 'to enable disadvantaged individuals to become more effective citizens' by one-to-one visiting and casework which led to specific acts of welfare.[64] The second approach was carried out under the auspices of the Settlement Movement and was more collective and spatial in its scope. This saw the construction of what would now be called community centres in the heart of slum areas. Their founders' intention was to create sites where middle-class citizens (who would live in the settlements, as Oxford graduate Jellicoe did at the Magdalen mission) could be brought together with the local working-class population. Through the provision of education and other communal activities, the poor would be helped to achieve their potential in a context which reminded them that they were not just individuals, but members of a larger body politic.[65] An important corollary of this process was the commissioning of often striking new buildings whose design was intended to connote the possibilities contained within for betterment and progress.

Philosophies like these would have a particular influence on the housing policies of neo-Idealist groups like the SPHIS and KHT. Their leaders interpreted the housing designed by the state as concerned solely with meeting the material needs of its occupiers, thereby creating passive citizens whose acquiescence in the social order was secured. For Jellicoe, Alexander *et al.*, the provision of new accommodation, and on such a scale, represented an unrivalled opportunity to create environments which would realize the potential of those who inhabited them, making active citizens of them all. They therefore developed a model of housing which catered for both the material and social needs of the rehoused. Centrally located, close to places of employment, the voluntarists' model flats would be soundly constructed, self-contained and easy-to-clean. With separate bedrooms, a living room, kitchen and bathroom, running water and powered by electricity (SPHIS) or gas (KHT), they provided the context in which domestic life could be conducted free from the overcrowding and filth of the slum. Such programmatic advances were not matched, however, by a radicalism of form, and their architecture was typical of the decade's preference for neo-Georgian designs (Figs 1.1 and 1.2).

Alongside these re-formed dwellings, and serving as their complement, went considerable programmes of communal amenities. Both organizations established social clubs for all age groups on or near their estates, and instigated holiday schemes. Loan funds were established to help tenants pay for new furniture and the KHT would pioneer the practice of differential rents. Much time was devoted to nurturing the lives of the tenants' children: the SPHIS built a nursery school on the roof of one of its new blocks, the KHT content to build its at street level. The final aspect of this programme was the insistence that all schemes were overseen by women housing managers: their job to visit the estates regularly to collect rent but also to act as social workers when necessary. This socio-spatial approach to housing reform would, the voluntarists believed, make of the poor active and responsible citizens, ready to take their place in the progress of modern life.

Towards a collectivity of action

Such endeavour had emerged against the background of the inactivity of central and local governments against the slum problem. In 1928, however, circumstances began to change when the then Conservative administration indicated that in the next parliamentary session it would seek to dismantle the subsidy system introduced by the post-war housing acts and resume the pre-war sanitary policy of slum clearance. This policy subsequently became part of the election manifestos of all parties. In response, a new phase in the voluntarists' housing campaign was entered: their task to persuade the state that it should be their model of housing which was adopted and they who should be its suppliers.

They were already well prepared to promote their activities collectively. Prior to the Conservatives' shift in housing policy, the volunteers had made, for largely

Figure 1.1
Saint Pancras
House
Improvement
Society Flats,
Somers Town, late
1920s

Figure 1.2
The Kensington
Housing Trust's
Crosfield House,
North Kensington,
late 1920s

pragmatic reasons, preliminary moves towards collective self-promotion and unity of action. Many associations were faced with considerable problems in raising the necessary funds for construction. So early in 1928, the London groups had met to explore ways of joining together for more effective action in raising investment. This meeting produced two resolutions: to improve the organization of the London societies by sharing knowledge and fund-raising techniques, and to campaign for more public awareness of the slums and the work of those groups which were working to improve them.[66]

A collective campaign required additional techniques to the ones the SPHIS or the KHT had deployed. Rather than addressing a local and probably familiar public, the sector was now appealing, on the one hand, to a largely unknown metropolitan public whom they needed to persuade to lobby future MPs for action and, on the other, to national policy makers. Their first attempt to speak to this audience came through the establishment of a housing propaganda group called the Under Forty Club (UFC).

Described in its publicity leaflets as 'an appeal to the younger generation; an appeal for youthful energy, brains and sympathy', the UFC was intended as 'a collecting and distributing centre for workers and money'.[67] Working on behalf of the London societies it sought to raise awareness of their work, directing funds raised to wherever they could be used most effectively. It also aimed to be a resource for housing workers and began to acquire a library of information in its headquarters in Westminster.

The UFC's work drew considerably on the propaganda methods established by groups such as the SPHIS and KHT. It led students on tours of slum housing and produced a film 'showing the sordid and tragic home life of a slum family', which was available for loan to any organization interested in housing.[68] In important respects, however, it differed. In keeping with its need to promote the sector as a 'corporate' body, the UFC sought out more prominent platforms from which the voluntary groups' work could be publicized. So in 1929, and again in 1930, the UFC took a stand at the populist *Daily Mail* Ideal Home Exhibition (DMIHE). The 1929 display showed a large-scale model of an ideal tenement flat.[69] In 1930, models of flats built by several of the London housing societies were on show.[70] Where better to draw attention to the plight of the slum-dweller than at an exhibition devoted to the fantasy dwelling?

The introduction of a wholesale slum clearance programme in 1930 by the newly elected Labour Minister of Health, Arthur Greenwood, may have seemed to many in the sector a vindication of their campaigns. The Act offered both the first coherent anti-slum legislation since 1890, and specified that the sector should work alongside local authorities to provide the new housing. The onset of the Depression, and the fall of the Labour government, however, curtailed Greenwood's vision. The new National Government, anxious to limit public expenditure, put his plans on hold. Reluctant to lose the opportunities presented by the 1930 Act, the volunteers determined to keep slums and the sector's work in the public eye until more favourable economic circumstances returned.

Drawing on the precedent of the UFC's stands at the DMIHE, it was therefore decided to keep slums in the headlines by holding a housing exhibition.[71] If the displays were sufficiently graphic they would draw press attention and ensure the exhibition's message would reach a national audience. So, a small committee was assembled to work on what became the 'New Homes for Old' (NHFO) exhibition which opened at Westminster Central Hall in December 1931. Among its visitors would be Wells Coates and also Mansfield Forbes, who spent much of his morning there talking to its co-organizer Elizabeth Denby.[72]

It is not clear whether the exhibition was intended as a one-off, or the first of many, but within a few months of its closure the organizers were given the chance of a regular home. Mr H. G. Montgomery, owner of the biennial Building Trades Exhibition at

Olympia, an international trade fair, offered them a stand at the show to be held in September 1932 and, subsequently, the rest of the decade.[73]

Since NHFO 1931 and 1932 were held at a time when central government was hampered in its ability to implement a full-scale slum clearance programme, the organizers' aim was to keep the tragedy of the slums in the public mind, and show how the sector had resolved the problem in London. At NHFO 1931, the organizers, the KHT's Denby and Elizabeth Alington of the UFC, took this contrast between the existence and resolution of the slum problem as their basic theme. Their display featured the SPHIS's 'Chamber of Horrors', a stand of giant models of the vermin and insects which infested the slums of Somers Town. This was complemented by a full-size model of a typical one-room slum dwelling with six wax-model inhabitants, alongside which stood, as a sign of things to come, the living room from a brand new flat. Denby and Alington also included posters of housing statistics to underpin the message of the more sensationalist stands.[74]

The mixture of attention-grabbing displays with sober statistics was repeated at NHFO 1932. Its centrepiece was a model flat, built to Ministry of Health space standards, in order to give a physical demonstration of what the sector advocated. The volunteers also introduced a new theme that year, that of town planning. In true New Philanthropy spirit it had found a gap in state practice which it now proposed how to fill.[75] Central government was only beginning to acknowledge the concept that the wholesale replanning of districts might form a vital element in any slum clearance programme. Another innovation was the production of a catalogue. This contained short essays which complemented each display, and acted as a permanent reminder, and reference source, to other potential activists or converts to the cause.

When NHFO 1932 closed, it had attracted twenty thousand visitors in a fortnight and much enthusiastic press coverage. The *Architect and Building News'* reporter, for example, noted that, 'taken as a whole, the exhibit is stimulating and provocative, and should have a useful influence'.[76] For proto-modernists, the influence of the exhibition, and the decade of campaigning on which it built, would lie in three particular fields. First, it demonstrated the importance of collective action. Second, the sector's absorption of the building into its armoury of propaganda techniques, alongside more conventional media like the film, photograph, exhibition as well as the report, magazine or pamphlet, would be of particular importance for a movement whose architectural output would never be prolific. Finally, the unabashed determination of the volunteers to campaign from the peripheries – its seizure and celebration of its vanguard status – would establish a modus operandi which, like that of the DIA, showed that, however marginal a group might be, change could nevertheless be achieved.

Sites of campaign III: the architectural media

While encounters with the DIA and the housing volunteers were significant in providing contexts in which the nature of space and form might be re-thought, neither was primarily concerned with modernizing the principles and practices of contemporary architecture. This, like the political scene in the 1920s, had, for the most part, settled into a state of polite consensus against change. The innovations of the Arts and Crafts movement had, by and large, mutated into a neo-Georgian or a Voysey-esque domestic architecture, while variations of classicism tended to prevail for public buildings. The latter style was increasingly underpinned by the schools of architecture which, by the 1920s, were superseding pupillage as the main form of architectural training. Most, like Liverpool University, where Fry trained, and London's Bartlett School and the Architectural Association, had adopted curricula based on the French *Beaux-Arts* system, an approach which, in the longer term, suggested that Britain's national language of architecture would be classical.

For architects who were disconcerted by this adherence to historicism there were few places to turn in the 1920s. Their professional body, the Royal Institute of British Architects, was a bastion against change, one reason why so many looked to the DIA instead; education, as noted, was similarly hidebound. There were, however, a few pockets of resistance. From the early 1920s, a small band of editors and journalists would use their publications as weapons in a campaign to modernize British architecture. Deploying form and content as their ammunition, they would bring to architectural discourse the same level of engagement with modernity that the DIA had brought to design. And like the Association, they would look to continental Europe for a model of how to proceed towards a modern idiom of expression.

To suggest that the architectural press was influential on the British movement is not, of course, an innovation. Of all the sites discussed in this chapter, it is the only one which has been widely acknowledged in the existing literature. Where the discussion here differs from the standard account is in its concern to see the architectural press as one among several sites, many inter-related, from and through which the modernization of British architecture was achieved. Such an approach allows a shift in emphasis away from the more usual characterization of the press as a deus ex machina through which the passive architectural world was finally awakened to the 'saviour' of modernism. It also allows a wider range of journal to be considered – the *DIA Quarterly Journal*, already discussed, *Country Life* as well as *The Architectural Review* – and a new understanding constructed of the intersection of personnel among these journals and other progressive sites.

Country Life

It is only relatively recently that awareness has grown of the not insignificant part played in debates about the modernization of British architecture by the weekly magazine *Country Life* and, in particular, its chief writer, Christopher Hussey. We are more accustomed to award *The Architectural Review* this accolade yet, as John Cornforth has shown, Hussey was among the first moderns to use a magazine both as a medium to promulgate exemplary forms, and as a rallying point for like-minded campaigners.[77]

The tardiness of this recognition reflects, perhaps, the fact that in many respects both Hussey and *Country Life* seem unlikely protagonists in the evolution of a British modernism. A member of the landed gentry, Hussey was Eton and Oxford educated. On coming down, he joined *Country Life* in 1921, a magazine which, since its founding in 1897, had built its reputation on its detailed articles about the nation's country houses as well its reporting of the social comings and goings of the country set. This apparent unlikeliness serves, however, as a useful reminder of the broader consensus on which the British movement was built. For despite its fondness for the great houses of the English past, *Country Life* had always combined this with coverage of new country houses, especially those by the pre-war moderns in the Arts and Crafts movement, and had shared their desire to move towards a style of the age.[78] Hussey revived this aspect of the magazine after the war, looking particularly to Europe in the absence of a native modern architecture.

From 1925, a slow stream of articles, some by Hussey, some presumably commissioned at his instigation, were placed in the magazine. There were reports on modern Swedish architecture and a series on work in Germany. New York skyscrapers were discussed in 1927 and Hussey himself would write on the use of concrete and steel in housing. In 1928 there was coverage of the new workers' estate at Silver End in Essex, and by the early 1930s the first articles on British modernist work would be published.[79] Hussey did not, however, confine such propaganda work to fomenting change through the medium of text and half-tone photographs. Alongside this effort, he was also embarking on a more active strategy to achieve the modernization of contemporary architectural culture.

In 1923, Hussey became one of the first British people to own and read Corbusier's *Vers une Architecture*. Galvanized, he decided that it was the moment to form a small group dedicated to promulgating the Corbusian message, and around him gathered Noel Carrington, to whom he would present a copy of the masterpiece, Serge Chermayeff and Frederick Etchells.[80] They were an interesting bunch. Chermayeff, Russian-born and Harrow-educated, was just embarking on a career as an interior designer at this point, having spent much of the early 1920s as a professional ballroom dancer in Argentina, perhaps the most unlikely background of all the British movement's members. He seems to have been recruited because he worked in the office in which the group met.[81] Carrington was an old friend of Hussey, and his colleague, but his recent membership of the DIA would have anyway signalled him as an ally in the modernizing cause. Etchells was the most significant member and brought to the group an impeccable pedigree and, in 1923, the most experience of being a 'modern'.

A decade older than his contemporaries in the group, Etchells had been associated with the Bloomsbury Set before the war. A painter, and associate of the Omega Workshop, he had then changed sides, joining Wyndham Lewis's Vorticists in 1914. Equally at home in Paris and London, after the war he remained allied to Lewis and kept in touch with the latest developments in French art, although he ceased to paint, turning his attention to architecture from 1923.[82] His awareness of the Parisian and British artistic avant-garde made him an obvious target for Hussey, as did the fact that he was either in the process of, or about to embark on, the translation of *Vers une Architecture*.[83]

Ultimately the group would be short-lived. It seems to have devoted itself primarily to discussion: Hussey giving a speech, 'Mechanics and Architecture', in its 1924–5 session. But the very idea of gathering together, of trying to institutionalize a shared interest, was important, even if a little premature. Of equal significance was the group's attempt to present the principles of modern design to the public by means of an exhibition, as it proposed to do in 1925. Although this was again unsuccessful, it likewise provides valuable evidence of a modernizing impulse in British architectural culture well before the period to which it is usually dated.

The Architectural Press

By the mid-1930s, Hussey's allegiance to things modern was beginning to wane as he became increasingly preoccupied with a different sort of Britishness in the picturesque.[84] This diminution in support might have been more serious had not another journal already superseded *Country Life* as the mouthpiece of the emerging British movement. This was *The Architectural Review*, the flagship publication of the Architectural Press. Its sister publication, the weekly *Architects' Journal*, would also back up the cause.

Like *Country Life*, *The Review* was a journal predisposed to the modern. Established in 1896, its founding purpose had been to promulgate the Arts and Crafts movement. By the early 1920s its combative origins had been somewhat diluted by a propensity to cover the contemporary preference for the classical.[85] A series of changes to the staff during 1927 would, however, lift *The Review* from its adherence to the architectural status quo, and see it resume its campaigning zeal.

That year saw the proprietor's son appointed editor of *The Review*. Under the helm of Hubert de Cronin Hastings, both it and *The Journal* would henceforth be dedicated to bringing British architecture into communion with modernity. Hastings' motivation to do this, and his ability to achieve it, lay in his background. Unlike the patrician Hussey, he left school at 16 and immediately went to work for the Press. This on-the-job training was combined with attendance at the Bartlett School of Architecture, then presided over by Albert Richardson, renowned for his firm adherence to *Beaux-Arts* classicism. This experience was to prove Hastings' epiphany. Encounters with students at the Slade School of Art, which like the Bartlett formed part of University College London, introduced him to the principles of modern art and, in particular, Clive Bell's concept of Significant Form. The contrast between this and his classes at the Bartlett seemed unfathomable and led him, he recalled, 'to reject the horrors of Richardson's world and the overblown monumentality of the neo-Georgian buildings of the day'.[86] Throwing his T-square across the studio, he abandoned his architectural training for good, committed himself to the Modern Movement, and set about persuading his father that *The Review* and *Journal* could survive if they too were dedicated to the cause.[87]

Although Hastings was appointed editor to both journals, his concern was not with their day-to-day running but the ethos which underpinned them. Very much an impresario – John Summerson would call him the 'Diaghilev of English architecture' – he gathered around him those who would help him make the Press's journals the appropriate mouthpieces of the modern age.[88] As Assistant Editor he appointed Christian Barman, another stalwart of the DIA, and brought in 'bright young things' such as John Betjeman, Robert Byron and Evelyn Waugh as contributors.[89] Undoubtedly his most significant appointment was Philip Morton Shand. Educated at Eton, King's College, Cambridge and the Sorbonne, Shand combined a flair for languages – he spoke French and German fluently – with extensive travel. Journeys to Holland, Switzerland, Finland and Germany brought him into firsthand contact with leading European modernists and his photographs of their work would be published frequently by Hastings. Such knowledge made him the leading authority on modernism of his day.[90]

Hastings' concern was not simply to modernize *The Review*'s content by publishing articles which considered the latest architecture in Sweden or Germany but to ally this with a completely new approach to the way that the architectural periodical was designed. Again, such a policy looked back to the earliest days of the Architectural Press when, like its contemporaries *Country Life* and *The Studio* (founded 1893), *The Review* had taken advantage of new technologies of photographic reproduction to transform the representation of buildings. Spindly engravings gave way to sumptuous half-page photographs.

Thirty years later, through new combinations of image, text and layout, Hastings sought to realize the idea, as John Gloag recalled, 'that the pages of the magazine should have the same effect on the reader as a modern building would have on the viewer'.[91] Photographs were trimmed or, conversely, and innovatively, allowed to bleed across whole spreads. Coloured inks were also used, and writers like Betjeman encouraged to demand alternative typefaces if it suited the content of their article.

Such a command of form and content, and the harnessing of technology to synthesize it into a coherent mode of expression, was the result, as Gloag put it, of Hastings' passionate belief 'in a new way of thought … not a new style'.[92] In the late 1920s, such a stance was what distinguished Hastings' journals most from that of his contemporaries. So while *Country Life* published modern work, as did *The Studio*, and the otherwise trade-oriented *Architect and Building News* had pursued a policy since 1925 of publishing photographic essays on European modern work by Howard Robertson and Francis Yerbury, their coverage lacked the moral imperative which underpinned policy at the Press.[93] Hastings shared, then, the programmatic modernism of the generation his journals would, in part, inspire; a position which would mean that for the next thirty years the Architectural Press and the British movement were synonymous.[94]

That there would be a movement for the Press to champion reflects the more particular conditions in which 'an architecture for to-day' emerged in this same period. These were the moments which, in Freeden's model, saw the broader context of a mass of people and ideas intersect with a smaller group of individuals' thoughts and deeds, giving rise to a new system: in this case, a British architectural modernism.[95] Labelled here sites of encounter, these moments were often contingent, a chance meeting, and nebulous, the shared experience of particular types of social space. Their ephemerality means that it is not always possible to document them with precision, nevertheless, as the final part of Chapter 1 seeks to show, they were of the utmost importance for the movement's evolution. On the one hand, they would bring a set of formal and spatial influences to British modernism which would complement the institutional and informational sources already outlined. On the other, by providing the contexts for like-minded architects and clients to meet, they provided the catalyst for the movement's crystallization into built form, and the formation of a collective identity.

Sites of encounter

One day in 1925, the young Max Fry, newly qualified and in his first job at the architecture-planning practice of Adams and Thompson in London, looked up from his desk to see someone emerging from Adams' office. It was the successful applicant for the post of the firm's secretary, a young man named Wells Coates. Fry recalled the moment:

Smoothing with one hand his crimped wavy hair and with the other taking a cigarette from his mouth in sweeping arabesques performed for the theatrical pleasure of it, he surveyed me … for what I was and what I might be worth to him, and deciding in my favour, gave me a conspiratorial wink … In a matter of days we were boon companions.[96]

On such a chance encounter, it might be said that a movement was founded. In this office on Victoria Street came together for the first time the two men who would do most to lay the foundations of modernism as a definite and manifest part of British architectural culture. In 1925, they could, of course, have had no notion that this would be the ultimate outcome of that meeting. That it was reflects two factors. As Fry's recollection suggests, it is clear that both men recognized in the other an as yet inchoate desire to change and to progress, and saw that this was a journey of discovery on which they might embark together. It would then be the synthesis of this desire with the particular territories and knowledges that they traversed which brought them to the realization that their cause was the modernization of British architecture.

Of the two journeys, Fry's was the simpler. Although he seems to have joined Coates in his forays into the salons of Bohemian London, discussed below, and read his fair share of advanced literature, Fry's modernization was, as we have seen, conducted primarily through his membership of the DIA.[97] The exemplary work he saw in its lectures and journals gave a vocabulary to his discontent, and showed him that there were alternatives to the ersatz forms of contemporary architecture which he saw going up around him in central London. It would be some considerable time before Fry was able to find a client who would give him the freedom to express the new ideas such work inspired in him.[98] Nevertheless, in the shorter term, he was able to use his membership of the DIA to carve out an organizational base from which, when the moment came, some of the first steps to build the movement would be taken.

For Coates, the journey was a much more complex one. From the autobiographical writings which survive from this period emerges a vivid picture of a man conducting an urgent search for a vocation, as well as a new way of life, eager to join forces with those who, like him, were hungry for change and who might guide him towards his destination.[99] It was, perhaps, the job at Adams and Thompson, and the encounter with Fry, that first gave Coates the inkling that architecture might form his ultimate goal but the fact that he was there at all reflects an earlier epiphany.

Coates' journey

On the surface, Coates' background, unlike that of his solidly bourgeois friend, Fry, was utterly exotic. Born in Tokyo in 1895, he spent his formative years in Japan, leaving only at the age of 18 to return to his native Canada. This exoticism was, however, tempered by the fact that his parents were Methodist missionaries, the gravity of their calling reflected in a son who, back in Vancouver, quickly assumed the well-worn path of a dutiful scion of the colonies. Hence his journey home had been to take up a place at the University of British Columbia to read engineering: the prelude to a life in an eminently useful profession. As a loyal subject, he suspended his studies to enlist in the Great War and served in the Artillery before becoming a pilot in the Royal Naval Air Service.[100]

Resuming his studies in 1919, he graduated in 1922, and was awarded a small grant to attend Imperial College, London, where he researched a thesis on 'The Gases of the Diesel Engine'. It was the achievement of his doctorate in June 1924 which seems to have awoken Coates from this colonial trajectory. Its bestowal led not to celebration but to a period of crisis and self-reflection. Realizing that engineering was not, after all, his vocation, he applied himself to the task of discovering what, instead, was.

Reflecting his training, Coates' search for a vocation would be a systematic one, conducted with the utmost seriousness according to what he described as 'a well-defined plan'.[101] It would be funded by the temporary jobs he took in offices like Adams': jobs that would sometimes become educations in themselves. Not long after meeting Fry, for example, an opportunity to work for the *Daily Express* took him to Paris for a few months, an experience from which he returned, his friend recalled, 'metamorphosed'.[102] More typically, the plan entailed the pursuit of a detailed programme of study which encompassed, so he explained, 'every development of modern knowledge and culture' as well as the 'rediscovery of knowledge and culture of the past'. His outline of the programme gives some idea of what this meant. He wrote:

> First, I re-read with a new vision … the great names in English literature, especially poetry and the drama … In science I read all the literature of relativity physics and the new astronomy … Einstein … Bertrand Russell … and on the metaphysical foundations of science … Wittgenstein (Tractacus-Logico-Philosophicus); in psychology all the published works of Freud, Jung and Adler, … in anthropology … Malinowski, WHR Rivers; Biology and bio-chemistry: scientific papers in publications of institutes etc. In philosophy I re-read Plato, Aristotle, Lucretius etc. Bacon, Descartes, Kant, Hume, Locke, Berkeley, and for the first time Pascal, Schopenhauer, Hegel, St Thomas Aquinas etc. Philosophy and psychology of art and criticism: the above, and TE Hulme, TS Eliot, Ogden Richards and Wood, Matthew Arnold, Coleridge, Marianne Moore, Robert Graves, Herbert Read, LP Smith, Wyndham Lewis … modern literature: TS Eliot, Marianne Moore, EE Cummings, Graves, Read, David Garnett, Virginia Woolf, the Sitwells, D H Lawrence, Norman Douglas, James Joyce, Marcel Proust, Jean Cocteau, Drieu la Rochelle, Paul Morand, Ezra Pound, Arthur Waley (Chinese translations) and a host of others. In modern painting I made a special study of the origins in Cezanne, VG [sic], Gauguin, Monet and Manet etc., and of the living painters Picasso, Derain, Matisse, Duncan Grant, Braque etc., and in sculpture Epstein, Dobson, Brancusi, Maillol, and in modern music, Prokofiev … Honegger, Hindemith etc.[103]

The scope of this programme offers a fascinating insight into what a young man in search of modernity thought would be relevant to his quest. Assimilated with the other conditions outlined in this chapter, it is also indicative of the intellectual basis on which the British movement would stand and suggests how Coates was, in due course, able to project himself as the movement's leader. Quite simply, he knew more than anyone else did.

Bohemian London

Alongside reading, Coates also sought out less solitary, though equally progressive, forms of self-education, spending his evenings in London's Bohemia, a site rarely mentioned in histories of the movement but one which would exert much influence on its final genesis. He gravitated to Fitzrovia, in the western half of Bloomsbury, which was occupied by a slightly more rough and ready set than those who flocked around the Woolfs in Gordon Square further east.[104] In the clubs of Soho and Gower Street, and the bedsits of Charlotte Street (to which he would soon move), he had much to learn. Their denizens offered him models of how a self-styled avant-garde might organize and operate. Further since they tended to live unconventionally, the environments they fashioned to accommodate such spatial practices hinted at the form a new architecture might ultimately take. More simply, in providing Coates, and his contemporaries, with an environment in which, at last, they felt 'at home', they became embedded into a social network from which the first modernist commissions would arise.

One site in Soho would be of particular importance for the development of Coates' political sensibility and his awareness of how a group with a cause might organize to develop and impart ideas. This was the 1917 Club in Gerrard Street which had been founded by Leonard Woolf and friends to celebrate the Bolshevik Revolution. Described as 'a home of political idealism, democratic fervour and serious progressive thinking', it gathered to its dusty rooms all those dedicated to creating an alternative to the Edwardianism which prevailed in contemporary political life. On any one evening, an engineer in search of modernity might meet and hear there Ottoline Morrell, Clement Attlee, Osbert Sitwell, H. G. Wells, Alec and Evelyn Waugh or Aldous Huxley.[105]

A less highbrow, but similarly influential, site was another club, the Cave of Harmony, which was founded in 1921 by the dancer and actor, Elsa Lanchester. Located in an old stable in Chenies Mews, off Gower Street, she ran the club with the painter John Armstrong, who doubled up as caterer, costume and set designer, and the future film director James Whale. They put on cabaret and one-act plays, including Chekhov and Pirandello, and hosted after-hours dancing sessions. Here Coates encountered artistic Bohemia for the first time, and acquired a social circle which included the clubs' founders, painters such as John Banting, Cedric Morris, Nina Hamnett, and the publisher Francis Meynell, and through them acquaintance with Edward Wadsworth, Paul Nash, Ben Nicholson and Frederick Ashton.[106]

Such friendships serve as another example of the influence of an emerging generation of avant-garde painters on those who would forge the British movement. We have already seen the liaison among Etchells, Hussey and Carrington which was developing at this time, and the inspiration from the Slade School on the young de Cronin Hastings. It would also be a significant influence on the reformers at the DIA.[107] These encounters did not, however, just provide precedents in how to re-think the language of form, but also of how to re-think space.

In the interiors of the clubs and bedsits of London's Bohemia we can find what were perhaps the first attempts to establish the spatial expression for new modes of life – whether that be of entertainment or daily existence. In contemporary descriptions of such spaces there is a very palpable sense that existing types of building could not do what our Bohemians demanded of them. Too poor to build anew, they therefore improvised, re-built, added or took away from such spaces in order to make them accommodate better their modus vivendi. In this respect, Lanchester's choice of an old stable to host her club is significant. A relatively neutral space, she and Armstrong could construct within it the settings for whichever activity the club would pursue on any particular night. The fact that the club also served as Lanchester's home signals changing sensibilities of where and what home might be for Bohemians like her and, hence, of what might constitute a modern domesticity. She recalled:

> I lived at the studio and slept in a kind of balcony-loft which I had built at one end; I climbed up a ladder and through a trap door to get to it. In this comfortable den I really felt independent and secure. I could see down on to the dance floor through a little square window, and could retire if I wanted to and just listen to the music and general babble.[108]

The spartan and ad hoc qualities of Lanchester's loft are echoed in the description of another Fitzrovia interior, this time the bedsit in Fitzroy Square occupied by the painter Kathleen Hale (whom Coates knew through Cedric Morris). Hale's recollection is also of interest because it points to the sensibility which motivated so much of what these Bohemians did, and which would have such an impact on new forms of space making in the 1930s. Although her room was furnished only with a fourth-hand table, a bed, a chair, bucket and jug, it was, she wrote, 'beautiful'. And she recalled how,

> Early each morning I would blissfully survey my humble possessions. The spacious bareness around me was heavenly after a childhood spent among heavy furniture, thick carpets and pictures in ponderous gilt frames ... the sense of freedom, the lack of responsibility, was quite wonderful.[109]

Despite all this searching, it would not be until 1927 that Coates finally found his vocation. Its achievement was caused by perhaps the most contingent factor of all, love. That summer he married Marion Groves, a young graduate of the London School of Economics, whom he had met at the Cave of Harmony in 1925, and who now worked for Francis Meynell at the Nonesuch Press. It would be in the act of setting up home, in the two rooms they shared in Doughty Street, that Coates discovered that his metier was, in fact, architecture. This first interior, although it survives only as a description, suggests that his modernism was in place almost from the start, its vocabulary evolved from the sites and spaces he had occupied in his journey through Fitzrovia. Groves described it thus:

> Wells went to Heals and chose the plainest furniture and haircord carpet and had plain curtains made of corduroy with a line design painted on them by John Banting, who painted another on a cupboard. Wells took aluminium sheeting and covered the fireplace. He enclosed the gas cooker near the door in a sort of lobby.[110]

Coates may have found his metier, but the fact that this interior would form the first step of a career offers a clear demonstration of how the particularities of an historical moment allow the intimate to intersect with wider events. In this instance, the synthesis of his personal epiphany with the friendship network of Fitzrovia allowed Coates to realize that he was not just articulating his and Marion's sensibilities in space and form but those of a wider generation. For, having seen the Coates' new interior, Arthur Lett-Haines, partner of Cedric Morris, recommended him to a friend who needed 'modern' furniture for her drawing room. Then, a chance meeting with another set of friends resulted in an introduction to the manufacturer Alec Walker who ran Crysede Silks, winning Coates a commission to design a store.[111] This in turn led to a fruitful association with the firm, Cresta, founded by a sacked employee of Crysede, Tom Heron. It would be his extensive use of plywood in the interiors of the stores he designed for these men which would lead, as we shall see in Chapter 3, to the liaison with Jack Pritchard. While, a little later still, Coates' Fitzrovian friend made good, Elsa Lanchester, now married to the Hollywood actor Charles Laughton, would commission him to transform their marital home in Gordon Square, from an 'old Victorian flat into the open liveable space it is now' (Fig.1.3).[112]

So by 1928, both Coates and Fry had found the answer to their search. For them, modernism offered the way out of the impasse into which both architecture, and their lives, had fallen. Now sure of their path, their task became to convert others to the cause, and ensure that this new way of thinking became the future of British practice. The circumstances in which they were able to achieve this goal were not entirely of their own making, however, and had much to do with a young architect and his patron who, like them, had met in a similarly chance encounter.

Figure 1.3
Interior of 34
Gordon Square,
London, designed
by Wells Coates
for Elsa Lanchester
and Charles
Laughton,
c. 1933–4.

Finella

A teashop in Museum Street, close to the British Museum, was the unlikely setting for the meeting in 1926 which would lead to the creation of the centre around which the British movement would first begin to coalesce. It was there that a young Australian architect, Raymond McGrath, struck up a conversation with a Cambridge English don, Mansfield Forbes. McGrath, a classically trained graduate of the University of Sydney, had arrived in England at the beginning of 1926 with a travelling fellowship, intending to pursue some sort of postgraduate study in his discipline. This proved difficult to achieve, and after a failed attempt to enrol at the *Ecole des Beaux Arts* in Paris, McGrath had improvised a programme of study in which he divided his time between classes at Westminster School of Art and the Brixton School of Building, and reading in the British Library.[113] Although he seems not to have shared their anxiety about the contemporary world, McGrath was, nevertheless, like Fry and Coates, a young man in search of a direction.

In Mansfield Duval Forbes he found a mentor.[114] An extraordinary polymath, Forbes had pioneered the study of English Literature at Cambridge, combining this with interests which ranged from history to folklore and economics. Above all he was devoted to the fine arts, architecture and sculpture in particular, and was at the centre of a 'very lively art group' in the city.[115] On hearing McGrath's predicament, Forbes immediately suggested that he apply to become a research student at his college, Clare, and within a few months the Australian found himself in Cambridge, pursuing a thesis on 'The Development of the Theatre and Buildings for Public Entertainment'.

The thesis would never be completed and the pair instead embarked on another project. Keen to expand the stage on which he pursued his artistic interests, Forbes leased a house from the university which he intended, in addition to becoming his new home, to serve as a meeting point for all those who, like him, 'were genuinely concerned with contemporary expression'.[116] Such a purpose required a very particular setting, and Forbes saw in McGrath an architect young, and perhaps manipulable, enough to create what he envisaged. Like his Bohemian contemporaries in Fitzrovia and Bloomsbury, then, he recognized that a new mode of life required innovations in the language of space and form.

Between 1928 and 1929, the two men transformed the dull Italianate villa which was 'The Yews' into the astonishing house, 'Finella'. Forbes seems to have been the driving force in this process. For him the basis of a contemporary mode of expression lay in new materials and he insisted that he and McGrath attend every building exhibition, and inspect any new material, which came onto the market. This delight in materials was fused with a decidedly camp sensibility; consequently Finella's modernism would be very different from that which Coates would produce.

Typical of Finella's heady combination of materials and campery was its forty-foot-long entrance corridor (fig. 1.4). This featured silvery-green glass ceilings and walls covered in silver leaf, while the junction where corridor met staircase hall was marked by a silver-leafed elliptical vault. Visitors were intended to proceed down this passage, then pass through a gold-leafed door into the house's salons: the 'Pinks'. These were two drawing rooms, occupying the width of the house, separated by a pair of folding doors made from copper Plymax, a metal-faced plywood. As their name suggests, the salons were painted, walls and ceilings both, in pink, their 'rosy room-skies' further lightened by the new steel-framed French windows which opened on to a new grass court into which a fountain was set.[117]

It was to the 'The Pinks' that, as he had hoped, Forbes attracted those concerned with 'contemporary expression'. Among the artists known to have mingled there were John and Paul Nash, Jacob Epstein, Henry Moore and Eric Gill. While Forbes' interest in the new materials led to a friendship with Jack Pritchard and through him introductions to Wells Coates, Max Fry and, on one occasion, a visit from Charlotte Perriand. McGrath, of course, was a frequent visitor and Serge Chermayeff, de Cronin Hastings, John Gloag and Morton Shand were also guests.[118]

Although individual modernists like Coates and Fry had known each other for some time, their coming together at Finella with all the other key proto-modernists made it evident to them that a critical mass was emerging and that they were ploughing not a lonely furrow but a common cause.[119] Joining forces with Pritchard, they therefore

Figure 1.4
The corridor and hall at Finella, Cambridge, Raymond McGrath and Mansfield Forbes, 1928–9

initiated what turned out to be the first of a series of attempts to establish a permanent institutional base for those who advocated modernism in architecture.

The Twentieth Century Group

Forbes would be the catalyst for the first of these moves to institutionalize.[120] In the wake of the completion of Finella, he had proposed the formation of what he described as a 'Company to float modern ideas in England'. Variously named, 'Décor Ltd', 'Newtopia (Housing Design and Furnishings) Ltd' and 'Chapter One (House Designs and Furniture) Ltd', his notion was to promote what he called 'aesthethics' – aesthetics, according to him, being 'the ethics of the future' – through the execution of design work.[121] By late summer 1930, this had become the Twentieth Century Group (TCG), founded not as a commercial venture but 'to define the principles to which contemporary design should conform', its ultimate goal, 'the achievement of architectural unity'. And although Forbes was among the Group's officers, its committee included Coates and Pritchard, as well as Noel Carrington, Raymond McGrath, Serge Chermayeff and Howard Robertson.[122]

Coates and Pritchard had, in effect, hijacked Forbes' proposal. Such a tactic was typical of their first attempts to engineer individuals into a movement. At this point, their strategy seems to have been to link up with anyone who showed a propensity towards the modern, hoping thereby to gather strength in numbers and perhaps to effect a transition from within, pushing the moderns towards the modernist. Hence, on receipt of the letter in which the don outlined his plans, Pritchard replied positively but noted, 'I know of another similar organisation which is about to be formed and it would be just as well to explore how the two could work together.'[123]

The short life of the TCG hinted at the weakness of this strategy. Although the members did manage to agree that they should hold an exhibition about contemporary design, this came to nothing. Surviving documents suggest that members spent most of their meetings in discussions about whether new members should be allowed to join, or whether this might contaminate the Group's founding goal.[124] It was clear that there were tensions between those who would define themselves as modernists – Coates (almost certainly responsible for the mission to define the principles of contemporary design), Pritchard, Chermayeff and, perhaps, McGrath – and those such as Forbes, Carrington and Robertson, who were concerned for the modern but less inclined to the doctrinaire. By February 1932, this first effort at collective activity had therefore petered out. A letter from Forbes hints at the general exasperation members felt: 'I am, indeed, much sick with the inability of the practitioners to pull together, and feel I have wasted d____d [sic] sight too much time and money on this kerboodle.'[125]

The failure of the TCG did not mean that all was lost for the modernists. In parallel with their efforts with Forbes, Coates, Pritchard and Fry were also pursuing another alliance, this time with the DIA. The Association had much to attract them. It was a well established organization, unlike the TCG, and had good connections to the design establishment. Fry was already a member, as was Pritchard, so they already had links within the Association. There was also the fact that in 1930, it was beginning to experience some turmoil of its own on which they might hope to capitalize, thereby building a modernist stronghold within an existing group.

Alliance with the DIA

At the beginning of this chapter we saw how, from about 1924, as the British economy endured another lull, young industrialists had sought to revivify the DIA's campaign to modernize manufacturing through the instigation of a plan of research and the publication of a quarterly journal. Their efforts were, however, to be sidelined as preservationists took over the Association and the first of the *Cautionary Guides* was published. The Wall Street Crash, and the onset of the Depression, however, came as timely reminders of the Association's founding goal. By February 1930, its Annual Report would signal that the beginnings of a change of direction were underway when it recorded the resolution taken at the AGM 'for a more aggressive policy' in a period of 'new economic changes'.[126]

Over the following eighteen months, a small group within the DIA used this resolution to reorient the DIA back to a direct engagement with design. Comprising Fry and Pritchard in league with William Crittall and Noel Carrington, their concern was to manoeuvre themselves and potential allies onto the DIA Council and, from that position, launch a new strategy for the Association's work.[127] By April 1930, Carrington was Vice-Chairman and Basset-Lowke, Gloag, Pritchard and Thorp were all on Council; the following year Carrington became Chair and Pritchard his Vice, their President, Frank Pick.

The faction announced its first plans for the DIA in May 1931.[128] Under the headline 'Design: A Necessity', Carrington outlined the Association's 'New Economic Policy'; the allusion to Soviet practice a clear sign of the seriousness of his and his collaborators' intentions. His message was simple. In a period of national crisis, the only way to sustain the economy, and regain export trade, was to look to those industries where 'skill and design count most', and to inaugurate a renewed campaign to persuade manufacturer and consumer alike that design was the way forward. The first proposal was therefore for an 'Exhibition of Industrial Arts, planned on a worthy scale, and expressing fully the twentieth-century movement'.[129]

In September 1931, phase two of their plan was launched. 'A Plan for the DIA' sought to place the organization of the Association on a much more systematic basis so that it could target its campaigns more effectively. Hence a first proposal was to divide members into different categories: manufacturers and distributors, architects and designers, and ordinary members. The next step was to focus the Association's resources on persuading manufacturers of the merits of design. Closer contact would be sought with trade organizations and a programme of propaganda drawn up which, in its first year, would focus on key areas of manufacturing, those related to the office, bathroom, dining or living room, kitchen. A series of lunch meetings would be held, bringing together designers and manufacturers according to each of these themes. These activities would then be complemented by the founding of a new journal to replace the *Quarterly Journal*. Overseen by an Editorial Board which comprised John Gloag, Crittall and Pritchard, the intention was that each issue would be devoted to one of the Association's chosen themes, and assembled by a specialist guest editor.[130]

The decision to effect a liaison with the DIA would be much more successful than the attempt to work through the TCG. This, perhaps, reflected the fact that it was Fry who led this particular charge, a man who, unlike Coates, was more able to effect compromise if it meant the achievement of a goal. It would always be his task, as he commented wryly later, to act as 'manager to a prophet'.[131] It may also be attributed to the fact that by 1931–2, their understanding of what constituted their modernism was more developed than it had been eighteen months earlier, a status reflected in Coates' desire to make the formulation of the principles of contemporary design part of the TCG's work. A year's worth of practice – Coates was then working on the BBC project – and Fry's immersion within the DIA had helped them to strengthen their theoretical position.

Fry's quieter approach, and the men's greater maturity, would have three significant outcomes. The first was the commitment of the proposed exhibition to the 'twentieth-century movement'. The second, Fry's guest editorship of the inaugural issue of the DIA's new journal, *Design in Industry*, which was published in the spring of 1932. Its subject matter, the office, is of less interest than the fact that in Fry's main essays, 'The Modern Office – What Is It?' and 'The Management of Space Organization, a Word to the Architect' he offered what may well have been the earliest public articulation of this newly articulated modernism.[132]

In both essays Fry was careful to rehearse the party line on what he called the 'revolution of mind' in contemporary design. His definition of modern architecture was practically word perfect. It was the result, he wrote, 'of a new analysis of programme, material and structure, which can be expressed in the materials which prove economic and fitting, whether they be brick, stone, concrete or steel'.[133] It was only when he moved to a more detailed discussion of the starting point for this new analysis, that a more personal, and British, inflection was brought to the debate. For Fry, the abiding principle of the new architecture was 'just economy', an approach which, he argued, had its 'jumping off point', though not its stylistic precedent, in the traditions of Georgian building, 'and a taste for things well made'.[134] The pages of the journal would demonstrate what this meant, and why it was so important to adopt this new approach. His readers would therefore notice 'the absence of that superficial ornament which the words *luxury*, *de luxe*, *super* and so on, call to mind' and see instead

> something cleaner, more wholesome and better proportioned, *better designed*. Something with a much stronger chance of developing into a virile national style of doing things, than the make believe products of this passing age of reproduction and stunt.[135]

The final outcome of the liaison with the DIA was the involvement, this time, of Coates, in the Exhibition of British Industrial Art in the Home which was held at Dorland Hall in London's Regent Street, in June and July of 1933. This was not, strictly speaking, an initiative of the Association, but had, in fact, been mooted by Christopher Hussey in 1932, who felt that circumstances were now, at last, ripe to hold the exhibition he had first proposed in 1924–5. He recruited the architect Oliver Hill to oversee the design of the show and secured some financial backing from *Country Life*. Hussey's friendship with Carrington suggests that he would have been aware that a similar exhibition formed part of the DIA's plan, and he therefore approached the Association in the hope of obtaining both further funding and support, particularly through its contacts with manufacturers. After much debate, the Association agreed to become a silent partner to the venture as it was reluctant to associate itself publicly with an exhibition over which it did not have ultimate control.[136] Such niceties did not worry our DIA modernists. The exhibition offered the chance for public exposure, as well as the building of further contacts both with the cognoscenti who would visit the show, and the manufacturers who would contribute to the displays. Thus Coates would serve on several of the exhibition's selection committees. He was joined by John Gloag, while Hastings was a member of its Executive Committee.[137] Coates would also be an exhibitor, having persuaded Pritchard to sponsor a full-size mock up of their project for the Lawn Road Flats.[138] Likewise Chermayeff would exhibit a Weekend House, fully furnished.[139]

The production of the DIA Plan, and their participation in the Dorland Hall exhibition, marked the culmination of the efforts of Fry, Coates and Pritchard to work within the progressive design establishment. Although the DIA would continue to be an important base for the men, Fry becoming its Chair in 1934, there nevertheless remained the sense that they had achieved as much as they could within a forum whose primary preoccupation was to improve the design of things not buildings. There was also the fact that, as a group within a group, they would always lack autonomy and, at a time when they were still developing their ideological position, risk confusing their aims and ideals with those less committed to the ultra-modern. Authority and a clear identity would only come if they committed themselves to one cause alone: the transformation of contemporary architecture.

It must, then, have been the very happiest of moments when Coates received, some time in the autumn of 1932, a letter from Siegfried Giedion, Secretary of the Congrès Internationaux d'Architecture Moderne (CIAM), asking him to

> Please let us know if interest in the new architecture is still so lukewarm in England, and whether there are really no young men to be found there who have the courage, and feel it is their duty, to form a collective organisation, and establish contact with us.[140]

Towards MARS

The invitation owed much to the network of allies and sympathizers in which Coates and Fry had embedded themselves since the late 1920s. The link in this instance was Philip Morton Shand whose previous suggestion of his cousin, Howard Robertson, had failed to result in a British chapter of CIAM, although he had attended the first two Congresses in Frankfurt and Brussels.[141] Hence Giedion's rather pleading tone in his letter to Coates, Shand's next suggestion, three years later. This time the response was very different. Here was the opportunity for which Coates and Fry had been waiting, perhaps since that first meeting in 1925.[142] Over the next few months, further letters would be exchanged between Giedion and London, as the two men set the necessary structure in place to form what, on 28 February 1933, would be formally constituted as the British affiliate of CIAM, subsequently named the MARS Group.[143]

Coates and Fry brought to the organization of MARS their experience of failure with the TCG, the tactics which had worked with the DIA, as well as the countless lessons learnt from their journeys through the various sites of encounter and campaign that this chapter has outlined. Fundamental to the creation of the MARS Group, therefore, was the fact that it would be a group devoted solely to architectural reform and one whose central and leading members were architects; Pritchard would play no role in this group. MARS was to be, then, an architectural avant-garde, its goal only achievable if the group were a tightly knit and progressive organization. Among its founding principles and policies, therefore, was the agreement that:

> the membership of the group must … be kept select and small, and be restricted to those who are willing and able to carry out effective work for the group and for the Association, according to their qualifications and functions.

Echoing the DIA Plan, they therefore proposed three categories of membership:

> Architects, engineers and allied technicians, non-professional adherents to the ideals of the professional members … and Professional or non-professional snob names of the intellectual or 'international' variety.[144]

Such strictures were manifested in the founding members of MARS: Coates, Fry, and David Pleydell-Bouverie (Coates' then business partner), all described as 'Architects', and three 'Non-Professional Adherents', Morton Shand, Hastings and John Gloag.

Although the membership would expand, it was always carefully vetted.[145] This may be attributed to the experience of compromise in the TCG, and also at Dorland Hall, where the austere modernism of Coates sat awkwardly alongside the more decorative modern forms of Oliver Hill. This had convinced MARS' founders that only those committed solely to the new architecture should qualify for membership. Hence Coates, in his second memorandum as Chair of MARS would write:

> Certain people who are popularly and notoriously known as 'modern' architects obviously do not qualify in our sense, eg Howard Robertson, Grey Wornum, Oliver Hill, Walmesley Lewis, Oswald Milne, etc.

He had already excluded Joseph Emberton as a potential member in the founding Memorandum, 'on the evidence of the published designs of the New Olympia Exhibition Building'.[146]

As well as addressing the structure of the new group, the founder members also had to agree what its precise programme of work would be. Like all chapters of CIAM, they were required to prepare material for its Congresses. By May 1933 the members had agreed that a programme of research into slum conditions would form the basis of their contribution to CIAM 4 held on board the SS *Patris* that summer. Alongside this their activities would largely be framed by the central organization's guiding principles:

> To formulate contemporary architectural problems; to represent the modern architectural idea; to cause this idea to penetrate technical, economic and social circles and to work towards the solution of the contemporary problems of architecture.[147]

While it was relatively easy to formulate contemporary architectural problems, since this could be achieved hypothetically when commissions were few and far between, it was in approaching CIAM's two other goals that Coates and Fry faced their greatest challenge. However certain they were that modernism was a live movement in Britain, its advocates were very much in a minority. They needed to persuade nearly everyone, not least the state and the architectural establishment, of the necessity of the new architecture. That they recognized these conditions was evidenced, first, in their decision to embrace their vanguard status and constitute MARS as a close-knit, solely architectural, group and their carefully defined categories of membership. A decision which was informed, perhaps, by the example of their contemporaries in the voluntary housing sector and the self-conscious political and artistic avant-gardes of Bohemian London.

The corollary of this decision to place themselves outside the mainstream was their acceptance that the minority nature of their work would make it difficult for them to engage with a general public in the same way that an organization like the DIA had sought to. Their campaign of persuasion would have to be more indirect. By working outwards from those closest, and thus most sympathetic, to them, they would create, in the longer term, a ripple effect which would draw more and more into the fold. Fry would later explain their rationale:

> We as a group, and I always insisted on this very strongly, had nothing to do with the general press, the general media, because the ideas were too diffi-cult to bridge the gap between ourselves and the *Daily Mail*. We had to go through another stage to spread our ideas. We had first to present our ideas to the talkative intellectuals of our age.[148]

Such a stance was clear from the start, not only in the desire to include intellectual or snob names as a category of membership but also in the list Coates drew up of those to whom the press release announcing the Group's formation should be sent. This included only architectural or engineering journals, professional societies such as the RIBA, the Town Planners' Institute, the DIA and the Royal Society of Arts, newspapers such as *The Times* and the *Manchester Guardian* and periodicals such as *The Weekend Review*, *New Statesman and Nation* and *The Listener*.[149]

Towards action

Since that first meeting in 1925, Coates and Fry had travelled far. Eight years of prepara-tion had imbued them with the sense of duty, and rendered them sufficiently coura-geous, to be able to move into the next phase of work. The time was now ripe to make Britain modernist.

Part 2

Rhetorical Modernism

Part 2

Part 2

Introduction

Between 1925 and 1933, Wells Coates, Max Fry and their co-conspirators had succeeded in creating an identifiable group of modernists within British architectural culture. Manifested in a growing number of commissions for interiors and buildings, their participation in, and co-organization of, events such as the Dorland Hall exhibition, it was reinforced by the movement's institutionalization in the MARS Group.

Its foundations secured, after 1933 the movement left its pioneer phase and entered the period of its first maturity. This new phase, which continued until 1939, was characterized by an expansion of ambition within the modernist camp. So while the task of effecting a take-over of the architectural establishment was sustained, they also pursued Fry's strategy of engaging with the 'talkative intellectuals' by extending the field in which they operated through the elision of their advanced ideas about form with advanced ideas about social reform. This was to be achieved through the formation of a series of progressive 'fronts': mutual alliances with reformers in other disciplines whose campaigns encompassed a need for new forms and spaces. With them they would create a series of model environments and discourses which would demonstrate how modernism as a social, spatial and formal practice could bring Britain and Britons, and not just architecture, into a complete reconciliation with modernity.

That the formation of such fronts was possible may be attributed to two main factors. The first was that in organizing themselves as a cohort, and forging links with cultural sympathizers like Mansfield Forbes and organizations such as the DIA and the Architectural Press, architects like Fry and Coates not only gained access to potential clients, but also became embedded within networks which extended beyond the world of culture into the realms of political, social and economic reform. Through such means, reformers in different disciplines became aware of the work of others. While the economic circumstances of the late 1920s, and the nascent state of architectural modernism, prevented any concrete results emerging from this mingling of narratives of reform, these encounters nevertheless created the pre-conditions for potential unions, should circumstances change. By the early 1930s they had.

The first years of the new decade saw the beginnings of economic recovery in Britain and, alongside that, a more general optimism about the possibilities of achieving change. This was evidenced in an enthusiasm for planning across the political spectrum and a raft of government legislation (which owed not a little to the propaganda campaigns of social reformers in the twenties) that sought to address some of the worst social problems of the inter-war period. The specifics of such legislation will be discussed in more detail in the chapters which follow. It is sufficient to say here that this newly constructive attitude on the part of the establishment created among modernist reformers – architects included – the growing sense that the moment was now ripe for their propositions and prototypes to exert a real, and influential, command over this discourse of change.

Part 2 of *Re-forming Britain* explores the progressive fronts which came together to formulate and proselytize such propositions and prototypes and takes as its organizing principle the two inter-related arenas of reform with which modernist architects sought to engage in this phase: health and housing. Both were the subject of significant, and high-profile, debate in the 1930s for it was widely understood that in their un-reformed state they constituted substantial obstacles to the achievement of modernity, whether social, domestic or economic. As will become apparent from the different case studies explored here, by joining forces, modernist architects and modernist reformers were able to achieve a more complete realization of their agendas of reform through the creation of buildings or other artefacts. These, in turn, rendered their agendas more visible, especially when mediated further through other discourses such as film or photography and thus, it was hoped and intended, more likely to direct and dictate the blueprint for social change.

The section begins with a discussion of what was the most fundamental social problem of the inter-war years: the health of the nation. Chapter 2 considers how two sets of alliances articulated and enacted, through the commissioning of new forms of space, two very different but equally progressive practices of health care that they had developed as a response to that problem. The first was created by Owen Williams and Fry, along with the doctors Innes Pearse and George Scott Williamson, the philanthropist Mozelle Sassoon and the housing reformer Elizabeth Denby, and expressed in the Pioneer Health Centre and the adjacent block of workers' flats, R. E. Sassoon House in Peckham, south London. The second is the campaign to improve citizens' health in the north London borough of Finsbury. This was the work of local councillors and the practice Tecton. It was manifested in the Finsbury Plan, of which the Finsbury Health Centre was the only part built before the outbreak of war in 1939.

Attention then turns to the housing problem. Chapters 3, 4 and 5 offer a detailed consideration of the way in which progressives developed a distinctive philosophy of housing reform in this decade, one which addressed the re-shaping of the homes of both the middle and the working classes. This is explored first through a discussion of the work of Coates and Jack and Rosemary Pritchard at Lawn Road in Hampstead and their attempts to create an appropriate setting for modern middle-class life in the Isokon Flats. The following chapters consider the collaborations which produced model environments for a modern form of working-class domesticity. Discussion focuses first on the writings and exhibition work of Coates, Fry and Jack Pritchard. It then turns to a consideration of the collaboration between the MARS Group and those who organized the New Homes for Old Exhibition of 1934 and their joint development of a new theory of social housing. The realization of this theory in built form is then explored through analyses of Amyas Connell and Basil Ward's Kent House, built for the Saint Pancras House Improvement Society in north London, and Kensal House, a collaboration among Max Fry, Elizabeth Denby and the Gas, Light and Coke Company. Emphasis is placed on the way this theory of social housing assimilated other contemporary narratives of reform in the hope of creating completely transforming environments. This approach saw the principles of the labour-saving dwelling fused with notions about working-class citizenship, while the way in which these new dwellings might be furnished was viewed as an opportunity to educate their inhabitants as modern consumers.

While the discussion in Part 2 considers some of the most well-known buildings, events and texts of early British modernism, as well as introducing some hitherto little-known works, the intention here is not to reiterate the familiar story of its unfolding. Instead, by framing the discussion of their creation in terms of their makers' engagement with contemporary debates about social – as well as architectural – reform, the intention is to set these projects within the broader theme of this book. That is, a concern to move away from the notion that modernism in Britain was an extraordinary idiom, unconnected to prevailing architectural and social preoccupations, and imposed upon an unsuspecting public. In each of the following chapters, therefore, the objective is to locate and explain each project, and those involved in it, within a very specific set of historical circumstances, thus allowing some significant revisions to prevailing assumptions. The first of these is the contention that modernism should be understood as one part of a broader attempt to address the obstacles which prevented British progress towards modernity in the inter-war period. Viewed in these terms, what becomes important is the way in which its advocates sought to direct such attempts towards specifically modernist solutions.

The second is that by seeing projects such as the Finsbury Health Centre or Kensal House as the product of collaborations between two sets of reformers, due acknowledgement is given to those who commissioned the buildings as well as to those who designed them. In some instances, moreover, it is suggested that the client should be considered co-designer, such was their impact on the final building. This attention addresses a significant gap in many histories of British modernism: their failure to consider the clients who created the opportunities for modernist architects to realize their ideas and thereby helped to push modernism towards hegemony.[1] This disregard reflects two historiographical prejudices: the architect-focused methods of the majority of the historians who have written on the period and, more recently, the desire to paint modernism as an idiom imposed rather than one which was a response to a genuine demand. The evidence suggests that, on the contrary, by the late 1920s and throughout the 1930s, modernism was not something launched on an unsuspecting audience. Rather, it was more typically the result of a shared recognition of the emergence of new modes of life, which required new forms of spatial expression.

Third, this approach provides an insight into the meaning of the form and style of the buildings here discussed. In this respect, it is important to note that it was only in this second phase of modernist activity in Britain that a substantial number of modernist buildings were constructed. Between 1925 and 1933, the very nature of a pioneer phase, as well as economic circumstances, had meant that modernism had operated primarily in the form of texts, interiors or discussions and a very small number of buildings. From 1934, however, the quantity and types of the latter increased significantly. As a result of the alliances outlined above, this period saw the construction not just of private houses, the traditional 'first step' for any new architectural idiom, but large-scale projects such as blocks of flats and public, or quasi-public, commissions for health centres, zoo buildings or seaside pavilions.

Though modernist principles were now additionally expressed in built form, modernism had not yet, by any stretch of the imagination, reached a position of dominance and it would remain, quantitatively, an entirely marginal practice throughout the period. This situation created particular demands of those buildings which did exist and meant that, like the un-built modernisms which preceded them, projects such as Kensal House operated primarily as persuasive discourses whose form and programme became rhetorical tools through which the modernist agenda of reform could be advanced. This tendency is labelled here 'rhetorical modernism'. It meant that for architects and clients alike, both the building type and, in particular, the form of the buildings they created, were carefully crafted to ensure that they drew attention to the cause, both *in situ* and in reproduction through assorted media; a lesson well learnt from the propaganda practices of the DIA and the voluntary housing sector in the 1920s.

So rather than seeing the Le Corbusier-influenced work of Connell, Ward and Lucas, or the Miesian borrowings of Fry, as a wholesale and thoughtless copyism, and evidence of the lack of a true modernism in Britain, we might, instead, understand their deployment of such radically different forms as a rhetorical device to propagandize whichever cause their building served. Furthermore, a look beyond the rhetorical form to the rhetorical content might also allow a reassertion of the Britishness of this modernism. For while their surfaces may have been borrowed from elsewhere, they cloaked programmes which derived from peculiarly British approaches to social reform. It would be through this hybridization of progressive form with progressive content that modernism was able to capture some of the most significant discourses of inter-war reform.

Chapter 2

A new landscape of health

> In the last resort, all progress, all empire, all efficiency, depends upon the kind of race we breed. If we are breeding the people badly neither the most perfect constitution nor the most skilful diplomacy will save us from shipwreck.[1]
>
> Cecil Chesterton (1905)

If there was one preoccupation which, above any other, can be said to have underpinned the reformist agenda in inter-war Britain, it was the state of the nation's health and, in particular, that of its urban working classes. The poor health of the majority of Britons raised serious doubts about the possibility of the country retaining both its imperial and industrial position. Reformers from across the political spectrum therefore sought to develop new models of health care which could create a nation of healthy citizens and thereby maintain Britain's status as one of the world's great powers.

As the quotation from the political journalist Cecil Chesterton at the head of this chapter suggests, it was around the twin poles of empire and efficiency that these anxieties revolved. Although these concerns had their structural roots in the 1870s, they had first begun to be widely recognized in the 1890s.[2] The researches of the social investigator Charles Booth had shown that 30.7 per cent of London's population lived in poverty with 'means ... barely sufficient for decent, independent life' and documented the poor housing in which most workers lived.[3] The ramifications of such conditions became apparent when it was revealed that only two-fifths of those who volunteered to fight in the Boer War (1899–1902) were fit to do so, a statistic which led to the establishment by parliament of an Interdepartmental Committee on Physical Deterioration in 1904.[4] Its report confirmed Booth's observations, and noted widespread physical unfitness which was caused by poverty, malnutrition, environmental pollution and what were perceived as bad personal habits.[5] The realization that Britain's engagement in an imperial war had been seriously jeopardized by the abject health of its soldiers was compounded, as noted in Chapter 1, by evidence of Britain's economic eclipse by competitor powers such as Germany, Japan and the USA. By the turn of the century all these countries, at the same as they competed with Britain for empire, were also exceeding her in both reproductive and productive output. Their birth rates were higher than Britain's, while their industries were both more efficient and more modern. The 1890s, for example, saw Germany and the USA exceed Britain's level of steel production. Germany, in particular, led the way in chemical manufacturing, optical glass and electrical goods, all of which Britain imported rather than manufactured.[6]

This intersection of anxieties in the first decade of the twentieth century resulted in what Geoffrey Searle has called the quest for National Efficiency: the attempt to restructure national life so that Britain could retain its imperial and industrial dominance. This was manifested in many ways: attempts to modernize industry,[7] an increase in the machinery of government, and, in particular, by interventions by the state into the bodies and lives of the working-class population. Between 1906 and 1914, for example, the Liberal government introduced a raft of welfare legislation. This included the discretionary provision of free school meals and school medical inspections, old age pensions and, in 1911, a National Insurance Act which introduced compulsory health and sickness insurance for the majority of those in industrial employment.[8] The ultimate aim was to create a citizenry which was fully capable of working, and fighting, in modern conditions. Such state intervention was unprecedented and highly controversial.[9]

In the inter-war decades these debates, and the general anxiety about the health of the race, as it was then called, were further inflected by the loss of 700,000 men of child-producing age in the Great War and the severe wounding or maiming of over 1.5 million more.[10] This exacerbated concerns about the nation's reproductive health while, as Searle has noted, the gloomy state of the post-war economy caused another crisis similar to that occasioned by the Boer War, as Britain's heavy, and most 'virile', industries entered their death throes.[11] This period therefore saw further legislative attempts to ameliorate the lives of the working poor. The 1918 Maternity and Child Welfare Act provided for the establishment of ante-natal and infant welfare clinics. A year later state-subsidized social housing was introduced for the first time, a subject discussed elsewhere in this book. Such 'improvements in housing, sanitation, hygiene and medical skill', as a 1937 social survey put it, did have concrete results. Whereas two-thirds of conscripts to the Great War had been unfit for service, this had been reduced to a third of soldiers in the Second World War.[12] Nevertheless, despite such progress, access to proper health care remained extremely patchy. The National Insurance Act did not cover the families of workers and services such as dentistry were not included in its terms. Most people had to rely on private insurance schemes or had no health care at all. The fact remained that a substantial number of working people lived in poor housing and experienced poor health: enough to produce the third of men unfit for military service in 1939.

The issue of how this phenomenon might be addressed in an urban context is the focus of this chapter. It explores two projects which attempted to grapple with the problems of urban modernity, their creators deploying methods that encompassed the social, medical and spatial in order to bring about a reconciliation with this condition so that society, and its working-class citizens in particular, could progress. These were the south London Peckham Experiment, which was begun in 1926, and manifested in the purpose-built space of the Pioneer Health Centre of 1935, and the north London 'Finsbury Plan', initiated in 1935 and embodied in the Finsbury Health Centre of 1939. Two prototypical environments – spaces both re-formed and reforming – their founders hoped that they would be widely emulated. They also tell us a great deal about the intersection among modernist architects and architecture, the evolution of social welfare debates in this period, and the effecting and dissemination of reformist agendas.

The two projects have much in common. Both exemplify the way in which modernist reformers in complementary fields – health, housing, architecture – came together to form an alliance to create and promote narratives of change. This is the process which this book has signalled as being one of the central ways in which modernist architects were able to promote their cause in this decade. Further, in both cases, a new form of architecture was central to their instigators' achievement of prog-ress, a belief augmented by their conceptualization of health care as part of a wider programme of reform which would require further significant interventions to the built environment. Finally, given that these were both exemplary projects, they acted as works of rhetorical modernism, at once accommodating a new vision of health care and connoting it through their form.

Both schemes can, then, be understood as having been enacted by programmatic modernists. Their optimism about the possibilities of modernity allowed them to at once criticize its negative impact while at the same time locating its resolu-tion in the technological, administrative and organizational techniques modernization had created.[13] Yet, as both contemporaries and later historians have recognized, this commonality, and the corollaries to it outlined above, resulted in two projects which also had significant differences.[14] It is because of these that the Centres are of particular interest. They serve as reminders that in the inter-war years there was not one monolithic Modernism but rather co-existing, complementary, sometimes competing, modern-isms, any one of which might ultimately have prevailed. So while in hindsight the Finsbury Health Centre, and the Plan of which it formed part, might be seen as the epitome of the modernist project in so far as it was funded by local government, focused on a curative model of health care, and through treatment and education sought to inculcate in its users a state of health, the suggestion here is that in its day, it represented only one potential modernism of health. The theory and practice which underpinned the Pioneer Health Centre is evidence of a contemporary modernism which was then equally valid, and one which indeed might be understood as the more radical of the two. Unlike Finsbury it was predicated on a model of preventive medicine. It was supported partly by philanthropic donations but chiefly by the weekly subscrip-tion paid by its working-class members, and it functioned through the medium of a social-cum-health club in which conventional medical treatment was not dispensed. Through this technique it sought to facilitate in its members a sense of responsibility for their own health. The fact that both projects could coexist on opposite sides of London is testament to the experimental nature of this decade. This was a period, unique perhaps, when differing ideas about the nature of social welfare and health care and its spatial form could be freely debated. It is to a detailed discussion of these two proto-types that this chapter now turns.

The Peckham Experiment

The Peckham Experiment was initiated by two doctor-biologists, Innes Pearse and George Scott Williamson,[15] and a small committee of philanthropists in 1926.[16] The Experiment, as its title suggests, was to be a highly focused investigation. Through the establishment of a club, the Pioneer Health Centre, it sought to ascertain the exact state of health of a small working-class community in south London. From that base its objective was to develop techniques of care which could improve or enhance the health of that community. Investigations were conducted in two phases. The first spanned the years 1926 to 1930 and convinced the doctors that further research was necessary and that there was a demand for the services they offered. Consequently, after several years of fundraising, a second larger experiment was started in 1935 which was housed in a new purpose-built Pioneer Health Centre, designed by Owen Williams. It continued until the outbreak of war in 1939.[17] This second phase also encompassed plans for similar centres elsewhere, as well as a new venture into social housing, of which one small test project, R. E. Sassoon House, designed by Elizabeth Denby and Max Fry, would be built on a site adjacent to the Centre.

To the prevailing concern for the effects wrought upon working-class bodies by the conditions of modern urban life, the doctors brought a particular, and sometimes peculiar, set of preoccupations which stemmed from their definition of what constituted health. Whereas many contemporaries would have defined it as the absence of disease, the doctors instead called health 'the physiological condition of an organism living in mutual synthesis with its environment'.[18] For them, the nature of urban life meant it was almost impossible for this synthesis to be achieved. They pointed to two especially overwhelming obstacles to this: the breaking up of traditional communities and environments, and the social welfare policies of successive governments which had placed too much effort on improving the lives of the unfit at the expense of developing the health of the fit. The latter factor, in particular, had led to the creation of what they called 'C-ness', people who were '"invalid" for work or fighting – devitalized'.[19] This resulted in considerable numbers of the population who were unable to operate at their most productive. Furthermore, if reforms were not made to urban life and medical welfare soon, there would be grave implications for the reproductive and racial health of the country. For the doctors, then, the real issue, was that

> We face two problems ... to see that only the fit marry and beget, and that having married and begotten, they have an environment in which the achievement of potential is possible.[20]

As the doctors' preoccupation with reproductive health and their concern for the loss of community life suggests, their attempts to mitigate the problem of 'C-ness' were informed by a distinct set of contemporary philosophies of social welfare and medicine. First, the ideological blueprint which would underpin the conceptual framework and organization of the successive Experiments came directly from the

Idealist politics of the voluntary sector. These emphasized the development of a sense of citizenship and responsibility among the poor alongside the necessity of both social and material improvements to their environments. These beliefs were then complemented and medicalized by those of the contemporary movement of Social Medicine. Its advocates believed that conventional medical practice had 'lost sight of the fact that individuals were both biological and social beings'.[21] They therefore characterized the body as an organism, something from which no part should be singled out for treatment or study; instead it should be treated as a complete entity. This twin emphasis on the body as both a corporeal and social being was then further intertwined with the ideological field of another branch of Social Medicine, that of reform eugenism.[22]

Like the National Efficiency movement of which it formed a strand, the eugenics movement sought to create an improved and modern society, but this was something it believed could only be achieved through the controlled reproduction of the race.[23] Its policy of Positive Eugenics focused on encouraging the middle classes to breed and defined the entire working class as unfit to reproduce (dysgenic). By the inter-war years, a sub-group within the Eugenics Education Society, the main institutional body for the discipline, was attempting to develop a less class-biased eugenics. Its advocates argued that among the working classes were submerged many individuals of good stock who were presently thwarted by their circumstances from realizing their full potential. This position was advocated by the scientist Julian Huxley, who would become a member of the Experiment's advisory committee in the 1930s.[24]

Huxley, though a eugenist through and through, was also a socialist, and uncomfortable with the Society's class bias. He argued for the application of Positive Eugenics across the classes, a position which he summarized in a 1936 article for *The Eugenics Review*, 'Eugenics and Society'.[25] His main thesis was the need 'to equalise the environment upwards before we can evaluate genetic differences'. He hoped, therefore, for a 'more generous social environment' in which people could develop, and argued that if everyone shared the same environment, then, so to speak, the wheat would truly be sorted from the chaff. The ways to achieve this 'single equalised environment' were to raise the standard of diet, the provision of facilities for healthy exercise and recreation, and the upward equalization of educational opportunities. He concluded that 'as eugenists we must therefore aim at transforming society'.

The Peckham Experiment can, then, be understood as an attempt to create an equalized environment so that the true quality of the working-class individual could be ascertained and realized. Before discussing what constituted this equalization, it is worth noting that, as might be expected, the doctors' definition of environment was not the typical one. It was a term they used extensively, and was one they conceptualized broadly, so that it could comprise both a material and a corporeal landscape. The body (especially that of the mother) was just as much an environment as the club, the home or the town; all of it required attention and reform:

> The power of the environment may yet be potent enough to save the individual. If environment can be changed *early enough*, the child at least may be saved from the twin shackles of disease and devitalization.[26]

In 1926, however, the doctors' ideas, and their fears for workers' health, were as yet theories. Hence, their first step, drawing on the narratives of reform which they espoused, was to put together an environment in which their suspicions could be tested. The solution was, as A. D. Lindsay wrote in his Preface to the first of the books in which the doctors promoted their work, 'a settlement, but one founded on medicine'.[27] At 142 Queen's Road, Peckham, the doctors set up a family club in a converted house. There, for a subscription of sixpence a week, member-families were entitled to the use of a nursery, social club, poor man's lawyer, laundry and dress-making facilities. In return they agreed to submit to what the doctors called the 'periodic overhaul', an extremely thorough medical and dental examination. From the data gathered, the doctors would be able to establish the state of health in this carefully selected area of London, a site which contained 'a moderately good artisan population, capable of benefiting from educational work'.[28] The combination of these procedures would establish and test techniques through which members could be brought to (the doctors' definition of) health and thus be enabled to become fully (re)productive members of society.

Such a concern reiterates the eugenic nature of the project, a position reinforced by the fact that it was possible only for families to join the club. This reflected the doctors' belief that the basic unit in society was, '*homo sapiens* ... an organism embracing man + woman' and neither was capable of significant function without the other.[29] It also meant that couples of childbearing age were regarded as proto-families and were therefore as eligible as those who already had offspring. A more tacit eugenism was evident in the choice of location. This area of Peckham was not populated by the very poor. Rather the majority of its residents were the sort of 'decent' working-class stock that was seen by reform eugenists as the backbone of a new society, were it not for the fact that its development was jeopardized by the problems of urban life.[30]

Thus the combination in one location of a health service with leisure facilities, what the doctors called 'instruments of health', was not simply a means through which the doctors could collect data about health but also a technique through which the doctors could combat 'devitalization'. Cut off from nature by town life, from a natural supply of food by industrialized production and packaging techniques, and the sense of community inherent in village life, individuals, they argued, particularly women, had lost touch with their true nature and their real role in society which was to form the organic entity of the family.[31] Crucially, and in keeping with their own modernity, the doctors did not believe it was possible to go back to the country like their garden city contemporaries advocated. Instead they believed it was possible to create a reformed space within the urban context through which members would be enabled to achieve a state of mutual synthesis with their environment and thus attain health. And it was because they defined health as such a synthesis that they thought 'cures' could be achieved by social rather than medical treatment; thus a member could be 'prescribed' learning to knit or chatting to another young mother. Hence a club whose focus to its member was a set of social facilities was, they firmly believed, the means through which the process of revitalizing the sense of community which had been lost in the modern city could be initiated.[32]

The device of a family club also solved another problem which modern urban life had caused for the promotion of health. Before mass urbanization, as Pearse and Williamson argued in *The Case for Action*, doctors had lived in the same areas as their patients and had been able to observe them as they went about their daily lives. They saw their clients in a state of ease as well as disease. Urbanization had caused the separation of the classes which meant that doctors now dwelt in different locations from their patients and they saw them only once disease had fully developed. This was a matter for great concern. Previously, constant neighbourly contact with their patients meant that doctors were able to observe subtle changes in health and consequently act to prevent them from becoming more serious; as they no longer saw their patients on a daily basis through social contact, such preventive work was not possible. People were becoming more ill than they needed to. They were unable to operate at full strength and thus were devitalized.

The club was, then, also an attempt to re-establish the beneficial gaze of the neighbourhood doctor. Had it only been a health centre, members would only have come when they believed themselves to be ill. The establishment of what was, in effect, a social club with a medical practice on the side would attract people on a daily basis. This enabled Pearse and Williamson to observe the members 'when operating unrestricted within [their] environment, unencumbered by illness' and thus be able to note change, whether that be for the better or not.[33]

The Centre was, as Lindsay observed perceptively, a medical settlement. At Queen's Road, and later in the purpose-built club, the middle and working classes could be re-united with the aim of regenerating both health (through the perpetual gaze of the doctors and their team) and community (through leisure facilities). And, in a further echo of settlement practice, the doctors also placed great emphasis on personal work and techniques to enable members to take responsibility for themselves: 'educational work, we consider, cannot be a matter of general propaganda; it must be a matter of personal and individual contact'.[34] Improvement only had meaning, and permanence, if it was something which the individual initiated her- or himself. Like their British Idealist ancestors, the doctors believed in immanent potential, something which could be brought out from individuals by

> continuous individual contact with a better example … the only sure and natural method of which we are aware of stirring the feeling, which alone is capable of giving the necessary urge to action.[35]

Better example could take many forms. It could be both moral, the example of other people's actions, hence the importance of individual contact – the chat with another mother – or the gaze of the neighbourhood doctor. Or it could be physical: the provision of amenities or an improved environment. This technique they gave the quasi-medical label of 'personal infection'.[36]

Such ideas and techniques were implemented and refined during the first phase of the Peckham Experiment. Over a period of three years, the Centre attracted 112 member-families.[37] This proved to the doctors that there was a demand for such a club and it was a major factor in their decision to launch a second and larger experiment. The other was that their investigations had revealed an alarming degree of disease and devitalization. Of those who had joined the Centre, only nine per cent were without any form of 'disease, disorder or disability'. In 32 per cent 'disorder was accompanied by disease' and despite the fact that the remaining 59 per cent appeared in a state of 'well-being', this surface masked actual disorder.[38] Such statistics had alarming implications for the future of the race and required further investigation. As the doctors declared, 'we had to go forward'.[39]

The Pioneer Health Centre

The creation of a new centre was to be a lengthy and drawn-out process. Although a two-acre site on the nearby St Mary's Road appears to have been secured as early as 1927, financial problems led to several revisions to the brief and the budget. The doctors would also reject a complete set of designs by the architect E. B. Musman before Owen Williams' scheme was finally approved in November 1933.[40] No copy of the final brief has survived, but it is possible to gain some sense of what Pearse and Williamson sought from the Centre's *Annual Reports* and their other publications.

Having established a basic set of instruments of health at Queen's Road – the club, the overhaul, the assorted amenities – the task now was to develop and augment these in a new building which would allow more 'scope for exercise of latent potential in the individual' and 'the means of lifting the organization out of the category of charity'.[41] This required a structure that was large enough to accommodate sufficient member-families whose subscriptions would allow the project to be self-supporting. In Phase One, charitable donations had subsidized operations, a situation which fitted ill with the doctors' insistence on the necessity of their members' self-reliance and responsibility. They therefore wanted a building which could accommodate the 2,000 families which they estimated would bring in an annual income of £10,000 on a two shilling weekly sub.[42] It also needed to be sufficiently spacious to house the other functions which the doctors believed necessary for the full development of the members' health and potential. In 1927 they envisaged that

> A complete health centre will have not only a swimming bath, gymnasium, practise grounds, dance floor etc, but will also have a reading room presided over by some genius quick to fan the latent potential to mental flame.[43]

One final aspect of the brief was that the new building itself should be an instrument of health. In the first phase of the Experiment the possibility of using space in this way had been severely limited by the establishment of the centre in an existing building. And while it is possible to consider the transformation of a building's purpose, in this case from a villa to a health centre, as a spatial intervention, as far as can be told few alterations were made to the building during its occupancy.[44] In a new structure, however, the very arrangement of space and form could be dictated in order that, alongside all the other instruments, it too could bring the member-families to a state of health. Such a brief, as the doctors wrote, required, '[a] new building, which is of necessity unlike any other'.[45]

Discussion about the design began in 1929 when the doctors were described as working 'in conjunction with' their architect, Musman, on the internal planning of the new building.[46] In 1930, the scheme was unveiled at the Royal Academy's annual exhibition and then published in *The Case for Action* a year later. It is hard to imagine a building more like any other than this design. While it did provide the requisite space for the gymnasium, medical area and the flame-fanning reading cubicles, and so forth, it housed them in an axially planned, neo-Georgian building which could easily have been mistaken for a municipal welfare centre (see Figs 2.1 and 2.2). In *The Case for Action* the doctors wrote positively about the design, but their subsequent actions suggest the realization that Musman's scheme did not provide them with the instrument of health they required.

The realization was also precipitated by the fact that during 1932 it became apparent that the Experiment's finances were not sufficient to retain both the site and construct a building which would have cost approximately £44,000.[47] Galvanized, from this point on the doctors seem to have become more demanding clients. So whereas in 1929 the description of their working 'in conjunction' with Musman on the design is belied by the result, this time they took matters directly in hand.

The first stage in this process was to revise the plans in an attempt to reduce costs to £30,000. To this end, Pearse and Williamson enlisted the help of a young graduate of the Architectural Association, J. M. Richards. He worked with them to draw up a set of indicative plans and specifications which would explain to potential designers what they wanted.[48] Another year, and a further set of revisions to reduce costs to £25,000, passed before the doctors were finally ready to present a new brief to prospective architects. This, in the informed re-imagining here, would insist on the need for economy on the one hand and, above all, that the building itself should function as an instrument of health.

What did this mean precisely? The very building – somehow – should allow its occupants to achieve synthesis with their environment. It could do this in a functional way by providing space for the other instruments of health but the doctors wanted more than this. Here the allied notions of 'infection' and 'continuous individual contact with a better example', and the characterization of the Experiment as a settlement, are useful in bettering our understanding of the Centre's potential design. In plan and form the building needed to attract or infect people with the desire to use it. Very simply, it needed to be a magnet for health. It should then be a beacon, emanating the possibility of a new life. Such a concept was not new. Most purpose-built settlements had been deliberately designed to stand out from their surroundings in order to signify the transforming environment inside. What had changed since the main period of settlement design in the 1880s and 1890s, was the emergence of the new materials of steel, concrete and plate glass. These could allow both more radically different looking buildings, and structures which could magnetize through their transparency, and it was these materials which the doctors appear to have favoured in their discussions with their Committee.[49] Such specifications the doctors summarized in their demand of their prospective architects that they design a building in which the 'sight of action was an incentive to action'.[50]

In October 1933, the Centre's Committee agreed to approach a number of architects and ask them to produce preliminary sketch plans within the costing (including fees) specified. These included Wells Coates, H. S. Goodhart-Rendel, and Owen Williams.[51] Apart from Goodhart-Rendel, who refused to comply with the conditions, all submitted designs either in ferro-concrete or brick and steel and all, with the

Figure 2.1
E. B. Musman,
Design for the
Pioneer Health
Centre, Perspective,
1930

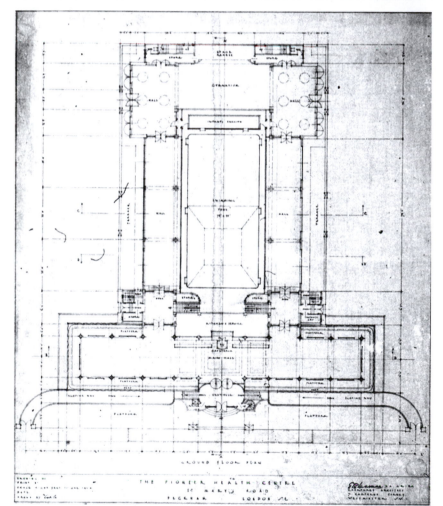

Figure 2.2
E. B. Musman,
Ground Floor Plan
for the Pioneer
Health Centre,
1930

exception of Coates, were within budget.[52] Following discussions the Committee decided, in November 1933, to choose the engineer Williams as their designer.[53] Although this decision may be partly explained by the fact that his work was already known to the Committee through the Sainsbury family who were benefactors of the Centre, Richards points to two further deciding factors. First, he noted that the doctors admired the relation between function and structure Williams had achieved in his other work. Second, and for Richards the primary reason, was that given the doctors' experience with Musman, he was chosen because they did not want someone 'with his own architectural theories' who would allow his dogma to get in the way of the building's true purpose.[54]

Eighteen months later, on 27 March 1935, the new Pioneer Health Centre was opened by the King's Physician, Lord Horder (Fig. 2.3). This time the doctors could declare themselves unequivocally delighted:

> The outstanding suitability of the building for its function as a health centre is beyond criticism. Just as the grouping of the family-member for health required a new technique, so the building was required to be of a character previously unknown.[55]

Set back from the street line, nestled on its two-acre site behind newly planted gardens, the new Centre was a remarkably effective response to the brief. At the same time as it had met the need for functional spaces to accommodate the swimming pool and medical rooms, it was also able to use space and form to achieve the doctors' more nebulous demand that the building function as a site for personal infection.

The key to this was Williams' structural device of a central concrete frame with mushroom columns supporting floor and roof slabs which was bookended by load-bearing sections. From the exterior this created a building which had a sufficient mass to connote its significance, but none of the unfriendly municipal munificence or monumentality of Musman's design. Instead, as the building came into view along St Mary's Road, a street which, with one exception, was otherwise strung with brown brick

Figure 2.3
Owen Williams,
The Pioneer Health
Centre, Peckham,
1935

villas, the overwhelming impression was of transparency and openness. This was especially so when the windows were folded back as they could be, or when it was illumi-
nated at night. Thus, in good settlement tradition, passers-by were able to glimpse a
sign of a potential future, something signified not just by the overt modernity of the
façade but also by the views its frame-like form allowed into the building.

Once inside, the transparency of the building established a different form of
communication (Fig. 2.4). The structural frame enabled a free plan in which all dividing
walls, except those in private areas, were made from glass panels. Echoing Huxley's
prescription of healthy exercise and recreation as the means to a healthy nation, the
building was then further divided into distinct zones. Each was nominally assigned to a
specific floor: the ground was for physical culture; the first for social culture; and the
second for mental culture and the medical rooms. In fact, the doctors' primary emphasis
on the facilitation of physical exercise permeated the entire building and it was reflected
in the plan's orientation around the central swimming pool. As a key area of potential
activity it could be viewed from the cafeteria and main hall on the first floor which overlooked it. In addition, an open-air nursery and a gym were sited on the ground floor. The
first-floor hall could be used for keep-fit classes, as could the flat roof, which was also
available for roller skating. Space for social activity was also sited across the building
through the provision of the cafeteria as well as a theatre and clubrooms.

The merging of physical and social culture was not just implicit in the plan
and designation of spaces, but also in the way they were intended to be used. Although
the doctors did 'prescribe' physical activity, the intention was always that self-motiva-
tion and -reliance should be enabled by the physical form of the environment. They
noted, 'It is essentially a building *designed to be furnished with people and with their
actions.*'[56] So watching swimming from the cafeteria windows might inspire someone
to think about learning to swim (Fig. 2.5). Or a sudden desire to form a discussion group
would be facilitated by the nature of the Centre's furniture. This related to the doctors'
concept of 'Self-Service Technique' which led to the furnishing and equipment of the
Centre being conceived as a set of tools which members could pick up when necessary. Commissioned from the architect Christopher Nicholson, he produced a range of
unit furniture which could be easily moved together or apart into a variety of configura-
tions (Fig. 2.6).[57] The concept was extended to the cafeteria which was also designated
self-service. This practice the doctors described as 'not an expedient but a principle'
and they declared that it had 'the merit of engendering responsibility and of enhancing
awareness as well as of increasing freedom of action'.[58] In addition, the cafeteria served
another function as a site in which women members could learn to cook nutritious
meals: a practice which not only brought them into contact with real food again but also
served to remind them of their primary nurturing roles as wives and mothers.[59]

That the Centre was a highly gendered site is not really surprising, predicated
as it was on a view of the human race as comprising 'man + woman'. All the doctors' writings expressed the conviction that their interventions to corporeal and material environments were intended to return men and women to their appropriate gender roles. So the
cooking lessons in the cafeteria were complemented by the women's workroom on the
top floor of the Centre, which was equipped for needlework and dressmaking; while the
men's hobbies would have been woodwork or shoe-mending.[60] It is, however, too

Figure 2.4
Owen Williams,
Plan of the Pioneer
Health Centre,
1935

SKETCH PLANS

The general construction of the building is that of flat slabs on cruciform columns allowing of maximum flexibility of planning : no immovable partitions.

Whole building planned on a grid 18ft. square, varied at either wing to give a 24ft. span for gymnasium and theatre.

All single lines on the plan represent easily removable brise block partitions.

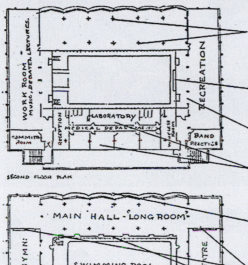

Cruciform pillars carrying the concrete floor spaces, and affording conduits for power, water, etc., allow flexibility of internal planning.

Window giving view of swimming bath.

Billiards, table tennis, darts, etc.

There is privacy in the Physiological Department.

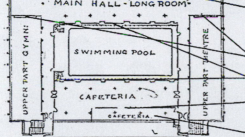

Sliding windows the height of the room can be thrown back in Summer. Bays between the pillars forming natural points of congregation for groups of people.

Windows giving on to gym and theatre.

Windows surrounding bath.

Cafeteria counter and window into kitchen.

Kitchen for preparation of cafeteria meals, including Nursery teas by mothers.

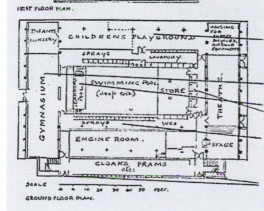

Covered playground for children of all ages, with Infants' Nursery located to catch the full afternoon sun.

Gymnasium with easy access to the Nursery, playground, and to the garden.

Infants' and learners' pool. Slipper baths
Lavatories and spray-chambers for men and women on either side of the bath chamber.

The main entrance is at the back, leaving the front unobstructed for maximum utilisation of sunshine and open aspect.

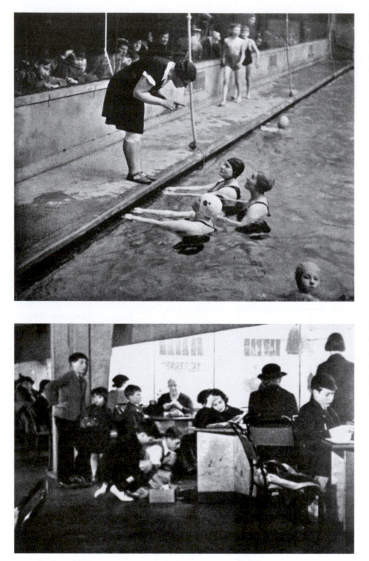

Figure 2.5
Centre members
watch a swimming
session from the
cafeteria

Figure 2.6
View of cafeteria
showing
Christopher
Nicholson's
furniture

simplistic to dismiss this division as overly conservative. As will become apparent in the
other projects discussed in this book, however progressive they were, they all operated
from the then commonplace belief that men and women had specific biologically given
roles in society. Nevertheless in important ways the Centre did, if not subvert gender roles,
then offer some more enlightened interpretations of them. Like many progressives at this
time, the doctors saw marriage as a complementary partnership in which neither
husband nor wife had the upper hand. They also believed that modern urban conditions
prevented a fully companionate married life from flourishing so they were at pains to
create opportunities for couple-members' relationships to develop. Hence they included
a nursery in the Centre to which children could be banished for usefully long periods of

time. They also encouraged couples to see birth control as a shared responsibility and to plan the conception of their children. Pearse, in particular, was ahead of her time in her approach to maternity care. She rejected the traditional period of confinement before and after the birth – pregnant Centre women were often to be found swimming in the pool days before their babies were due – and she encouraged new mothers to breastfeed at a time when this was not the norm. The Centre was, then, a gendered environment, but one gendered in a particular way and always with the end in mind of revitalizing the family and hence society.

At the same time as it provided an environment which could allow the immanent potential of member-families, whether *in utero* or not, to be realized, Williams' design was also required to provide the doctors and their team with the instruments through which the Experiment could be continued. It is worth quoting at length from Pearse's description of the building to convey how it met this need:

> Here then is a modern building designed as a laboratory for the study of human biology. The general visibility and continuity of flow throughout the building is a necessity for the scientist. In the biological laboratories of botany and zoology, the microscope has been the main and requisite equipment. The human biologist also requires special 'sight' for his field of observation – the family. His new 'lens' is the transparency of all boundaries within his field of experiment. Sixteen steps down from the consulting room and he is engulfed in the action going forward, and which, by reason of the very design of the building, is visible and tangible to his observational faculties at all time.[61]

The instruments of the glazed partitions and the open plan allowed the doctors and their assistants to move unimpeded throughout the building and to observe the members as they went about their social and physical activities. Thus they were able to assess, discreetly, the social welfare of the members, and how each changed as she or he grew into health and family life.[62]

This purpose-built Centre, the primary instrument of health, was intended as an enabling environment, not a didactic one. It created a setting in which member-families would be facilitated to take responsibility for their own health and thus embark on the process of revitalization, and through that the achievement of a harmonious modern urban life. And in bringing this selected portion of the working class into health it also created reformed maternal environments in which babies could be conceived. Parents and children could then continue to benefit from the enabling environment of the Centre and a race of modern and model citizens would result. There was, however, one flaw in this otherwise perfectly re-modelled space. This was the problem of the members' domestic environments. A significant lesson learnt during phase one was that although a centre could provide an environment rich in the instruments of health, on leaving it member-families returned to homes of a distinctly less improving nature. Most, despite being relatively well off, lived in one- or two-room dwellings in overcrowded and subdivided houses.[63] Pearse noted that 'if individuals after their "cure" remained in the environment in which they had been living ... disorders were prone to recur'.[64] Without decent housing, all their hard work to improve health and social life was in danger. Was it possible to find a way to improve all the environments to which their member-families were exposed?

A single equalized environment

The first attempt to explore the issue of reformed dwellings was made in 1932 when the Centre's Committee discussed the possibility of linking the new building with housing schemes in other boroughs. This came to nothing, and it would be another year before a realistic opportunity to involve itself in a housing project presented itself.[65] In October 1933, in an instance of one set of modernists finding another, Mrs Mozelle Sassoon approached the Committee with a request for a site on which to build 'sixteen working men's flats'.[66]

Mozelle Sassoon was a wealthy Mayfair philanthropist whose fortune derived from the merchant and banking company ED Sassoon of which her late husband was Director.[67] The death of her son Reginald in a steeplechasing accident in January 1933 had led to her decision to commission a block of workers' flats in his memory. This may have been due to the influence of an ambitious young housing reformer of her acquaintance, Elizabeth Denby. At this time, Denby was seeking to capitalize on her experience in the voluntary housing sector and develop a career as an independent housing expert, a figure she would call a housing consultant. It is not clear how the two met. It is, however, evident that Denby saw Sassoon's desire to memorialize her son as a means firstly to launch herself in the role of consultant and, secondly, to advance the cause of modernist architecture to which she had been converted through her work on the New Homes for Old Exhibitions. By the summer of 1933, she had recruited another modernist, the architect Max Fry, to draw up a set of designs.[68]

A failed attempt to persuade Denby's then employer, the Kensington Housing Trust, to provide a site led them to Peckham, a project with which Denby was already familiar.[69] A collaboration had much in its favour. On a pragmatic level, it would provide a much-needed site, but the doctors' philosophies also echoed Denby's own and their consent would allow her to enact a more complete demonstration of her ideas on housing than might have been possible had the scheme gone ahead in Kensington.[70] By this time, Denby was at the forefront of the development of a philosophy of housing which infused the values of her voluntary sector background with the ideals of architectural modernism.[71] The resulting theory emphasized that working-class lives could only be improved by housing which was both well designed and incorporated extensive social amenities such as those which could be supplied by the Centre. It was also a firmly pro-urbanist theory, based on the premise that cities should be re-formed: a modern urban realm serving as a prophylactic against suburban sprawl. Her emphasis on re-forming both the social and physical environment thus echoed the doctors' concern to transform their members as both corporeal and social beings.

On 26 October 1933, therefore, the Centre's Committee agreed to give a portion of its two-acre site on St Mary's Road to Mrs Sassoon. There was one condition, that the block would be administered by a Trust on which the Centre would be represented.[72] A week later Sassoon formally accepted the offer and the Pioneer Housing

Trust (PHT) was formed to oversee the scheme with Williamson and Jack Donaldson on its Board.[73] Denby joined the Centre's Committee; the intention was that it should have a say in the selection of tenants.

That the two were complementary schemes, and the start of something bigger, is evidenced not only in the composition of the committees of the respective organizations but also in the *Articles of Association* which were drawn up when the PHT was registered as a public utility society in June 1934. It had three main goals: first, to acquire land on which to build or improve accommodation for the poorer classes at low rentals in Camberwell and elsewhere 'for the promotion of the health, decency and comfort of the persons so accommodated'; second, to establish or take over ante- and post-natal clinics for mothers and babies; and third:

> by education, instruction and advice, nursing, medical and other assistance and otherwise, to promote the health and welfare of parents and families, to develop the sense of parental responsibility, to promote the comfort, health and happiness of families.[74]

The vision, though it never came to fruition, was that the Pioneer Health Centre and Sassoon House should be the first steps towards a revolution in health and housing provision: a new landscape of health.

In the same way that the Centre's architecture would perform the rhetorical function of drawing attention to itself and the activities it housed, in their design of Sassoon House Denby and Fry used plan and form to connote the new domestic life which could be performed within it (Fig. 2.7). It too would be of a character 'previously unknown'. Their cream-painted five-storey block was thus a textbook exercise in modernist planning from its concrete frame, flat roof and cantilevered balconies to its *existenz-minimum* interiors (Fig. 2.8). It is not often remembered that this was the first occasion on which modernist techniques were used in workers' housing in Britain. They served to produce a block which was not only dramatically different from the other housing in St Mary's Road, but also to provide twenty three- and four-roomed flats which could be let at the low rents of nine and eleven shillings per week respectively.[75] In every way therefore, Sassoon House was intended as a model dwelling, demonstrating an economy and philosophy of housing which Denby, Fry, Sassoon and the doctors hoped to see repeated elsewhere.

In each flat, as *existenz-minimum* principles dictated, circulation space was reduced, the largest space was given to the living room, and the kitchen was planned on the galley lines favoured by the planners of the New Frankfurt, although its equipment was not nearly as sophisticated as in their German counterparts.[76] Nevertheless, at 8 by 6 feet, the kitchen was substantially larger, and better equipped with sink, gas cooker and gas copper, than anything tenants would have been used to; most would formerly have been lucky to have a separate space in which to cook. The kitchen opened into the living room which was, by virtue of its size (13 × 12 ft), the main focus of family life. Warmed by a brightly enamelled slow burning coke stove, it was lit by large south facing windows and a glazed door which led onto what was called a 'family' balcony (11 × 4 ft), which spanned the exterior of the living room and the rear bedroom. This reflected Denby's belief that if workers must live in flats then they should have

Figure 2.7
Elizabeth Denby
and Maxwell Fry,
R. E. Sassoon
House, Peckham,
1934

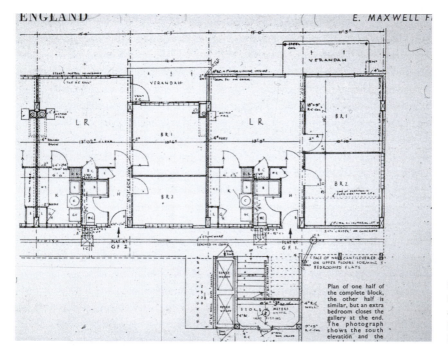

Figure 2.8
Elizabeth Denby
and Maxwell Fry,
R. E. Sassoon
House, plan, 1934

some sort of breathing space in compensation for lack of a garden, to which end it also contained a built-in flower box. This efficiently planned, labour-saving flat, which was free from dust-gathering mouldings, would, like the Centre, serve as a 'training' ground in which the woman tenant could develop her role as wife and mother. The block was, Fry recalled, 'a perfect receptacle for close family life'.[77]

The extent to which Sassoon House served as a receptacle for Centre families is hard to ascertain. It seems that because the flats were opened in advance of the Centre, in November 1934, that the original intention that the doctors should have some say over the choice of tenants was difficult to achieve. It would be Denby, in her newly appointed role as the flats' housing manager, who would take on this task, but she does seem to have tried to select the sort of families who would be ideal members of the Centre. From the 500 applications received, Denby was reported as saying that 'Finally, we chose young people with families', mostly from the Peckham district.[78] All the families had moved in by the first week of December 1934.[79]

At this distance the exact composition of the population of Sassoon House can probably never be known, but at its inception, its role in forging a new landscape of health in this ordinary street in Peckham was clear. It was all part of the process through which urban life could be transformed. The Centre itself certainly was able to attract member-families. 135 joined in the first week,[80] and by the time war broke out and the Centre was closed, just over 1,200 families had undergone periodic overhauls.[81] It was clearly popular among the local community but how was it received by the world outside?

The response to the Centre

Following its official opening in March 1935, the Centre received extensive coverage from the daily press, the architectural and other specialist media.[82] The response was entirely positive and much of it demonstrates a clear understanding of, and support for, the doctors' theories and their attempts to reorient urban life.[83] The response of the architectural press is especially interesting and a number of journals, notably *Country Life*, the *Architects' Journal* and *The Architectural Review* wrote detailed analyses of the Centre and its architecture,[84] rather than producing the standard spread of photographs, plans and descriptive text.[85]

The *Journal* and *Review* were particularly impressed. Their articles provide important insights into what was deemed significant for architects about events at Peckham. It should, of course, be remembered that by that time J. M. Richards had become editor of the *Journal* and was therefore almost certainly the author of the Editorial, 'Pioneer Work at Peckham', which was devoted to the Centre on 4 April 1935. He also wrote the main feature on the Centre, 'The Idea behind the Idea', in *The Review* and conceivably the accompanying text as well. For the *Journal*, Peckham represented where the future of architectural practice lay and Richards wrote that it was important:

> First, because it is an example of enlightened scientific enterprise that is planning for a future far finer than is ever envisaged by officialdom – an example of the technician taking his place as a pioneer of social progress; secondly, because it has produced a building which itself reflects the

function of modern architecture to express the spirit in which it is conceived and the ideas behind its conception rather than the ideas or personality of the particular technician commissioned to design it.[86]

The Review devoted 14 approving pages of its May 1935 issue to the Centre. This comprised a series of magnificent photographs by Dell and Wainwright, interspersed with Richards' essay on the doctors' theories and an introductory essay which focused on the urban implications of the Centre. It was in this, above all, that its lessons lay for *The Review*, and this short text, no more than 350 words, provides further evidence of a defiantly pro-urban stance in progressive British architectural circles. The essay opened by noting the 'centrifugal tendency of the present-day urban population' and the fact that for the town dweller the town had become 'merely the entourage of his work or business'.[87] His instinct therefore was to escape,

> If he can afford it, to the country; if not, to a suburb or garden city where some illusion can be maintained of the more civilized country gentleman's existence, which is his ideal – or to the cinema, and such-like distractions from actuality.

Such tendencies led to 'the wasteful decentralization of building' and 'the progressive disappearance of the countryside', a process which could be prevented, not by abandoning the city, but by creating new nuclei about which a 'genuine urban life' could revolve. Hence, the writer declared,

> The difference between town and country must be redefined. They must be appreciated as two distinct things with different uses, not as different degrees of the same thing. This can only be done by making a full and energetic life possible in terms of urban existence; that is the great social value (quite apart from the medical value) of an organization like the Pioneer Health Centre. It provides a focal point at which the town as workshop coincides with the town as community. It is one of the answers to the town-planner's question: I know where people ought to live, but how can I make them live there?

In the back pages of *The Review* its commentator 'Junius' passed further favourable comment on events in St Mary's Road. He pointed to the revelatory impact both the Centre and Sassoon House would have on the inhabitants of the street. Noting that modern buildings usually had the effect of intrusion in such an environment, he wrote that, in this case, 'it is not the new building that appears to be called upon to offer discreet apology but the solid solemn surrounding Peckham houses which have the air of being entirely in the wrong century'. This discrepancy, he believed, would lead their occupants to cry 'what extraordinarily heavy, clumsy, dark, grotesque, irrational boxes we're living in. Can we stand it much longer?'. In concluding, Junius quipped, 'Mr Maxwell Fry's sane inviting little block of flats nearby may well have begun the process of disillusionment.'[88]

As a model of progressive town planning and health care, the Peckham Experiment continued to be extolled and promoted throughout the 1930s. There was a broadcast on the BBC in early 1937 and a major article in *The Spectator* in 1938.[89] Above all, there were the doctors' own publications. In addition to the *Annual Reports* issued from the onset of the Experiment to those who supported the Centre with dona-tions, from 1931 Pearse and Williamson made deliberate use of the book to convey their message beyond the boundaries of Peckham. The first of these, *The Case for Action*, provided a summary of the Experiment to date and served as an attempt to raise funds for Phase Two. In 1938, an interim report, *Biologists in Search of Material*, was published and during the war Pearse and one of the Centre workers, Lucy Crocker, published *The Peckham Experiment* (1943). These were persuasive texts, intended to infect their readers to convince others that the Peckham way was the future of health care, thereby creating a critical mass of opinion in its favour. In achieving this, Williamson had already made some headway through his membership of the planning lobby group Political and Economic Planning (PEP). Its 1937 report, *The British Health Service*, advocated many of his and Pearse's practices, and it gave a clear sign that at this date, at least, the preventive message was shared across the progressive spec-trum.[90] Through such means the doctors could reasonably have hoped that the Centre's existence would reach policy makers' ears. Indeed, Frank Singleton, the author of *The Spectator* article, observed that it was 'pointing a way which local authorities might profitably follow'.[91]

Finsbury

A year after PEP's report was published, and a week before Singleton's article came out, another prototype of health care was unveiled on the other side of London: the Finsbury Health Centre. This had been commissioned by the Public Health Committee of Finsbury Borough Council under the conditions of the Public Health (London) Act of 1936, and was designed by the modernist architectural practice Tecton. Like Peckham, it was an attempt to form a response to prevailing anxieties about the health of the race and it likewise used architecture to both accommodate and connote its newness of purpose. In significant other respects, however, as Singleton observed, it 'differed so widely in form and function that it is profitable to compare and contrast them'.[92]

Many of the reasons for the differences between Finsbury and Peckham were to do with location. Finsbury was the most overcrowded borough in London. None of its predominantly poorer working-class citizens owned their homes,[93] and most lived in slum housing, the majority of which was sub-divided houses but which also included 2,500 cellars used for sleeping or living, or both.[94] The incidence of tuberculosis was high, as were mortality rates. The founding of a health centre at Finsbury was, as Singleton observed, 'a magnificent rearguard action' against well-established disease and decay.[95] The Pioneer Health Centre functioned under very different conditions. The borough of Camberwell in which it was situated was far from prosperous, but it contained better quality housing and a wider social mix than its north London counter-part. The Centre served only a circumscribed area of the borough – streets within walking distance of its location – rather than its entirety, and its focus on health not disease was a stance undoubtedly facilitated by its artisanal address.

Nonetheless the two schemes do bear comparison. Not least because both were modernist projects which sought to transform urban environments in order to effect change in both individuals and society. But chiefly because in both instances we see modernist reformers of space, like Denby and Fry at Peckham, and Tecton in Finsbury, allying their particular cause to two very different, though equally progressive, solutions to the most pressing social issue of the day.[96] Solutions which, in fact, represented the two directions in which health care could have been directed in this decade, and which operated under fundamentally opposed views of the purpose of social welfare and the source of its provision. These positions might usefully be characterized as framed by the concepts of a citizenship of responsibility or a citizenship of entitlement.

The Peckham model started from the belief that health care should be paid for, hence the instigation of the weekly subscription. This was seen as a way to instil a sense of responsibility in the individual and the intention was that this, in turn, would foster a sense of responsibility to a broader community, whether that be the Centre's or society as a whole. If the services at the Centre were dispensed freely, expectation rather than responsibility would result, and passive rather than active citizens would be created. This reflected the British Idealist belief that any intervention in an individual's life by the state should have a moral purpose. While this belief did not preclude the state administering projects like the Peckham Experiment – the doctors depended on the local borough for its right to exist – it did go against the model of state healthcare provision which had developed since the turn of the century.

The state-led approach had emerged less from a preoccupation with discourses of citizenship and more, in the context of the National Efficiency debate, from the pragmatic realization that it was in the state's economic interest to have a healthy work force. As Abigail Beach has noted, by the inter-war years this pragmatic concern had developed into the more socially concerned, and fairly widely held, belief that every citizen was entitled to a basic level of health and that it was the duty of the state to provide medical care free at the point of delivery. The citizen reciprocated this provision by operating as an efficient worker and observing the laws of common decency.[97] In municipal Finsbury, the concept of a citizenship of entitlement was clearly the starting point for the Centre's instigators but, as the results suggest, it was always intended as more than a mere re-organization of a borough's health provision. Finsbury Health Centre was to represent nothing less than 'the dawn of a new era in public health service'.[98]

The Finsbury Health Centre

The Finsbury Health Centre was born of two modernist narratives of reform – one socio-medical, one architectural – which intersected by chance. As noted above, by the early 1930s housing and health conditions in Finsbury were in a dire state, and the assorted forms of medical service which were dotted throughout the borough formed an inadequate defence against this pitiful state of affairs. It was not until 1934, when the Labour Party was elected to the leadership of the borough, that this situation showed any real prospect of resolution. This shift in power formed part of a London-wide swing to the left which saw fifteen boroughs elect Labour councils and the supra-metropolitan government, the London County Council, likewise change leadership. As Beach has noted, this inaugurated a period of concerted and self-conscious effort by Labour-led boroughs to implement Party policy; Finsbury's councillors took to this task enthusiastically.[99]

At the helm of this crusade were Alderman Harold Riley, Council Leader, and Dr Chuni Lal Katial, Chairman of the Public Health Committee, both of whom were committed to improving the conditions in which their citizens lived. Katial had long wanted to build a health centre and had even picked out the site in Pine Street which would eventually house the Tecton building, but that plan had come to nothing.[100] Finally empowered, they grasped the opportunity to demonstrate what a socialist model of welfare could be. They began to develop a programme to improve health services, clear slums and replace them with new housing and new amenities, what became known informally as 'The Finsbury Plan'. Health, understandably, was their first priority. In May 1935, following a proposal from Katial to the Public Health Committee for a standardized and rationalized health service, the Council received a report from the borough's Medical Officer of Health which recommended the formation of a new Public Health Department, with new facilities.[101]

While these proposals made their way through the machinery of government, it would be March 1936 before the Council could approve the scheme, Katial sought out an architect who could create a form appropriate for the building which would inaugurate the transformation of Finsbury. In November 1932, he had attended the centennial conference of the British Medical Association at which hypothetical plans for a TB Clinic for East Ham, by an architectural practice called Tecton, were exhibited.[102] Deeply impressed, but unable to do more than admire the project, Katial noted the name in the hope that the moment might come when he could commission its creators. Three years later, in autumn 1935, he was able to approach the practice and invite it to discuss, initially informally, how the site in Pine Street could be used to best effect. Within six months Tecton had been formally appointed as architects. Work began in spring 1937 and the building opened in October 1938, the first time, as John Allan stresses, that a municipal commission had been awarded directly to a modernist practice.[103]

That Tecton won the commission as a result of the exhibition of a hypothetical scheme tallies with the proposition of this book that it was through a command of the discourses of persuasion that modernism ingratiated itself into acceptance in this period. The ways in which Finsbury Health Centre would itself operate as a persuasive discourse will be discussed later in this chapter, but for the moment it is important to reflect on the skill with which Tecton, and Berthold Lubetkin, in particular, operated as propagandists for their own cause. Further, it is also important to consider a second aspect of Tecton's modernity, its attempt to formulate a way of practising appropriate to the modern age.

Tecton had been founded in 1932 when the Russian-born Lubetkin joined forces with six modernist-minded graduates of the Architectural Association.[104] Lubetkin had trained in the Soviet Union and practised in Paris before he settled in England in 1931, drawn there by his awareness that interesting developments in modern architecture were then underway. He would bring a theoretical mind, and first-hand experience of French modernism, to what was still, even among modernists, a gentlemanly and largely empirically driven architectural culture. It is tempting, though Allan suggests his motivations were largely pragmatic, to imagine that Lubetkin saw this liaison as the opportunity to create the perfect modernist practice.[105] That goal is certainly suggested by the decision to give the practice a collective name, something entirely new at that date. It was indicative of the method of group working which Lubetkin would develop with his team of young architects, none of whom, as yet, had completed a building.

The method was initially developed through the device of a hypothetical project which, since the firm had no substantial commissions in its first year of existence, Lubetkin decided would be a fruitful way for his team to spend their time. Via an introduction from Godfrey Samuel, he approached Dr Philip Ellmann, the Medical Officer of Health for East Ham and a tuberculosis specialist. This was an astute choice. Lubetkin had selected a topical subject and one with a potential for publicity. It was also a project which looked towards a future when such large publicly funded schemes would become the norm and for which architects needed to be adequately equipped. Ellmann provided a brief, though not a very thorough one, for a TB Clinic for East Ham so Lubetkin therefore set his team the task of first assessing and analysing it as a prelude to its recasting. Then, in order to produce a design, they were to break down the programme into component parts, analyse their relationship the one to the other and carry out studies into the factors which would influence the planning such as patterns of circulation, and the need for appropriate ventilation and insolation. All was to be carefully documented as a means to reflect upon the design process and evaluate it. Finally, all the investigation and experimentation would be worked up into a series of annotated presentation drawings and a model. It was these that Katial saw. It can be imagined that Lubetkin was delighted that this project had at once provided his team with an exercise in design technique and served to publicize what the practice could do, as well as the sort of work with which they wished to be associated.[106]

Three years later, when Katial sat down with Lubetkin to discuss plans for a health centre in autumn 1935, they embarked on a design process not dissimilar to that for the TB clinic. In sharp contrast to Peckham, where Pearse and Williamson had gone to great pains to define their programme, at Finsbury, the clients were less articulate and Tecton appear to have taken on the role of translating for Katial precisely what it was he and the Public Health Department required. In this sense, Tecton acted as experts, a relationship which worked well in a borough ordered on the socialist model of a centralized state organized and administered by such figures. What emerged from this discussion was a programme for a building which could house under one roof municipal health services which included a dental clinic, chest clinic, a solarium for ultra-violet ray treatment, a cleansing station for verminous people, disinfecting stations, a mortuary and a laboratory. It also needed to provide office space, a reception area and waiting room and a lecture theatre.

These services were what the Centre needed to accommodate but, as at Peckham, there were less tangible aspects to the brief. There was a sense that the building itself needed to be a didactic space which conveyed the message of the importance of public hygiene to its users. Related to this was the idea that since it was a flagship for a socialist model of health care, its form should be striking and noticeable. The result was what quickly became known as a 'megaphone for health', a building which Katial described as 'essentially modern and business-like, and which, by its general open expression, automatically associates itself with hygiene and public health'

(Fig. 2.9).[107] On a cramped site on Pine Street, close to the Farringdon Road, this cream coloured, H-plan building emanated modernity to all who passed by. Like Williams' design for the Pioneer Health Centre it was an eminently satisfying and sophisticated solution to the brief.

Tecton had elected to address the programme by separating the building into two zones. There were those which had fixed functions, such as the reception and waiting area and the lecture theatre, and those, like the clinics and treatment rooms, whose use was likely to change over time or which needed spaces adaptable to differing types and sizes of equipment. Hence the design was anchored around a central entrance core, with load-bearing internal walls and columns, which was flanked by the two legs of the 'H' (Fig. 2.10). These wings were constructed as a series of clear spanned 'cells' in which all services were gathered into channels within the external wall surface with access via removable duct covers.

The building itself was set into an island site; the entrance block placed to the rear of the site, framed protectively by the two wings, and accessed by a footbridge. This placement made the Centre stand out from the dark housing which surrounded it; a difference further enhanced by the cream tiles with which the entrance block was clad and the light-coloured concrete paint which covered the rest of the building. The extensive glazing on the outside walls of the wings, and the glazed bricks of the curved entrance façade, also emphasized its extraordinary nature and allowed the building to glow with light at night.

As Katial proudly declared, the very form of the Centre signified health and cleanliness. Likewise, the careful ordering of the plan, which included placing all clinics on the ground floor so no patient would have to climb stairs to reach them, signalled a systematic and rational approach unusual in its day. As the dawn of a new era in public health service the Centre, at the same time as it addressed a unique programme, was also intended as a persuasive device. And so, once it was opened, it served not just to administer cures, but as a site to be visited by medics and local politicians and, of course, architecture students,[108] and as a prototype to be photographed and reported in the media.

The dissemination of the Centre was helped considerably by Tecton's own publicity skills. It produced an explanatory exhibition to accompany the opening, 'Getting it across to the Layman', which was reproduced widely in the architectural press alongside its series of annotated presentation drawings.[109] *The Architectural Review*, in recognition of the scheme's significance, devoted a similar amount of space to coverage of Finsbury as it had done to Peckham. Its content was, however, rather different. Whereas in 1935 *The Review* had found it necessary to locate the Pioneer Health Centre in terms of both medical and urban theory, by 1939 its report focused simply on an outline of the Finsbury Plan and a detailed analysis of the Centre's design.[110] A number of factors may account for this. Richards had had a personal interest in Peckham which came through very clearly in the articles he wrote. It was also the case that four years on, Finsbury, though undoubtedly a tremendous achievement, represented a culmination of several years of modernist activity, rather than being a precursor of it. It therefore required less contextualization for much of its message would by now be familiar to *The Review's* readers. Finally, and perhaps most

Figure 2.9
Tecton, Finsbury
Health Centre,
Finsbury, 1938

interestingly, the article comprises Tecton's own account of the scheme which, in its detached and analytical manner, allowed the practice to present itself as the expert problem-solvers it believed architects should be.[111]

The non-specialist media also covered the Centre, and the article by Singleton, already cited, offers some useful insights into its reception, especially as he compared it with the Peckham model. He clearly understood the differences which have been outlined here, commenting, 'Finsbury is not really a health-centre in the same sense that Peckham is. It is a poly-clinic organised for disease. Peckham is organised for health'. In the end, he was rather pessimistic about Finsbury and he wrote that it

> braces itself to fight disease with the best weapons and in the most efficient ways that man has yet devised, but in so far as its main operations begin after disease has established a hold, its whole existence is an acknowledgement of human failure to achieve or retain health.[112]

Paul Reilly, writing in the left-wing *News Chronicle* was more positive. He saw the implications the Centre might hold for the future, writing:

> The actions of the Finsbury Council ... will give a fine fillip to the spirits of our younger architects who know what progress there is in the new methods of building and the new conceptions of architecture. At present their talents are employed in the satisfaction of the whims of a rich and snobbish clientele. There is a far wider scope for them in the service of the public.[113]

In histories of the Centre, it is Reilly's view, rather than Singleton's, that has prevailed. Here, the concern is not to challenge its significance as an attempt to resolve appalling health conditions, which cannot be denied, nor to deny its importance as the

Figure 2.10
Tecton, Finsbury
Health Centre, plan

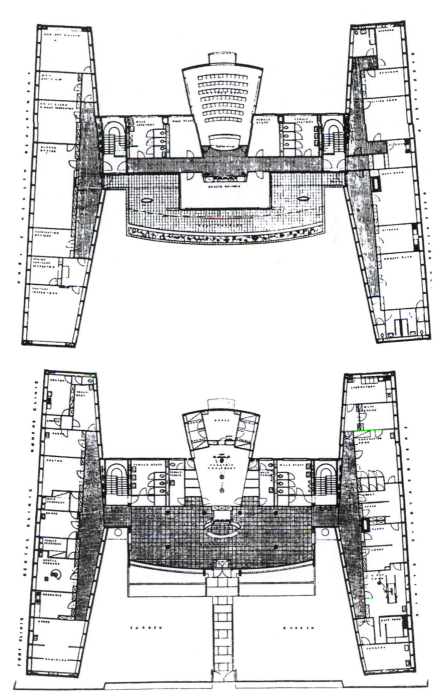

Figure 2.11
Foyer of the
Finsbury Health
Centre

first modernist building to be commissioned by a municipality. Instead it seems impor-tant to consider Finsbury within the framework of the model of health care which it sought to promote, if not initiate, rather than in terms of what it foresaw. This can be explored through a comparison of the entrance areas of Finsbury and Peckham.

It is well known that when they designed the Centre, Lubektin and his team invoked the idea of an open-access club. Their concern was to create an environment which did not intimidate users. Mindful of the need for the building to convey the message of public hygiene, they also deployed the Soviet concept of the social condenser. The question raised here is whether the final design achieved these goals. Starting with the exterior of the Centre, there can be found a quasi-monumentality to Finsbury's form, especially in its central block, flanked as it is by wings, and denoted by its richer treatment and the deeply framed entrance door which is approached by a footbridge. This is a much more conventional treatment for a façade than at Peckham and is more reminiscent of the municipal neo-Georgian conventions of Musman's work. The exterior treatment also creates a building which is impossible to see into, though light could emanate from it. Set back from the street line, and glazed with glass bricks, its function – other than as something 'modern' – could not then be discerned by the glimpse of a passer-by.

If this exterior was surprisingly monumental, then the entrance hall was much less so. Once across the footbridge and through the rather magnificent doors, the patients entered an open-plan reception area which was furnished, not with serried ranks of fixed benches, but by informally placed pieces of furniture (Fig. 2.11). The walls were decorated with murals designed by Gordon Cullen which combined scenes of healthy living with slogans such as 'live out of doors as much as you can' and 'chest diseases are preventable and curable' (Fig. 2.12). While this plan can be explained, as it

Figure 2.12
**Mural in the foyer
of the Finsbury
Health
Centre**

usually is, with reference to the condenser and club analogies, a more helpful analogy in understanding and explaining this space, and indeed, this building, is that of it being a 'megaphone for health'.

By using this as a device for interpretation, we can see the Centre for what it was, rather than as it has come to be seen. A megaphone amplifies the voice and directs it more effectively; it is used to address a crowd. This is precisely what the Centre did. In fact it spoke to, or rather at, two 'crowds'. The first was those who shared the expertise of the people who had commissioned and designed it. Here the rhetorical form, and the annotated diagrams reproduced in the architectural press, sought to spread the Finsbury model to those who understood the language in which Tecton and their clients spoke. The other crowd comprised the citizens of Finsbury, a mass who had no choice but to come across the borough to seek treatment in this strange looking building.[114] Once over the footbridge and into the Centre, a transforming journey in itself, the reception area becomes the condenser to which it is so often, and for once rightly, referred. Here was a space in which the waiting patients were exposed to the ever-present message of the murals and thereby inculcated, in tandem with the invasive treatments they underwent in the clinics, of the necessity of hygiene.[115]

The sheer magnitude of the health problem in Finsbury goes some way to explaining the overwhelmingly didactic, if not dictatorial, character of the design, but its origins lie also in the model of health care which the Centre embodied. Centralized, bureaucratized (there is space for offices and archives here), designed by architectural experts and run by health experts, Finsbury leaves the sense of a building created as a production line for health with little room for personal sentiment or self-responsibility.

Peckham, as we have seen, operated from a very different model, one which placed the individual and their family at the centre of what it did. While the suppositions which underpinned it were not without their problems and, in the surveillant practices of the doctors, not a little peculiar, it created a far less dictatorial environment: one which talked with its occupants rather than at them. It was a magnet rather than a megaphone. Potential members were attracted to the Centre through the transparency of a façade which, at the same time as it allowed people to see what was going on inside, also served the rhetorical purpose of drawing attention to itself. Here, there was no formal approach to the entrance, instead it was sited at the rear of the building. On entering, members either headed straight for the changing rooms, ready for action, or ascended the staircase into the social space of the first-floor cafeteria. There were no murals. Education resided in the sight of what others were doing and the individual became healthy only if they had the (eugenic) potential to take responsibility for themselves.

Despite such fundamental differences, the schemes at Finsbury and Peckham had one further element in common: both were seen as component parts of larger plans to improve the urban environment. At Peckham, a voluntary effort, this was inevitably of a piecemeal nature, but in Finsbury, the Centre was just the first part of Alderman Riley and his fellow councillors' grand vision for the borough, 'the Finsbury Plan'. This was a full-blown attempt to demonstrate what a socialist munici-pality could achieve and comprised a major scheme for slum clearance and re-housing,[116] new public gardens, civic squares and amenities and a programme for air raid precaution.[117] Tecton was appointed the Plan's architects and, had it not been cut short by the outbreak of war, it would have been a ground-breaking piece of municipal patronage.

By 1939, two progressive models of health care had been established in London. Although it was as yet unclear whether the statist, curative and inculcating model of Finsbury, or the preventive, voluntarist and facilitating one of Peckham would ultimately prevail, what was clear was that the forms of modernist architecture had been firmly aligned with the modernization of health care. Further, in addressing the social problem which underpinned all the other social ills afflicting Britain at this date, these prototypes had established some common principles from which the other protago-nists considered elsewhere in this book did not depart. First, that such problems required new solutions and new forms of building to accommodate them, something which might entail a considerable degree of research into the potential programme. It thereby created, as Richards had put it, the architect as a pioneer of social progress. Second, that the resulting buildings should not be isolated beacons of possibility but should form part of a more concerted attempt to transform the urban environment. Hence the close attention which was paid to housing in both schemes, a subject which will be considered fully in the chapters which follow.

Chapter 3

Modern Dwellings for Modern Needs

> How do we want to live, what sort of framework must we build round
> ourselves to make that living as pleasant as possible?
>
> Rosemary Pritchard (1934)

In Chapter 2 we saw how the techniques of self-promotion, the limited competition
and friendly opportunism brought modernist reformers of health and modernist
reformers of space together to address the most significant social problem which
faced inter-war Britain: the health of its working-class population. Through the forging
of prototype landscapes and their mediation through text and image, they succeeded
in rendering modernism synonymous with modern practices of health care. In
entering the arena of housing reform, modernist architects sought to achieve a similar
synonymy but in so doing they took on a challenge very different from the one they
had assumed in health reform. At Peckham and Finsbury, whether in collaboration
with voluntary sector or municipal modernists, their task had been to create environments for modern practices of health care for which no exact precedent – socio-
medical or spatial – existed. In the case of housing, no such *tabula rasa* existed and
modernists had to bring their propositions and prototypes to an arena already well
stocked with new forms of housing.

   The first of these were the types of dwelling which had been developed
under the aegis of central government following its assumption in 1919, in the circumstances outlined in Chapter 1, of some responsibility for the provision of housing for
rental by the working classes. In the 1920s, this produced the cottage estate (Fig. 3.1).
In the 1930s, as policy shifted from general needs to slum clearance, a process
discussed in detail in the next chapter, the first blocks of flats began to be constructed in
inner-city areas. Soundly built to generous space standards, with indoor lavatories and
bathrooms, both provided a form of housing which was dramatically and noticeably
different from the cramped slums and terraces in which most workers lived.[1]

Figure 3.1
Huntingfield Road,
Roehampton
Estate, west
London, LCC
Architects'
Department,
completed 1927

Alongside this, and aimed at the middle classes, from the mid-1920s onwards building societies and speculative builders developed the market for owner occupation. Like the state, they favoured the suburban low-density model but in order to differentiate their products from council housing their preferred model was the 'three-up two-down' house (Fig. 3.2). More often semi-detached than in a terrace, their conventional façades – debased Arts and Crafts or Tudorbethan – masked interiors far better planned and equipped than anything which had been available to middle-class consumers before the Great War.[2] Together, local authorities and private enterprise would have built just over four million new dwellings by 1939,[3] one third of the country's entire housing stock, and in so doing made suburbia part of the British landscape.[4]

If this sharing of provision between state and private enterprise, and the general preference for a suburban modernity, represented the establishment position on re-formed housing, then this same period also saw the consolidation of what might be called the official opposition to these practices in the Garden City and Town Planning Association (GCTPA). While it agreed that the house was the appropriate site for modern domesticity, hardly surprising since both the state and private sector drew heavily on garden-city principles for the design and layout of their estates, its primary concern was with the location of such dwellings.[5] Under the leadership of F. J. Osborn, the GCTPA established the basic tenets of an oppositional orthodoxy which demonized the industrial city and suburban sprawl and advocated, instead, a policy of decentralization and the planned development of garden cities enfolded in a protective green belt across the country.[6] Such an approach was paralleled in other organizations such as the Council for the Protection of Rural England founded in 1926, and the DIA's campaigns for planning reform through its publications of the late 1920s.[7]

Modernist architects could not compete, quantitatively at least, with these prevalent narratives of modern housing, either establishment or opposition. Yet the problem of the dwelling was a subject upon which they could, with some justification, feel qualified to comment. Most had first explored the language of modernist architecture in domestic commissions, something which reflected the fact that, as a building type, the dwelling had long been the site for architectural experimentation. Its small

Figure 3.2
Typical 'semi-ds'
on a London estate
of the 1930s

scale, and the existence of a sympathetic client, had historically created the context in which new ideas about space and form were developed and refined. Indeed, it was fast becoming a part of orthodox British modernist theory that the house, as Max Fry wrote, was 'part of a much wider sphere of enquiry' and 'provides the architect with the means of putting into practice ideas which have their final application in the service of the wider community – when the community is prepared to receive them'.[8]

Fry's observation, written in 1934, signals both the problem modernists faced but also the solution. Their approach would be to assume the mantle of pioneers of social progress and deal with housing not as it was but as it might be. Placing themselves in a territory of critique, they would construct a narrative of reform which exploited their putative affinity with the design of the dwelling and centred around the postulation of the insufficient modernity of current housing design and practice. Through both built and textual discourses they then sought to persuade policy makers, and those with influence upon them, that there were better ways to re-form housing.

This trio of chapters explores the British movement's attempts to assume control of the future of housing in the 1930s. As in the case of health reform, this was something to be achieved through collaboration, and they formed a housing avant-garde with the small number of individuals and groups who, like them, were similarly excluded from the dominant modes of practice and provision. In this chapter, discussion focuses on how their efforts were addressed towards the reform of the middle-class dwelling and it explores the collaboration among Wells Coates and Jack and Rosemary Pritchard between 1929 and 1934 which resulted in the Isokon Flats at Lawn Road, Hampstead, north London. This block formed part of a more ambitious project including a series of prefabricated house prototypes, as well as plans for several other blocks of flats. The ultimate intention was to demonstrate how the principles of

turned psychotherapist, bought a plot of land on Lawn Road, Hampstead. On this they intended to have built a home for themselves and their two children. As their architects they chose Molly's sister Jill and her husband Harry Harrison, who produced a design for a pair of houses, one large and one small, plaster-rendered and with flat roofs and metal-framed windows (Fig. 3.3). The scheme was duly exhibited at the Royal Academy,[12] and published in *Decorative Art: The Studio Yearbook*.[13] It would never be built. By the end of the year, the Pritchards had abandoned this scheme and turned to the young architect-engineer Wells Coates for a new design. Five years later this commission would finally be realized, not as a house, but as the Isokon Flats, a block of 29 minimum dwellings.

No precise reason for the Pritchards' rejection of the first design has been recorded. It is only Jack's gnomic observation that 'we had not yet learnt the importance of the brief' and their subsequent actions, that give some hint as to why they took what could not have been an easy decision, given its potentially uncomfortable familial repercussions.[14] Here, the suggestion is that on receipt of the Cooke-Harrison scheme they underwent an epiphany very similar to that which had been experienced by the doctors in Peckham at more or less the same time. It was only at the moment of being confronted by their architects' (mis)interpretation of their needs that they recognized what it was they wanted or, perhaps, did not want and that it would be necessary to find

Figure 3.3
Cooke and
Harrison, design for
a pair of houses for
Jack and Molly
Pritchard for a site
on Lawn Road,
Hampstead, 1930

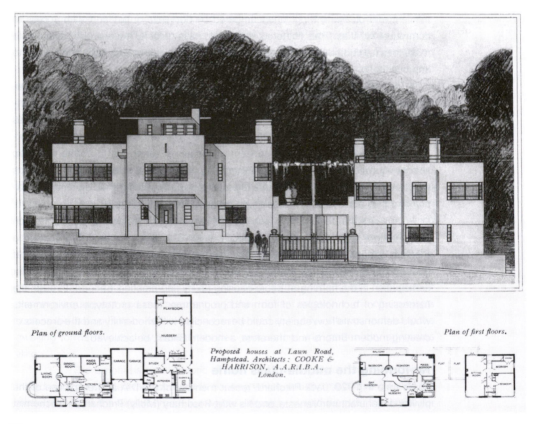

Plan of ground floors.

Plan of first floors.

Proposed houses at Lawn Road,
Hampstead. Architects: COOKE &
HARRISON, A.A.R.I.B.A.,
London.

designers who would be more sympathetic to their progressive practices of living and working. In Peckham, this led the doctors to formulate a revised programme and work with an engineer. In Hampstead, the Pritchards would collaborate with Coates, a man who had no formal training as an architect.[15]

The paths which led the Pritchards to Coates, and the houses to become a block of flats, epitomize the accidental and deliberate intersections of people, preoccupations and milieux which created modernism in inter-war Britain. Fundamental to these, as is true of all the projects discussed in this book, was the self-conscious modernity of their protagonists. All had in common identities and values which can be seen as quintessentially modern: something formed by the coincidence of their dates of birth, their family origins and their upbringings. In the case of the Isokon project, which typifies this condition almost to the point of caricature, all were born in the 1890s: Coates in 1895, Pritchard in 1899 and Rosemary Cooke (as she was then) in 1900.[16] They grew up in an era that itself was highly conscious of its modernity.[17] The new technologies such as electricity, the aeroplane and the automobile, the consolidation of middle-class women's political and educational emancipation, and new forms of mass communication and transport, went hand-in-hand with the move to modernize empire and industry under the aegis of the National Efficiency movement. For well-educated, middle-class figures such as they, these conditions created an awareness of and openness to change which to many only ten years their senior would have been unthinkable. The Great War, in which both Coates and Jack Pritchard saw service, moreover, left in many of their ilk, as their contemporary Noel Carrington noted, 'a readiness to take a fresh look at the physical structure of civilization'.[18]

The son of a barrister, Jack Pritchard was educated at the public school Oundle and then served for two years in the Navy.[19] It was at Cambridge, which he attended between 1920 and 1922, that his 'modernization' was accelerated for, as he recalled, 'Edwardian smugness showed signs of giving way and a rebirth seemed a real possibility'.[20] That he might be equipped to participate in this rebirth is indicated by his choice of degree: not for him Classics or Mathematics but the decidedly modern subjects of Engineering and Economics. It was the latter which particularly interested him and he attended Maynard Keynes' lectures and forged a friendship with the economist Philip Sargant Florence.[21] It was at Sargant's home that he met Henry Morris, Secretary to the Cambridge County Education Office and founder of the Village College movement. Morris would prove to be an important influence on the young Pritchard, especially his dictum that 'a job was not just a means of earning a living; it must be life itself'.[22] This sentiment seems to have instilled in Pritchard the very real sense of mission which would play such an important part in the development of the Isokon project.

It was in his first week at Cambridge that Pritchard met his future wife, and Isokon collaborator, Molly Cooke. She, like Pritchard, came from a professional family and shared his predisposition to modernity. Her father was a solicitor and her mother had worked in an infant welfare centre before her marriage. They sent their daughter to one of the new academic girls' day schools, the Godolphin and Latymer School in west London, from which she entered Cambridge to read medicine. On graduation she worked initially as a biochemist before she retrained as a psychotherapist, that archetypally modern medical profession. The pair married in 1924 and their sons were born in 1926 and 1928. An early sign that this was not to be a conventional family is clear in Molly Pritchard's decision to continue to work full-time after the birth of her children. To accommodate this, she and Jack established a nursery school in their Hampstead house, which was run in collaboration with the educationalist Beatrix Tudor Hart. From there, the boys were sent to Dora Russell's progressive school, Beacon Hill, whose aim was to produce

> not listless intellectuals, but young men and women filled with constructive hopefulness, conscious that there are great things to be done in this world, and possessed of the skill required for taking their part.[23]

Just the sort of people, in fact, who fill the pages of this book.

At the time of his marriage, Pritchard was working for the Michelin Tyre Company at its offices in Clermont Ferrand, France, and London. There he was trained in the techniques of Scientific Management and market research: systematic methods of business which were only just beginning to make a major impact on British manufacturing. Pritchard left Michelin in 1925 to join the Building Uses Department (BUD) of the plywood importer and manufacturer Venesta.[24] At the BUD, his role was to promote the uses of the company's products, to which end he applied the methods learnt at Michelin. These included the then innovative policy of consulting with a statistician in order to predict and estimate the extent of demand for their products.[25] When it became apparent how limited this was, a concerted campaign was initiated to promote new uses for plywood in which emphasis was placed on expanding the company's contacts with builders, designers and architects.[26] Central to this was collaboration with another modern type of business, the advertising industry. Pritchard developed a close relationship with John Gloag, Director of the firm Wood, Pritchard and Partners, which was owned by Jack's brother Fleetwood Craven Pritchard. It was a crucial encounter, for it brought him into the then centre of progressive design in inter-war Britain, the DIA. This, he recalled, enabled him 'to meet a variety of people with somewhat similar interests and provided confidence to experiment with new ideas'.[27]

More importantly, it almost certainly led him to the pages of the design press. There he saw the work of a young architect called Wells Coates who was using plywood in just the sort of new manner which Venesta was seeking to promote. In a shop interior for the silk manufacturer Crysede he had made extensive use of plywood sheeting for the fittings, an approach which, Pritchard wrote, demonstrated 'the logical use of the material', and provided 'the needed stimulus and *guidance* at the most useful moment'.[28] In March 1929, therefore, the company contacted Coates to request permission to use images of his work in their advertising campaign.[29]

Through the interface of representation, Pritchard had discovered a man very much like himself. Just as he was seeking to modernize his sphere of practice – manufacturing – so too was Coates seeking to modernize his world, that of architecture, as we have seen in Chapter 1. Although it is not clear when they finally met in person, the encounter represented a significant merging of what in Britain had been two rather separate worlds and inaugurated one of the most important design collaborations of the early 1930s. For Coates, at least, this was apparent from the start and he would later confess to Pritchard, 'from the moment that I met you I knew instinctively that we were destined to do a job of work in this world, together, someday'.[30]

From the house to the flat

It was presumably the birth of the Pritchards' second son, Jeremy, that led to their decision to buy the site on Lawn Road and commission the Cooke-Harrisons for a design. Having abandoned that scheme, the Pritchards then set about revising their ideas with a tenacity which reflects how profound was the epiphany they had undergone. The first step was to recruit Coates as their architect and to commission him to design them not just a house but also a nursery school for Beatrix Tudor Hart on the Lawn Road site.[31] Next, aware that the Cooke-Harrison design did not fit the open and free way in which their middle-class life was lived, they sought to establish precisely what it was they wanted in this future home. This quest would lead to a two-year long investigation into the form the modern dwelling should take.

The Pritchards' determination to achieve the appropriate form for their house was shared by Coates. As their architect this was, of course, his primary obligation but it also provided him with the opportunity to experiment in a field in which he was much interested but had had relatively little experience. With the exception of his very first commissions, Coates' work between 1929 and 1931 was primarily shop interiors and fascias for the silk manufacturer Cresta, and the series of studio designs for the BBC.[32] A letter to Pritchard in the first year of their collaboration allows a clear understanding of just how important this job was:

> Here I am, a young man in a profession, self-labelled for the sake of a practical strategy, but practically outcast, a rebel and a revolutionary too [...]. For years I have been fed up with...[sic] etc. and for years I have determined to do something about it, to build up the technique and the knowledge and the experience to cope with this great problem which I believe to be at the root of all social disorder and distress; this problem of the *kind of place* a man and a woman and a family should live in, this problem of the *theatre* of ordinary daily life, the theatre of modern living...[33]

The house at Lawn Road would form his masterpiece: the opportunity to prove his complete command of the modernist language and thereby to demonstrate his eligibility for the leadership of the emergent movement in Britain.

How then did the Pritchards and Coates set about creating a theatre of modern living? As Coates' metaphor suggests, their concern was how everyday practices of living could be choreographed most effectively. This implies that the house plan should not dictate the activities within it; rather, it should act as a backdrop, or a tool, to facilitate daily activities. This in turn suggests a conceptualization of modern life which sought to escape from conventions and seek the means to find and accommodate new ways of living. Such premises therefore led their work to commence with an interrogation of the potential functions of the proposed house and in January 1930 they embarked on a six-month-long programme of research into contemporary re-definitions of the dwelling. Through discussions, visits, and correspondence, the three exchanged ideas about the project.[34] The evidence which survives points to the three main influences which guided their research at this stage.[35]

The first was Pritchard himself. Here was a man who, once he had realized the necessity of re-thinking the brief, was eminently well equipped to do so. At the root of this was the fact that his education as an economist and his training in Scientific Management had imbued in him the method of reducing any activity into its component parts in order to consider the ways in which it could be conducted most efficiently and effectively. This was then augmented by the awareness of how such principles might be manifested in design, which came from his membership of the DIA. This organization, whose very motto, 'Fitness for Purpose', had Taylorist echoes, also provided him with an early window onto continental modernism through its journal and lecture programme, while his role at Venesta took him frequently to the continent and allowed him to see such work at first hand. Indeed, a year or so before work began on Lawn Road, Pritchard had seen Le Corbusier, Charlotte Perriand and Pierre Jeanneret's model flat interior at the Salon d'Automne in Paris, in which he perhaps recognized the DIA's maxim translated into the more sophisticated dictum that the plan is the generator.[36] In the long term, Pritchard's familiarity with contemporary design, and the concomitant development in his knowledge of what he wanted from the project, would lead to some spectacular arguments between him and his architect. In the short term, however, it seems to have allowed him to direct Coates to very specific references and concepts, and to enjoy a genuine dialogue with his architect. He was, then, one of the best-informed clients of his day.

It is clear from their correspondence that Le Corbusier's work, and that of other French modernists, was another significant early influence on both men. In February 1930, Pritchard would send Coates photographs of Le Corbusier's work. These Coates declared 'inspiring', and he requested that he might be allowed to retain them as they kept him in the right frame of mind while working on designs for the house.[37] Further evidence of Le Corbusier's influence, as well as Coates' desire to re-define the dwelling, is found in a letter to Pritchard in which he declared:

> I can plan a house – a machine to live in – which will give you better accommodation than that provided by the present plan … at a price strictly within the limits you set provided you are willing to accept radical alterations in principle, construction, design and finish.[38]

The dialogue continued the next month when Pritchard asked Coates to read an article in the French periodical *Art et Décoration* about the designer Djo-Bourgeois. His instructions to Coates are of particular interest, for he asks him to pay attention to the references to the relative merits of built-in furniture against open spaces in which furniture could be moved around. He wrote

> There is, in my view, no one solution. The one principle being 'what are the conditions that will govern the use of each space, or each room?' and that if it is probable that a certain space can only be used for a certain function then there is a good reason to fix furniture.[39]

The interest in the use of space is echoed in another influence: German modernism. In April 1930, both Pritchards joined with Coates in a visit to Germany, during which they went to the then Mecca of modern housing, the Weissenhof Siedlung in Stuttgart.[40] While this would have allowed them to experience a range of modernist aesthetics in addition to the Corbusian Purism with which they were already familiar, the visit also exposed them to the link made by German modernists between new forms of living and new forms of space. This reflects the linguistic trick in German by which the word for dwelling, *Wohnung*, refers both to the dwelling itself and the living practices within. The Weissenhof had originated as an exhibition devoted to *Die neue Wohnung* and given Pritchard's preoccupations, it seems likely that the duality of meaning and purpose which underpinned German modernism would have appealed to these British visitors.[41]

Two schemes resulted from this initial phase of work. The first was for a single house and was produced in March 1930 but this was abandoned and a second scheme followed in the July. This was for a pair of linked houses, one for the Pritchards and one for Coates and his family; both were highly reminiscent of Le Corbusier's work.[42] The second scheme, in particular, bears a strong resemblance in plan and site layout to his Villa La Roche of 1925 and, in the treatment of the elevations, to the Villa Stein de Monzie of 1926–7. In the context of the evolution of Isokon, however, the Corbusian influence is less important than the fact that the development of this second set of plans led to another epiphany for the protagonists. A week after receiving the designs, Jack Pritchard wrote to Coates to say: 'They are good. Shall I say important? Anyway, they are going to be important.'[43] This comment signalled the realization that the project might form the beginning, as Fry would put it, of a wider sphere of enquiry.

Isokon

In the eighteen months which followed the production of Coates' second set of plans, he and the Pritchards gradually expanded what had begun as a personal quest to find a modern home into nothing less than a project to take on the house building industry. There is not space here to consider in detail what was ultimately an unsuccessful venture, with a very convoluted history.[44] However it is important to draw attention to the particular aspects of this episode which relate both to the evolution of the Isokon flats, and the broader themes of this chapter.

Chief among these are the need to register the scope of the ambition which Coates and the Pritchards brought to the project. The amount of time and money which they exerted during these first years of the decade, suggests they genuinely believed that it was possible to develop and promote a different method of design and building from that which then prevailed in the speculative housing market.[45] For Pritchard, this expansion of aim can be attributed in part to his experience at Venesta in bringing together designers and new materials. It also owed much to his membership of the DIA in whose recommitment to persuading government of the centrality of design to the progress of British trade he was then playing a guiding role. His patronage of modern housing, not just the house, would contribute to this campaign and serve to reiterate the principle that 'design has an economic importance as well as [a] decorative [one]'.[46] From late 1930, therefore, he and Coates worked to develop a system of 'modern unit construction', prefabricated component parts which could be combined in various ways to create a series of prefabricated house-types which they called 'Isotypes'.[47] These would be manufactured and constructed by the newly formed company, Isokon.[48] The idea was also extended to the intention to 'design and sell standardized unit equipment' for these dwellings. Their ultimate aim was to show that 'a really scientific house [could] be made' and sold at a low price.[49]

Such optimism and zeal is typical of this generation of reformers, but it does seem to have been somewhat misdirected in this instance. It is understandable that Coates and his collaborators should have wanted to exert influence over an industry which, by the time their project began, was producing over 150,000 potential theatres of modernist living a year.[50] It was, however, doing this very successfully through the employment of traditional construction techniques and the creation of house-forms which, as noted above, were at once as up-to-date inside as their exteriors were not.[51] The prefabricated system proposed by Coates, and the Corbusian forms in which it resulted, would have had little appeal to either the producers or consumers of semi-detached suburbia.[52] It is surely significant that the scheme for Isokon furniture was the only successful outcome of this phase of activity; it was the sole sphere in which any of those involved had any direct experience.[53]

However deluded the Pritchards and Coates may have been in their ambitions; their scheme nevertheless offers an early instance of the ways in which British modernists, echoing the practices of their German and Swiss-French counterparts, conceptualized the future of the building industry. In appointing Coates as Consultant Architect to Isokon, the intention was to reinstate architects as a central figures in an industry from which they had been largely excluded and thereby make design central to the building process. This was reinforced by connecting this status, under the banner of science, to the exercise of expertise over systems of prefabrication, the use of new materials and other high technologies of construction. However unrealizable such a vision was at this date, at the powerful level of theory, it served the valuable purpose of associating modernist architects with another arena of progress.[54]

The most significant outcome of this period of activity was that, regardless of the feasibility of the Isotypes, the aim of all involved remained to create an appropriate form of modern dwelling. And it was as part of the ongoing discussions to achieve this goal that an alternative or complement to the Isotypes was first suggested: the building of a block of flats. The moment at which this idea was first mooted is unclear. Cheryl Buckley cites a letter from Coates to Jack Pritchard dated August 1931 in which he states 'I note you agree to "minimum" flats and will proceed on these lines'.[55] A letter from Pritchard to Coates of February 1932 makes reference to the inclusion of a 'grand one [flat] of our own' in the scheme,[56] but it was not until the next month that this additional project seems to have been formalized.[57] Writing to his brother Fleetwood, Pritchard declared:

> Instead of building houses on our site in Lawn Road we will build minimum
> flats each one consisting of a large room with bays for sleeping and eating,

a compact kitchenette, bathroom, balcony garden and use of garden. Service will be supplied to the extent of hot and cold water, clearing of refuse, cleaning and the supply of a small breakfast.[58]

Having worked through assorted schemes for houses, and having finally elected the flat as their chosen form of dwelling, the Pritchards and Coates had proved a modernist dictum, or rather established one that British theorists of the modernist dwelling would shortly ratify in print. For, at more or less the same time that the first briefs were issued for the Isokon flats in late spring 1932, F. R. S. Yorke was embarking on the research which would result in *The Modern House*, published in May 1934.[59] Three years later, with Frederick Gibberd, he would write *The Modern Flat*. Both texts would enshrine a notion fundamental to this generation of modernists: that however significant was the house, it was but a step in the evolutionary process towards the flat (a process embodied, incidentally, in the chronology of the books' publication). As Yorke wrote in 1934:

> In so far as the modern architect is concerned the villa has had, and will continue to have, a great importance as the cheapest complete building unit for examination and experiment, and it is most often in this small structure that modern architecture goes through its complete revolution.[60]

But, as he continued, these experiments served as the basis of the real solution to the housing problem which undoubtedly lay 'in a re-formed type of flat dwelling and controlled land development'.

In both books, their authors also established the standard arguments which modernists would rehearse in defence of the flat. These revolved around the assertion that the mass production of the 'individual villa type of house' had caused the town to spread 'more rapidly than in the past'. The only logical response to this sprawl was 'that dwellings must be grouped and built higher', with facilities such as laundry and hot-water supply arranged communally. Yorke did acknowledge that flats, however necessary, might not be to the taste of all. He sealed his argument, however, with the assurance that provided flats were well enough designed and laid out sufficiently well, re-formed in other words, as the examples in *The Modern Flat* would demonstrate, then people would want to live in them. This point also related to the fact that, for those who hated both the form and content of suburban sprawl, the modern flat served as a corrective to the damage wrought by the speculators on the city. In tones which have strong echoes of the discussion of the Pioneer Health Centre cited in the previous chapter, Yorke wrote ruefully:

> as long as the town is unable to offer the people a healthy life in pleasant surroundings, in flat dwellings that are of a very much better type than those existing, the villa will be built on the outskirts by the people who work in the city but who escape after business hours from its ugliness and noise.

It is now widely understood that the flat was no more necessary or inevitable a dwelling type than the house.[61] What lent it this framework of necessity was the fact that for this generation of modernists it was, especially in the forms presented in

The Modern Flat, the most noticeably different form of contemporary dwelling and it therefore constituted a dramatic contrast to what was then being built in England. As Yorke and Gibberd would declare, 'The flat has produced a building type peculiar to our own era; without precedent in the architecture of the past.'[62] The flat – specifically the Modern Flat – was, then, a rhetorical device in its own right. To deploy it was to gain an immediate shorthand for modernity and progress, and to guarantee attention for the projects in which it was used.

At a more pragmatic level, as the Pritchards would discover, a project for a block of flats was more likely to reach fruition than any number of schemes to create modernist housing without the backing of a building company or the state. One reason for this, and what still allowed them to claim that their work was a corrective to the speculative builder, and a demonstration that design was an economic proposition, was that, in commissioning the flats from Coates, they were addressing a market which the speculator had overlooked. The market for owner occupation was primarily one for the family house; and there remained sections of the middle classes who failed to fit the suburban model. Middle-class professionals, unmarried or in couples, who wished to live in the city, close to its amenities and their places of work, found it hard to find decent accommodation, and for them the housing shortage continued into the 1930s. They often found themselves resigned, as Yorke and Gibberd would note with more than a hint of pathos, 'to liv[ing] alone in single rooms ... [in] an old ready-to-be condemned, originally one-family house, with common bathroom and w.c. that no one takes pride in'.[63] In meeting a demand which, in 1931, was only beginning to be tapped, the Pritchards and Coates could hope to define the form of the modern flat for some time to come and stake it out as a modernist territory.

Given the significance of the modern flat, the matter of who first came up with the idea that the Isokon company should become its patron was of considerable importance, both at the time and subsequently. The most common assumption has been that it was Coates' idea. Several historians describe him as persuading the Pritchards that they ought not to build a house on a site in London.[64] As will be discussed later, both during and after the flats were being built, Coates was much concerned about the way the scheme was publicized and was always anxious that he should be duly acknowledged for what to him was his primary conceptual lead in the venture. This is entirely understandable: as the self-styled leader of British modernism and pioneer of social progress it was vital that he should be understood as the expert, rather than his clients.

The actual course of events was, like the building process itself, far more complex, and it seems most probable that the idea was Molly's. Jack, writing in 1984, recalled that it was in the course of discussions with Coates that she mentioned that it seemed wrong to use the plot for one family alone. To this, he said, Coates responded, 'in one of his superior moods, "Of course, I always knew that the right thing to do was to build flats rather than a house."'.[65] Jack's recollection is supported by a letter from Molly to Coates of January 1935. It is diplomatic but makes her feelings clear. She wrote:

> You accuse me of putting over the flat idea as mine – well so it was – I have
> felt you to be unkind when I have heard you put it over as yours – therefore

the truth must be that, as a result of a germ dropped from you and another from me, the idea came to us both independently.[66]

Although this does signal Molly's ultimate authorship of the proposal for flats, her notion of mingled germs does allow another conclusion to be drawn.[67] In keeping with the thesis of this book, it offers further evidence in support of the contention that it was the consensus between client and architect that created new spaces and forms in this decade.

Following the decision to commission a block of flats in spring 1932, the Pritchards spent the next six months finalizing the brief for their first building prototype. Although it was, as Jack wrote to Coates, 'a relatively small job', it was nevertheless important that they get the brief correct. For, as he continued, the scheme was 'a cornerstone for the future' and the means to demonstrate their thesis that design could transform both the processes and products of industry. That this consideration may have been amongst the many which Coates brought to the resolution of the brief, Jack recognized. In the same letter he observed, 'you look on it as an opportunity to show what you can do – it will help to make you'.[68] As ever in this period, then, brief and design were formed by both pragmatic and rhetorical demands.

The efforts to create a brief culminated in a long Memorandum from Molly to Coates in September 1932 in which she noted 'we hope to be able to proceed with this scheme immediately'.[69] It was comprehensive and elaborated the description which Jack had given to his brother earlier that year. Her basic requirement was 'a block of one-roomed service flats consisting of about 20 flats, the type to be suitable for dupli-cation in principle in other areas'. She asked that 'if practicable' each should have a large living room; kitchenette, fitted and very small; bathroom or bath-dressing room; facili-ties for bed space, dressing space and dining space; and arrangement for a spare bed. For their equipment she referred Coates to a memo on Isokon houses which has not survived. To this basic outline was then added the request that, if it were convenient to the plan, Coates should see if it would be possible to have two-room flats and extra balcony space, as it would then be possible to let these at higher rents. She also listed specifications for gas and electricity, the provision of telephones and adequate ventila-tion. Finally, Coates was asked to provide accommodation for the service aspect of the flats which included cleaning of rooms and the provision of meals for tenants. This required a central kitchen with offices, a staff sitting room and a cloakroom. The maximum outlay would be £5,000.

This detailed Memorandum is interesting for a number of reasons, not least because it demonstrates Molly's command of modernist terminology. She uses the words 'equipment' and 'space' in her specifications. It also addresses, very deftly, the desire to produce flats which would simultaneously allow architectural experimentation, be lettable and provide an adaptable prototype. This was achieved through the device of what Jack called, in the letter of March 1932, the minimum flat: a concept which had the merit of fitting in with a number of existing narratives of modernity, and which thus made it comprehensible across a range of reforming communities. First, and most obvi-ously it spoke to modernists by referencing the European concept of the *existenz-minimum*. At the same time, however, it gave Coates the opportunity to anglicize this by linking it to the form of the flat, to tendencies within British modernism and the theories of the dwelling which he was developing at this time.

Re-termed the 'service flat', the Isokon scheme, however avant-garde its final form, could also be made to fit in with existing attempts to modernize the spaces in which middle-class living was conducted. An early publicity pamphlet for the scheme declared that the flats were designed for 'businessmen and women who have no time for domestic troubles',[70] an audience which, as has already been noted, was only beginning to be catered for by the speculators at the time the Isokon project was conceived.[71] To build for them was an astute business move which could allow modernist spatial forms to enter, and potentially shape, a more mainstream concern.

A similar elision of modernist concepts with modern ones can be found in the reference to 'domestic troubles'. To contemporaries this would immediately have placed the flats within this era's ongoing attempts to create living environments which addressed the so-called 'servant problem'. Although the extent of this problem has been exaggerated, it was nevertheless true that many middle- and upper-class families and individuals found it increasingly difficult to find the servants upon whom they had become dependent to run the large Victorian and Edwardian houses in which they lived, or to conduct professional lives unencumbered by the exercise of daily domestic duties.[72] Such dwellings were what the leading domestic expert of the day, and erstwhile patron of the Pioneer Health Centre, Mrs C. S. (Dorothy) Peel called 'the labour-making home'. These were spaces which 'seem to have been planned with the express desire of providing an unnecessary amount of hard work for the unfortunate persons who inhabit them'.[73] These problems had given rise to a widespread enthusiasm for the principles of labour-saving design as a technique to transform such homes and make of them environments which were easier for the middle-class housewife to manage with only a daily 'char' or which would attract servants to work in them.

Peel was amongst many experts who advocated the application of the Taylorist principles of Scientific Management to the planning of the home in inter-war Britain. In so doing she helped to bring into debates about a re-formed middle-class domesticity some tenets which would take on a particular significance for modernist reformers of space.[74] These principles were articulated most clearly in her book *The Labour-Saving House*: chief among them were her insistence on the harnessing of technology and the transformation of space as the means to create a manageable environment in which to live and work.[75]

Mrs Peel was, therefore, highly enthusiastic about gas and electricity, and keen that coal should henceforth be banned from houses as it created so much dirt and drudgery.[76] She was also a keen advocate of simplifications of plan and space in order to further reduce labour. Hence she recommended using basements only for storage, and the transferral of the functions usually accommodated therein to ground level. The ground floor plan could then be reconfigured into one which comprised a large reception room, a kitchen and a pantry, with bedrooms and bathroom upstairs. She also advised on how these re-formed spaces might be equipped and furnished appropriately. The kitchen, for example, should have 'as few utensils as possible, and these shall have their proper keeping places'.[77] Further, she exhorted that 'all rooms should be under rather than over furnished and free of heavy, stuffy draperies', and recommended that floors were covered with linoleum, covered by rugs when necessary, because fitted carpets were 'taboo'.[78] Such concepts, though they were not aimed directly at flatted accommodation, could be applied very easily to its (re)design.

For Mrs Peel, as her support of the Pioneer Health Centre suggests, the ultimate aim in writing *The Labour-Saving House* was to restate 'the incalculable value to the nation of the good housekeeper'. The principles she outlined would enable this housekeeper, and those who worked with her, 'to bring up a race of decently behaved, clean, well-fed people, and to make of her home a place of peace and good will, a centre from which radiates a right influence'.[79] Peel's engagement with technology was one means to achieve this but it was not, as it would be in the modernist project perhaps, an end in itself. Nevertheless, in her domestication of technology she, and other writers like her, were able, by stealth, to make one of the key manifestations of modernity an integral part of domestic discourse from the late 1910s onwards. And in this way they created a potential shared ground between lady experts and card-carrying modernists.

The link between Mrs Peel's principles, which would of course have been familiar to the Taylorist-trained Jack Pritchard, and those of the Isokon flats is evident in the publicity pamphlet cited above. It reads:

> In the first place everything that is unnecessary, ugly, inconvenient and 'labour making' has been eliminated, and yet everything essential is there, and is there in exactly the right position. In the second place the flats although not furnished in the usual sense are absolutely ready to live in … When you take the flat you bring with you your favourite rug – a vase or two for flowers and perhaps a small table, and your room is completely furnished. Beyond these things – which are just those which bring your own personality to the room – all you need to provide are your bedding and crockery.[80]

This text also has much in common with Coates' theoretical writings on the design of the modern dwelling. It reflects, perhaps, the fact that British modernism has not been taken as seriously as it deserves, that we are not accustomed to think of its advocates as having devoted much of their time to the development of architectural theory. While it is true that most chose not to frame their discussions of what they did as 'theory', Coates and Fry individually, and the MARS Group collectively in the second half of the 1930s, did attempt to articulate in text, and exhibition, the principles which underpinned their practice.[81] From early on in his career, Coates began to write about the modern dwelling and its furnishing.[82] This articulated an approach to its design which was formed from the assimilation of the extensive reading he had undertaken in his period of self-education in the mid-1920s, the writings of Le Corbusier, his early experience of Japanese domestic architecture, and contemporary narratives of domestic modernity such as Mrs Peel's penchant for Scientific Management in the home and his growth into artistic consciousness in the anti-Edwardian interiors of Bohemian Fitzrovia.[83] These ideas were then fed into, and further refined by, his work on the various schemes for Lawn Road and the other domestic commissions which he had won in the early 1930s.[84]

Fundamental to Coates' theory was the premise that 'the requirements of the society in which we live must determine the things we make and live with'.[85] This allowed him to posit a definition of society which created the conditions in which the sort of architecture, and architect, which he advocated, were the only logical outcome. Pointing to 'the general collapse of feudal society … which is taking place all round us today', he argued that 'the task of the architect is clearly defined'. They should 'invent and exhibit, a better architecture which will quite naturally be accepted and demanded by the people, for the people, and of itself produce a finer society'. This task he described as:

> A new service which he alone of all 'experts' can provide. The natural starting-place for this new service must be the scene in which the daily drama of personal life takes place; the interior of the dwelling – the PLAN [sic] – and its living equipment, the furniture.[86]

If the architect's task was to build a way out of contemporary chaos, on what requirements, what daily dramas should he base his design? In terms which would be repeated by many a British modernist, Coates specified that:

> Our society is above all determined to be free. The love of travel and change, the mobility of the worker himself, grows with every opportunity to indulge it. The 'home' is no longer a permanent place from one generation to another … we move away from the old home and family; we get rid of our belongings and make for a new exciting freedom. A new freedom which demands a greater comfort and a more perfect order and repose, also a new type of *intricacy* in the equipment of the dwelling-scene.[87]

From such precepts, Coates formulated a system which was based on a dramatic simplification of the dwelling form. This entailed both a rationalization of the plan through zoning of function and a reduction in what he called 'the burden … [of] permanent tangible possessions'.[88] He proclaimed:

> The dwelling-scene of tomorrow will contain as part of its structure nearly all that today is carried about for the purpose of 'furnishing' one house after another … Thus furniture…will take its place in the logic of construction, becoming an integral part of architecture. For the rest, clothing, bedding, crockery, utensils, books, pictures and sculpture will have the select value of a personal environment; will be, in fact, the only 'furniture' (personal belongings) in use.[89]

Although Coates' system offered a method for the planning of the dwelling it was less specific about how these units might be built or where, or whether one particular type was more desirable than any other. A hint that he envisaged some form of prefabrication is apparent in his reference to the lack of permanence in contemporary society. This suggests that he was arguing that dwellings needed to be both more flexibly made and more adaptable in their plans. As for the location of these dwellings, it was only when Coates began to criticize what was actually being built in the early 1930s that his position as a pro-urbanist became apparent. Discussing the development of suburbia he argued, in terms which could very well be applied to the Isokon project:

> What is the use of moving out of overcrowded towns, merely to overcrowd the country? Every year larger and larger areas of England are becoming a no-man's land, neither town nor country. No; the next step in the design of dwelling-units must be the block or group of dwellings with every centralised service which makes the sharing of costs economically possible ... The community structure is the only one that will give us better buildings, more open space, better living facilities, freedom to move and breathe and rest, and cheaper rents and transportation costs.[90]

From an intersection of narratives of domestic and spatial reform, and entrepreneurial zeal, the Isokon Flats were formulated as a modernist manifesto. By April 1933 the final form of the block had been agreed as comprising 29 flats in four storeys with service quarters on the ground floor and a flat for the Pritchards on the roof; a budget was also set at just over £13,000.[91] It had also been agreed that a full-size mock-up of one of the minimum flats should be exhibited at the Dorland Hall exhibition which would open in June 1933. This had been at the instigation of the publicity-aware Coates, who saw it as a medium through which the 'economic, social and formal value' of the 'new service' could be demonstrated to an informed and potentially influential public.[92] Despite their apparent agreement about the economic necessity of design, Jack Pritchard was initially unsure about whether to participate, telling Coates:

> My preliminary thought is that it would be dangerous to co-operate with this as the Committee appears to me to consist of those who are either able individualistic designers or their supporters, instead of being those who believe that design has an economic importance as well as decorative.[93]

His reluctance to associate his project with the wrong tendencies in design reform was mitigated by the appointment of Coates and Fry to the exhibition's organizing committee, and his own growing influence over the DIA by this time, so it was eventually agreed that Isokon would exhibit.[94] It was a wise decision. The project enjoyed considerable publicity and approbation, earning the company sufficient downpayments on leases to allow the scheme to be finalized. It also ratified Coates' position as the leading figure in the shaping of new forms of domestic architecture: a useful boost to the leader of the newly founded MARS Group.

Thus emboldened, tenders were sought in July 1933 and the application for the design's approval under the Building Acts was sent to the LCC. After a slight delay due to the Council going 'into recess' for much of the summer, the necessity of seeking further permissions from Hampstead Borough Council, and a last-minute request that Coates pare down costs from the original £13,587 to £12,500, work commenced on site at the end of September 1933.[95] A bitterly cold winter held up construction by 37 days but on 26 June 1934 the builders were able to hand over the more-or-less completed block to the Pritchards.[96]

The most modern building in England

Five years after she and Jack had first attempted to build at Lawn Road, Molly welcomed guests to the opening ceremony of the Isokon Flats on 9 July 1934. It was a momentous occasion, not just for those who had been involved in this modernist odyssey, but also for the development of architecture in Britain. Its completion marked a key moment in the process in which modernism moved from a movement concerned to re-form its own discipline to one which sought equally to engage with other narratives of reform. It is true that there were earlier, and more conventionally 'public' modernist buildings, such as Joseph Emberton's Royal Corinthian Yacht Club of 1931 or Tecton's Penguin Pool of 1933–4. However, their significance resided less in their architects' attempts to resolve a particular obstacle to progress through design (bringing penguins to modernity was not a commonplace concern) and more in their unification of the formal principles of modernism with non-domestic building types. They were three-dimensional proof that modernism was moving beyond the pioneer phase. The Isokon Flats, by contrast, were the first realization of the attempt to use design to resolve contemporary social problems: in this instance, those of achieving economic and domestic modernity. Further this was done with the expectation that the flats would operate as a prototype, 'a cornerstone', for wider application. For this reason, Molly was perhaps more accurate than she realized when, at the start of her speech she declared: 'This building ... is perhaps the most modern building in England. It is not only modern as an Architectural piece – it expresses a revolutionary idea for living.'[97]

It was Coates' ability to assimilate innovations in design and notions of how life might be lived that makes the Isokon Flats such an intellectually and formally satisfying building.[98] As will become evident in the analysis which follows, every element of the design – the planning of the flats, the way their interiors were equipped, the treatment of the elevations and the siting of the block – served to demonstrate how a

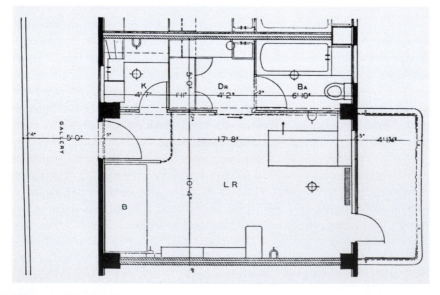

Figure 3.4
Wells Coates, Plan
of single flat at
Lawn Road, 1934

modern theatre of living could create a finer society and that design could serve economic ends.[99] In Coatesian fashion the analysis of the design should start with the plan, and here the single flats which formed the majority of the accommodation will serve to exemplify his resolution of the brief.

The businessman or -woman who chose to live at Lawn Road would have acquired a minimum flat, 17' 8" deep by 15' 4" wide (Fig. 3.4). Such a compact space required a careful choreographing of use, with areas zoned for circulation, service, sleeping and living. Approximately a third of the area was given over to a 5' wide strip which comprised the electric kitchen (4' 7" by 5' 0"), which contained a cooker and refrigerator as well as cupboards and sink; and a dressing room (4' 2" by 5' 0") which opened into the bathroom (6'10" by 5'0"). Sliding doors closed these spaces off from the main living area when not in use. The remaining 17' 8" by 10' 4" space was divided into an area for sleeping, marked by the divan's frame and plywood panelling to dado level and a living zone demarcated by a built-in cabinet which contained bookshelves, cupboards and an electric fire. At the window end, a built-in table marked the dining area (Fig. 3.5). All the furniture was made to Coates' specifications since it was impossible to buy such fittings off-the-peg at this date, a problem which had the virtue of making the flats' interiors, as well as their plans, visibly different from those of contemporary dwellings. Into this setting, whose dominant colours were the browns of the plywood and light creams and white of the paintwork, the tenant needed only to bring a vase or painting, as that early publicity pamphlet had suggested. This would add, in Coates' terminology, the 'select value of a personal environment' to the space. This was

Figure 3.5
Interior of single
flat at Lawn Road

its true furniture, 'what is personal and individual, as distinct from what is social and universal in the equipment and arrangement of the dwelling'.[100]

This was not just a rhetorical distinction on Coates' part. It linked with the concept of the serviced flat as an integrated whole and, as he had written in 1933, the idea that a building should enable freedom to move and breathe and rest through the provision of better living facilities. The social and universal equipment of the built-in furniture would limit the amount of domestic troubles experienced by the tenant but also work in tandem with the services provided on-site. Depending on the rent paid – between £96 and £170 per annum – tenants were entitled to services which ranged from daily bed-making and cleaning to the provision of meals; a reminder that although the flats may have been revolutionary in many ways, they did not disrupt prevailing economies of social relations.[101] Nevertheless, liberated by equipment and the labour of others, Isokon tenants were able to venture into the modern world beyond their doorstep.

The block itself comprised four, gallery-accessed storeys. Each contained a larger 'double' flat at the south end with bedroom alcove; three single flats and, at ground floor level the staff accommodation, and at first to third floor level, another single flat and then a studio flat. The service space was extended to the front by a bay to contain the entrance and staircase tower which was further abutted by a single-storey row of garages. In keeping with its purpose of demonstrating an alternative to conventional methods of building, the construction of the block was as radical as its planning.

That this was so was partly due to the site. Beneath Lawn Road sat two London, Midland and Scottish Railway tunnels which carried the East Coast mainline. These ran east–west, one beneath the south end of the block and the other beneath the north. Even if Coates had entertained the thought of using traditional load-bearing foundations and construction techniques, such a form of building would not have been possible in this context. It was this factor which allowed him to make two decisions which would have a significant impact of the form and appearance of the Isokon Flats. The first, and inevitable one, was to use a framed-system of construction and to cantilever that frame over the tunnels, therein finding his design motif. The second was to use monolithic reinforced concrete for the frame. This was a construction system of far greater complexity than the more standard frame and infill technique used by many of his contemporaries. Whereas that system was almost invariably expressed in a rectilinear form, with its component parts clearly articulated, the monolithic system, which formed frame and wall together, encouraged the conceptualization and formation of the building as a seamless, sculptural whole.

By using monolithic reinforced concrete Coates was able to fulfil his dogma that the exterior of a building should 'make explicit externally the processes, functions and qualities included in the whole scene'.[102] A system which cast the building as a whole allowed the precise union of function with form which was central to the conception of the Isokon Flats. But Coates was not interested in functionalist reasoning alone and although he expressed these ideas in standard modernist phraseology he did, unusually for this period, also acknowledge that this almost inevitably implied some element of aesthetic judgement. Indeed, for Coates this was one of the things which

Figure 3.6
View of Lawn Road
Flats from Lawn
Road (present day)

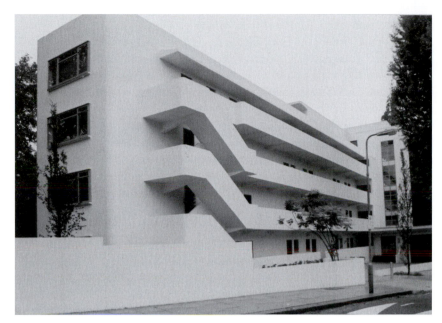

gave the architect his status and it was his task, once he had synthesized furniture and plan, 'to give to the whole a formal aspect of significance'.[103]

Coates located the formal significance of the block in the contrast between the smooth surfaces of the exterior walls – the result of being cast in metal sheeting – and the tiers of deep cantilevered access balconies.[104] This was emphasized further by the extruded canopy which protected the top floor balcony and the extravagant turn of the staircases at the south end. These projections were, in turn, counterpointed by the cantilevered canopy over the entrance which was carried round to form the roof of the garage. The motif was continued on the west façade, where a series of individual balconies, also cantilevered, punctured the building's surface. Here was proof that at the same time as reinforced concrete reduced building costs and met the practicalities of the site, its inherent material and structural qualities could be used to considerable formal effect (Fig. 3.6).

Framed by boundary walls, its smooth surfaces covered in pink-tinted cream paint, the block offered a supremely simple and effortlessly confident façade to Lawn Road. Easily the equal of anything built on the continent, it showed a real command of both spatial and formal expression and signalled not simply the advent of Coates' mature style but also that British modernism was beginning to develop its own language of form.

Having finally achieved their prototype, the challenge for all involved was now to promote it. It was in doing so that some of the differences in the motivations which underpinned the project began to manifest themselves. For the Pritchards, in July 1934, their primary concern was to use publicity to attract tenants for the flats and thereby prove its economic viability for further emulation. They remained concerned to promote the flats as a solution to modern living conditions and so forth but in the short term their actions were more commercially driven. For Coates the project had always been the means to achieve his reputation, and that of modernism, as the only medium through which modernity could be expressed. Because of this, as already noted, he was particularly concerned that his role in the project should be duly acknowledged and that the flats should receive sympathetic coverage in the appropriate journals. In fact, tracing Coates' correspondence with various architectural journals, as far as it is possible, allows some significant insights into they way modernism was 'marketed' in the 1930s, and how the networks traced in Part 1 worked together to promote the cause.[105]

Coates' first concerted effort to promote the Isokon Flats began, as we have seen, in July 1932 when he pressed the Pritchards to agree to participate in the Dorland Hall Exhibition. In parallel with this he was also able to see published a number of articles in 1932. Although they did not make direct reference to either the flats or to the Isotypes, the texts were nevertheless rationales for the principles they embodied and helped situate him as an expert on the design of dwellings. During 1933, his propaganda work was tied more directly to the Isokon project, most obviously when the full-size replica of the minimum flat went on display at Dorland Hall in June. The publicity garnered during this time was then augmented by Coates' contribution to the BBC talks on 'Design in Modern Life' and by the extensive coverage which the formation of Unit One gained. *The Listener*, for example, included Coates' axonometric rendering of the flats as an illustration to an article on the group by Paul Nash; the following week he wrote to admonish them, gently, for printing it upside down.[106]

As the flats neared completion in spring 1934, both Coates and the architectural press started to make plans for reporting them. In April 1934, Raymond Postgate, sometime left-wing journalist but then working as Secretary to Isokon, reported to Coates that *The Architectural Review* was willing to commission Dell and Wainwright to take pictures of the flats 'provided they had the rights of first publication'. Noting that 'applications for this must be made by the architect, not the company' he urged that Coates did so with some urgency as in order for the photographs to appear in the June *Review* they needed to have been taken by the first week of May.[107]

The Architectural Press's interest in the project was not surprising given the significant role its staff had played, and would continue to play, in the promotion of modernism in Britain. The Isokon Flats were an affirmation of how far the movement had progressed and warranted substantial coverage in its journals; a status indicated by the fact that it was Hastings who assumed editorial responsibility for the building's coverage. He decided to delay the photography until the end of June because he felt the building was not yet ready; he also recruited John Havinden in place of Dell and Wainwright. These plans he outlined to Coates in a letter of 15 June 1934 and it is clear that he viewed the Press's coverage as something to be produced in collaboration with the architect. In response, Coates sent Hastings what he called 'some preliminary dope' which offered a detailed outline of what plans and drawings should be included (site plan and typical floor plan and plan of the minimum flat) and the specification that most photographs should be exterior shots. He also included a list of the angles from which the various images should be shot. He further stipulated that interior shots should only be taken of the single flats because the larger flats had not yet been properly furnished:

'I will not [sic] have published the flat furnished by Heals'. He finished by agreeing to provide 'general notes for copy but suggest PMS [Philip Morton Shand] or one of your lads should write it – say in interview with me'.[108] Coates' censorship of the images shows how carefully he guarded his public image and his eagerness to associate himself with the flagship journals. He was therefore much agitated when Hastings wanted to delay the photography. Aware that the Pritchards, as will be discussed, were taking their own steps to promote the Flats, he responded 'very well, but tell him [Hastings] other papers may "get" the job – although I myself will not release to others before Arch Press'.[109]

The Review would publish the article in August 1934 – very much to Coates' specifications – and *The Architects' Journal* would publish a series of articles on the block the following month, reflecting the decision by Hastings to reserve 'the art for the Archi [sic] … the technical for the AJ'.[110] Coates appears to have collaborated similarly with Mr Greenhalgh, the editor of *The Builder*, and *The Architect and Building News*. He also sought to persuade *Design for Today* of the project's merits. In a letter to its editor, Anthony Bertram, Coates hinted at why this level of control was so important:

> I have been wondering whether you would like some dope on LRF [Lawn Road Flats] … If you do, I should much appreciate a talk with you on this matter as some of the dope which has been pushed out about the flats has been done without my knowledge and approval, and difficulties have arisen between me and the client in regard to it.[111]

The comment referred to the ongoing argument between Coates and the Pritchards about authorship of the idea of the flats. It also reflected the always difficult relationship among them occasioned by competing egos, the Pritchards' inexperience as clients, Coates' delays in producing plans, and the many faults found in the design subsequent to completion. These differences may partially account for the Pritchards' separate pursuit of publicity for the flats, but it is also to be explained by the fact that, as already noted, they had produced a block which needed to be let in order to prove its viability as a model for future practice. Molly was quite clear about this in her opening day speech:

> The intention of ISOKON is to provide … 'good living' for as many people as possible. If this block is a success and we make money on it, we shall use that money for building another block and so on. In fact we hope to be able to have a chain of this kind of flats over the country … but obviously we cannot launch out on these till we have succeeded with this our first scheme. The press can help us. You can help us. You can spread news of these flats among your friends and so help us quickly to fill them up so that we may be able then to start on a new scheme.…[112]

Like Coates the Pritchards had started their publicity work early on. It has already been noted that Jack's letter to his brother of March 1932, announcing the intention to commission the flats, was written with the intention of finding out what sort of publicity his brother's advertising agency could provide as the project developed. They were similarly systematic when the flats were complete and employed a press agent, Andrew Reid, to feed copy to the press. They also appear to have used Philip Morton Shand on a freelance basis to 'plant', as he put it, material in the newspapers. While this might be considered something of a conflict of interest given his role at the Architectural Press, which was working with Coates, it may be explained by the fact that his wife Sibyl was working as a secretary to the Pritchards at this time. She too seems to have spent much of her time on publicity work. It was certainly successful. In addition to the coverage which Coates had solicited, the flats were reported across a wide range of the daily and weekly press, from the *News Chronicle* and *Daily Mirror* to the *Southern Daily Echo*.[113]

The Pritchards also used the opening ceremony to make personal contact with decision-makers who might be persuaded of the project's merits as a prototype. The MP Thelma Cazalet opened the block, and they invited Lancelot Keay, Liverpool City Council's Chief Architect (who could not attend); the Minister of Health, Hilton Young; Herbert Morrison, who passed the invitation on to Lewis Silkin, Chair of the LCC's Housing Committee; and Archibald Scott, Chief Architect of the Ministry of Health. To Young they wrote:

> May we take the liberty of calling your attention to a block of new flats which we are erecting in Lawn Road and which, we feel, might interest you as an example of modern tenement building … We believe that the style and general arrangement of the block might give some interesting ideas for new buildings of this kind.[114]

It is unclear whether he attended, while Silkin, who, judging by his reply, had received a similar letter, albeit via Morrison, responded through his secretary:

> Mr Silkin is advised that the type of construction employed for the flats in question is one which on the score of cost, is not so suitable for the erection of working class dwellings as the type of normal brick construction used for the Council's block dwellings, and, in the circumstances, he does not think any useful purpose would be served by his availing himself of your kind invitation to inspect the building.[115]

This, it can be imagined, was not the response the Pritchards were hoping for, and it signalled that it would be a while before governments, local or otherwise, were persuaded of the merits of the principles embodied in the work of Isokon. For the time being, they had to be content that, at least among their fellow intellectuals, there was recognition of what it was they had achieved. In the *News Chronicle* Gerald Barry would declare,

> the experiment is the signpost to a new order – it represents in concrete and steel the new attitude towards this business of living which is beginning to emerge from our present-day chaos.[116]

They may not have been able to persuade officialdom to back them, but in the months following the opening of the flats at Lawn Road the Pritchards worked hard to demonstrate that their prototype could be reproduced elsewhere. In Molly's speech that day she mentioned plans for schemes at Manchester, Birmingham and

Nottingham. No designs for these survive, and none was realized. It was only a subsequent scheme for 69 flats on a 33-acre site at St Leonard's Hill, Windsor, that might have continued the Isokon 'brand' and demonstrated how the flat could also conserve the countryside.[117] This scheme was designed by a partnership of Walter Gropius and Max Fry, a relationship engineered by Pritchard and Morton Shand as a means to release Gropius from the emerging horrors of Nazi Germany.[118] Coates was furious with the Pritchards for doing this, but given the problems they had experienced and the fact that Coates himself had, earlier in the year, sold the Isotype idea to the builders Berg, it was hardly surprising. Unfortunately, circumstances conspired against its realization: Jack became ill and it proved impossible to raise the finance.

The Isokon Flats at Lawn Road would, then, remain the sole building produced by the Isokon Company but it was, and remains, a hugely significant scheme. In unifying modernist design principles with narratives of economic, social and domestic modernity it was very much a signpost to a new order. Within a year, Frederick Gibberd's block, Pullman Court, in south-west London, would be completed and the rest of the decade saw a steady stream of similar projects constructed across London and the south-east of England and disseminated to a wider audience through the pages of *The Modern Flat*.[119] By 1939, when Coates' sublime block at 10 Palace Gate in west London was opened, the British movement could reasonably claim considerable success in the re-shaping of the middle-class dwelling. A greater challenge was the reconciliation of modernism with the reform of working-class housing, and it is the media through which this was achieved which form the subject of the following chapters.

Chapter 4

New Homes for Old

Slum clearance is not enough, we must build with pride and hope

Marjory Allen (1934)

The Isokon Flats had been conceived of primarily as an attempt to articulate the future form of the middle-class home and to influence the practice of the speculative builder. Yet, as the Pritchards' overtures to local and central government politicians suggest, there was also the hope that the Isokon prototype might exert an influence over a state social housing policy which, since 1930, had been focused on the problem of slum clearance and promised a major programme of building in the years ahead. Silkin's terse rebuffal of their invitation, however, was a sign of the challenge British modernists faced if they were to achieve such an influence.

The quest to render modernist principles synonymous with social housing would not simply be a matter of the accidental forging of alliances with like-minded co-conspirators, and the creation of prototype forms through which a territory, either unoccupied or undergoing formation, could be seized, as it had been in Hampstead, Peckham or Finsbury. It necessitated instead the development of a much more strategically plotted and controlled campaign. For the British movement needed to persuade not an individual client of the validity of its methods but the civil servants and politicians who were responsible for the state housing programme and the campaigners and intellectuals who had influence upon them.

It is the concern of this chapter and the next to trace this campaign of persuasion and conversion from its earliest manifestations at the end of 1931 to the outbreak of war in 1939. They will show how British modernists, recognizing that the present of housing provision was monopolized by the state, sought instead to deliver ownership of the future of housing policy and practice into their hands.

This chapter focuses on the first years of the campaign, and considers how the movement, under the leadership of Fry and Coates, sought to achieve this goal by the establishment of a territory of critique. The men constructed a number of bases from which they initially articulated and then disseminated a modernist theory of housing in parallel to prevailing orthodoxies. These included a proposal for a housing and planning exhibition, produced by Fry, Coates and Jack Pritchard in November 1931, and a pair of journal articles by Fry written in 1933. Alongside this they sought to further develop their campaign through the formation of a strategic alliance with the voluntary housing sector, a body which, by the early 1930s, was similarly marginalized from the contemporary programme. Discussion focuses on the way this liaison was developed and its first public expression in the third New Homes for Old Exhibition, held in 1934.

The alliance between the modernists and voluntarists would create a distinctive socio-spatial blueprint for the dwelling as it *should be*. They rejected what they argued was the purely materialist approach of the state to the design of the working-class home, and in its place proposed a housing praxis which linked material and social reform with new practices of living and management. Synthesized in the medium of the Modern Flat, their ultimate goal was to transform society through the revitalization of the family and the creation of active citizens from former slum-dwellers. This blueprint also encompassed new conceptions of the architect's role, and the development of models of practice that emphasized research and teamwork as essential components of successful reform and planning. The chapter concludes therefore with an analysis of a scheme in which all these processes were embodied: Kent House. Commissioned by the Saint Pancras House Improvement Society, and designed by Connell and Ward, it heralded a new era for the modernist-voluntarist praxis of housing.

The campaign begins

That members of the British movement should have felt themselves qualified to contribute to debates about the re-forming of the working-class dwelling is hardly surprising. As noted previously, such a position was informed by their putative affinity with the house as a building type, and reiterated by the fact that the notion of architecture as a social service was a prerequisite of modernist practice. Yet a mere adherence to dogma does not explain the thoroughgoing nature of the movement's campaign nor its ultimate success. The explanation lies, rather, in the coincidence of the movement's evolution with the changing approach of central government to the shaping of the built environment.

As we have seen, it was from about 1930 onwards that Coates and Fry began to make their first efforts to create an organized movement and, subsequently, to initiate the process of marrying their concern to reform design culture with those who sought to reform society. This may partly be attributed to these men's personal ambitions but can also been seen as a response to signs that a legislative climate, more in tune with modernist preoccupations, was emerging in the wake of a Labour victory in the 1929 general election.

The signal came in 1930 when the new Minister of Health, Arthur Greenwood, introduced the first post-war housing legislation to tackle directly slum clearance, the problem which for so long had been highlighted by the voluntary housing sector. Intended as a complement to the subsidies available under the 1924 Wheatley Act, which were targeted primarily at the provision of housing in urban rather than rural areas, the Greenwood Act created subsidies for the costs of re-housing families displaced by clearance, and made higher sums available for building on expensive inner-city sites.[1] It also required local authorities to develop and submit five-year programmes of work to the Minister, and ordered that provision was to be the responsibility either of municipalities or of housing associations working by arrangement with them.

If this Act was significant for its move towards a more decidedly pro-urban housing policy, one which recognized both the flat and the house as desirable forms of re-housing, it was also important in signalling a shift towards a more thoroughgoing centralized control of the built environment. This was evident in Greenwood's demand that local authorities provide him with planned programmes of work, but more particularly in the fact that the Act was intended as the first stage in a broader tranche of town-planning legislation. The downfall in August 1931 of the Labour government as the Depression deepened prevented the full realization of this vision, but a Town and Country Planning Act was passed the following year by the National Government which replaced it. This, though many of its provisions were permissive rather than statutory, brought both developed and undeveloped land under planning control for the first time. It meant, therefore, that it was now possible for local authorities which so wished to pursue plans for the redevelopment of their cities.[2] The days of the state-sponsored development of suburban, low-density cottage estates were over. A more complex economy of urban housing and planned slum clearance and flat building in the inner cities had begun.

The shift was an important one for the emerging British movement. It was not that any of its members expected that modernist flats would be built under this legislation, nor that they would be called upon to re-plan the cleared areas. Rather, it was the very fact that flats had become a favoured form of re-housing, and that planning was being recognized by government which was significant, for it established a common ground between modernists and the state which could be exploited. It set in place, therefore, one of the conditions which this book has proposed as enabling the modernist project to be achieved: the creation of a narrative of modernity onto which their principles could be grafted. We saw this process enacted in the previous chapter with the Pritchards' conflation of the minimum flat with the more familiar narrative of the serviced flat. This allowed them to translate the modern into the modernist and colonize a territory, hitherto unmapped by the movement, with a new language of form and space. The adoption by the state of the modern flat, and the principle of planned development, meant that a similar translation might now be engineered in the arena of social housing. This had two distinct merits. First, now relieved of the problem of persuading the state of the worth of the flat and of planning *per se*, the British movement was enabled to pursue a more positive campaign. Their task became the altogether more constructive one of capturing the realm of ideas by demonstrating that their techniques and practices could create better, more modern flats, in better planned environments, than anything yet built. Second, the prospect, however distant in 1930, that this goal might be achieved, provided a pole around which the nascent movement could cohere.

The establishment of this narrative of modernity was, therefore, important. Yet the legislation of 1930 onwards served only to open a door to the modernists' proselytizing. To render this narrative modernist, members of the British movement needed to site themselves and their ideas very carefully, and highly visibly. That they understood this, and were able to do so, was evident from the very start of their campaign.

EPIC

In November 1931, Fry and Coates sent Jack Pritchard a report that outlined what appears to have been a joint project for a display to be held in conjunction with the Building Trades Exhibition (BTE) which would open at the exhibition halls at Olympia the following September. Entitled an 'Exhibition for Planned Industrial Construction' (EPIC), their proposal was for an exhibit which demonstrated the necessity of planning – both economic and physical – in the development of industrial areas.[3] The display would, they wrote, open with 'The Story of Un-Planning', a tale of how the uncontrolled development of a factory and the area around it inevitably brought about 'stagnation and decay' and hence a move away from 'Unplanning'. This would be followed by an *'Entr'acte'*, entitled 'The Story of Planning', which outlined the 'essential elements' of industrial planning. The exhibition would culminate in a display of 'Planning in Practice'. This, its largest section, would comprise a complete town planning scheme for an industrial zone which included a factory as well as a workers' housing scheme alongside it. Using charts, diagrams, aerial photographs, scale and one-to-one models, this was a highly ambitious project,[4] a worthy opening salvo to the modernists' housing campaign.

It came to nothing. In the same way that Pritchard and Coates' contemporary plans to take on the speculative house builder were wildly optimistic, so too were their plans for EPIC. Quite how two unknown architects and a virgin entrepreneur thought they could convince, as they proposed, manufacturers and bankers to fund their display, remains unclear,[5] and no further correspondence relating to the proposal survives after the end of November 1931.[6] In the context of this discussion, however, its failure to be realized is less important than the fact that, in its content, it provides the earliest existing statement of the movement's theory of social housing. And further, that in its proposed format and location, it demonstrates the considerable acumen which its authors brought and would bring to the projection of that theory. This is most evident in the choice of the exhibition as the medium through which the campaign would be inaugurated. Although the text would remain an important and primary tool of propaganda, the exhibition provided a more tangible as well as appropriately spatial articulation of the modernist position. Moreover, if this display were as striking as Fry and Coates' memorandum suggests – at one point they mention 'a moving exhibit, presented very dramatically' – then they might reasonably have hoped to attract an audience beyond the exhibition through the medium of the newspaper journalist.[7]

The choice of the BTE as host exhibition for the EPIC project was also significant. Since its foundation in 1895 as a 'shop window for the building industry' it had evolved into a large-scale biennial event.[8] Typically each Exhibition included manufacturers' displays, stands for all the major architectural journals, and a strong emphasis on architectural education fostered by a long-standing relationship with the RIBA. This was combined with a concern, especially in the inter-war period, to address contemporary social problems through specially commissioned displays. An important meeting ground for the building industry, the architectural profession and politicians, the BTE therefore guaranteed access to precisely the sort of audience that the modernists needed to convert.

Had EPIC been realized, that audience would have seen a display whose content was a careful blend of the familiar with the unfamiliar, something most evident in the primary emphasis on planning in the proposed display. This allowed its authors to benefit from their identification with what was becoming a widely supported concept, especially amongst visitors to the BTE, and, in this guise, introduce some rather more radical ideas about housing.[9] Thus Coates, Fry and Pritchard were careful to demonstrate their grasp of the language of town planning in displays such as 'The Story of Planning'. Through a 'graphic and dramatic diagram', this rehearsed the 'ABC' of the survey: land use; transport links; sources of power; population; social needs and so forth.[10] Further, as a complement to this attempted assimilation with the familiar, the men also sought to effect an alliance with perhaps the most influential planner of the day, Raymond Unwin. The intention was to offer him space to exhibit one of the schemes he had prepared in his capacity as Technical Adviser to the Greater London Regional Planning Committee.[11] Its inclusion would have signalled the tacit approval of Unwin, and linked the movement, by association, to the RIBA, of which Unwin was President, and to the GCTPA, of which he was a founder.[12]

The rehearsal of a consensus on planning evident in the primary content of the EPIC proposal served, then, as a smokescreen for the more defiantly modernist propositions it included on housing. Although they were not extensive, they are significant for they represented the basis on which a modernist theory of social housing would develop during the rest of the decade and they demonstrate how early some of its key principles were established. Chief among these was the conception of housing as something which should not be produced in isolation but as an integral part of a planning scheme, in this instance that of an industrial area. This was complemented by the insistence that its siting should be logical and take into account not just the location of the proposed factory but also open space, recreation, shopping and transport. Of equal significance, and evidence that the movement was concerned to specify a distinct role for itself when the opportunity came, was their specification that 'large-scale planning is not merely a builders' job, but … requires the brains of sensitive and experienced planners'.[13] Finally, and indicative of the men's as yet unmediated absorption of continental European models, the proposal was that this new scheme would comprise an estate of minimum houses. There is little precise detail of their form but the emphasis elsewhere in the document on the need to use 'last-word Construction and Design' gives some idea of what this might have entailed. Moreover, the fact that they intended the proposed model of the scheme to demonstrate that 12 houses to the acre 'involves waste', because it used only the short terrace or semi-detached pairs, suggests a preference for terraced housing on the *Neue Frankfurt* model. And, as in Frankfurt, the proposal also envisaged that the model could be expanded to include plans for larger houses or tenements.[14]

The lack of specific detail in EPIC, and the grandiosity of the scheme as a whole, points to a more fundamental reason for the project's failure than its authors' youthful exuberance. This was that neither Coates' nor Fry's modernism, nor the movement itself, were sufficiently well developed or established, to engage so publicly with a major social problem. More work remained to be done to secure the place of modernism and modernists in contemporary architectural discourse. Over the next eighteen months, therefore, the two men would scale down their ambitions and instead pursue the dual process of effecting the institutionalization of the British movement and creating a more sophisticated theoretical position to underpin its practices, a process outlined in Chapter 1.[15] Once this was secured, the campaign to seize the territory of social housing could be resumed.

A mass attack on the slums

They could not have known it in late 1931, but the decision to put the issue of social housing to one side would ultimately prove to be of immense benefit to the campaign. Although Coates' and Fry's primary concern in this period of hiatus was to argue for the necessity of a new architecture, and to articulate its guiding principles, this very process caused the theory of social housing first elucidated in EPIC to evolve into something both more sophisticated and wide ranging. This process was also influenced by the fact that the hiatus saw both men, but particularly Coates, mature as practising architects, and their social circles widen so that they encountered new individuals and organizations who held new ideas about housing and social reform. Finally, this evolution might have come to nothing had it not been for the advent of further government legislation which, as in 1930, heralded a new era in the housing programme.

The Greenwood Act had promised much but its execution had been largely thwarted by the onset of the Depression. By December 1932, as economic conditions began to improve, however slowly, Hilton Young, the Minister of Health in the National Government, sought to re-start the campaign by declaring a 'mass attack on the slums' and introduced a new housing bill to parliament.[16] Law by the following March, the 1933 Housing Act took the dramatic step of abolishing state subsidy for the building of houses and thereby established the principle that slum clearance would henceforth be the sole focus of government activity. Most significantly of all, this decision meant that the flat would now be the dominant form of social housing.

The passage of the new Housing Act coincided with the formation of the MARS Group. A sign both of the movement's maturity within British architectural culture, and that its reputation had been established and was recognized abroad, circumstances were now much more propitious for Coates and Fry to address the issue of social housing. The research work they would carry out for CIAM congresses would further develop their housing theory, while MARS as an institution would lend the authority and weight to the campaign which had been absent in 1931. It was against this context that the first moves were made to re-engage with the issue of social housing. This time the approach was more cautious, and Coates and Fry would favour the more accessible, and more controllable, medium of the journal article as the means to re-launch the battle.

Fry would take the lead in articulating a modernist theory of social housing. He had written, and drawn, for the architectural press, most prolifically for the *Architects' Journal*, since the late 1920s. It was perhaps as a result of this relationship that he was able to seize the opportunity when it came to expound the modernist position.[17] Like many other periodicals in 1932–3, the *Journal* devoted a substantial amount of space to considerations of the way the slum problem could be resolved. It was, after all, an issue in which many of its readers had a considerable interest, not least because the Act presaged a revival of building after two long years of Depression.[18] Of particular interest are two articles by Fry which formed part of special issues of the *Journal*: one devoted to 'Planning', published before the Act was passed in January 1933, and the other, on 'Slums', in the wake of the Act in June 1933.[19]

In his first article, 'De-Slumming' Fry looked, janus-faced, to EPIC. As then, and suggesting his primary authorship of that proposal, he insisted that re-housing was impossible without planning, and that a technological solution to the problem was imperative:

> We have got to solve the new problem by absolute planning, using new materials and new constructions, and, where necessary, bringing building laws forward to meet these basic methods, and this we must do on a basis of town-planning that rejuvenates the rotten areas and makes a town fit to live in.

The reference to the town was significant for it was evidence of the first of the two most substantial shifts in the modernist position from 1931, the move towards a pro-urbanism. As Fry wrote:

> The problem must be solved from the centre … The fallacy that herding is ignoble led the garden-city movement down their garden path. One of the really central purposes of slum clearance should aim at ennobling, by finely-designed dwellings, the human wish to live a neighbourly and an urban existence. How are we citizens otherwise?[20]

Fry's second article, 'The Architect's Problem', repeated many of the themes of the first, but extrapolated further on why modernist techniques were relevant to the contemporary programme and the outcomes their application could achieve. In addition, and indicating the second key shift in the movement's position by this time, it showed that the flat, rather than the (minimum) house, had become the movement's accepted dwelling type for slum clearance: Fry's discussion is framed solely in reference to the flat. This change in position may be attributed equally to the new legislative climate, to the influence on the movement of the liaison with CIAM and, as will be discussed below, the voluntary housing sector.[21]

The starting point for this article was Fry's assertion that 'slum clearance is not enough'.[22] To support his argument he drew on the research of Dr M'Gonigle, Medical Officer of Health in Stockton-on-Tees, in the north-east of England.[23] M'Gonigle had shown that when slum-dwellers were moved to suburban estates they suffered higher mortality rates because they could not afford the increase in rent in addition to the costs of travel to work (in the town's centre) and food. Fry therefore declared 'dwellings are not "model" *unless the rent is within the means of the tenant*'.[24] How then could this dilemma be resolved? The problem he thought had three aspects: rent, land and construction, of which rent alone was fixed. The solution lay, therefore, in terms of land

and construction, of which the latter was specifically the architect's problem. Their challenge was to reduce the costs of construction, which, he argued, was possible only by turning to industry and the standardization of building components. Here he made considerable play in contrasting the standardization of constructional elements in contemporary LCC flats. In these, he argued, a 'blind faith that the only decency is Georgian' meant that the principle was applied, but only to external elements and expensive ones at that: sash windows, stone pediments and high-pitched tiled roofs. This was made worse by the fact that when economies were required, as they had been as the Depression worsened, this could only be met by lowering the standard of internal finishes.

For Fry, standardization started with the construction of a building. The use of steel and concrete, he wrote, allowed the regular disposition of structural members from which economies naturally resulted. Following on, bathrooms and kitchen units could be standardized. With this principle as the basis of design it was possible to plan space far more efficiently than was possible in buildings designed on the Georgian pattern or 'the even more rigid and less logical patterning of recent Westminster housing'. This latter remark was presumably a snub to the Grosvenor Estate, Westminster, designed by Edwin Lutyens, for the local council.[25] In making his case for the standardized form, Fry was careful to reiterate that 'a repetition of standard parts is the material of grand design'. He would sign off the article with the observation that it was another standardized unit, the brick, which had revitalized domestic architecture in the wake of the Great Fire of London.

For Fry, the reduction in construction costs allowed by standardization, and the concomitant reduction in the need for skilled labour to erect such blocks, meant that the architect was able to deliver flats at considerably lower rents than had previously been possible. This then left only the problem of land to be resolved and it was here that the necessity of planning came to the fore. He wrote:

> It is obvious at once that slum clearance has been so far an act of local surgery upon a diseased body; piecemeal; unconnected … without the operations of town planning, freeing vastly larger units for the erection of *really cheap dwellings* with sufficient open space, the slum problem is not solved but aggravated.[26]

In concluding his article, Fry turned his attention to design and in so doing pointed towards some of the wider motivations for his concern to marry technology with town planning. In a further snub to Lutyens' Westminster work, he wrote that it was hardly worthwhile 'indulging oneself in a fanciful chequer-board of solid and void if blocks are so closely spaced that they must be separated by arid and anti-social strips of hard tar paving'. Nor should architects overlook the need for the correct orientation of buildings so they received maximum sunlight: 'any other arrangement is not slum clearance but barrack building'. He finished:

> Nor is design good that places style before use, fearing the outcome of a complete and brave solution of the programme; for the purpose of slum clearance is to provide cheap dwellings for poor but otherwise normal

people. Anything less than this is an indulgence of private taste at someone else's expense.[27]

Fry's articles are important because they brought together for the first time the central ingredients of what would henceforth become the modernist orthodoxy on social housing. This linked a preoccupation with technology and town planning with a new concern for the social, and expressed this in the medium of the flat. It also encompassed a turn to the urban and a concern for the promotion of citizenship. The emphasis on the technological and on planning may be attributed equally to the men's adherence to modernist dogma, to the influence of Pritchard's interest in planned solutions to contemporary problems, and the ongoing Isokon project in which prefabrication was intended to play a significant part. The incorporation of sociological concerns into a theory of housing is not, at first glance, remarkable. It too was an inherent part of modernist theory, but the content of Fry's emphasis on social concerns was not, and it brought a new inflection to the modernist project in Britain. Its origins lay not in European modernism but in his and Coates' growing awareness of the philosophies and practices of the voluntary housing sector from late 1931 onwards.

Modernism and voluntarism

The earliest evidence of what would become a marriage between modernism and voluntarism is to be found in a memorandum from Pritchard to Coates sent during the discussions for EPIC. In it, Pritchard drew Coates' attention to the advance notice in *The Times* for the first NHFO exhibition, noting 'that they were attempting to do there something which you, Max Fry and I are thinking of and it might be a good idea if we three went to this Exhibition'.[28] It is known that Coates did go to the exhibition when it opened in December 1931, and that he met Elizabeth Denby there.[29] It is Fry's writing, however, rather than Coates', which suggests the more thoroughgoing assimilation of the sector's approach to housing. Whether this was learnt from attendance at this or the subsequent NHFO exhibitions in 1932 and 1933, or his relationship with Denby, however, remains unclear. If his autobiography is to be believed, his interest in social housing dated to the epiphany wrought by his membership of the DIA and, in particular, to his witnessing the building of Devonshire House on London's Piccadilly. Fry described how the slow covering of its steel-framed structure with 'a crust of stonework' caused a moral revulsion against his *Beaux-Arts* training. Consigning his student work to the dustbin he began work on the hypothetical block of working-class flats which would eventually be realized as Sassoon House.[30]

But Fry's concern for housing as a means to citizenship, the preoccupation with the urban, and the desire to use economies of technology and construction to bring decent dwellings to the poorest of the population can only have come from an engagement with the voluntarists. As we have seen in Chapter 1, they were the only group in this period to forge these concerns into a coherent philosophy of housing and to ally this with an emphasis on the necessity of town planning. The displays at NHFO 1932 had been devoted to slums, reconditioning and demonstrating 'the fundamental need' for planning. They also reflected the sector's primary focus on working within the context of the city and its advocacy of the building of flats 'if families are to live reasonably near their work, and if there is to be adequate open space for light and air, health and communal recreation'.[31] This latter comment was, as we have seen, echoed in Fry's 1933 articles, while his railing against 'barrack building' also had a precedent in the exhibition.[32] The NHFO catalogue had urged that 'it is … vital that the pre-war barrack tradition [of flat building] should be discarded, and that flats should be planned as centres of happy, family life'.[33]

The assimilation of modernist ideas with voluntarist ones represented in Fry's articles of January and June 1933 would first be translated into built form by the following November when R. E. Sassoon House was opened. Although this project had been occasioned by the serendipitous encounter among him, Denby and Mrs Sassoon, it nevertheless mirrored a more general, and significant, merger between two oppositional groups at this time. Each group was at a pivotal moment in their histories; alliance would help both further their respective campaigns.

For the voluntarists, the central impetus for this merger was the 1933 Housing Act. Its passage had represented a shattering blow to their ambitions. While Greenwood had envisaged that both housing associations and local authorities should provide the new housing, the 1933 Act, following a period of intense lobbying of central government by local authorities, awarded primary responsibility for its provision to municipalities.[34] The exclusion was further reiterated by the report of a departmental committee of the Ministry of Health which had been set up under the chairmanship of Lord Moyne to investigate the supplementary role the sector could take in the wake of the Act. It recommended only that it might play a role in the reconditioning of old housing, a practice which most of the post-1918 housing societies had either abandoned early on or never pursued.[35]

By 1933, it was also becoming apparent that the sort of housing likely to be built under the new slum legislation would owe little to the exemplary work of the sector in the 1920s.[36] Like the two-storey cottages they superseded, the blocks of flats built to re-house slum-dwellers represented a solidly materialist approach to housing practice. Though qualitatively far superior to the slum accommodation from which their tenants came, landlords like the LCC provided none of the amenities or management systems which the sector understood as necessary in the transition from slum to new dwelling and for the restoration of family and community life. Perilously close to the 'barrack building' criticized at NHFO 1932 and by Fry in 1933, schemes such as the LCC's Wapping Estate, Stepney, east London, on which construction began in 1928, comprised only a series of five-storey neo-Georgian blocks. No amenities were provided other than some shops and the asphalted courtyards which each block overlooked (Fig. 4.1).[37] The interiors were no more imaginatively planned (Fig. 4.2).

Faced with marginalization, and confronted with models of housing which, in its view, were far from ideal, it was time for the sector to rethink what it could achieve in this new climate. As we shall see in the example of Kent House, individual societies would, whenever possible, continue to provide social housing on the model the sector had developed and, in that instance, specifically seek to unite experimental form and practice. But circumstances required more strategic activity if the sector were to recapture the ground it had lost to municipalization and maintain its tradition of 'pioneering, and … helping to create, public opinion'.[38] Building on the collective work initiated

Figure 4.1
Wapping Estate,
East London, LCC
Architects'
Department,
1928-30

through the NHFO exhibitions, the volunteers sought a more public and permanent platform from which they could articulate their critique of state policy and develop models for the future of housing provision.[39] The efforts resulted in the formation of the Housing Centre in spring 1934, its aim 'to promote better housing conditions for the people of Great Britain, through organised Publicity, Information and Research'.[40]

Part think-tank, part campaigning body, the Centre positioned itself as the focus for progressive housing debate in this decade.[41] As such its Executive Committee both sought, and was sought out by, all those whose concern it was to reform the built environment but who operated outside of government at this time. A natural ally was the GCTPA with whom it shared premises, a relationship reinforced by the appointment of Patrick Abercrombie as the Centre's chairman in 1935. The desire to promulgate a model of housing better than that offered by the state, however, precluded the Centre from taking an exclusively garden-city approach to reform. Thus, in the very earliest months of its existence, the Centre would approach what it clearly recognized as another potential ally, inviting the MARS Group to collaborate on the preparation of the next NHFO Exhibition which would form part of the BTE at Olympia that September.[42]

The British movement which received this invitation could not have been more different from the one whose leaders had tried, three years previously, to participate in the BTE.[43] Coates and Fry were now at the helm of a group which was sufficiently mature in its organization, and confident in its theory, to take advantage of such an offer. In its first year of existence, it had participated successfully in CIAM 4, was six months into its own research programme into the problem of slum clearance and re-planning,[44] and would shortly host a CIRPAC meeting.[45] What it had not yet done, however, with the exception of Fry's two articles in January and June 1933, was to

Figure 4.2
LCC 'normal' plans
for block dwellings,
1930

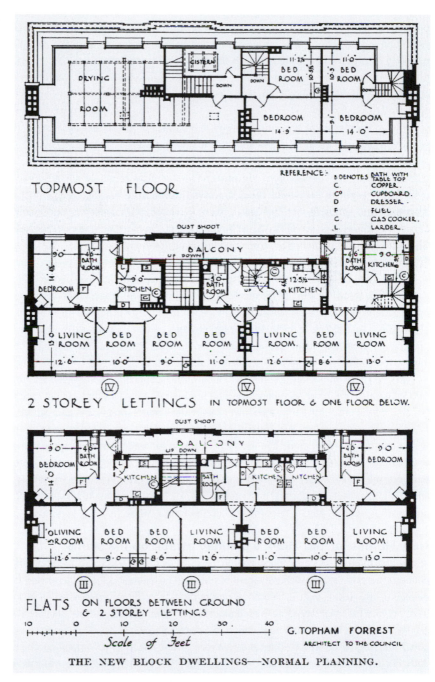

present its ideas to a British audience. To collaborate with the Centre on the NHFO exhibition would provide the immediate means to inaugurate this process as well enabling it to make direct contact with the sort of audience it needed to convert. More strategically, an ongoing alliance with the Centre would ensure permanent access to a wide range of policy makers and intellectuals thanks to the catholicity of its constituency.[46]

For the Centre, the British movement brought a progressiveness of form and space to a sector whose progressive approach to housing was not matched by its architecture nor provided by its other ally the GCTPA. The emphasis the Centre placed on publicity would also benefit from the use of the rhetorical forms of contemporary modernism. Likewise the MARS Group's avowed devotion to research suggested a shared ground and aims with the Centre, thereby reinforcing a sense of oppositional consensus. It was, then, a relationship of mutual benefit. On receipt of the invitation, the Group's Executive Committee's recommendation was therefore a simple one: '[we] feel that this opportunity should be grasped by MARS'.[47]

If the tendering and acceptance of this invitation provided the specific catalyst for a new stage in the British movement's housing campaign, it also formed part of a more general, and highly significant, shift in the evolution of housing reform in Britain. The process was akin to the DIA's quest for 'modern design' in the 1920s. That had brought together traditionalists, moderates and radicals into a consensual alliance which would effect the beginnings of a deeper shift in British design culture, something manifested more immediately in the formation of the Council for Art and Industry in 1931. Likewise, the Housing Centre was able, through its primary emphasis on better housing conditions for the British people, to unite volunteers, modernists and garden-city advocates in a progressive oppositional front. During the rest of the decade, both within and outwith the Centre, this front would go on to conduct a campaign against prevailing orthodoxies through rhetorical sites which encompassed the exhibition, the building, the documentary film and the text. In so doing, the distinctive modernist-voluntarist approach to housing first hinted at in Fry's 1933 texts would be developed and promulgated. Its path to hegemony began at NHFO 1934.

New Homes for Old 1934: a planned attack on the slums

In the first three NHFO exhibitions held in 1931, 1932 and 1933, the predominant concern had been to establish the extent of the slum problem and the necessity for its resolution. By 1934, with a clearance programme now firmly established, and in keeping with the voluntary sector's reconfiguration into an advisory, rather than purely provisory, body, the emphasis now shifted to a demonstration of how that programme could and should be executed most effectively. In the hands of its organizing chair, Judith Ledeboer, and her right-hand woman, Elizabeth Denby, this direction was made clear. In a nod, perhaps, to Hilton Young's declaration of December 1932, they called for 'a planned attack on the slums',[48] in which clearance formed only a part of a 'completely comprehensive policy' for housing.[49] This, they argued, should include 'Town Planning, traffic regulation, the placing of Industry and of schools, preservation of open spaces, and the organisation of the building industry, etc.', and was the only way to ensure that the problem was ended once and for all.[50]

In many respects, the innovation of this call for a comprehensive policy lay less in its content – it had been a familiar refrain of garden-city, voluntary and modernist dogma for some time – than the fact that it was conveyed through the medium of the progressive front of the Centre. It implied a critical mass, even an inevitability, to this approach since it was so widely held. The more profound innovation in NHFO 1934, however, was its demonstration of the method through which this comprehensive policy should be enacted. Writing about the exhibition in *Design for Today*, Ledeboer argued that the successful execution of the programme required the bringing together of 'the best brains of the country'.[51] Perhaps for the first time in Britain, the notion of teamwork was proposed as an integral part of any housing praxis, a technique demonstrated in the organization of NHFO 1934. Under the over-arching eye of an architect (Ledeboer), a team of experts was assembled, each of whom could bring insights – social or spatial – into a different aspect of the problem. Thus in form, content and structure the exhibition sought to persuade the BTE's audience of builders, architects, politicians and journalists of the future direction of housing policy.

Visitors entered NHFO 1934 through 'Slum Alley', a reconstruction of a recently demolished slum court in Shoreditch (Figs 4.3 and 4.4). This, the Catalogue observed, would serve as a reminder of what 'are likely to become things of the past'.[52] It was complemented by a display called 'Slum Clearance and Re-housing' that demonstrated the extent of the slum problem and the development of housing standards. These two sections were then followed by a series of displays which outlined the portfolio of responses which should be brought to the problem's resolution. This was organized to proceed from the general to the particular, as the Centre would argue any

Figure 4.3
Slum Alley

Figure 4.4
View of NHFO
1934

proper clearance scheme should. It began therefore with two bays devoted to town planning, the first of which, entitled 'Suggestions', was the work of the MARS Group.

The Group had worked on its display since June 1934. At Fry's suggestion, the original intention had been to use information about the east London district of Bethnal Green which formed part of the research programme it had been conducting since the previous October to produce a universal model for urban planning.[53] Demonstrating the members' awareness of current planning technique this would have exemplified the practice pioneered by Patrick Abercrombie, drawing on Geddes, of survey, diagnosis, plan.[54] Lack of time, and characteristic over-ambition, however, meant that the final display comprised only the survey. This, the Group called an 'Analysis' of Bethnal Green. Presented on a series of panels, it began with 'a graphical representation of the CHAOS [sic] that is modern London' and proceeded to an analysis of the district under three categories: density, circulation and surface utilization (Fig. 4.5).[55] This represented 'the first step … to solve the problem of urban replanning' and formed part, they assured, of a continuing investigation.[56]

The display may not have been as complete as the MARS Group would have liked, but it garnered extensive coverage in the architectural press as well as more general approbation in reviews which considered the exhibition as a whole.[57] The Group's participation also gave its members the opportunity to control their entry into this more public realm of debate and thereby frame the role the modernist architect could assume in a re-formed housing programme. Central to this was their presentation as disinterested experts, evident in the catalogue's description of the MARS Group as 'architects and allied technicians united by a common belief in the necessity for a new conception of architecture and its relation to society'. And just in case this clinical anonymity was misconstrued, the Group stressed that its aim was the 'scientific and architectural solution of social and economic problems. Its work is to collect and analyse FACTS [sic] and to present them synthetically, as a foundation for contemporary architectural design.'[58]

Figure 4.5
MARS Panel from
the 'Suggestions'
section of NHFO
1934

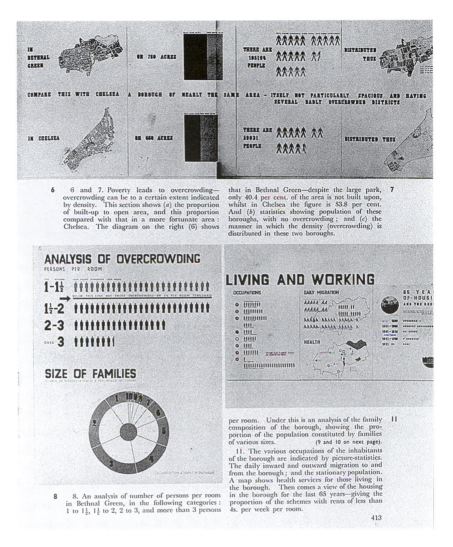

At the same time as the MARS Group's presence at NHFO 1934 raised awareness of it as an independent organization, as the coverage in the architectural press suggests, it also located the Group within a continuum of reformist practice, one from which the modernist-voluntarist position on housing would evolve. This was apparent in the rest of the exhibition. On leaving, 'Suggestions', a section devoted more generally to the theme of planning was entered. Organized by Jocelyn Abram, the first woman member of the Town Planning Institute,[59] this used examples of good planning by both public and private enterprise to underline the message that 'rehousing without planning may do more harm in the end than temporary good'.[60]

From the more general matter of the planning of the region and the city, visitors then entered the sections which addressed the most effective way to design the new dwellings which would replace the slums. The first of these dealt with their planning and equipment. Drawing on her experience in the voluntary housing sector, and her research on continental housing in Europe, Denby's display offered a prescription for what the ideal clearance flat should be.[61] She stressed the importance of the incorporation of high quality technologies of lighting, heating, cooking and water heating in the new accommodation. Such facilities were noticeably absent from contemporary LCC housing which still tended to incorporate a range in the living room, but they were, she argued, 'the core of successful house planning and construction'. She also noted that there was considerable scope for the provision of 'good inexpensive furniture'. Another vital element in successful flat design was the incorporation of what she called a 'balcony extension to the living room', a substitute for the garden which, she observed, was 'an unquestioned part of all cottage rehousing estates'. Its urban equivalent was necessary 'both for health and recreation ... and [was] a direct means of contributing towards civilised and homely living', a point reiterated by the inclusion of a model balcony in the display. Looking beyond the balcony she signalled the importance of 'allotments, club rooms, meeting halls, children's and adults' playgrounds' on the new estates but left this matter to be addressed in the next section of NHFO.[62]

The design of the public spheres of clearance schemes was the focus of 'Amenities'. Here the display stressed the need for 'the new [housing] schemes [to] incorporate facilities for a happy home life and a successful community life', and illustrated the facilities which would achieve this from nursery schools to community centres. Its organizer, Lady Marjory Allen of Hurtwood, was a landscape gardener and campaigner for nursery education and it was that particular expertise which had led to the invitation to contribute to NHFO 1934.[63] Nursery education was a subject at the forefront of contemporary progressive debate in education and its absorption into the Centre's remit is further evidence of its command of reformist debate as a whole. The display therefore devoted considerable space to the need for nursery schools – including a model of a nursery on the flat roof of a block of flats – as well as stressing the necessity for individual and communal gardens and playgrounds, and allotments. In concluding her catalogue entry Allen summed up the message and purpose not just of her particular display, but that of the Centre as a whole:

> The public must demand, not only that the slums be cleared away, but also that the new housing schemes must include facilities for a full and happy home life. Slum clearance is not enough, we must build with pride and hope.[64]

The 'planned attack' presented by Ledeboer and her team received extensive coverage in both the national and architectural press. The response of a correspondent of *The Times* was typical. It was also perceptive:

> Several qualities make the NHFO exhibit ... the most interesting thing at Olympia; but two in particular give it importance at the present moment. First, it is itself planned, it is a whole made up of selected and arranged parts ... And next the NHFO shows clearly that the housing problem does not include building only.[65]

As the coverage in *The Times* suggests, the MARS Group's participation in NFHO enabled it to project its radical ideas from the broad-church base of the Housing Centre and thus introduce modernist principles to an audience which may not have been aware of the movement. This was an important step in spreading the modernist approach to reform to a wider constituency, and discursive media like the newspaper article and the exhibition would continue to be central tools in the movement's campaign of persuasion and conversion. But proof of the viability of the movement's ideas, particularly in relation to housing – not houses – resided in the building, and for architects this remained their ultimate medium of reform.

In fact, as noted earlier, it would not be long before the modernist-voluntarists were able to add buildings to their arsenal of propaganda tools when, in November 1934, R. E. Sassoon House was opened. A timely reiteration of the exhibition's message – something both Fry and Denby were surely aware of as NFHO was planned – it was a sign of a new phase in the movement's housing campaign in which the socio-spatial came to the fore.

Over the next three years, two further schemes would be built which saw the theory of housing presented at NHFO 1934 become a praxis of housing. Kensal House, another design by Denby and Fry, which was commissioned in November 1933 and completed in late 1936, would constitute the supreme expression of progressive housing reform in this decade and as such will be considered in detail in the next chapter. Here attention turns to Kent House, a collaboration among Connell and Ward and the Saint Pancras House Improvement Society, which was commissioned in March 1934. Very much a response to the exhibition's exhortation that flats should be planned 'for a full and happy home life', it was opened in December 1935.

Taken together, these schemes in south, north and west London, brought a critical mass to the movement. Furthermore, exemplars of rhetorical modernism as they were, they were quickly assimilated into the progressive front's ongoing narratives of written and exhibitionary discourse as well as being deployed in a newly harnessed propaganda medium, the documentary film. It was through such devices, it is suggested, that by the end of the decade the blueprint for a modern working-class domesticity which they embodied was well placed to become the dominant narrative in debates about the way British citizens should be re-housed. This process began in a dingy street in north London.

A small corner of the New Jerusalem

As we saw in Chapter 1, since its foundation in 1924, the Saint Pancras House Improvement Society (SPHIS) had worked in Somers Town to replace the dilapidated and vermin-infested slum housing in which most of the local working-class community lived. Relocated into new blocks, SPHIS tenants found themselves in soundly built, electric-powered homes and with access to the many amenities and support systems which the Society, like the voluntary housing sector as a whole, saw as integral to the practice of housing. Through this combination of material and social reform its intention was to 'resurrect a beautiful place of homes' from the dirty and cramped streets of Somers Town,[66] while at the same time demonstrating 'that rehousing a slum population was a practical business proposition'.[67]

In late 1929, at the instigation of Society members who were active in voluntary social work in the north of the borough, the SPHIS Executive Committee agreed to expand the scope of its activities beyond Somers Town to address the slum problem in Chalk Farm and Kentish Town.[68] To lead this work, a new sub-committee of the Society was formed, the North St Pancras Group (NSPG). Operating more or less autonomously, though all its decisions were ultimately ratified by the parent body, the NSPG seems to have conceived of itself as a vanguard within a vanguard, pushing the main Society towards an ever more experimental position.

Given that the membership of the NSPG included two businessmen and members of the Rotarian Society, Stanley Shaw and Leonard Day, two aristocrats, Lady Marjorie Pentland and Lady Frances Stewart, and a priest, the Reverend Nigel Scott, this stance may seem surprising. Yet, as in the case of the Housing Centre, to which it was a significant precursor, this serves as an important reminder of how an ideological field – in this instance, the improvement of society through the reform of housing – could accommodate people from otherwise diverse backgrounds and enable the most radical solutions to a problem to enter the (progressive) mainstream. In Shaw, Day and Pentland, the NSPG members who seem to have done most to promote experimentation, we find therefore three protagonists usually disregarded in histories of modernism. They may not fit the caricature of the typical modernist client, but, in their own patrician and benevolent ways, they too were concerned to engage with the problem of modernity through design. Without their patronage, the movement would have been hard pressed to escape the pioneer phase.

Day and Shaw were businessmen and nonconformists, and it is known that the latter was both a prison visitor and a volunteer social worker.[69] Like many of their class, generation and faith, they saw it as part of their responsibility as citizens to use their personal wealth and abilities to improve society.[70] A similar concept of service underpinned the work of Lady Pentland. Born Marjorie Gordon, she was the daughter of the Earl and Countess of Aberdeen who, in their roles as Lord and Lady Lieutenant of Ireland, had invited both Raymond Unwin and Patrick Geddes to work with them on the development of plans to resolve the problem of the Dublin slums.[71] When Gordon married the Liberal MP John Sinclair (later Lord Pentland) in 1904, she found a partner equally committed to modernity. A former resident at Toynbee Hall, he was founder of the London Playing Fields Association and a keen advocate of housing reform and garden cities. As Governor of Madras (1912–19), he would invite Geddes to India, perhaps at his wife's suggestion. Given this pedigree, it was almost inevitable that when Lady Pentland became involved in voluntary work on their return to England in 1919, she did so in the sphere of housing and was active in the SPHIS from its early years.[72] She also played a significant role in the sector's propaganda campaigns and in the founding of the Housing Centre, on whose Executive Committee she served during the 1930s. She was, as a contemporary recalled, 'far more than just a titled do-gooder, bringing a mind and a personality to housing which everyone respected'.[73]

It was this mind and personality which appears to have been the driving force behind the development of Kent House as a corrective not just to local authority practice, as all the SPHIS schemes were, but also to that of the Society itself. Initially, the NSPG had conformed to the usual building conventions of the SPHIS. Its first scheme,

Athlone House, which was opened in Kentish Town in July 1933, comprised ten four-roomed flats designed in the Society's neo-Georgian house style by its architect Ian Hamilton.[74] Each flat had three bedrooms, a living room and a kitchen and, in what was then a very high, and imaginative, standard of provision for social housing, was fuelled by a combination of electricity and coal. In the warmer seasons, cooking could be carried out on an electric cooker, but in winter a coal-fired range in the living room could be used both for cooking and for heating; throughout the year electricity was used for the lighting and to heat water.[75]

Yet neither the technological modernity of these interiors, nor the progressiveness of the SPHIS as a whole, was apparent in its form. Such a discrepancy took on a new significance in 1933 as, in the circumstances outlined earlier in this chapter, new housing legislation changed the context in which the volunteers operated. Paralleling the sector's collective efforts to reclaim and re-orient housing debate which were manifested in the Housing Centre, the Society sought, on a much smaller scale, to explore the ways in which it too could raise the sector's profile.

So, in the autumn of 1933, as the NSPG began to plan the second phase of its building programme, it was agreed that one of its sites, one-fifth of an acre on Ferdinand Street, Chalk Farm, should be used for an experiment. Following a proposal from Lady Pentland, no doubt influenced by her growing knowledge of modernism gained at the NHFO exhibitions, it was decided that the resulting block of flats should constitute an investigation into how building costs might be reduced through the use of reinforced concrete design and construction.[76] This was a significant decision. At this point in state housing practice, the use of concrete was highly unusual. By linking reinforced concrete with the SPHIS approach to housing a new era of domestic reform could be entered. Reflecting its command of propaganda, the NSPG had recognized that experimentation would ensure that the Society's progressiveness was finally correlated in form. This would increase the scheme's visibility as a prototype and, in turn, serve as a riposte and signal to central government of the appropriate way forward in the clearance programme. The only challenge was to find the designers who could achieve this.[77]

The NSPG required architects who understood the principles of designing in reinforced concrete, were sympathetic with its aims, and were also attuned to the notion that the building itself, and not just its mediation through text and image, should signify its purpose as an exemplary prototype. Modernist architects were then a natural constituency for the Group to approach since they were, in this era of rhetorical modernism, accustomed to combining the reformist message in the medium of building form. Quite how and when the NSPG elected to award the commission to Connell and Ward is, however, unclear. It seems most likely that it was Lady Pentland who, through her connections with the organizers of the NHFO exhibitions, especially Denby, would have had access to the modernist community.[78]

They were certainly well suited to the task. As early members of the MARS Group they understood that modernism would be achieved as much through propaganda as through building. And, although the pair had built very little by 1934, Connell, in particular carried with him the acclaim gathered from the house High and Over. The practice was also establishing a reputation for its commitment to the use of new materials, something enhanced by Colin Lucas who joined the firm in 1933.[79] That they also shared the SPHIS's conflation of design and society is apparent in Basil Ward's rationale of the practice's work. This, he argued, 'arose … out of reappraisal of technique, the technique of using reinforced concrete … also … out of a reappraisal of needs in architecture as a social function – "a new way of life in building form"'.[80] Whatever, or whoever, brought them together, by March 1934 they had been asked to prepare detailed plans for the new block.[81]

In May, Stanley Shaw formally announced that the NSPG was 'embarking on a sound and economical scheme in the contemplated block of concrete and that the experiment would be an enterprising and useful one'.[82] The next month the *Architects' Journal* published a drawing of the scheme with what turned out to be an optimistic by-line of 'work to be started immediately'.[83] In fact, the LCC would challenge the proposed density of 20 flats on the site and require Connell and Ward to reduce this quantity. Approval for a scheme of 16 flats was not given until May 1935 and in the July of that year building work finally began.[84]

As it always did on these occasions, the SPHIS marked the onset of construction with an official ceremony, an event which served both as an opportunity to publicize the Society's work and, equally importantly, to signify that a process of transformation was about to commence. This time the ceremony centred around the burning of a small bundle of timbers, taken from the old houses which had occupied the Ferdinand Street site, on top of a block of concrete. The resulting ashes were then poured into the concrete foundations of what would become Kent House. As the SPHIS's reporter declared: 'with God's blessing the new building will be another small corner of the "new Jerusalem" which Father Jellicoe gave his life to build'.[85]

Kent House: a new way of life in building form

The mingling of the ashes of dilapidated houses with the concrete of Kent House serves as a powerful metaphor for the elision of voluntarist and modernist principles which it embodies. Indeed, it may be taken as a metaphor for the emergence of British architectural modernism as a whole and the way it was able to assimilate existing narratives of modernity, many with roots in late nineteenth-century social and cultural philosophy, with a new language of form and space.

At Kent House, the existing narrative of modernity hinged around the SPHIS's desire to use the re-forming of the domestic environment as a means to rebuild family life and through that society. In this respect it had much in common with the doctors in Peckham. The Society's position was informed, however, not by a quasi-biology but by a High Anglicanism and its Committee's first-hand knowledge of the conditions in which slum-dwellers lived. Some idea of what these were, can be gathered from the film *Housing Problems*, made for the British Commercial Gas Association by Arthur Elton and Edgar Anstey, and released in 1935.[86] It is an immensely powerful film for it features, in what was then a highly innovative technique, working-class men and women talking directly to camera about the slums in which they dwelt. Typical of them is Mr Norwood who lived in two rooms with his family and paid ten shillings a week rent. Noting that 'we haven't room to swing a cat around', he added that the rooms were 'not only overrun with bugs but I've got mice and rats'. Every drop of water had to be fetched from the yard. His wife cooked on a gas ring which stood by their bed, and they ate in the other room where the children slept. Like many of the parents who spoke in the film, he had also suffered the loss of children in such an environment. In his case two had died, one aged only seven weeks.

Others spoke of how the combination of their poverty, and the cramped conditions in which they lived, made it impossible to buy food for more than one day at a time. Many had no cupboards and, as Mrs Graves remarked, 'if we leave anything on the table of a night-time we have the rats'. Perhaps the most moving testimony came from Mr Burner. Filmed alongside his wife and three children, and barely able to conceal his anger from the camera, he began his testimony with the observation, 'Of course a lot of people don't understand what it is living in one room.' He went on to reiterate the difficulties of living, eating and sleeping in such a small space and looked to the day when:

> Every working-class man will have a hygienic flat to live in where cooking conditions is [sic] better, living accommodation better, sleeping accommodation better and what's more we have a bath.

The philosophy which the SPHIS had evolved in response to such needs was articulated very forcefully in a 1933 SPHIS publication, *Challenge*, written by Nigel Scott.[87] In a section tellingly subtitled 'Home-Breaking and Home-Making', his starting point was the common voluntarist one that 'slum clearance is something more than a simple question of knocking down old houses and rebuilding new ones'. For the Society any new housing, therefore, should be built 'in accordance with the Christian ideal of family life' and the design of the flats – and there is no question that it was flats that would be built – should promote home-making. This he admitted was a 'complex matter' and was 'intimately concerned with the size and shape and positions of the rooms'. It also required that each flat should be self-contained with no communal kitchens or wash-houses for these were 'the kind of thing which tends to destroy all individual personality of the family and its members and which is so definitely against the basic principles of Christianity'. Finally, 'they must be such as to encourage breadth and beauty of outlook', which for him meant the development of both a cultural and Christian way of life.

Connell and Ward's task was to create the conditions for family life through the forms of a reinforced concrete building. At the same time, they needed to demonstrate how that material could reduce the cost of building and, in its form, plan and equipment, make the block as (rhetorically) modern as possible in order that it could act as a riposte to both the SPHIS and local authorities. This they achieved by deploying a range of techniques.

The site at Ferdinand Street was narrow but deep, so Connell and Ward elected to place the accommodation in two blocks; they also had to find space for a fish-and-chips shop whose premises had been demolished when building began (Fig. 4.6). Therefore, the front block, five storeys high, was set back ten feet from the pavement to allow the shop to be re-built, a device which also meant a small flower bed could be created between the building line and pavement. A second block, four storeys high, was placed to the rear. Each contained three-room flats and pram sheds

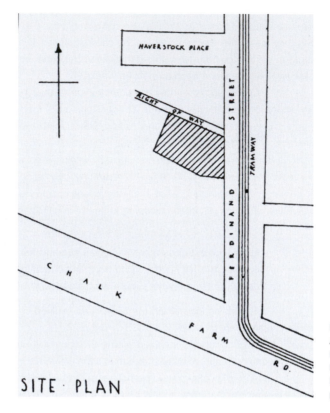

Figure 4.6
Amyas Connell and
Basil Ward, Kent
House, Chalk Farm,
London, 1935, site
plan

at ground floor level with a pair of four-roomed flats on the floors above. These were reached by an open external staircase cantilevered from the rear of the block which led to a small lobby which the two flats shared. As the cantilevered staircase suggests, the building was carried on a reinforced concrete frame with four-inch concrete walls faced with plastered half-inch building board internally (Figs 4.7 and 4.8).

By placing the staircases on the exterior of the building and through the use of concrete, the design fulfilled the Society's requirement of reducing expenditure and maximizing space. The final total expenditure on the block was £7,525 which worked out at one shilling and threepence per cubic foot, or just over sixpence per cubic foot for the structure alone.[88] An analysis by the surveyor Cyril Sweett showed that this compared well with the cost of the LCC's preferred method of brick construction with concrete and filler joist floors and tiled mansard roof which was approximately seven-pence per cubic foot.[89] He also noted that in a larger block than Kent House, economies of scale could substantially reduce the figure of sixpence.

Compared with its two concrete contemporaries, the Isokon Flats (on which Sweett was the Quantity Surveyor) and R. E. Sassoon House, Kent House represented the median. Its total cost of one shilling and threepence per cubic foot was undercut by Sassoon House's one shilling and a half-pence and exceeded by Isokon's one shilling, four and a half-pence.[90] Taken together, they signalled that it was possible to make substantial reductions in cost if clients were prepared to experiment.

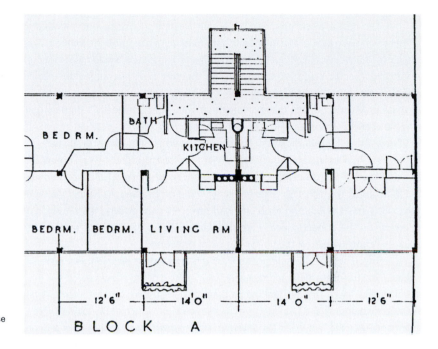

Figure 4.7
Plan of Kent House
flat

Figure 4.8
View of Kent House
from Ferdinand
Street (present day)

The cost analysis executed by Sweett was propaganda work, intended to show that there were logical and economic, rather than stylistic, grounds for the use of concrete in social housing. Further, the savings effected by its use would mean not only that more blocks could be constructed to resolve the slum problem but that they could also be qualitatively better than anything else then being built. It thus met Scott's exhortation that, above and beyond material improvements, slum clearance's primary goal was 'home-making' and exemplified Fry's 1933 assertion that the architect's problem was to bring about the reduction in costs which allowed an increase in amenity.[91]

In the planning and equipment of Kent House therefore, it was Connell and Ward's and the NSPG's concern to create the sort of hygienic flat Mr Burner dreamed of, and the context in which a Christian family life could be enacted. As he and the other workers interviewed in *Housing Problems* had revealed, this required the provision of what might, on the surface, seem commonplace spaces, unworthy of remark, but whose significance would, at the time, have been profound.

The process of re-starting such a life began with a decision as apparently simple as using direct staircase access to each flat instead of the access balconies then more commonly used. This avoided the problem of people walking past a family's flat on the way to their own and helped to create a sense of privacy and ownership, something enhanced by the fact that it also allowed each resident to have their own territory in the landing space. It thereby helped to fulfil Scott's prescription that spatial planning should preserve the individuality of each family and, as noted above, it also reduced costs.

Once inside, Kent House tenants entered an interior which was the antithesis of the slum. In place of its hostile environment, in which the conduct of daily, let alone family, life was a constant battle against dirt, infestation and the perpetual presence of others, Connell and Ward brought space and calm through their adherence to modernist practices of zoning. The space was carefully divided into living-room-plus-kitchen and bedrooms-plus-bathroom. The tenants may not have noticed this, though specialists would, but they would have recognized a site where hygiene was achievable. Here there were separate spaces for cooking, living, washing and sleeping, and plenty of cupboards in the kitchen where food could be stored, thus allowing staples to be purchased on a weekly rather than daily basis and reducing strains on the family budget. For many this would be the first time they had hot and cold running water inside their homes; no longer would they have to fetch every drop of water from a yard several floors down nor heat it up on a gas ring. Such environments were nothing less than miraculous.

In addition to the way the spaces of the interior were arranged, careful attention was paid to their equipment. In the discussion of Athlone House, it was noted how, in the spirit of better 'home-making', the SPHIS had sought to bring modern technologies to their tenants. In what was an early example of the extension of labour-saving principles to the working classes, the intention was to reduce the drudgery experienced by the housewife. She would then have more time to spend on, and with, her family; a further reminder of the gendering of modernity throughout this period.[92] Kent House, like Athlone House, was designed to be run on a combination of electricity and, in wintertime, coal, but its equipment was more sophisticated. In addition to electric lighting, each flat had a back-to-back coal grate, with hot-water cylinder above, which was placed between living room and kitchen and could be used for cooking, heating and hot water in winter. In the warmer months, an electric cooker and immersion heater could be used instead. This avoided a problem commonly experienced in workers' housing, which derived from the practice, to save costs, of having a range in the living room, with the consequence that there was constant heat in the living room even in hot weather. Removing cooking into the kitchen, as happened at Kent House, was both hygienic and cost-effective.

The final aspects of the design were the inclusion of a surrogate garden to each flat in the form of the cantilevered individual balconies on the front elevations, each with a flower box. This was the place, perhaps, where beauty and breadth of outlook was to be achieved. There was also a playground on the roof. As a whole the scheme could not have been more different from SPHIS or LCC provision. To ensure that the message of its modernity could not be overlooked, this was further accentuated by its colour scheme. Carefully chosen to emphasize its most structurally dramatic features, Kent House had pink walls, light blue (steel) window frames, blue staircases and bright red balconies.

On 2 December 1935 the opening ceremony for the flats was held. It was presided over by Sir Wyndham Deedes, whose speech made it clear that he understood well the significance of the restorative and transforming environments the Society and its architects had created.[93] He proclaimed:

> Each flat is an Englishman's home. God knows, enough people do not know what it is to have an Englishman's home. Your Society is not only opening flats. You are opening avenues, windows, doors to new lives for men, women and, most important of all, the rising generation.[94]

His response was not unique. *Housing Happenings* reported that the 'bright colours and novel architecture' of Kent House had attracted a great deal of attention from experts and the general public, and that the internal planning was particularly admired.[95]

Unusually for SPHIS schemes, Kent House was reported in the architectural press, suggesting that the NSPG's decision to work with progressive architects had succeeded in bringing its work to a new constituency.[96] It was also included in the first edition of *The Modern Flat* in 1937.[97] Perhaps the most perceptive of the architectural coverage it received was that in *Design for Today* which discussed the flats in an article that surveyed the housing constructed during 1935. Noting that 'the greatest progress is, as usual, recorded in the housing by the public utility societies located in London', it declared Kent House 'an extraordinarily interesting and arresting piece of work'. It also commented on the flats'

> light, colour, simplicity, ease of operation and entirely efficient modern equipment. The use of colour is extraordinarily fine and it must have a stimulating effect on those late slum dwellers translated now into light and comfort.

The journal found the LCC's flats 'disappointing' in comparison. Even more perceptively, and here it referred to all the SPHIS's work, it commented 'they are the realization in bricks and mortar and concrete of a new and entirely admirable social conception and that, of course, is what design ought to be'.[98] A response which suggests that, at least within progressive circles, Kent House's status as the child of the union of modernism and voluntarism was well understood and greeted with much approval.

Surveying St Pancras

The innovation and experimentation represented in Kent House would not be the only collaboration among Connell and Ward and the SPHIS. In the spring of 1935, while plans were still being finalized for the flats, the architects brought a new proposal to the building sub-committee of the NSPG. The suggestion was that they might carry out a survey of the borough in order to ascertain potential sites on which they could build what Ward described as 'a scheme for putting up good modern flats to house the largest number of people healthily and well'. More comprehensive than anything yet worked out, and 'something quite new', he thought that it might be of use to the local authority.[99]

Ward's reference to the local authority gives some clue as to why he and his colleagues might have embarked on such a proposal. Under the 1930 Housing Act, all councils had been required to prepare five-year programmes of work. Further, among the clauses of the 1935 Housing Bill, then going through parliament, there was also the requirement that they conduct surveys into the level of overcrowding in their areas. Connell and Ward's project, which combined survey and design, was then an attempt to simulate these processes and demonstrate, particularly through the development of the clearance scheme, how modernist principles could be used to resolve the slum problem in the borough of St Pancras. They would thereby bring modernist ideas to another new audience.

If this turn to urbanism was, on the one hand, about taking modernism to the wider world, it was also about asserting its principles within Connell and Ward's own discipline of architecture. Although the two men would have an ambivalent relationship with the MARS Group, their efforts in St Pancras can be seen as contributing to its attempts to develop a distinctly modernist form of planning.[100] This had its origins in the EPIC scheme of 1931, and had evolved into the work carried out for CIAM 4 and NHFO 1934. During 1935 the Group would be working on its contribution to the 'Functional City' exhibition to be held in Amsterdam in June.[101] The addition of another survey to this work helped to widen the territory the movement could claim to cover. It also reiterated its insistence that planning should always be considered as part of a 'completely comprehensive policy' on housing. Through such activity the movement hoped to position its approach to planning alongside the better known oppositional urbanism of the GCTPA.

That Connell and Ward sought to carry out their survey in tandem with the voluntary sector served to strengthen further the affiliation between these two 'outside' groups and the correlation between progressive form and content. They also benefited from the considerable expertise the sector had in survey and planning work. Barclay and Perry had conducted many investigations into housing conditions in London,[102] while the nearby Kensington Housing Trust had combined survey and plan in their 1932 'Plan for Kensington' which proposed the reconstruction of an area to the west of Paddington Station.[103]

It was after some months of discussion, that in April 1935 the Executive Committee of the SPHIS accepted Connell and Ward's offer. Initially, the Committee had expressed some concern that such a survey might interfere with the work of both the borough council and the LCC. This was an important consideration for societies like the SPHIS whose freedom to operate was dependent on the tolerance of municipalities, especially in the 1930s, but when it became apparent that neither authority objected and furthermore were interested in the potential results, this concern was abated.[104] A Survey Committee was then formed which comprised Connell, Ward, and now Lucas, Shaw, Scott and Stewart of the NSPG and representatives of the parent Executive.[105] Its task was to first organize, and then supervise, what would turn out to be a two-year investigation.

The survey used the same technique that MARS had partially implemented at NHFO 1934 of survey, diagnosis, plan. Hence a series of sub-committees were set up which would report their findings to the Survey Committee and from which the architects would produce a final scheme and report. There were five sub-committees: social conditions, transport, industries and commerce, social amenities and technical. The latter was further divided into existing buildings, technology, engineering, building and structure, and planning. Each sub-committee was staffed by representatives of the SPHIS and, in a further reiteration of the practice pioneered at NHFO 1934, by co-opted members, brought in for their expertise. Of particular interest, and again signalled in 1934, was the way in which this expertise was distributed across the committees, and we can see emerging a clear demarcation, if not yet a division, of areas of expertise between the voluntarists and the modernists.

Thus we find the more sociological aspects of the survey overseen by SPHIS members. The social conditions sub-committee was chaired by Miss Hill and the social amenities by Edith Neville, both of whom had long experience of social work in the area. The more technologically oriented sub-committees, transport and technical, were chaired by Connell, Ward or Lucas or co-opted members, a method which brought additional modernist co-conspirators into this progressive front. The critic Geoffrey Boumphrey, for example, chaired transport and recruited Philip Morton Shand as a member. The building and structure sub-committee was organized by the architects and Cyril Sweett. Colin Lucas was given responsibility for the existing buildings sub-committee.[106]

Once organized, each committee was expected to carry out research independently but it is clear from the surviving minutes of the Survey Committee that progress was erratic and some teams were more productive than others were.[107] This may explain why no complete report seems to have been written, although there are references to what was clearly a substantial Memorandum to the local council, as well as to the design scheme produced by Connell, Ward and Lucas. The Memorandum, of May 1936, was directed to the Estates Committee of St Pancras Borough Council and was intended to be forwarded by it to the LCC. It appears to have been a response to the Council's own investigations into overcrowding in the area. The letter which accompanied it, which is all that survives, is of great interest for it offers a useful summation of the modernist-voluntarist position on redevelopment and of what they hoped would be achieved by their collaboration on the Survey. The SPHIS's particular concern was for the provision of amenities in replanned areas and it urged the Council to learn from the Society's experience in rehousing people. It wrote:

> It is now widely recognized that all schemes for rehousing families in considerable numbers run the risk of destroying old associations and breaking up neighbourhood units and neighbourly traditions. It has also been demonstrated that with careful forethought and planning, and particularly by provision from the first of opportunities for community life, rehoused families may gain in these respects as well as in that of improved housing conditions. We wish therefore to urge that provision for neighbourhood and community life, Nursery schools, playgrounds, occupation centres etc should be included in every redevelopment scheme. The SPHIS would be glad to assist with all the manes [sic] in its power with the provision and running of such amenities.[108]

Just over a year later, in July 1937, there are references to the preparation by Connell, Ward and Lucas of a scheme, possibly two, which translated these ideas into three-dimensional forms. None has survived, but it seems likely that, in keeping with the architects' original proposal 'for good modern flats to house the largest number of people healthily and well', that they would have comprised blocks higher than the usual five storeys.[109] Indeed, there is a note of a meeting between SPHIS members and the LCC about plans for high building in June 1937. The sites on which the flats would have been built were carefully chosen to fall under the terms for clearance and redevelopment of the 1935 Housing Act.[110] It is clear that they were intended as prototypes to guide the borough's, and the LCC's, future work.

References to the survey end suddenly in the SPHIS's minute-books in mid-1937 and no buildings appear to have originated from its two-year-long investigation. Nevertheless, the collaboration among Connell and Ward and the SPHIS which was manifested in that project and, more permanently, in Kent House, represented an important moment of synthesis between two vanguard traditions in the mid-1930s. It was also reiterated by the contemporary collaboration at Peckham which had resulted in R. E. Sassoon House. Together, these schemes were evidence of the growing maturity and scope of the British movement. But neither, however well received, constituted the sufficient critical mass, nor was able to achieve the command of reformist propaganda, that the cause required. It would take a much larger, and better financed, scheme, one in which the socio-spatial ideas enacted at Chalk Farm and Peckham were writ large, to achieve such authority. Kensal House, commissioned by the Gas, Light and Coke Company in November 1933, designed by a team led by Elizabeth Denby and Max Fry, and completed in late 1936, would achieve this goal.

Chapter 5

The Modern Flat

really the last word in working-class flats

Anthony Bertram (1937)

In November 1937, Anthony Bertram, design critic and sometime editor of *Design for Today*, made a BBC broadcast on the subject of 'Housing the Workers'.[1] The talk, which focused on a series of visits he had made to new municipal estates across Britain, concluded with an account of three 'outstanding' schemes he had seen in London. These were not LCC flats, however, as his listeners might have anticipated given the rest of his discussion. Rather, they were the work of voluntary housing associations, being Kent House, Sassoon House and Kensal House. Bertram was unequivocal in his praise for each. Kent House, he declared, was remarkable in its accommodation and equipment while Sassoon House was 'another excellent scheme'. However, he did not devote much time to either of these, choosing instead to introduce his listeners to Kensal House. Lauding its design and the collaborative process which had produced it, and commending in particular the provision of two balconies per flat, he proclaimed the scheme 'really the last word in working-class flats'.

Bertram's comments were not simply the hyperbole of a modernist sympathizer. Indeed, he was complimentary about many of the municipal schemes he had seen,[2] but his singling out of these three modernist-voluntarist schemes was significant. For the talk demonstrated that the new model of housing which these projects embodied had been absorbed by someone beyond the 'inner circle' of the MARS Group and the Housing Centre and, as a consequence, was being promoted to a wider audience through the relatively new medium of the wireless talk. Furthermore, Bertram's structuring of his talk suggests that he recognized a clear progression in the development of this model from the more modest schemes at Peckham and Chalk Farm to the 'last word' at Ladbroke Grove.

Bertram's approbation was deserved. The conjunction of a client committed to the process of modernization through design, and the leading conceptual roles its creators had in the worlds of modernism and voluntarism, meant that Kensal House would constitute the most complete expression of the praxis of progressive housing reform before the outbreak of war in 1939.[3] Here, as nowhere else, what Fry labelled 'the technical and the social' were synthesized to create a environment which comprised not simply a re-formed private sphere, as had been the case in Peckham and Chalk Farm, but also a re-formed public sphere.[4] The whole constituted what Denby would call 'an urban village'.[5]

This blueprint for a modern Britain might have assumed the unobtrusive mantle of its predecessors, had not its creation been paralleled by the other factor which made the scheme so central to the advancement of the modernist project in the 1930s. For Kensal House was the most thoroughgoing example of rhetorical modernism explored in this book. The combination of its form and programme, with the propaganda skills of those involved in its making, ensured that it would be made known to a far wider array of contemporary audiences, and become absorbed into a greater number of progressive discourses, than any other project in the thirties. It became, in effect, a narrative of modernity in itself, ultimately serving as a signifier of a new Britain.

Modernism and capitalism

Unlike Sassoon House and Kent House, Kensal House had its ultimate origins in commercial, not philanthropic, activity. Its client, the Gas, Light and Coke Company (GLCC), was one of the country's oldest and largest public utility companies, and a major supplier of both power and equipment in London. From the early 1900s onwards, however, it had faced increasing competition from the emerging electricity industry.[6] To counter this, the Company developed a series of strategies which centred on the use of design and advertising to modernize both itself and its products. These strategies would culminate in Kensal House. They provide further evidence of the diverse narratives of modernity which allowed architectural modernism to develop in Britain.

Although electricity had been viewed as a threat to the gas industry since before the Great War, as a source of power it had not been sufficiently widely available to consumers to make it a serious competitor to the market for gas. That prospect became more real after 1926 as the construction of the National Grid linked an ever-growing number of dwellings to the electricity network. It was further compounded by the advent of slum clearance programmes in the early 1930s and, to a lesser extent, by the growth of the speculative house-building market. To a company like the GLCC, among whose primary markets was working-class housing, the new legislation should have offered the opportunity for an increase in sales, but this was not necessarily to be the case. Many municipalities owned electricity supply companies and were under no obligation to include gas power on their new estates, especially as the Grid was expanded. If the GLCC were to retain its market, it was necessary to face the challenge of electricity head-on. It therefore launched a concerted campaign to demonstrate to consumers and politicians alike the supremacy of gas as both fuel and appliance.[7]

Under the instigation of the Governor, David Milne Watson, and the new General Manager, Robert Foot, appointed in 1929, the GLCC's campaign entailed nothing less than a thoroughgoing modernization of the business. Inspired by a trip to the US to inspect modern office systems, they streamlined the Company's structure and introduced such basic innovations as replacing handwritten ledgers with typed ones.[8] Alongside these administrative changes they also focused on reforming the Company's product range, creating what they called 'a modern gas service'. This combined a new line of re-designed products with cheaper tariffs and was aimed directly at the low-rental flat market, especially following the introduction of the 1933 Housing Act.[9] The final element in this strategy was to increase the budget for advertising and public relations. The GLCC had long enjoyed the services of the progressive London Press Exchange for this purpose; it could also draw on the resources of the industry's promotional body, the British Commercial Gas Association, which had been formed in 1912. In 1931, it augmented this work with the creation of its own specialist Publicity Department, headed by A. P. Ryan. Together their task was to 'sell' the reformed Company and its modern service to municipal and private consumers alike.

That the GLCC saw design and advertising as integral to its process of modernization is significant. It should be understood as part of that narrative of modernity, originated within the DIA, which conceptualized design as an economic proposition,[10] and something central to the revitalization of the British economy in the 1930s. The GLCC had links with the DIA through its Controller of Sales, Sir Francis Goodenough, who served on its Council in 1932.[11] Its declaration that the new product range was intended as 'our contribution to the ideal of art and industry', further indicates an allegiance to the Association's aims.[12]

The means through which the GLCC undertook modernization through design is also significant. Prior to the re-structuring, and on Goodenough's initiative, the Company had employed the architect W. J. Tapper to improve the quality of its displays and exhibition stands, but the plans for the modern gas service required a more wide-ranging and strategic design effort.[13] In early November 1933, Watson and Foot therefore appointed a committee of what was described as 'architects and others' to advise it 'on architectural and kindred matters of common interest'.[14]

The Committee had nine members. Two were representatives of the GLCC, Watson and Foot. They were joined by S. C. Leslie who then managed the Company's account at the London Press Exchange, an appointment which underscores the rhetorical nature of both this Committee and its activities.[15] To the 'gas men' were added the advisers: five architects,[16] Robert Atkinson, G. Grey Wornum, Fry, C. H. James and Michael Tapper (convenor, secretary and son of W. J. Tapper); and one 'other', Elizabeth Denby. There can be little doubt that this was a carefully chosen team of experts: each member selected for an ability to make a specific contribution to the promotion of the modern gas system. Furthermore, as well as providing advice, the appointment of such a Committee served as another sign of the Company's modernity. The notion of employing a team of specialists to assist in the development of industry was quite new in the early 1930s. It was more commonly found in progressive social and economic circles such as PEP and the Housing Centre. Through the adoption of such a strategy, the GLCC could present itself as pioneering new practices of management as well as of design.

The work of the Committee was carefully apportioned to the skills available. Atkinson, Wornum, James and Tapper were each given the task of designing either offices or showrooms for the GLCC as part of its ongoing policy of overhauling its public image. These men had wide experience of commercial and public architecture, and as moderns, rather than modernists, could be guaranteed to produce designs of sufficient novelty to connote the Company's modernity but not to the extent that they frightened the consumers at whom they were aimed.[17]

The final part of the Company's process of reform was the most ambitious. Catalysed by the 1933 Housing Act, the intention was to bring design and advertising together through the commissioning of a block of model flats in which the cheapness and efficacy of the modern gas service could be demonstrated in action. In Denby and Fry they had the perfect advisers to achieve this. Now an independent consultant, Denby could bring to the project her ten years' experience of re-housing slum-dwellers for the Kensington Housing Trust and was well placed to advise on the equipment of the proposed block.[18] Fry, as co-leader of the MARS Group, could be expected to produce an architectural form which through its advanced modernity would attract publicity to the services it housed. In mid-November, therefore, the Court of Directors of the GLCC agreed that

> The Governor arrange for the erection of a block of working-class tene-ments for employees of the Company and others, either on the Pancras Gasholder site or on some other site to be settled by him and reported to the Court.

In January 1934 a section of the gasworks at Ladbroke Grove, Kensal Green, west London, was finalized as the site. By February the Court had seen and approved in prin-ciple architect's sketch plans for the scheme.[19]

At this point, Kensal House was a project driven by technological and commercial concerns: its purpose to offer a definitive demonstration that gas was supe-rior to electricity. Fry's modernism served merely to create an appropriately dramatic setting for the sale of a system. However, by the time a set of complete plans had been submitted to the LCC and Ministry of Health in November 1934, there were the first indications that the project was beginning to move beyond this purpose.[20] Over the next six months a social club, playground and nursery school were added to the plans,[21] and it would be recast as a scheme which, through the combination of technological and social services, offered a solution to 'the problem of providing the right living conditions for re-housed slum-dwellers'.[22]

A number of explanations can be offered for this shift in aim. The fact that Denby and Fry were awarded primary responsibility for the scheme suggests that it was always a likely development. Both were at the start of their careers as fully fledged modernists, and the greater resources offered by the GLCC created a unique opportu-nity to carry the principles and practices of their modernist-voluntarist approach to housing on to an expanded and much more public stage.[23] It also brought the British movement into contact with another useful ally, and potential source of work, in private enterprise. In this respect, it is important to note that despite the growing level of state intervention in social welfare provision in the inter-war period, not least in housing, this remained a matter for much debate. It was as yet by no means inevitable that what became the Welfare State would emerge. In allying themselves with the GLCC, Denby and Fry were, so to speak, hedging the modernists' bets and making the movement's models of progress available to, and synonymous with, as wide a constituency as possible.

For the GLCC, the re-casting of the purpose of Kensal House provided the culmination of the process of modernization initiated in 1929. This had been partly achieved through its policy of linking of design (and advertising) with industry in order to achieve economic progress. Now it added the notion that a modern industry might involve itself in social progress by assuming the role of a provider of social housing. While this located the Company within contemporary traditions of citizenship, the association of the GLCC with social service also provided it with a significant weapon in its competition with the electricity industry.

The problem for the GLCC, and the gas industry as a whole, was that however advanced its technologies actually were, and however much it re-designed its products and showrooms, its efforts were always confounded by what Leslie described as 'the prevalent identification of electricity with the millennium'.[24] It needed, therefore, to rehearse its modernity elsewhere if it were to be associated with progress in the public mind. Through the re-presentation of Kensal House as a scheme which offered a solution to perhaps the greatest social problem of the decade, the GLCC could identify itself as a company concerned with the future shape and well-being of society.

Kensal House: 'the right living conditions'

Once the decision to expand the function of Kensal House had been made, the GLCC then embarked on the creation of the necessary legal and financial frameworks to effect this. The first significant step in this process was the formation of a housing association to build and manage the scheme. This allowed the Company to enter into co-operation with the local authority in order to gain government subsidies to fund the flats, a procedure made possible under the terms of the 1930 Housing Act.[25] Such co-operation had two advantages. The erection of the scheme in conformity with the standards required by the Act would enable the GLCC to receive public funding to achieve its own aim of proving the suitability of gas for social housing. It would also reiterate the contention of progressive housing reformers that with more imagination and insight state housing could be significantly improved. By the end of the year, therefore, the Company had formed the Capitol Housing Association. Following negotiations with both the local council and the Ministry of Health, a programme of subsidy for the building was then agreed.[26] Most of 1935 was devoted to refining the different aspects of the design and securing planning permissions for them;[27] early 1936 saw building work commence. In the December of that year, three years after the idea had first been proposed, the estate was completed and the tenants began to move in.

In approaching the design of Kensal House, Denby and Fry drew on many of the same techniques and narratives that they had used at Sassoon House and which Connell and Ward had deployed at Kent House. In design terms, then, the estate is perhaps best understood as a reiteration, albeit a highly sophisticated one, of a progressive consensus about the form and plan of the workers' flat.[28] The first rule of this 'lexicon' was that reinforced concrete should be the main building material and so it was at Kensal House. Each block was carried on a reinforced concrete frame and clad with concrete panels (faced internally with cork and then plaster). Such a system served at once the rhetorical purpose of signifying difference but could equally be justified by the fact that the Ladbroke Grove site was a difficult one, sloping sharply upwards from south to north (Fig. 5.1). Concrete-framed construction also allowed Fry to reduce building costs,[29] and to produce another prerequisite of the modern workers' flat, a standardized *existenz-minimum* type-plan.

To suggest that the design of the Kensal House flats was iterative is not to suggest it was not innovative. What made, and makes, the scheme so significant was the way in which the technical tropes deployed there were dovetailed so precisely with the social programme of the estate. While anti-modernist critics might see the *existenz-minimum* plans or *sachlich* exteriors as evidence of the British movement's seduction by European precedent at the expense of native traditions and inhabitants' needs, these, and other elements of the design were, in fact, intrinsic to the estate's function as a dwelling place. Indeed, in many instances, they were not so foreign as they might at first appear.

The dovetailing embodied Fry and Denby's contention that it was only by assimilating the technical (the modernist) with the social (the voluntarist) that a satisfactory model of housing could be achieved. In creating Kensal House, they therefore devoted the same attention to the design of the new types of amenity, welfare systems and management practices which would support the tenants in the transition from slum to modern dwelling, as they gave to the design of the flats. It was an approach which, as Fry wrote, stemmed from the simplest of motivations:

Figure 5.1
Elizabeth Denby
and Maxwell Fry,
Kensal House,
Ladbroke Grove,
London, 1937

The idea that animated both sides of the work was the desire to build a group of homes where people whose incomes allow them little above sheer necessity could experience as full a life as can be.[30]

Kensal House: the private sphere

In terms of the discourses within which Denby and Fry were working, the domestic context of this 'full life' would first be achieved by the reinstatement and fostering of the family as a social unit. Following the lexicon established at Peckham and Chalk Farm, the flats were intended as a device through which each member of the family could (re)learn specific familial roles. The mother could become a better housewife and parent, the father affirm his role as bread winner and *pater familias*. At the same time, these re-formed dwellings would also provide a better environment in which children could grow up and, in turn, learn their appropriate future path.

An emphasis on a renewed form of family life owed much to the broader contemporary movement of Positive Eugenics and the desire to create a healthy working class, fit to reproduce. It might therefore be seen as unremarkable, and highly gendered, had it not been augmented by a wider sense of what the scheme's synthesis of plan, equipment and management programme could achieve. For at Kensal House the creation of a modern working-class family was part of a more ambitious project. Informed by modernist-voluntarist housing praxis, the doctrines of design reform, and the principles of labour-saving, the transformations effected in the private sphere were intended to prepare each family member, but especially the adult women, for participation in the public realm (both that of the estate and the world beyond its walls) as citizens and consumers. Viewed in this light, the *sachlich* forms and spaces of Kensal House were deployed to fulfil very British concerns.

This anglicization of continental European tropes is nowhere more apparent than in the deployment of *existenz-minimum* principles in the planning of the 68 flats at Kensal House (Fig. 5.2). Their use achieved several goals. Rhetorically they signified the modernity of the scheme, its difference from state practice and the expertise of its designers. Most importantly, however, they allowed the provision of the requisite spaces which would instigate the process of reinstating family life. In place of the messy promiscuity of the slums from which many came, Kensal House tenants were removed to an interior in which space was discrete – a kitchen, bathroom and WC, separate bedrooms for parents and children, a living room – and ordered in its size according to function and occupancy. As at Kent House, such a plan helped to facilitate and enhance the individuality of the family as a unit, as well as the individuality of each of its members. This sense of privacy was further enhanced by the fact that each pair of flats was reached not by balcony access but by an internal staircase.[31]

If these differentiated spaces allowed family members to begin to 'find their place', their rationalization and orientation worked simultaneously to articulate particular ideas about how these spaces might ultimately be performed. Although the extent to which these spaces were used as intended was beyond their originators' control, the interaction between spatial and management practices at Kensal House served, at least in the short term, to ensure some level of correlation between intention

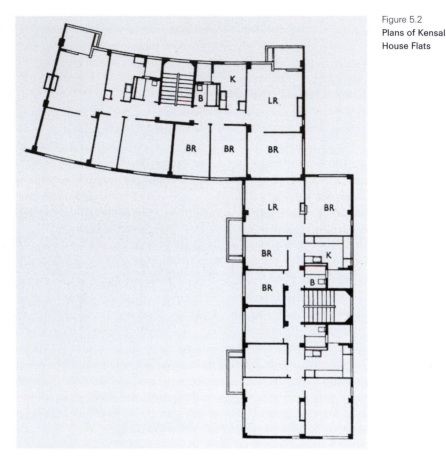

Figure 5.2
Plans of Kensal
House Flats

and inhabitation.[32] In addition, the desires of the new tenants themselves to assimilate the designers' aspirations for them should not be discounted.[33]

On entering their flat, tenants walked into a hallway off which opened, to one side, one or two bedrooms (depending on the size of the flat) and, to the other, the bathroom and kitchen.[34] The hall extended only as far as the entrance to the living room from which the main bedroom was entered. This reduction in circulation space was at once a technical device – using space efficiently so that the room in which the family was intended to spend most of its time could be as large as possible – and a programmatic one. For, once the children had gone to bed and the living room door was closed, the parents had the zone of the living and master bedroom to themselves. Such privacy was important. It reflected the contemporary anxieties, discussed in Chapter 2, about the impact living in slum conditions had on married life. The plan form used at Kensal House therefore created a discreet space in which the parents were able to develop their relationship as companions and lovers and thus enjoy a complete relationship.[35]

The limiting of circulation space was not the only device which allowed the living room to be the largest in the flat and thereby assume a central role in each family's everyday life. Fry stuck rigidly to *existenz-minimum* practice and kept the sleeping

Figure 5.3
Living room of
Kensal House flat

quarters relatively small, 'because you don't live in bedrooms all day'.[36] In collaboration with Denby, he also produced the highly rationalized bathroom-kitchen working unit, although in this case the reductions served a further purpose, as will be discussed later in the chapter. As a result, the living room was a space slightly larger than 185 square feet.

Here was where family life would be lived to the full. The small dimensions of the kitchen meant that meals would have to be eaten in the living room. It thus became the location for the daily coming together of the family. A coke fire provided the modern equivalent of a hearth, its role as the heart of the home reinforced by the positioning of the flat's wireless speaker above it. A modernist inglenook, the intention was surely to reinforce this space as one for congregation. The combination of heat and amusement would draw family members together (Fig. 5.3).

The living room also contained the door to the flat's sun balcony, a feature already used at Sassoon House. This was a substitute garden for each family, serving to relieve the closed-in feeling of living in a flat. At 8 by 5 ft, it was designed to be large enough to hold a table or give sufficient space to allow children to play within sight of their mother. A deep window box was fixed into the balconies for tenants to use for growing flowers or propagating vegetables to be cultivated on the estate's allotments; the hanging out of washing here was strictly forbidden. Each balcony also offered the families a view of their estate: kings and queens of all they surveyed.

In such a setting, families broken by slum conditions could begin to be mended. But this was not something which would be achieved solely through the medium of space. Intrinsic to the transforming potential of the flats were innovations in the way they were furnished and equipped. These served both to further the achievement of family life and, once this was underway, to begin the process of enabling the inhabitants to engage with the demands of life beyond their front doors.

A citizenship of consumption

The interest in the furnishing of the domestic interiors at Kensal House had its origins in the activities of the voluntary housing sector for which Denby had worked in the 1920s. Like many of the new housing associations formed in that decade, her former employer, the Kensington Housing Trust (KHT), had provided furniture loan funds for its tenants. On becoming an independent consultant she had adapted this practice and at Sassoon House undertook what a contemporary described as

> a very interesting experiment. She realizes that if you move a family from 2 slum rooms, or less, into a flat of 3 or 4 rooms, the tenants will probably need more furniture. Normally they would be tempted to buy this through the usual hire-purchase shops. She is eager to help them choose suitable furniture at a low cost. Consequently, she had furnished two of the flats, simply yet beautifully, and inexpensively. The prospective tenants are invited to see the furniture, which is all clearly priced. They can either buy the furniture outright or make an arrangement with the property manager to pay an agreed price every week with the rent.[37]

The practice was repeated at Kensal House. Again a show-flat was furnished and was visited by the new tenants as part of what seems to have been an induction to the estate. At this tea parties were held, guided tours conducted, and the families given access to their new homes so that they could measure up for any new furniture and fittings they might need to buy. By the end of the scheme, about £126 worth of goods, 'mainly beds and bedding', had been bought.[38]

The source of the goods on display at the show-flat was a new venture with which Denby was involved, a shop called House Furnishing Ltd (HFL). This had been opened in April 1936 by the ever-experimental Saint Pancras House Improvement Society (SPHIS), and had been conceived to address its concern that

> labour-saving devices and most well-designed furniture, designed specially for cleanliness, can only be afforded by wealthy people, whereas it is people with limited incomes who need such furniture more than the rich.[39]

To address this gap, the shop was stocked with 'good, strong, serviceable and well-designed furniture and fabrics',[40] which could be bought at hire-purchase rates substantially lower than then common.[41] Denby's existing expertise in this field of reform led to her involvement almost from the start. She was appointed one of the shop's directors and its chief buyer.[42]

Given that the voluntary sector did little in this decade that was not exemplary, the founding of HFL, and the instigation of the scheme at Kensal House, were more than acts of intelligent philanthropy. Rather, they should be seen as a response to one particular ramification of the Housing Acts of the 1930s. This was that the clearance programmes they had inaugurated had made potential consumers of all those removed from slums to new dwellings. In addition, the 1936 Housing Act would authorize local authorities to provide furniture on fair terms to their poorest tenants. For reformers like Denby and the SPHIS, who were preoccupied with the reform of everyday life and things, and believed in the ameliorative and modernizing powers of design, the formation of this mass market offered an unparalleled opportunity. Their concern, therefore, was to show the state how it could be seized. Through the establishment of shops like HFL, a generation of virgin consumers could be 'trained' in the merits of good design before they were exposed to the horrors of the High Street. This training, in turn, would enable them to participate fully in another aspect of modern life: the progress of the British economy through informed acts of consumption.

The only problem in effecting this transformation in taste, and creating a race of modern consumers, was the difficulty, as Denby reported to the HFL directors, of finding furniture which combined 'good design with strength and low price'.[43] While contemporaries such as Pearse and Williamson, and Coates, had the budgets to commission new types of furniture, Denby had to rely, for the most part, on distilling from the commercial market goods which fulfilled the SPHIS's eminently DIA-esque criteria. Some idea of what this produced may be seen in these photographs of the show-flat at Kensal House (Figs 5.3, 5.4 and 5.5). As they show, much of the furniture was of the white-wood variety which the purchasers could paint or stain themselves. Simple and serviceable this may have been, but it created somewhat utilitarian interiors, a quality which Denby and the HFL directors sought to mitigate, as can be seen, by the use of textiles, goods which the shop stocked in quantity. For those who could not afford new furniture, or perhaps had some to bring with them, they provided an effective and inexpensive means to create, as Coates would have put it, 'the select value of a personal environment'.[44] And, as *Housing Happenings* noted, such textiles could also bring some delight 'among people

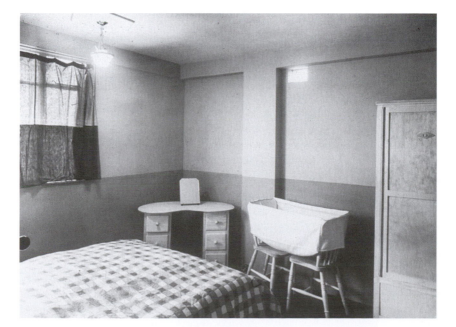

Figure 5.4
Main bedroom of
Kensal House flat

Figure 5.5
Second bedroom of
Kensal House flat

who have suffered from drabness all their lives'.[45] Merchandise included washable hearth rugs, checked cottons and casement cretonnes, and embroidered cushions which were described as 'quite à la Liberty'.[46]

The exceptions to these goods were the settee and armchair seen in the living room, and the chest of drawers in the second bedroom. These were specially commissioned pieces of furniture, and had their origins in Denby's participation in an investigation into the furnishing and equipment of the working-class home which was then being conducted by a sub-committee of the government's Council for Art and Industry (CAI). This had been instigated by its Chair, Frank Pick, in late 1935, and reflected his shared recognition of the potential offered by the new housing legislation to design reformers.[47] The sub-committee's investigation would take eighteen months and pursue three main areas of activity.[48] The first was to assemble three collections of furniture and equipment, using budgets which ranged from £50 to £100, in order to assess the type of goods currently available to the working-class consumer. Denby would conduct the £50 survey and use it to source, and attempt to commission, goods for HFL.[49] A study of the supply of articles to be bought at sixpence and under was also made, and the furniture designer Gordon Russell was commissioned to investigate the feasibility of making the main articles of furniture for a new household at low cost from deal.[50] This effort was brought together in a report, *The Working Class Home, Its Furnishing and Equipment*, published in May 1937, and an exhibition of approved designs at the Building Centre in London held the following month.[51]

The report reiterated Denby's difficulty at finding goods which were at once affordable and well designed. As an attempt to resolve this dilemma, the furniture which the sub-committee commissioned is therefore of great interest. It embodies what can be understood as a progressive consensus about the sort of modern design deemed appropriate for a working-class market. In the development of this, the sub-committee spoke of the need 'once more [for] a living tradition of furniture design'. The basis of this they saw not in 'the uncompromising severity which some modern tastes dictate' but in goods which 'while of good and pleasant design in themselves, might be expected to meet the popular taste by some added decoration'.[52]

'Good and pleasant' are useful words with which to describe the chair and settee used in the living room of Kensal House. Made from beech wood and upholstered in corduroy, they were intended to be easy to clean and easy to move. Their 'decorativeness' resided in the contrast between fabric and timber, something to be complemented by one of HFL's many embroidered cushions. At £1 17 shillings and 6 pence, the chair was also approximately half the cost of the upholstered chairs the sub-committee had examined; an economic advantage which supported its criticism of the three-piece suite ('unhappily … often a mark of prestige').[53] The set was the subject of wide approval. A reviewer in *Art and Industry* singled it out as a representative of 'the new type of plain, sensible design which is replacing gimcrack imitations of luxury'.[54] Certainly, it was an improvement on the white-wood furniture on which HFL mostly relied for stock.[55]

The other furniture commissioned was that produced by Gordon Russell. Ultimately produced in oak, rather than deal, he designed a bedroom suite of chest of drawers, dressing table and wardrobe.[56] The simple forms of the range, their effect derived, as the report noted, from 'good proportions and simple construction', meant that they also met with *Art and Industry*'s approbation. Its reviewer described them 'as pleasing and practical pieces'. Their cost, however, hinted at the difficulties of making such things available to the wider market; the wardrobe was just over £10.

The linking of Kensal House with the CAI investigation served to embed the scheme within another progressive discourse, that of design reform. More particularly, the instigation of the scheme with HFL, by connecting the private realm of the family with the public realm of the market place through the act of consumption, served to remind each inhabitant that actions within the home had implications beyond it. Such a mapping of public concerns onto domestic spaces can also be traced through another set of interventions to the environment of the flats; this time more gendered in focus. They were manifested in the adherence to the reformist narrative of the labour-saving home in their planning and equipment.

Housewives and citizens

The origins and nature of the labour-saving home were explored in Chapter 3, and it was noted in the previous chapter that the SPHIS had pioneered the application of its principles in the design of its estates. Generally, however, as the social reformer

Margery Spring Rice observed in her 1939 study, *Working-Class Wives, their Health and Conditions*,

> The rationalisation of labour has passed over the working woman, leaving her to carry on in more or less the same primitive way that has been customary since time began; never specialising and seldom learning real skill in any of her dozens of different jobs.[57]

Yet, as we have seen in Peckham, the reinstatement and enhancement of working-class women's roles as housewives and mothers was considered to be central to their achievement of modernity. The absorption of what had hitherto been primarily a middle-class discourse into a social housing scheme, and the extent to which labour-saving ideas were applied, therefore further rendered Kensal House as an exemplary environment. The tremendous advantage in this context was, of course, the patronage of the GLCC. Its own publicity material had noted that badly designed equipment made women 'worse human beings, housewives and mothers than they might otherwise be',[58] and it is in the design of the flats that the collaboration between the Company, Denby and Fry is most evident. Together, they assimilated plan and equipment to create a training ground and workshop fit for a modern housewife.[59]

As Mrs Peel had exhorted, and likewise her contemporaries in continental Europe who were similarly in thrall to the Taylorist principles of Scientific Management, the process of becoming, or creating, 'a good housekeeper', of value to the nation, began with simplifications in plan and form.[60] These would reduce the amount of labour to be expended in cleaning and maintenance. Kensal House was exemplary in its rationalized use of space and its lack of dust-gathering mouldings and skirting boards. In addition, wall surfaces were plastered and painted in light, bright colours – pinks, creams, blues – in order to capture the light which streamed into the flat from the large steel-framed windows. Dark-brown linoleum, recommended by Peel, was laid throughout the flat. With rugs on top, and light movable furniture (both bought from HFL), cleaning was thus made easier.[61]

Such devices, however, were but complements to the most significant site in which the Kensal House housewife could achieve domestic modernity: the kitchen. And this was a kitchen like no other, undoubtedly the most well equipped, and arguably the best designed such space of its type, geography and time. A part of the flat's 'working unit', this standardized system would be repeated throughout each block.[62] In addition to the kitchen, the unit contained the bathroom and WC and a drying balcony (Fig. 5.6). The kitchen itself was planned to meet all the criteria commentators like Peel had laid down for an efficient kitchen. It was planned therefore as a working kitchen, 96 square feet in size, with space only for the housewife (and, perhaps, an assisting daughter, as the film made about Kensal House after its completion shows).[63] The space was zoned into areas for food preparation, cooking, and also laundry; eating would take place in the living room. Amenities which required hot water were ranged against one wall thereby sharing plumbing and flues with the bathroom equipment. There was a large butler's sink, flanked by generous draining boards, one of which was fixed and had storage space beneath. The other was hinged to allow access to the gas washing copper which was stored below it. The instantaneous gas water heater was

Figure 5.6
Plan of Kensal
House flat working
unit

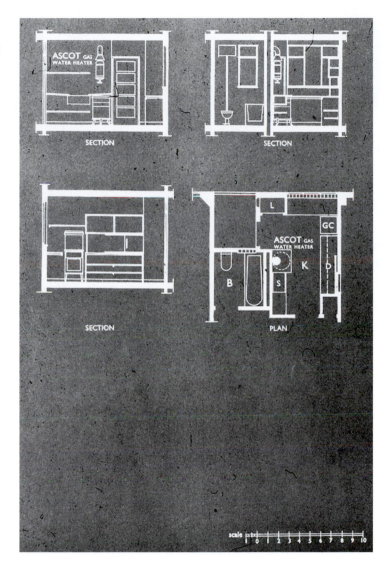

positioned above the sink and ensured a ready supply of hot water to both it and the bath (Fig. 5.7).

On the wall opposite was the space for food storage and preparation. This featured a long work surface with a recessed shelf beneath. Such an arrangement, also used for the table in front of the window, had been recommended by household management experts because it allowed the housewife to sit down while preparing food. Cupboards, supported on narrow poles, were hung on the wall. The gas cooker stood at the end of this row, within easy reach of the second food preparation table at the window. A gas point, for a gas iron, was also provided.

As well as fulfilling the GLCC's requirement that the kitchen should be a well-equipped workshop, Denby and Fry's concern, in correct labour-saving manner,

Figure 5.7
Kensal House
kitchen

was to see that it was also an efficient one. The fact that the working surfaces were continuous and at a regular height, that the cupboards were not positioned so high that they could not be reached, and the inclusion of a hatch between the kitchen and living room wall through which food could be passed, all helped to minimize unnecessary effort and facilitate ease of movement. Similarly careful attention was paid to the placing of the copper. Positioned opposite the door of the drying balcony, housewives had a direct, and short, route across which heavy washing would be carried to be hung out to dry.

The inclusion of a gas copper inside each flat, rather than having a communal laundry, was significant. It was another device to ensure individuality and privacy: as Anthony Bertram would observe, 'very poor people are sensitive about displaying their underclothes to the neighbours'.[64] Privacy was further enhanced by the inclusion of the drying balcony in place of the more usual facility of shared, and very public, washing lines in an estate's grounds. Washing could be hung up away from the direct public gaze but dry just as efficiently as if fully outside, thanks to the ventilation holes and large opening of the balcony (Fig. 5.8).

Such a level of equipment was remarkable for kitchens of this period. At Kent House, the provision of an immersion heater, continuous work surfaces and a good quantity of cupboards, could not make up for the fact that cooking was still expected to take place in the living room. The slightly later, but important, block at Quarry Hill in Leeds had a communal laundry, only one balcony per flat and provided an open coke range in the living room with a pair of gas rings and a baking oven in a scullery.[65] At Ladbroke Grove, in contrast, the GLCC's gas system not only comprised the copiously equipped kitchen but lighting throughout, the living room's coke fire, a gas panel heater in the parents' room and gas points in the other bedrooms for portable radiators. This, as the Company was at pains to argue, was all included within the very affordable weekly rents of 9 shillings and 6 pence (for two-bedroom flats) or 11 shillings and 6 pence a week (for three bedrooms).[66] That it had an immediate impact on those for whom it was designed was reported in a speech by S. C. Leslie in September 1937:

> It will not surprise you to hear that the housewives who use it, some of them from slum basements, but some of them moved from other rehousing estates with traditional fuel systems, say that their working life is quite radically altered and simplified in the new conditions. Their working day is shorter, they find themselves with unexpected and unusual hours of leisure.[67]

The thoroughgoing application of labour-saving principles to the planning and equipment of Kensal House was an innovation. Certainly it also constituted a very fine advertisement for the GLCC's system but this commercial motive should not be allowed to overshadow the fact that by the time the estate was completed the Company's products had become an integral part of a highly radical scheme.

A second, and less immediately tangible, innovation was the third purpose which these technologies of plan and form served. It is an aim which helps to reiterate the case for the ultimate Britishness of Kensal House and derives from an interrogation of commonly held assumptions about the ideology of labour saving. To date, most of the literature which has explored the meaning of the use of the principles of Scientific Management in the home has focused on the writings of its American doyenne, Christine Frederick, and its use in social housing schemes in Holland and Germany.[68] Such studies have shown how, especially in the continental European context, the application of labour-saving principles was intended to create a generation of 'professional'

Figure 5.8
Rear block of Kensal House showing sun balconies and drying balconies

153

working-class housewives and mothers: re-formed women who were meant to use their newly found leisure time inside their transformed homes.

In Britain, however, the time savings effected by the radical reconfigurations of the domestic interior implemented at Kensal House, and earlier at Sassoon House and Kent House, were intended to serve a rather different purpose. Precisely what this was, was articulated by the British women, Denby among them, who contributed to the Domestic Section of the Sixth International Congress for Scientific Management held in London in July 1935.[69] In an address which otherwise considered the role of communal laundries in lessening the housewife's workload, Denby took the opportunity to question the ultimate purpose of such labour-saving facilities for women. They would, she said, provide them with more leisure but, she asked, 'Leisure for what?'.[70]

As far as Denby was concerned, the leisure made possible by the rationalization of household work should not necessarily be put to domestic or familial ends. Instead she contended that 'the ultimate aim of improvement in material things is perhaps to free the individual to take part in all the other sides of life – the life of the mind and the spirit'.[71] The rapporteur of Denby's session, the prominent Labour politician Lady Shena Simon, made it clear what should constitute that life.[72] She argued that the application of technology in the private sphere meant that 'the special experience of women as well as the experience of men' could, indeed should, be brought to bear on the public sphere. She demanded, therefore, that each newly leisured woman should think of herself as 'a citizen as well as a housewife', especially given the times in which they were living.[73]

So however 'un-British' – or in this book's term, rhetorical – Kensal House's plan and form appeared on the surface, their application was in fact tied intimately to a peculiarly British concern for democracy and citizenship.[74] It should be remembered that in Britain equal adult suffrage had been achieved only in 1928 when women over 21 were given the vote. Furthermore, in the years when Kensal House was being designed and built, Britain increasingly found itself as one of the few countries in Europe whose government was untouched by extreme politics. In such a context the preservation and enhancement of a democratic state was vital; the bringing to active citizenship of the largest section of society, its working classes, equally so.

Simon's call for the housewife to also be a citizen was not solely a response to the newness of women's acquisition of the vote. Her ideas also owed much to the influence on debates about citizenship by developments in British feminist politics in the inter-war period which had seen the emergence of New Feminism.[75] In contrast to pre-war feminism, whose advocates had been preoccupied with the attainment of equal suffrage and access to the professions (especially for middle-class women), the adherents of New Feminism were less interested in equal opportunities than in the chance for each gender to develop its different qualities and attributes to the maximum potential. In particular, their concern was to campaign for reforms such as family allowances, birth control and better housing which would free working-class women from the burdens of poverty, frequent pregnancies and drudgery. Once liberated, such women would then be able to develop further as housewives and mothers and, in time, bring their knowledge and skills to bear on the public realm as citizens.

Scientific Management was therefore an ideal tool for the New Feminist. It served to develop working-class women's domestic skills, and to provide them with the leisure time to apply themselves to the world outside their homes. The potential this suggested was captured well in the conclusion of Simon's report:

> We are indeed at the dawn of a new phase in civilization, for, from the beginning of history until the present day, the home has been the provision of the housewife – and now, thanks to the advancement of science, the door is ajar, and the housewife is on the threshold.[76]

It was, however, a potential which was in danger of going unfulfilled. Although local authorities had had the powers to build community centres on new estates since 1925, few had taken up this right. It would not be until 1937 that the Physical Training and Recreation Act made it possible for municipalities to build centres in any location.[77] In the meantime there was a distinct lack of sites in which not just housewives, but all the other inhabitants of social housing schemes, whether in urban, suburban or rural locations, could begin to exercise the life of the mind and the spirit and develop as social beings. The deficiency was a matter for much contemporary concern and debate.[78] It had also been a constant theme at the NHFO Exhibitions that new schemes should provide both for 'a happy home life and a successful community life'.[79]

In a scheme such as Kensal House, it was therefore imperative to provide for community life in the planning of the estate. The resulting sites would then act as counterpoint to the inaction of the state and demonstrate a model of practice which it should follow. The principle on which this model would be developed, reflecting the preoccupations of the progressive front, was a didactic one. The provision of particular sorts of amenity, combined with the implementation of certain management practices, would train the tenants in 'the best use of leisure',[80] a socio-spatial strategy which ultimately served two purposes. In the first place, it facilitated the formation of a sense of community on the estate and, once this had developed, provided the physical sites in which it could flourish. Secondly, through their interaction with the small democracy of Kensal House, each resident would be equipped with the skills necessary for participation in the world beyond.[81]

Kensal House: the public sphere

While its creators' primary approach to facilitating community life at Kensal House was to assimilate the social and the spatial, a significant, though accidental, factor in effecting this process was the location. The estate was enclosed by the Great Western Railway to the south, the Grand Union Canal to the north, a gas holder to the west and Ladbroke Grove to the east, and had a ground level which was lower than the road (Fig. 5.9). In devising the layout of the estate Fry took care to exploit this insularity. His massing of the main blocks, and their *sachlich* forms, created the impression of a castle-like beacon when viewed from the main road or railway line. This motif was completed by the walkway which ran from the main entrance and spanned the drop-off in land between the front and rear blocks. A drawbridge by any other name, to traverse it was to gain access to a new world (Fig. 5.10).

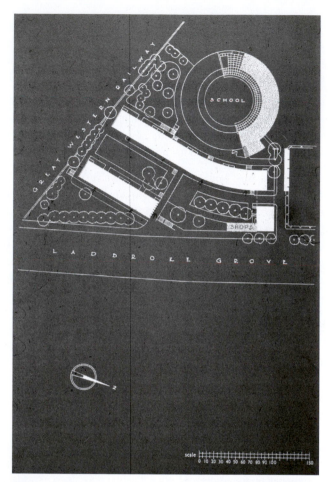

Figure 5.9
Site plan of Kensal
House

Figure 5.10
View of Kensal
House walkway

Each element of this new world – the modern flats, the nursery school, the children's playground, the two social clubs, the allotments and the tenants' committee – represented a long advocated but seldom realized entry from the agenda of progressive housing praxis as it had been articulated since the early thirties. Such extensive provision also allowed the Company to demonstrate another aspect of its modernity: its recognition of 'the community's responsibility towards all its members '.[82] Its act of citizenship in creating, with Denby and Fry, the transforming environment of Kensal House, would in turn enable the tenants to become active citizens themselves. At a planning level, the completeness of the estate's public sphere also reflected Denby's recommendation that such amenities should be included in new schemes 'right from the start'.[83] It was only by doing this, and not adding them as an afterthought, that tenants would view the clubs or the committee as an integral part of their environment, belonging to them just as their flats did.

Although the range of amenities and practices provided was intended to instill a sense of belonging in all the estate's inhabitants, and place them on the path towards citizenship, there was one group which was seen as having the potential to respond more completely to the socio-spatial transformations which surrounded them. These were the children under five who lived at Kensal House. While the stain of the slum might prove harder to eradicate from their parents, the children were less irrevocably sullied by the environments into which they had been born. By including a nursery school in the scheme, the reform work begun in the modern homes they now inhabited could be continued. This process, would, as Denby wrote, 'cut off the slum tradition at the root' and show how a new Britain might be re-built from its youngest citizens upwards.[84]

Kensal House: the nursery school

As has so often been the case in the projects discussed in this book, the incorporation of a nursery into Kensal House represented the assimilation of architectural modernism with a pre-existing tradition of progressive reform. The campaign for nursery education had originated in the first years of the twentieth century as part of the National Efficiency movement, its advocates seeing the introduction of nursery schools in slum areas as a means to improve the quality of the race.[85] Among the leaders of the campaign were the Bradford-born social reformers, the sisters Margaret and Rachel McMillan. Working in south London from the early 1910s, they had developed a system of nursery education which sought to make of slum children healthy and useful members of society. The formula was a simple one. In open-air buildings set in large gardens each child could be improved both physically and socially through exercise, free play and basic lessons in the 'three Rs', an elision of social and material reform which reflected another influence on these women, that of British Idealism.[86]

Their model was taken up by the Nursery School Association (NSA), which was founded as a voluntary organization in 1923 with Margaret McMillan as its President. Its concern was 'to guide the development of children whose parents cannot give them all the care necessary from the age when they cease to attend infant welfare centres ... until they go to school at five years'.[87] The NSA believed that children were too precious a resource to be left to the care of parents in unhealthy and inadequately equipped homes. If they could be removed to a decent environment before the age of five, as Rachel McMillan had argued, 'much … physical and mental impairment can be prevented'.[88]

Yet however much groups like the NSA were convinced of the importance of the nursery school, central government was not. Under the 1918 Education Act, local authorities had only the discretionary right to establish nursery schools. In response, the NSA, as other bodies within the voluntary sector had done, adopted the technique of advocating the nursery school on the grounds of national responsibility while at the same time its adherents established model schools themselves. By 1937, half of the 87 nursery schools recognized by the Board of Education were run by the voluntary sector.[89]

The passage of successive slum clearance acts in the 1930s gave renewed impetus to the NSA's campaign. Its Organizing Secretary Phoebe Cusden noted that 'the opportunity for the comprehensive planning of new communities was unexampled'.[90] The Association therefore stepped up its work and urged that space be set aside for nursery schools in any new housing scheme. Again, central government refused to make such provision compulsory. A report issued in 1933 by a Board of Education consultative committee on infant and nursery schools merely noted that they were a desirable but not imperative addition to existing schools or new housing schemes.[91]

The disregard shown by the state for an amenity which was widely agreed to be of benefit to the nation's progress ensured the nursery school a place in modernist-voluntarist housing praxis. Both the SPHIS and the Kensington Housing Trust had incorporated nursery schools into their housing schemes in the 1920s. It was also central to the vision of housing Denby advocated. By 1934, a 'front' between the progressives at the Housing Centre and the NSA had been formed, evidenced in the curation of the 'Amenities' display at that year's NFHO exhibition by the Association's leading spokeswoman, Marjory Allen. The fact that the model of the nursery school she included in the display was designed for a flat-roofed block of flats clearly identified its provision with progressive forms of architecture.

It seems likely that it was Allen's involvement in the NSA, as well as the desire to reinforce the message of the NHFO exhibition, which planted the idea for a nursery school at Kensal House in its creators' mind. In the first of the collaborations which would produce the public sphere of the estate, Denby and Fry appear to have recruited Allen to help make the case to the GLCC and to advise them on its programme.[92] The logic for the inclusion of a nursery was clear. It identified the scheme with another sphere of progress and would be well received among reformers of education and child welfare as well as housing. Moreover, it did not require a huge financial investment from the Company apart from the initial outlay on the building. Through the Capitol Housing Association, the GLCC could apply for state funding for the school's upkeep in the form of grants from the Board of Education and the LCC.[93] Like the flats, which received MOH subsidy, the content of the scheme's public realm would again demonstrate that it was possible to work within the constraints of state financing yet produce an estate which did more than address its inhabitants' material needs. In May 1935, therefore, David Milne Watson announced that the GLCC would pay for a nursery school to be built at a cost of £2,500.[94]

The exemplary nature of Kensal House meant, however, that this could not be just any nursery school. In both its architecture and programme it therefore adhered to the principles of the most progressive model then available, the McMillan method. Fry followed precisely its key principles of open environments and the provision of sites for play. He placed the school on a sheltered site to the north-west corner of the estate overlooking the children's playground (Figs 5.11 and 5.12). A low semi-circular building, it was set back behind a terrace wide enough for the children to play on but safely so since it was bounded by a low retaining wall. The terrace was extended back round the north-west façade of the school to provide another area for outdoor play. Here were constructed a paddling pool and a sandpit. Inside, the school had three play-rooms, overlooking the terrace, each with large windows which could be folded back to let light and air into the interiors. There were also lavatories, stores, a kitchen, staff room and medical room. The whole was heated, of course, by gas; the playrooms by over-head gas panels.

In keeping with the McMillan method, the spaces of the nursery school acted as a setting in which each child could be brought to health and then develop both as an individual and as a member of society. To effect this, children were kept at school as long as possible. Mothers could leave them there at 8 a.m. and collect them at 5 p.m. Each day was then strictly ordered with regular naps and nutritious meals.[95] Such prac-tices had the simple purpose of addressing the malnutrition found in many of the chil-dren but also the more improving one of establishing health giving eating and sleeping patterns, habits impossible to achieve in noisy slum accommodation (Fig. 5.13). There was also much emphasis on hygiene. The school's nurse inspected each child on arrival and administered a dose of cod-liver oil if she felt it necessary which, it can be

Figure 5.11
Plan of the Kensal House nursery school

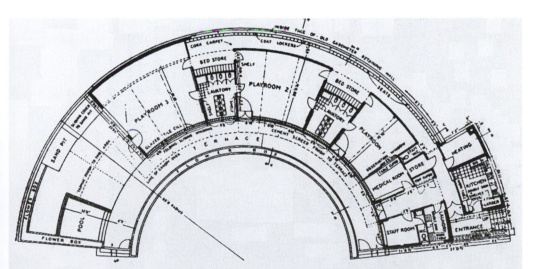

PLAN OF NURSERY SCHOOL, KENSAL HOUSE, LONDON

Architects' Committee : Robert Atkinson, F.R.I.B.A.; Elizabeth Denby; C. H. James, F.R.I.B.A.; G. Grey Wornum, F.R.I.B.A.; E. Maxwell Fry, B.Arch., A.R.I.B.A., Executant Architect.

Figure 5.12
Kensal House
nursery school,
terrace

Figure 5.13
Children's
afternoon nap in
the Kensal House
nursery

imagined, she invariably did. All the children were provided with a toothbrush and face-cloth and expected to clean themselves after meals.

Equal attention was paid to the cultivation of good manners and habits in everyday life. The children were encouraged to take responsibility for themselves and others. This tallied with what the Liberal politician Sir Ernest Simon defined as one of the four basic principles of citizenship.[96] Each child therefore took turns to serve their fellows at lunchtime and each had a personal cupboard and coat hook to encourage a sense of ownership and care (Figs 5.14 and 5.15). Likewise, the activities the children pursued during the day, although play-centred, also served a more serious purpose. As Cusden wrote:

> The child may indulge in pursuits that will satisfy his healthy curiosity, develop strength and imagination, self-reliance and courage; and by no means least ... learn to cooperate with others and to reconcile the legitimate claims of self with the equally legitimate claims of society ... this is what the normal child needs and which must be provided if the nation is to achieve for each of its citizens the ideal, desirable for Britain, no less than in ancient Rome, *mens sana in corpore sano*.[97]

In a practice which echoed the theories of the Peckham doctors, the hope was that the improvements to the children's lives and manners effected at the school would infect their parents. Much effort was also made to involve the parents in the school's educational programme as another means to foster family life.[98] The extent to which this happened is difficult to ascertain but in the short term Denby believed that the reforming environment was at least having an impact on the children. She wrote:

Figure 5.14
Children's towel
and mug shelf

Figure 5.15
Children's coat
racks

It is like a conjuring trick to see how infants entering at two years of age with the expression of men who have been through Borstal and Wormwood Scrubs are in a couple of months transformed into carefree happy babies.[99]

While the smallest inhabitants of Kensal House were being trained in good habits their mothers were expected to retire to one of the two social clubs on the estate. That they had the time to do so was the result of the labour-saving flats in which they dwelt and the fact that few of the estate's women went out to work.[100] Built into the basement level of the east block, the First Feathers Club, as it was called, was for the adult residents. During the day it served as a space for the coming together of the women for communal activity, and the exercise of the life of the mind and the spirit. This could entail participation in a dressmaking class or enjoying a chat over an afternoon cup of tea, as contemporary photographs show (Fig. 5.16).[101] Above all, the intention was that rather than staying inside her flat, the woman's presence in the club would form part of a process which would remind her that she was a member of both her own family and the community of Kensal House.

In the evening, the adults' club took on a different aspect. It became a venue where 'the men can come down with their wives for a pleasant social hour or two after the day's work is done'.[102] Here, couples might spend time together, socialize with their neighbours, or play a game of darts. The club also provided for more practical pursuits. It was equipped with tools for making and repairing furniture and for mending shoes (Fig. 5.17). Such facilities assisted the tenants in making ends meet but they were also intended, given the emphasis on regenerating the family which pervaded Kensal House, to help foster a sense of pride in homemaking among both the male and female

Figure 5.16
Main room at the
Kensal House First
Feathers Club

Figure 5.17
Male tenants at
work in the
Feathers Club
workshop

tenants. The fact that this also tended to reinforce gender roles – men made furniture (and also worked on the allotments outside) while women sewed – reflected the pervasive influence of New Feminism on the planning of the estate.

The concern for 'the best use of leisure' by the adult population, manifested in the First Feathers Club, and the mixture of worthy and social pursuits intended to be conducted therein, paralleled the way in which the nursery school operated as a site in which play served the more serious end of socializing the under-fives as proto-citizens. Such didacticism was also extended to the remaining population of Kensal House which comprised 130 children over five or adolescent.[103] While they might be expected to learn their lessons in citizenship at school, it is clear from the amenities which were provided for them that these were intended to reinforce, rather than provide relief from, their studies. Not for Kensal House youngsters the Saturday morning pictures. Instead, the younger children's primary entertainment was to be made in the circular playground, built on the site of the demolished gas holder. Equipped with goal posts and netball apparatus, the emphasis was on outdoor play and team sports.

The needs of the estate's adolescents were more complex. At 14, as the Capitol Housing Association's publicity brochure noted, most went out to work but their 'own special social needs' were rarely provided for in cities. As future citizens and parents, their evolution into adulthood could not be left to the contaminating world of commercial leisure. Instead, as the brochure's author wrote, 'these years of mental and physical coming to maturity require plenty of active sport, intelligent hobbies and cheerful mixed recreation'. For the adolescent population, the second club room on the estate, in the basement of the west block, provided the site in which they might make the transition into modern adulthood. They were provided with 'music, plenty of space and a good floor for dancing' and it was hoped that they would make their own equipment and develop their own study groups and sports societies.[104]

The incorporation of the two clubs into Kensal House represented another moment in the planning process when expertise was drawn on from outside the Architects' Committee: in this instance a voluntary organization called the Feathers Club Association. Founded at the instigation of the Prince of Wales (hence its name),[105] it had been working since 1933 to address the lack of community facilities in slum areas through the provision of clubs 'for friendship, occupation and recreation'.[106] Typically these combined a meeting hall with work rooms where members could use the carpentry tools and sewing machines provided to mend furniture or make clothes. In keeping with the voluntary tradition there was also the hope that in the process of coming together the members would benefit from 'the opportunities offered by them [the Clubs] both for the development of the individual and for corporate service to the community'.[107]

In calling on the FCA, with which Denby was already involved, to establish and run the clubs at Kensal House, the estate was again associated with those at the forefront of addressing a widely acknowledged social need. Such collaborations served, then, to enmesh the scheme into as many progressive, and potentially influential, discourses as possible. They were also testament to another innovation at Kensal House, the way it was designed.

Paralleling Tecton's approach to the design of the Finsbury Health Centre, Denby and Fry's concern in the making of Kensal House was to ensure that each aspect of the estate was designed to the precise specifications – material, technical, social – which would render it the most effective reforming environment possible. A team of experts, some in-house, some not, was then assembled to achieve this goal. In the case of the flats' design this was manifested in the close collaboration with the GLCC which resulted in the radical interiors that would bring the inhabitants to domestic modernity; a process further reinforced by the liaison with the SPHIS which produced the cheap furnishing scheme. Likewise, the advice of the NSA in the personae of Marjory Allen, and of the FCA, helped the pair to create the appropriate environments to inculcate civic modernity in each resident. In so doing they made design by teamwork an integral part of modernist-voluntarist housing praxis.[108]

The clubs and nursery school were one means through which the tenants could feel that they belonged to Kensal House and that Kensal House belonged to them. In seeking techniques to achieve this, the designers, and the modernist-voluntarists they represented, had recognized a fundamental truth. For social housing to work, its tenants needed to feel a sense of ownership and responsibility for the place. This was complemented by the belief that in acquiring such sentiments, each former slum-dweller might in time apply them to the wider world. The inculcation of a sense of citizenship both within and outwith the scheme, like the synthesis between the re-formed interiors and the affordable furnishing scheme, was something to be achieved by the synthesis between physical space and the way in which the estate was run. This was a particular preoccupation of Denby and something she was able to achieve because on the estate's completion the GLCC appointed her as its Housing Director in order 'to remain in touch with the estate and keep it on experimental lines'.[109]

Speaking in the Kensal House film, Denby explained what this entailed: 'the spirit of the estate is that the people run it themselves'. This was a radical approach for the time, but entirely in keeping with a philosophy of housing which sought to create active citizens from those who had previously lived in slums. The more usual practice was to have little or no formal estate management, common in municipal schemes which tended to rely on caretakers to keep a watch over daily life on estates.[110] The voluntary housing sector, in contrast, advocated the employment of women housing managers. Acting as an interface between the societies and their tenants, these women collected rent, dealt with tenants' problems and through the familiarity born of regular contact ensured that each of the blocks of flats for which they were responsible ran smoothly and co-operatively.

Denby's role as Housing Director encompassed some of the duties of the woman housing manager but the day-to-day running of the estate was given into the hands of its adult inhabitants. This began with the space outside the tenants' flats. Each family belonged to a staircase committee which was responsible for looking after the communal areas around their flats. From this two representatives were selected to serve on the estate's Tenants' Committee. On an already thoroughly innovative scheme, this was arguably its most innovative feature of all, and appears to have been unique for its day.

The Tenants' Committee was established very soon after the estate was opened at a meeting of all the inhabitants organized by Denby. The Committee's rapid inception reflected her understanding that the earlier amenities were included in the estate the more natural a part of daily life they became. The representatives met monthly with Denby to discuss business, each member being the conduit for grievances, issues or complaints from their staircase. A quarterly parliament of all the adult population was held in addition. While its primary concern was to ensure that everyday life on the estate was managed well, attention was also given to more light-hearted and, of course, community-building activities. Much time was spent during 1937 organizing a party in celebration of the Coronation.

Only Denby's word survives to indicate what the tenants thought of the responsibilities accorded them. In June 1937, she reported that they 'are aglow with pride at their new homes and their responsibility for managing them'.[111] Later, however, she acknowledged that in reality the practice 'was more difficult than it sounds' but stressed '[that] everyone seems quite happy as things are working out'. On balance, for Denby the experiment as a whole was a success, and she declared that 'the tenants are to my biased mind a fine example of the latent potentialities in every slum dweller which only need freeing from weed before they flower'.[112]

The collaboration among the GLCC, Denby, Fry, Allen and the NSA (and the tenants), and the deployment of a range of techniques which ranged from the spatial to the technological to the social, produced the total environment which Denby called an urban village. The term appears to have been one of her invention, but the ideas it embodied were not unique to Denby. Rather, it (and Kensal House) provided a shorthand for the pro-urbanism which had been an intrinsic part of the progressive tradition throughout the 1930s and which distinguished it most directly from the contemporary opposition of the garden city movement.

While the urban village concept arose from the same urge to stem the flight from the city which motivated garden-city advocates, Denby and Fry chose to address this urge not by abandoning the city but revitalizing it. At Kensal House, as they had done earlier at Sassoon House, they therefore brought the country to the city. The elements which made village life so desirable – community life, the proximity of nature, the house with a garden – were transplanted and translated through the medium of architectural modernism into an urban context. The cottage became a modern flat with a balcony for its garden. Well planned and well equipped, it was also affordable. The village hall became the Feathers Clubs. The allotments and the landscaping of the ground between the east and west block provided contact with nature for each resident. In such an environment it was possible to achieve the 'neighbourly and urban existence' that Fry had called for in 1933.[113] There would be no need to escape the city if it were re-planned on lines such as these.

In plan, form and programme, Kensal House was a remarkable scheme. There can be little doubt that the families who made the transition from tenement to urban village recognized this: 'we thought this heaven', one tenant declared.[114] Equally remarkable, is the speed and extent to which this extraordinary project was absorbed into the arsenal of propaganda tools of those who sought to modernize Britain and the British people. From the gas industry to campaigners against smoke abatement, from progressive educationalists to the MARS Group, all would use Kensal House as a signifier of what a better future could be.

Kensal House: the case for gas is proved

Although they never stated it publicly, it can never have been far from Denby's and Fry's minds that the collaboration with the GLCC gave them access to the considerable resources for public relations that the gas industry as a whole had been developing since the 1910s. They would not be disappointed. Through the media of press releases, house periodicals, promotional brochures, advertising and film the GLCC and the British Commercial Gas Association (BCGA) would launch extensive campaigns to promote the scheme and the system it incorporated. In so doing they would introduce the modernist-voluntarist vision to audiences to which the progressives had not previously had access.

The theme of the promotional work was consistent whichever its media and it pursued the corollary outlined earlier in this chapter of connoting the gas industry's modernity through its commitment to social progress. Although it has not survived, a press release was evidently issued at the time the scheme opened and the laziness, or loyalties, of journalists meant this message was swiftly translated into the press. Whether published in industry journals such as *Gas Bulletin*, *Co-partners Magazine* and *Gas World* or daily newspapers, the reports are interchangeable.[115] Typical are those in *The Times* and the *Kensington News and West London Times*. Both noted that the scheme had been set up 'to prove the merits of the all-gas flat or house for people of small means, besides which it is a definite contribution to the rehousing problem'.[116]

Journalists may also have drawn on the booklets issued by the BCGA and the GLCC to publicize Kensal House. The BCGA's *Kensal House, the Case for Gas is Proved* was written by S. C. Leslie and targeted, judging by its content, primarily at gas salespeople and those in the industry who lobbied municipalities to adopt gas, not electricity, in their new housing schemes. His emphasis therefore was on offering a thorough rationale for 'the effect on working class life, and of the cost to the landlord and tenant, of installing a "model" gas and coke fuel system'.[117] Leslie wrote in detail, comparing the facility of the GLCC's system with that of more traditional (and by implication, municipal) provision and the remedy it offered to the drudgery faced by working women. He also referred to the Company's research into working-class Londoners' budgets in order to show that Kensal House residents had six shillings a week more to spend on food due to the cheapness of the system.[118] In addition, he took care to assemble a case against the use of electricity, noting,

> When we consider Kensal House alongside other types of fuel installation and their cost, it is seen to prove, not merely that Gas [sic] can offer this full service below present average costs, but also that *only* Gas can do so. It thus offers to the Industry not merely a defensive platform, but a basis for a genuine forward policy.

The GLCC's own brochure, *Kensal House, a Contribution to the new London*, issued under the authorship of the Capitol Housing Association, was less didactic in tone than the BCGA's and more adventurous in design. Whereas the latter was in a traditional format – solid blocks of text, the odd diagram and the occasional photograph – the design of the Association's brochure was intended to evoke the progressive nature of the scheme as a whole. Printed in a mixture of black and white and colour, the text was placed asymmetrically and interspersed with images of the estate, some taken by the avant-garde photographer, Edith Tudor Hart. And while it included the Company's rationale for the gas system, its primary concern was to tell the story of 'why Kensal House was built' and to emphasize the social contribution the scheme made to London.[119]

Booklets and brochures such as these served, as Leslie noted, to demonstrate 'the kind of material Kensal House offers us for fundamental sales work and propaganda in the course of the next few years'.[120] Their audience was, however, not a particularly wide one. A more effective, and subtle, way to begin the process of eliding Kensal House and the gas system with the idea of 'a genuine forward policy' was through advertising. Constant reiteration in the pages of the daily press and specialist journals could bring the message of the GLCC's modernity to an audience which encompassed decision makers to consumers. The Company therefore ran a series of advertisements which linked Kensal House and its gas system with the resolution of particular social problems. One advertisement tied the scheme to the fight for better nutrition, its by-line: 'gas and coke, the complete fuel service for healthy rehousing'. It featured images of the estate's children drinking some of the five extra pints of milk which, the copy declared, the low rents now allowed the tenants to afford.[121] Another, which depicted children entering the nursery school, asserted that the GLCC's tariff could achieve three things: 'it can make better living conditions. It can ease the fuel charge on working-class incomes. It can make London clean. Gas and Coke – Fire without Smoke'.[122] The progressive message of the advertisements was reinforced by their design. In the same house style as the Company's *Kensal House* brochure, they were modern but not aggressively so, something evident in the use of both sans serif and the more traditional serif typefaces.

Suppliers to the gas industry also took advantage of the scheme to promote their wares. In 1938, Ascot Gas Water Heaters Ltd, whose water heaters were used at Kensal House, published a book called *Flats, Municipal and Private Enterprise*.[123] This documented, through plans, photographs and short descriptive texts, a wide range of recently completed British housing schemes. While these all happened to incorporate Ascot's products, the book was also intended to make a more serious point and its editor included a series of articles which argued for the wider application of the technologies such blocks incorporated. He argued, 'the people of England should, in future, be a healthier and more virile race, that is, provided the amenities and facilities that are now being made available to them are used to their advantage'.[124]

The authors of these articles, 'specialists who have something of real value and importance to say regarding various aspects of the [housing] problem', suggest that for Ascot, architectural modernism was the medium through which such a transformation was likely to be achieved. Yerbury of the Architectural Association and the Building Centre contributed an essay about housing on the continent, while Wells Coates contributed 'Notes on Dwellings for To-Morrow' in which he argued for the reorganization of house building on the lines of the motor industry. This series of essays culminated in two on Kensal House, the only scheme to be considered in this detail in the book. One was by Fry, which considered the scheme from a technological point of view. The other was by Denby who wrote on the social programme of the estate. Their chapters were followed by several pages of photographs, plans, and sections of the scheme, again substantially more in number than any other covered in the book. Leslie's *Case for Gas* was also included as an appendix. Such editorial choices were significant. They made the contrast between Kensal House and municipal schemes all the more apparent, and also point to another moment when an industry elided itself with architectural modernism to promote itself.

The most innovative way in which the gas industry sought to raise awareness of Kensal House and the technologies it embodied, however, was through the use of the documentary film. This was a medium with which the industry had identified itself since the early 1930s, its novelty proving one the most effective ways through which it could connote its modernity.[125] While the ultimate purpose of this was to increase sales, like Kensal House, the films need not have been quite as radical as they were. The choice of the films' subject matter, and their direction by pioneers such as John Grierson, Basil Wright, Edgar Anstey and Frank Sainsbury, reflected Leslie's view that there was an element of 'personal bonus' in the industry's film patronage. He described it as 'a contribution towards lifting us out of the morass of poverty in which so many were floundering'.[126]

Leslie's concern is evident in the use of Kensal House in the industry's films. In an early instance of its use as a signifier of the future, the scheme had made its first appearance in the 1935 documentary *Housing Problems*. Following on from the testimonies of former slum-dwellers, described in Chapter 4, it was featured in a sequence which showed the sort of new homes in which they might one day live. The narrator introduced this section with the observation that 'a great deal of thought from architects, engineers and other experts has gone into the design of dwellings for rehousing', a near perfect description of the process which had made Kensal House.

It is not surprising that the BCGA should have elected to complete the 'story' begun in *Housing Problems* by commissioning a documentary about Kensal House. Released in the summer of 1937, *Kensal House* was, on the surface, a very straightforward piece of film making. Twenty minutes long, its task, like the brochures and booklets discussed above, was to tell the story of the estate and convey how cheap it was to live there because it was powered by gas. But, like the estate itself, the content of the film was more complex and the commercial message was overlain with a more profound one. In its direction the film was a carefully composed attempt to mirror the way the estate was conceived and managed. There is no voice-over by a well-spoken unseen narrator, nor any surveillant tracking shots of the tenants. Instead, the viewer sees and hears all those involved in the project: the GLCC, Denby, Fry and individual tenants, all of whom are named. It is they who provide the voice-overs and, continuing the tradition begun in *Housing Problem*s, they all speak directly to camera.

The film opens with David Milne Watson introducing the idea of the gas 'system' and describing the recruitment of 'a group of first rate architects, Max Fry as executant, Miss Elizabeth Denby as specialist consultant' to design the estate. He then hands over the narration to the tenants for, as he comments 'they know more about what life at Kensal House is all about'. The majority of the rest of the film then cuts between scenes of estate life, the commentary offered by the tenants and a description of the design and management of the estate by Fry and Denby. The closing section of film reverts to the GLCC's representatives. Robert Foot explains how cheap the scheme is to run and various charts are shown of comparative tariffs. The camera then pans out over the roofs of Kensal House – showing how clean they were thanks to the use of smokeless fuel – and the film ends.

In the same quarter that *Kensal House* was released, two other BCGA-sponsored films went on show: *Children at School* and *The Smoke Menace*.[127] This was no coincidence. The former was a manifesto for nursery schools while the latter was an exposition of the pollution caused by the smoke from untreated coal. Kensal House, of course, offered a remedy to both these problems. If seen as part of a show reel at an exhibition, or shown to a film group, the cumulative effect of these three films would, at the very least, have ensured in a viewer's mind the equation of the gas industry with social welfare and social progress.[128]

The fact that the *Kensal House* film represented the resolution of a story first begun by *Housing Problems* and the careful scheduling of film releases, points to the sophistication of the gas industry's publicity machine. Under the leadership of Leslie and the BCGA, a thoroughly planned campaign was conducted to advertise the scheme which was consistent in its content and progressive in its form. Though primarily targeted at the promotion of gas, such techniques also had the effect of naturalizing the radical architecture and praxis of Kensal House through its reiteration in diverse media. In such a way, modernism could start to appear to be a part of everyday life.

Intersecting narratives

The gas industry was not alone in its recognition of the propaganda value of Kensal House. Indeed it would be adopted by progressives in many other fields and absorbed into their campaigns. For a group like the Nursery School Association, its advent would be welcomed as the embodiment of its crusade to include nursery schools on all new housing estates that it had been conducting since the early 1930s. Within months of the scheme's opening, Phoebe Cusden would feature it in her book *The English Nursery School*, describing it as 'an attractive example of planning to provide on a restricted area the essential features of a good nursery school'. She also included several photographs of the school.[129]

For New Feminists like Margery Spring Rice, Kensal House represented the sort of re-formed housing she advocated as one of the strategies to improve the poor state of health among the nation's working women which she documented in her book *Working-Class Wives*. Not only did the scheme incorporate labour-saving plans and equipment but it was also a corrective to what she observed was the lamentable government policy of building cottage estates rather than flats which she believed inhibited the development of community life. Cottages, she fulminated, 'occupied space that might otherwise have been … laid out in ornamental gardens, playing grounds, swimming pools, and all sorts of workshops, recreational and domestic for women as well as men and children'.[130] The allusion to Kensal House was made clear by her inclusion of a photographic plate of the interior of the First Feathers Club in the book. The fact that such views were disseminated in the popular paperback format of a Pelican edition further ensured Kensal House's entry into wider discourses of reform.

For Denby's peers in the voluntary housing sector, Kensal House represented the fulfilment of their work. The editor of *The Phoenix*, journal of the Fulham Housing Association and the KHT, for example, wrote of how 'architecturally and financially, these flats are immensely interesting to those of us who have been striving for years to discover the ideal'. Echoing Spring Rice's exhortations, she also singled out the Tenants' Committee and Feathers Club as likely 'to make for a permanent happiness and homeliness on the estate'.[131]

A rather different use of Kensal House may be found in the propaganda work of the National Smoke Abatement Society which campaigned for the use of smokeless fuels in order to bring clean air to Britain's cities. Its 1937 pamphlet, 'Britain's Burning Shame', described the daily grind of washing and cleaning faced by the housewife who lived in the smoky atmosphere of the city.[132] The reader was then presented with an alternative: 'Cleanliness House'. Described as 'an experiment in clean living, a block of smokeless working-class flats in London', this was, of course, Kensal House. In an echo of the techniques of the Kensal House film, the following pages were then given over to its women tenants. They testified to the reduction of labour that resulted from an environment in which 'every family warms its home, cooks its food and heats its water *by smokeless fuel*'. Mrs Tully declared 'My washing doesn't take me half as long' while Mrs Homans' exhortation 'give your children clean air at home' was a reminder of the ultimate aim of such reforms: a better future for the nation.

It would not just be campaigners against the smoke menace or New Feminists who used Kensal House to embody the reforms they advocated. This process may also be traced in the rhetorical purposes to which members of the British movement put the scheme. The sophistication of this use reflected the growing confidence of a movement which now had several years of building work under its belt and had benefited tremendously from its cohesion into the MARS Group and its association with CIAM and the Housing Centre. For these men and women, Kensal House would come to stand as a sign of the culmination of a decade's work, as a definitive statement of what a British modernism could be, and of the movement's right to assume leadership of the profession.

The architects' response

As a landmark building for the British movement, Kensal House received wide press coverage. *The Architect and Building News*, the *Architects' Journal*, *The Architectural Review*, *The Builder* and *Design and Construction* all reported on the estate's opening.[133] Of particular significance was the fact that the scheme was covered in the *Journal of the Royal Institute of British Architects*. Its seven-page article was a sign that the architectural establishment was beginning to acknowledge, and perhaps even accept, the modernist cause.[134] In a further sign of the broadening territory the cause was reaching, the scheme was also reported in the July 1937 issue of the American *Architectural Record*.[135]

Most of the articles on Kensal House were descriptive and extensively illustrated, their authors confident that by this date modernist buildings could be left to speak for themselves through the medium of the photograph. It was left to Summerson's *Architect and Building News* to take a more polemical tone. He would feature the scheme in two consecutive issues; the first had its picture on the cover. For the *News*, Kensal House was 'the latest and by far the most important contribution to the development of working-class housing in London',[136] and it is clear that the reporter understood the modernist-voluntarist ambition it embodied when he wrote:

> Mr Maxwell Fry's truly admirable design shows that 'housing' can mean more than the accommodation of a given number of people on a given area of land according to a given building code. In Kensal House, with its nursery school, and its playground cleverly accommodated within the hollow O of an ancient gas-holder, the modern spirit of urbanism is thoroughly alive.[137]

From the more ephemeral pages of the journal, Kensal House would soon be translated into more permanent forms of propaganda. Hastings' Architectural Press would play a central part in this process, absorbing the scheme into a canon of buildings included in the many books which it published on modern architecture and design. Typical of these was Yorke and Gibberd's *The Modern Flat*, published in November 1937. The complement to Yorke's 1934 book *The Modern House*, it likewise combined a polemical essay on the necessity for a new form of domestic architecture with a catalogue raisonné of exemplary projects from across Europe and North America. One significant difference between the two books, however, was in the way in which British work was treated. The earlier text grouped all of this together towards the end of the book, an organizing principle which was intended, perhaps, to suggest the European basis on which the national movement was founded and from which it would develop. In the 1937 book, there is no such obvious categorization. Rather they are arranged in an apparently random sequence: the plates open with a Dutch project followed by an English project followed by a German one.[138] This intermingling of examples was, however, not accidental and may have been intended to signal that the British movement now stood on an equal footing with its European counterparts, its response to the problem of the dwelling as valid as theirs.

The treatment of the British low-rental flats the book considered is also noteworthy. Testimony to the propaganda efforts of the modernist-voluntarists, the three schemes included in this category were Sassoon House, Kent House and Kensal House.[139] In a reiteration of the evaluation by Bertram with which this chapter opened, Yorke and Gibberd placed Kensal House at the forefront of radical praxis in workers' housing, according it four pages as opposed to the two pages given to its predecessors. They also, uniquely, arranged the two schemes by Denby and Fry in sequence, perhaps to further emphasize the particular efficacy of these prototypes. Through such editorial devices, Kensal House became the standard-bearer for the Modern (workers') Flat.

New Architecture

The culmination of Kensal House's role as the movement's standard-bearer came in the MARS Group's show, 'New Architecture, an Exhibition of the elements of modern architecture', which opened at the New Burlington Galleries in the West End of London in

January 1938. The exact nature and purpose of the exhibition had been a matter for prolonged debate among MARS' members but they had finally agreed that its main goal should be to win its audience's 'loyalty to the cause of modern architecture'.[140] They decided that the most effective way to achieve this was to demonstrate the necessity and inevitability of the new architecture through reference to tradition. The exhibition was therefore organized around the Vitruvian principles, as re-worked by the Englishman Sir Henry Wootton, that 'The end of architecture is to build well. Well building hath three conditions: commoditie, firmenes and delight'. Echoing Wootton's paraphrase, MARS interpreted each condition in the light of the contemporary situation, thereby linking the group to another revolutionary period in architecture, the English Renaissance.

On entering the exhibition, visitors went first into a small hall. Dominated by a huge photomontage which juxtaposed an English park with a view of London's Oxford Street, the catalogue declared:

> This is what we, our fathers and grandfathers have done to England. This is the product of a century of progress. The mischief is done. The monstrous town enmeshes our life and wealth. We regret, we condemn. But what can we do?[141]

The answer was to 'establish a new standard of integrity and realism in architecture, so that as we rebuild we recreate'. The basis on which this would take place was Wootton's principles, each of which was explored in turn in the displays which followed.

The first gallery of the exhibition was devoted to 'commoditie'. Interpreted as referring to present-day building needs, the displays considered, in good CIAM fashion, habitation, work, community, transport and town planning, with examples of modern buildings which met these needs. On exiting this room, visitors went next into a corridor where 'firmenes' was considered. This comprised 'a survey of the contribution of the scientist, the engineer and the manufacturer to structural technique'. In the last room, commoditie and firmenes reached their synthesis in 'delight', 'set forth in a review of the achievements of the modern movement'. This featured a model living room, children's room and garden. Panels and screens displayed photographs of modern buildings and a series of models was also included. The aim here was to demonstrate that 'the modern architect's aim is not to create a "style" but to pursue a realistic unity of form and purpose … Modern architecture is universal, infinitely adaptable'.

The moment of synthesis in 'delight' was reiterated in the exhibition's 'Epilogue'. This, as *The Architectural Review* observed, was the site where 'the exhibition frankly admits its propaganda purpose and demands the cooperation of the visitor in the bringing about of the new world that he has been introduced to'.[142] In a narrow corridor, two sets of panels were placed opposite each other. One set depicted a cross-section of the public – businessmen, housewives, week-enders, doctors, teachers, industrial workers – which represented those from whom co-operation was demanded. This faced a set of panels, entitled 'Historical Analogy', each of which depicted a different period in British history through an image of a building 'typical in kind as well as design'. The display was therefore at once a summary of the progress towards this new world and, in its final image, a sign of what form that world should take.

That image would be the last thing visitors saw when they left the exhibition; the memory of which would linger and convince them to support the cause or not. The choice of that building was therefore of immense significance. It needed to demonstrate how far the movement had come, the basis on which it could grow, and the territories it could, in time, occupy. In January 1938 only one building could fulfil this brief. In its synthesis of the technological, the social, the spatial and the formal, Kensal House stood for all the British movement wished architecture and its practice to be. In addition, as the Epilogue's explanatory panel declared, this synthesis also marked the onset of something new (Fig. 5.18):

Figure 5.18
Epilogue panel at the MARS Exhibition, 1938

> Many times in history architecture has been re-fashioned.
> Style gives birth to style.
> This is the only living continuity.
> To-day we recognise the beginning of a new phase in the English tradition.[143]

Part 3

Towards a new Britain

Part 3

Introduction

The New Architecture exhibition marked the penultimate moment in the evolution of rhetorical modernism. By the end of 1938, when the Finsbury Health Centre had been opened, this phase in the development of the British movement can be said to have been completed. As the discussion in Part 2 has shown, in a period of just over five years, Fry, Coates and their co-conspirators had, through their command of the persuasive discourses of the exhibition, article, building, and, latterly, film, succeeded in advancing the modernist cause in two arenas. First, they had continued to expand their inroads into British architectural culture, something signalled by the growing critical mass of the MARS Group which culminated in the exhibition of January 1938. Second, and of more significance for the longer term advancement of the movement, they had achieved a substantial presence within the progressive tradition through the liaisons formed with organizations such as the Housing Centre and reformers like Dr Katial and the Pritchards.

Yet, as the Epilogue panel's reference to a new phase in the English tradition suggests, there was also the sense that in achieving these advances, Fry's generation had left other aspects of the development of a British architectural modernism untouched. As Fry himself acknowledged in an article on the exhibition, 'We are only at the beginning of a new architecture. What will be its final forms we do not know.'[1]

Fry's question forms the starting point for the concluding chapter of *Reforming Britain*. It considers the emergence into the British movement of a new generation of activists for the modernist cause: those who, in seeking to resolve Fry's conundrum, would develop the new methods of practice and new architectural propositions which would complete the process of translating rhetoric into reality. Although this work was put on hold by the outbreak of war in September 1939, the combination of their efforts with the groundwork laid by the older generation would ensure that when talks about physical reconstruction began, architectural modernism would be the narrative of reform to which politicians turned.

Chapter 6

A living contemporary architecture

> Let's get one thing clear: the '30s and the '40s are not separate things –
> they dovetail.
>
> Erno Goldfinger (1980)[1]

In August 1938 a new set of protagonists announced its entry into the British move-ment. Infuriated by 'a civilisation whose leaders, whose ideals, whose culture had failed', and recognizing that 'the student in our profession to-day holds a greater responsibility than in all past history', these young men and women of London's Archi-tectural Association (AA) were the leaders of a revolution against outmoded methods of teaching and practice.[2] Pursued in the common room, the studio and the pages of their own radical journal, *Focus*, their campaign would ultimately transform both the move-ment and the profession, and secure modernism's domination over British spatial culture.

Earlier in 1938, these students had already begun the process of making a space for themselves in the movement. In February, the *Architectural Association Journal* had published their review of MARS' New Architecture exhibition under the collective authorship of the unit to which most belonged, Unit 15.[3] As much a manifesto as a critique, the article gave the first public indications of their willingness to assume the modernist mantle from Fry's generation, as well as the preoccupations, influenced by the communism many of them espoused, which they would bring to the cause. Thus, its content has much to tell us about the final narratives of modernity which would constitute British architectural modernism by the late 1930s.

The authors were careful to begin with a nod to their elders. They therefore acknowledged the importance of the exhibition as 'the first public statement of its kind by the progressive English architects', also noting the 'obvious sincerity of its inten-tions'.[4] This was to be, however, the only positive statement in a review whose over-riding tone was one of profound disappointment at an opportunity lost. In what was, in all likelihood, the first time the principles of historical materialism were applied to an article published in the AA's *Journal*, Unit 15 pointed to what it said was the central failing of the exhibition. This was the lack of rationale which its creators offered to its audience for the emergence of the new architecture. The students lamented the fact there was little reference to the 'historical situation out of which it grew', nor any attempt to trace 'the various influences, economic, social, and aesthetic, which have governed its development' (386). This was a profound and damaging oversight, they argued, for it meant that visitors would leave the exhibition unable 'to distinguish broadly between the sincere contemporary buildings and the merely meretricious' (386).

Unit 15 centred its critique of this oversight on the section 'firmenes', and the 'inadequate treatment' it gave to the matter of technique (386). The students argued that since new technologies were the primary cause of the 'revolutionary changes' which had happened in architecture since the nineteenth century, then

> by omitting to deal with the historical process since the Industrial Revolution which has gone to make up what we might call our contemporary consciousness, MARS failed to make clear why the 'new movement' has certain formal qualities essentially different from the architecture of previous ages, or from the greater part of the architecture produced in England to-day (386–7).

The lack of consideration given to technique led in turn to another problem. It gave the impression that 'modern architecture is a static affair'. For, the unit wrote, in giving

> no indication of the inter-relation of society, technique and architecture as a constantly moving and changing affair … not only was it not made clear how modern architecture arrived at its present stage of development, but it was not clearly shown how it would develop beyond its present stage (387).

The exhibition therefore lacked any sense of the imperative nature of the new architecture. Rather, the students mused, it was as if the MARS Group merely hoped that it might be applied on a wider scale.

It was this tentative tone that most irked the members of Unit 15. It was caused, it contended, by the Group's reluctance to engage with the political aspect of architecture and recognize 'the obstacles to the proper development of technique inherent in an anachronistic social system' (387). As long as 'profits or destruction are the end of the greater part of scientific knowledge', it was unlikely that the potential for technique to satisfy 'to-day's immense building needs' would be realized. By refusing to face that problem, MARS, the students declared, 'was forced to escape into formalism' (387–8). This resulted in an exhibition where, 'in an atmosphere of flippancy more appropriate to the display of "Daks" than of modern architecture … content … was submerged into form, and the form seemed to explain nothing' (388).[5] The students therefore concluded the review with a warning:

> One realised the dangers to which the new architecture is exposed as soon as it forgets its social responsibilities and starts playing parlour games, the

dangers of becoming divorced from social reality like so many so-called progressive arts of to-day, and retiring to the intellectual haven of a group existence (388).

In seeking to make their point, the students' review necessarily offered a somewhat caricatured account of the exhibition. Nevertheless, their critique did point to the obstacles which the movement itself needed to overcome if modernism were to become the permanent solution to the immense building needs of the day. This reflected the fact that Fry's generation had focused its energies primarily on the creation of demand, something achieved by bringing 'the talkative intellectuals' round to the modernist cause through a muted politics and an emphasis on the rhetoric of form.[6] The task to which the new generation applied itself was the more structural and long-term one of creating the supply of architects who could design the buildings to meet the call for a modernist architecture.

Who were these students? As they proudly declared, 'we were born in the war'.[7] They were therefore between ten and twenty years younger than Fry's generation. Their education at the Architectural Association, the leading school of its day, thus coincided with the era of rhetorical modernism. Unit 15, led by tutor Cyril Mardall (then Sjostrom), counted among its members many who would make their name in the post-war era. It included Anthony Pott and F. L. Sturrock, who entered the AA in 1932; A. J. Brandt, Elizabeth Chesterton, Anthony Cox and R. V. Crowe (1933); Peter Cocke, David Gladstone, Richard Llewellyn Davies and John Wheeler (1934). A little behind them came the members of another significant unit, Max Lock's Unit 11, who included Tim Bennett, David Medd and Bruce Martin (1936), Leo de Syllas and Oliver Cox (1937). There were countless others. Together, they formed part of a wave of student and tutor activism that would transform Britain's architectural schools.

Education was a matter to which the MARS Group had paid relatively little attention.[8] It had failed to realize that to reform architectural education was to secure the movement's longevity. Yet if there were ever a moment when attention to training held the prospect of achieving real change, it was the 1930s. That decade saw the culmination of the efforts to professionalize architectural practice which had begun in the 1860s and were ratified in two registration acts (1931 and 1938) which limited the use of the title 'architect' to those who had passed the examinations regulated by the RIBA.[9] This process was paralleled by the slow displacement of training under the pupillage system by academic training in schools of architecture: a process in which the AA played a significant part. There, as elsewhere, this shift to the academic was signified by the adoption of the French *Beaux-Arts* system of education which, in contrast to the empirical orientation of pupillage, was more theoretical in emphasis. Under the French method the architect's metier now became to produce drawings and coordinate work, not to be directly involved in the crafts or structural side of architecture.[10]

The legislation of 1931 and 1938 meant that participation in a regulated education system in an RIBA-recognized architectural school, and the successful acquisition of degree and diploma, would constitute the education of the future Registered Architect. It was, perhaps, the communist roots of the new generation which made them realize what this shift to professionalized practice meant for the British movement.

If its advocates could gain control of the means of production – making architects – they could change the nature of the profession through a steady supply of modernists into its ranks.[11]

This concluding chapter begins, therefore, with a discussion of the onset of this fundamental transition in the British profession. Taking as its focus the tumultuous series of events which unfolded at the AA between 1933 and 1939, it considers the process through which the hitherto dominant *Beaux-Arts* method of training began to be superseded by a curriculum based on modernist principles.[12]

Attention then turns to an analysis of the content of this curriculum. Taking two sets of AA students' work as exemplars, the discussion will show how new methods of training would achieve not just a change in the constitution of the profession, but also in the sort of modernism its members would practise. The first project to be discussed is Unit 15's 'Town Plan, for a site in Berkshire'; the second is Unit 11's 'Ocean Street Area' project of 1939. In building type, design process and ambition, each offered a significant expansion of the modernism practised by the MARS generation, although, as we shall see, they owed much to the example of Denby and Fry and Tecton. Their programmes generated by research, their architecture designed by group work, these were schemes whose purpose was to train architects for a world where large-scale 'public' socially-oriented projects (whether state-instigated or originating from some mix of state and private or voluntary effort) would prevail. For those born in the war, the future of the profession lay not in genteel private practice, as it had for the members of MARS, but at the forefront of social engagement. The modern(ist) architect would be an office-based professional who worked for the common good.

The combination of the narratives of modernity created by the MARS generation with those of the *Focus* generation – their synthesis of supply and demand – would bring to fruition the project begun by Fry and Coates in the late 1920s. This new phase in the English tradition would give form to the post-war world. The first steps towards its evolution were taken at the drawing boards of the AA.

The AA in the early 1930s

Since its foundation in 1847 as a meeting place and informal academy for architects in pupillage, London's Architectural Association had established itself at the forefront of the development of academic training in the discipline.[13] By the early 1930s, however, when the generation that became Units 15 and 11 entered the School, there was the sense that it was an institution somewhat at odds with itself: uncertain of its direction in a world where architecture and society were changing rapidly.

The dominant figure in the Association at this time was its Principal and Director of Education, Howard Robertson.[14] Appointed in 1920, he had presided over the institution of a curriculum based on the classical principles of the *Beaux-Arts* system. By the early 1930s, influenced by the investigations into contemporary building in northern Europe which he and the School's Secretary, Francis Yerbury, had undertaken, he had begun to instigate some minor changes to the course. Less emphasis was placed on the classical, and Robertson would show students European work to expound *Beaux-Arts* principles.[15] Soon Dutch and Scandinavian motifs found their way into students' projects.[16]

Although these shifts represented a turn towards the modern, that they reflected a stylistic preference, rather than a change in ethos, becomes clear from the outline curriculum included in the School's *Prospectus* for 1931–2. A description of teaching methods stressed that these were based 'on the setting out of definite problems embodying construction, function, expression, decoration, and historical precedent'. The first-year course included 'theory and projection of shadows' and 'analysis of pattern' and measured drawing in London's museums. Much emphasis was placed on the production of *esquisses* (sketches) in 6- or 12-hour sessions in order 'to allow the student an opportunity of expressing his own ideas rapidly and concisely'. In addition, students participated in 'a period of historical research including study of the basis of Post and Lintol [sic] construction including the "orders"'. By second year the students would have progressed to analysis of Roman and Byzantine forms.[17]

The janus-faced nature of education at the AA in this period was further complicated by the growing preference among the students not for the modern work presented to them by Robertson but for the forms and principles of architectural modernism. Awareness of Le Corbusier, whose work Anthony Cox described as 'difficult to justify intellectually but so exciting',[18] and, closer to home, the knowledge that six recent graduates of the AA were now members of a bona fide modernist practice in Tecton, made the contrast between 34–36 Bedford Square and the world outside even more apparent.

That the groundwork for the creation of a system of modernist, rather then quasi-modern, architectural education would ultimately be laid at the AA was due to a number of factors. Caused by the intersection of a series of new appointments to the staff and pressures on the School's governing Council from outside forces, its development was fomented and manipulated by an exceptionally politically motivated and politically sophisticated body of students. By 1939, the Orders would be banished from the curriculum, group work would replace *Beaux-Arts* individualism and, as one of the tutors recalled, 'it [would be] difficult to get the students to spend more than a fifth of their time on the drawing board, four-fifths had to be spent in sociological research'.[19]

The end of the *esquisse*

The first inkling that a profound change in the way the AA was run might be possible came in May 1933. As a sign that Robertson was beginning to loosen his hold on the School he had run for thirteen years, and reflecting his desire to focus more on private practice, an Assistant Director was appointed to work alongside him. The man chosen was E. A. A. Rowse. Before joining the AA he had spent four years as a lecturer at the Edinburgh College of Art, where he established the city's first Department of Civic Design.[20] In the absence of archival material, no reason for his appointment can be stated with certainty.[21] Indeed, he seems a rather curious choice given his decidedly odd character: a student described him as 'impervious to conventional thinking, contemptuous of honours, incapable of compromise'.[22] He also displayed a very non-*Beaux-Arts* commitment to the principles of Patrick Geddes.

The subsequent course of events suggests that it was Rowse's experience in the education of town planners that was the primary reason for his appointment. In

January 1935, he would become the Principal of a sister school to the AA: the School of Planning and Research for National Development (SPRND). The AA's governing Council had taken the decision to found such an institution in spring 1934,[23] reflecting its awareness of the recent wave of town planning legislation and a more optimistic economic climate, and its desire 'to widen the field of influence of its teaching on a national scale'.[24] Its founders hoped that the School would 'succeed in welding the work of the Engineer, the Surveyor, the Architect and the Local Government Official together with that of the Economist, the Sociologist and the Politician into that of the Planner'. Students took a two-year course which led to the award of both the AA Diploma and Associate Membership of the Town Planning Institute.[25] They attended classes that ranged from 'the collection of and distribution of food supplies' and 'hygiene and public health as related to planning' to 'surveying' and 'civics'. Teaching staff included Rowse, Thomas Adams, T. H. Marshall and L. Dudley Stamp, and among the members of the Advisory Board were Raymond Unwin (its Chair), Lord Balfour of Burleigh, Frank Pick and Percy Thomas (the President of the RIBA).[26]

In seeking to create 'a corps of trained men' who would 'ensure happy and ordered development in the place of the chaos which the nineteenth century has left us', the AA Council had demonstrated that, when it chose to, it could innovate and develop new models of education.[27] Despite this, it seemed reluctant to allow Rowse to bring any such changes to the architecture school's curriculum and the semi-modernized *Beaux-Arts* system continued to prevail, even though the students were increasingly frustrated by it. Nearly a year would pass before Rowse would be able to capitalize on the innovations embodied in the SPRND.

In December 1935, Robertson retired from the AA in order to enter private practice full-time. Rather than appoint Rowse in his place, the Council decided to split his job. A new, and superior, position of Director of Education of the School of Architecture was given to architect H. S. Goodhart-Rendel. Rowse was made Principal of the Schools of Architecture and Planning. The two men could not have been more different. Rowse, in Geddesian fashion, saw architecture as part of a wider range of activities. Now that he was freed from Robertson's command, he would encourage students to experiment with methods and practices of design. Goodhart-Rendel, though he has too often been dismissed as reactionary, was neither a modernist nor a planner.[28] It seems likely that his appointment was seen by the Council as a means to control the younger man and perhaps ensure that the methods he fostered in the SPRND stayed there. It did not work.[29]

Galvanized by his new position, Rowse set about transforming the way his students were educated. He thereby laid the basis for the ingress of modernism into the curriculum. Rowse's intention was to replace the individualist preoccupations of the *Beaux Arts* and bring to architectural education the team-led, sociologically based design methods he had introduced at the SPRND and which he had learnt from his mentor Geddes.[30] In the spring of 1936 he therefore ended the system of teaching by year and introduced a system of teaching by units: 15 in all across the five-year course, each led by a tutor and with approximately 17 students. Henceforth, staff would be encouraged to give the students live projects and to develop their analytical and group-working skills: enquiry would replace the *esquisse*.

The complement to this was Rowse's emphasis, derived from his interest in Scientific Management, on 'behavioural patterns as the generator of design'.[31] Although this was already a commonplace in kitchen design, the idea that it might form the basis of an entire design system was not. Interpreted both literally – design as anthropometrics – and metaphorically – behavioural patterns as systems of taste and custom – it would have a long-term impact on the design philosophy of the British movement.

Perhaps to Rowse's surprise, the move to the unit system was met not with delight by the students but with shock. This was due, as one of them noted, to the fact that it had not been introduced gradually 'but by the drastic method of changing the whole system of the whole school at the beginning of the Spring Term'.[32] The AA Council was also unimpressed by the move. The consequence was a tumultuous three years during which a battle over the nature of architectural training was conducted around the banner of the unit.

In opposition to the new method stood Goodhart-Rendel and the Council. For it stood Rowse, most of the staff, and the students, who, after the initial shock, realized the benefits of unit teaching and that it meant more individual attention from masters, more constructive criticism, and the freedom to work on their own ideas.[33] It would be they who would fight for the unit system most ardently. Under the leadership of Anthony Cox and Richard Llewellyn Davies, the *Focus* generation was able to structure and manipulate this battle so that its ideological principles would come to underpin the education of architects.

The Yellow Book

Cox and Llewellyn Davies had, in fact, been plotting against the irrelevancies of the AA's curriculum for some time before the events of spring 1936. Cox would later explain that their revolt had started as soon as he, and the group he called 'our gang' (Chesterton, Pott *et al.*), entered the School,[34] and were faced with the prospect of studying the basis of the post and lintel system. 'We felt strongly', he recalled, 'that AA education was useless, hopeless and that the right sort of information, technical, social, historical, was not being taught'. He added, 'so few of the tutors had glimpsed it [the New Jerusalem] that it was a nuisance to have them around the drawing board, sketching in their urns and axes'.[35] As already noted, the impetus for these feelings came partly from their knowledge of changes in the world of architecture: Le Corbusier's work in particular and that of the emerging British movement.[36] It was, however, the political situation which was the underlying cause of their disaffection. For Cox, the decisive moment was 1934 when an awareness of what was going on in Germany saw 'conscious politics, left politics' become a part of his life.[37] This was furthered by the arrival, that same year, of Richard Llewellyn Davies from Cambridge where he had been studying engineering. Described by Unit 11's Bruce Martin as 'a very powerful influence, he ran the whole thing',[38] Llewellyn Davies brought to this disaffected group the networking and political skills derived from his membership of the Apostles and the Communist Party of Great Britain (CPGB). With Cox he would form the nucleus of what is perhaps best understood as a communist cell within the AA which was dedicated to furthering the cause of a new society through the overthrow of the staid *Beaux-Arts* system. Indicating the existence of a political sensibility new to the British movement, Cox recalled that our policy [was that] it was no good just going round preaching revolution, because no-one would listen to us, what we had to do was be very good at our job. We said we'll work in architecture, in the school. It was all, in a peculiar way, muddled up with the potential of modern architecture as a, not a style … but as a social instrument.[39]

Rowse's decision to impose the unit system in spring 1936 provided what can be imagined as a long-awaited opportunity for the cell to act. Its introduction had galvanized the mass of students into political consciousness for the first time; in CPGB terms they were now ripe for exploitation. This metamorphosis would be facilitated by the fact that the new method of teaching had also transformed the way the School was organized. Hitherto, students had been locked into separate years and rarely had the opportunity to meet or speak with those ahead or behind them. The unit system, however, because it operated on a term by term basis, mixed people together. This meant, as Cox put it, '[we were able to] infiltrate that much more easily', a process he was very clear came from their training in Party techniques: 'we knew how to work the system'.[40]

If the unit system was the pre-condition for agitation, it did not necessarily follow that it would teach on modernist principles. In an echo of the modernist-voluntarist union effected by the MARS generation which had created a new praxis of housing, the challenge for the *Focus* generation was to marry the technological preoccupations of modernism to the social content of Rowse's Geddesian-derived process and forge from it a new method of education and practice. During the course of 1936, the cell therefore started to build the framework on which the modernist orientation of the unit system could be secured.

Having 'converted' students to the cause through the infiltration of the units, the next step was to fill the Committee which represented students in the School with their comrades. Following on from this, the Committee then sought to ensure the students' voice could be adequately heard and it secured a system of official meetings between the Student Committee and the staff (and thereby an implicit alliance between the two). This effort culminated in the agreement, in January 1937, that the students could prepare a report on their views of the form their training should take. The preparation of what became known, thanks to the colour of its binding, as 'The Yellow Book' received added impetus the following month when Goodhart-Rendel gave an address on 'Architectural Education' to the students.[41] Its content makes it clear how threatened the *Beaux-Arts* generation felt by new systems of education and how polarized the AA was becoming.

The main theme of Goodhart-Rendel's speech was the problem of how teaching could continue now that the Orders had been expunged, as they recently had been, from the curriculum. He bemoaned the 'absence of a norm; a system of conventions to which the designer can refer'.[42] The *Beaux-Arts* system had provided a solid framework on which preparation for practice could be secured; without it 'students are liable to fall out of architecture into copyism, into stunting, or into irrelevant sociology'. In concluding, and just in case any of his audience were in any doubt about his absolute disapproval of the approach to architecture which now prevailed, he averred:

> At the moment we are in an acutely romantic welter trying to stop the holes in our art with theories, with politics, with general benevolence and with a good deal of (rather bad) engineering.[43]

As this was an address to students, not a speech delivered to a General Meeting, no discussion of, or response to, the speech was allowed. Such disregard for the students' point of view lent the Yellow Book, when it was delivered in June 1937, an additional tone of protest.

The 'Report of Students' Sub-committee on the School System', as it was more correctly known, was intended, noted the anonymous author of 'The AA Story' in *Focus* 3, '[as] the first tentative step to clarify the basis on which a modern school should rest'.[44] In fact, it was far from tentative. Through the parsing of the existing curriculum which comprised the majority of the report, and the signalling of their approval or disapproval of particular aspects of the course, the students offered a definitive statement of what they believed a modernist architectural education should comprise.[45]

The Report makes fascinating reading and it is clear from it that Rowse's system, although it had turned the AA organizationally and attitudinally upside-down, had left much of the *Beaux-Arts* curriculum intact. In content the Book has much in common with the review of the MARS Exhibition of early 1938, making a causal link between new technologies and a new architecture. The students were, therefore, particularly concerned about the School's outdated teaching of construction. In their first two years of study they learnt only the techniques of load-bearing wall construction. It was not until the third year that steel and concrete systems were introduced and even then:

> The main task of the Unit Masters seems to be to prevent the mass of technical information acquired by the student from interfering with the development of his power to design and criticise a building as a whole (92).

The authors therefore looked to the day when frame (timber) construction was taught from first year (90) and when lectures on statics, structure, steel and reinforced concrete were introduced much sooner than at present (91).

The desire to see technology take a much more central role in the curriculum was echoed in the authors' observation of the tendency to compartmentalize different aspects of studio work into 'design', 'construction', 'decoration' rather than see them as part of an integral process of making (91). Decoration, for example, became something 'applied to otherwise finished buildings' and was, in any case, rather dubious; they noted that 'an undue proportion of the course is allotted to this work' (94). The students did, however, approve of the general content of the programmes which they were now given, something where Rowse's influence was most evident. As Anthony Cox later observed, 'Rowse … raised our sights from the building to the community'.[46]

The final part of the Report considered the teaching of history. At present the students felt that this was 'unsatisfactory' (94). Across the three years they studied Egyptian, Greek, Roman, Romanesque and Gothic Architecture, the Italian, French and

English Renaissances and the nineteenth century in England. Starting with more general lectures in first year, the emphasis shifted to historical methods of construction in second and 'more detail' in third year. Since, however, the precise aim of this last set of lectures was not explained, the students declared themselves unable to infer their particular purpose (94). As good Marxists, the Report's authors argued instead for lectures which were based 'on the historical rather than the architectural ... because the social, technical and aesthetic aspects are all interrelated'. They continued, 'what we want to emphasise is that the conditions determining the aesthetic character of a period must be understood before we can understand its art'. In particular, they concluded, study should focus on history since the Industrial Revolution (96).

From such new bases, the students proposed, a modern school of architecture could emerge. This, they likened to

> A laboratory in which each student profits by the successes and failures of experiments both outside and inside the school, and where architecture is regarded as something in development and not a static standard to be achieved.

Only in this way could 'a living, contemporary architecture' emerge (90).

Indicative of the extent to which the *Beaux-Arts* system was a pole around which the British architectural establishment could cohere, rather than stimulating progress the Yellow Book instead induced stasis and resistance. Not helped by the timing of its delivery – the end of the summer term – no formal response from Goodhart-Rendel was ever received. And while its contents were discussed in staff–student committees, it became apparent that tensions between Principal and Director were growing.[47] Matters came to a head in the spring of 1938. First, an attempt was made to bring an end to the practice of group working. Then, a second speech by Goodhart-Rendel, this time to an Association General Meeting, 'foretold an alarming step backward'.[48] Entitled 'The Training of an Architect' it was clearly intended, and clearly understood, as a prelude to the abandonment of the unit system and the return to *Beaux-Arts* principles.[49]

Right from the start of his paper it was clear how wide was the gulf which now separated Goodhart-Rendal from Rowse, most of the staff and the students. 'What,' he asked, 'should the finished product [of training] be?' Not the architect implied in the Yellow Book but 'a man capable of designing and looking after building works and of seeing that his employer pays a price that is fair for what he gets'.[50] He continued by noting that all the principles underlying sound architecture were French and dismissed the students' tendency for 'untimely and time-wasting research' when all the information they needed to design, he felt, ought to be in the programme or able to be covered in a preliminary lecture. His greatest disdain was, however, reserved for group working: 'a little practice in smooth teamwork ... may reasonably be in a school curriculum ... but should never replace individual students tackling the programme alone'.[51] No wonder, as Oliver Cox recalled, 'we all disliked him enormously'.[52]

As this was a General Meeting, discussion was allowed. Llewellyn Davies, representing the Students' Committee, took the floor. In a carefully worded piece of Marxist rhetoric he declared the *Beaux-Arts* system historically obsolete, musing 'to produce a French *Beaux Arts* Architect, the *Beaux-Arts* system was probably almost perfect, but how did it apply in the present time?' He concluded with the observation:

> In considering how to train the architects to-day the vital thing was to remember in what period in history they were working. They were living in a period of profound cultural and social change, and in architecture they were on the verge of a new style which should surpass all the previous ones in strength and human character. Their task was to work out in cooperation the basis of that new style.[53]

Goodhart-Rendel, and the architectural establishment he represented, would not concede. Further trials and tribulations followed until in May 1938, Rowse agreed to resign from the School with immediate effect.[54] If this was not a sufficient blow for the students, it was announced that until a permanent successor could be found, his replacement would be Fernand Billerey, a *Beaux-Arts* man.[55]

It was against this backdrop that the students embarked on a new venture. At a moment when they had lost the man who had introduced the basis for their educational revolution, and the return to *Beaux-Arts* principles seemed imminent with the arrival of Billerey, it was now the time to bring the necessity of the new style to a broader audience. The tool for this would be *Focus*, 'a journal where we can develop our still chaotic ideas on the foundations of those built by certain older men (in age not spirit) … To continue, the widest support is absolutely necessary'.[56]

Focus

Cox recalled that it was Tim Bennett and Leo de Syllas who were the main instigators of *Focus*.[57] In the wake of Goodhart-Rendel's second speech, they had approached the editors of the *Architectural Association Journal* with a request for some pages which could serve as a mouthpiece for the students' opinions. This was forthcoming, but when it transpired that anything they contributed would be subject to editorial veto they decided to try and produce their own journal. They then approached Peter Gregory, the managing director of the publisher Lund Humphries whose offices were on the other side of Bedford Square, with their idea. He was sympathetic, providing funds could be secured. They may have been critical of MARS, but when it came to promoting the cause of modernism generally the new generation looked to their elders for support. They contacted Max Fry and through him won the backing of Captain Fox-Williams of Williams and Williams windows (suppliers of steel fenestration to many a British modernist). This convinced Gregory, and he gave them the go-ahead to produce a quarterly magazine which would be entirely student-run.[58]

Bennett and de Syllas, with the by now graduated Anthony Cox as back-up and main contributor, would produce four issues of *Focus* between summer 1938 and summer 1939.[59] Mindful that the medium was the message, every issue was a carefully designed and beautifully presented object. Quarto in size and bound with the latest plastic spiral binding (in keeping with their commitment to new technologies), each had a striking cover design, the first by Cox's younger brother Oliver, then in his first year at the AA. Together these slim volumes form a remarkable body of evidence about British modernist sensibilities and abilities by the end of the 1930s.

Contributors included Le Corbusier, Siegfried Giedion, Walter Gropius and Max Fry. Subjects ranged from analyses of recent buildings and book reviews to discussions of economics and rent strikes. There was also, as might be expected, a strong emphasis on education. *Focus* 1 contained a riposte from Anthony Cox to Goodhart-Rendel's first speech (in the same issue which included Le Corbusier's musings on 'If I had to teach you architecture') and reports were encouraged from other students across the country. Extensive coverage was given to events at the AA and large sections of *Focus* 3, as already noted, were devoted to documenting the tumultuous events of 1936 to 1939.

With an initial print run of approximately 500 for *Focus* 1 and 1,500 for *Focus* 4, the editors' intention was surely to spread the AA message further and convert others. Such unsentimental purposefulness is testament to the systematic approach this younger generation brought to the promulgation of modernism. The gentlemanly contingency of the MARS Group was giving way to a thoroughly professional mode of operating. The single-mindedness given to the production of *Focus* and, indeed, all the campaigns at the AA in this period becomes apparent in this letter written by Cox to the planner-architect Max Lock, by then Head of the Hull School of Architecture, in December 1940. In it he discussed the failure to produce a fifth issue of *Focus* and how the cause might yet be continued despite the war. He wrote, 'we were just getting into the position of being able to see the immediate practical possibility of injecting younger and more progressive teachers into schools' when war was declared but, he continued,

> there is one thing that we can do – or rather, that perhaps you at Hull, as the secretariat of NASA [Northern Architecture Students Association] can do. It is this, plan a magazine that will keep things alive amongst the <u>students</u> in all the schools – make NASA into a kind of architectural vigilance association for education … If you have real contacts with the schools you might be able to make such an organisation a really useful fifth column, and a medium for keeping alive the rigorous thought in the schools that the oppression of war and the heavy hand of Authority is now blunting.[60]

The creation of *Focus* had come at what must have seemed the darkest moment of the students' campaign but, as the author of 'The AA Story' would recount, things did not turn out quite as expected. In July 1938 at the end-of-year dance, 'in an atmosphere of real fantasy', it was announced that the unit system would continue.[61] Then, when students returned to the School in October they were greeted with the news that Goodhart-Rendel had resigned. By January 1939 the decision had been taken to merge the post of Principal and Director back into one post and Geoffrey Jellicoe, a benign but nevertheless committed modernist, was appointed to this position. His inaugural address the following month indicated that henceforth things would operate on a more even keel. In a speech which was conciliatory but even-handed, he reported that he had read the Yellow Book and felt it a 'fair contribution'. He also felt that at the AA 'lots of things are done fairly well' but that the students were 'dissipating knowledge, learning too many things'. His immediate concern, however, was not to rush into the formulation of a new curriculum but to bide his time and seek help from an Advisory Panel to which he had appointed, among others, Anthony Cox.[62] In February

1939, therefore, prospects seemed good for these emissaries of educational revolution. For with the unit system retained, the path towards a living, contemporary architecture was set.

Realization

Innovations in architectural training were, then, one step towards the development of such an architecture. But they offered no prescription for its form or content, only (though significantly) the conditions in which they might be generated. If a complete architectural system were to evolve, one capable of meeting the immense building needs of the day or, as it turned out, the challenge of Britain's post-war reconstruction, then progressive modes of practice needed to be applied to advanced programmes and expressed in modern forms. The first attempts to achieve this synthesis are the subject of the final part of this chapter. It focuses on an analysis of two of the early products of the unit system: 'Town Plan' and the Ocean Street Area slum clearance scheme. The discussion will show how the younger generation brought together key aspects of the technique and praxis developed by the rhetorical modernists with a new set of architectural preoccupations derived from Rowse and informed by an acute political sensibility. The result was, in embryo, the modernism which would shape the post-war world.

The first project to be discussed is 'Town Plan', also known as 'Tomorrow Town', a renaming much disliked by Rowse.[63] This originated as a pre-thesis (fourth year) project by Unit 12, whose members included Elizabeth Chesterton, Anthony Cox, and Richard Llewellyn Davies, in the academic year 1936–7. It was presciently, if awkwardly, entitled, 'A plan for a town for 50,000 inhabitants for 1950 for a hypothetical flat site'. During 1937–8, the same students, now in Unit 15, re-worked the scheme as a thesis (Diploma) project, this time for a real site, a village in rural Berkshire.

Given that the project was created by the students who had been most vocal in their criticisms of the AA's method of training, and that they were given considerable support and encouragement from Rowse throughout the design process,[64] that 'Town Plan' was a highly polemical scheme is hardly surprising. Nevertheless, this was not polemic for its own sake. What makes the project so remarkable is the fact that at the same time that it constituted a noisy riposte to the individualistic, drawing-fixated *Beaux-Arts* system, the project offered a rational, carefully researched and professionally presented solution to the problem of the modern city.

'Town Plan'

To contemporaries, the polemical nature of 'Town Plan' would have been most evident in its subject matter. To elect to design a town was in contradistinction to *Beaux-Arts* educational principles. As Goodhart-Rendel had made so clear, that system was based on individual effort, measured by a student's progress through ever more complex projects with ever more difficult programmes. And while this might allow, at thesis level, a student to tackle a civic space as well as a major public building, to design a town was beyond an individual's scope. To choose, therefore, a project that necessitated collective enterprise was at once to demonstrate the (perceived) weakness of the *Beaux-Arts* method and to signal where, and how, modern architects' efforts should, instead, be directed.

Then there was the matter of the sort of town the students had imagined. They envisaged a town built for a population of 50,000, which number, they stated, experts agreed was the smallest able to maintain an independent existence.[65] Their client was the Co-operative movement. Having decided to relocate and concentrate many of its industrial activities on one site, it had bought a large area of land, close to transport facilities, on which to build factories and housing for its workers. Working from this basic set of conditions Unit 12 then developed a programme which, in a manner akin to Kensal House, drew on nearly every narrative of progress created by their elders. The result was a modernist utopia.

Here, the inhabitants worked a standard five-day week with a seven-hour day. At a time when paid holidays were a new phenomenon, they enjoyed a fortnight's worth each year. Pensions were received from the age of 55, there was equality of pay between the sexes and a comprehensive system of social services. Health services would be both curative and preventive, with centres attached to neighbourhood clubs on the model of the Pioneer Health Centre. A general hospital would be located outside the town. The provision for education was equally progressive. Nursery schools would be universal while elementary and at least part-time secondary education was compulsory. It was also intended that a technical school and combined agricultural college with experimental farm would be built. The latter was linked to the agricultural belt which would surround the town and supply it with vegetables and dairy goods. The Co-operative movement would, naturally, provide the central store and neighbourhood branches which sold all other necessary household supplies.

The living and recreation needs of the population were seen as integrated. Neighbourhood units would contain housing, schools, clubs, clinics, shops, restaurants and recreational facilities for the inhabitants. The housing itself was to be provided by the Co-operative movement, which would be 'landlord, architect and builder', with the individual given as much choice as possible among the different type of housing available. This was considerable, and combined detached or semi-detached houses, terraced houses and high flats. The final elements of the town were the industrial areas, which comprised factories, warehouses and service plants, and the central civic area. This contained the town's main commercial, administrative and recreational buildings: library, theatre and concert hall and a cinema, *inter alia*.

If the programme of the city was ambitious, so too was the method by which it was designed. Here the students drew directly from Rowse's method of group working. For both the pre-thesis and thesis schemes each student was assigned to either the Housing Group or Town Planning Group.[66] They were also given a different research topic, area of the town and building to work on, and required to produce the appropriate amount of drawings, models and supporting documentation.[67] When necessary, students also turned to outside experts for help. Cocke mentions that Dr Radford, the Medical Officer of Health for St Pancras, gave particularly valuable assistance.

The absolute seriousness with which the students undertook the research, as well as the design process, is evident in the detailed pages of notes on health services, divided into health centres, clinical services and hospitals, among Cox's papers. It can also be inferred from the references to numerous drafts of the final reports the students produced for each phase of 'Town Plan', as well as the extensive use of scientific data to support decisions made in the design process, such as the positioning of buildings in order to avoid overshadowing. This attention to process was, in student work at least, new for this date and was intended, like the town's programme, to be a prescription for practice henceforth.

These efforts were realized first of all in the pre-thesis project of a plan for a hypothetical site (Fig. 6.1). This was very much a preliminary planning exercise executed to work out the basic factors which governed the form of the town. At this stage, therefore, the students' primary preoccupation was with the organization of the two main activities of the population – living and working – to achieve maximum health and amenity. Factors which would, in reality, have limited this, such as a real site or finance, were put to one side for the time being. The plan was therefore a rectilinear exercise in zoning. It placed the administrative area in the centre and flanked it with residential zones of flats and terraced houses interspersed with schools, creches and garages. The placing of a railway line across the top of the 'site' allowed these zones to be separated from the town's main arterial road and the industrial area.

As evidence of the students' command of the process of town planning per se, and the modernist principles of zoning in particular, this first plan is of interest, but it is its reworking for thesis level which is of most significance in the context of this discussion. For, following what Cocke described as a 'post mortem' of the scheme and further

Figure 6.1
Unit 12 of the
Architectural
Association, 'A Plan
for a Town for
50,000 Inhabitants
for 1950', 1936–7

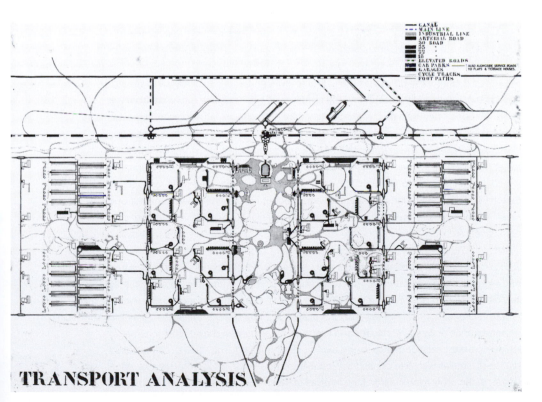

193

consultation with Rowse,[68] the students, now in Unit 15, decided to pursue the scheme at thesis level and apply the programme they had developed to a real site. In so doing they would produce the post-war New Town in all but name.

At this distance, it is impossible to know whether the members of Unit 15, as they embarked upon their thesis project, did so with the precise intention of designing a consensus about the re-formed city from a set of still disparate progressive architectural narratives. Yet this is what they did. That it was a likely aim was already evident in their choice of programme. A proto-welfare state, it is only the students' choice of a private, though social client, which dates it to a decade when, as already noted, it was still undecided whether the state or the voluntary sector should be the primary provider of social services. The political sensibility of the students too, evident in Cox's call for a modernist fifth column in wartime architectural schools, suggests a level of strategic awareness which would have seen the advantage, indeed the necessity, of bringing together seemingly opposed positions in order to ensure the prospect of change.

The first instance of hybridization came with the choice of the site on which the new town would be built. Here they favoured the model of the satellite town advocated by the garden city movement, selecting the village of Faringdon in Berkshire as their location. One of the Home Counties which encircled London, the county was typical of the regions which, after 1946, would be chosen to house the capital's over-spill population. Although the Unit's decision was contrary to prevailing modernist orthodoxy – the MARS Group was then planning to redevelop London as a linear city not to bypass it altogether – it was a canny one.[69] The command held over planning discourse by the GCTPA by the late 1930s would have suggested to most contemporaries that the state would ultimately favour a model of urban renewal primarily through the garden city rather than the urban village.[70]

Less controversial was the students' adherence to the principles of zoning, a practice common to the GCTPA and the modernists. Likewise their deployment of the neighbourhood unit was a new concept shared by both groups.[71] There was, however, one area in which Unit 15 departed from such overt conciliation with the garden city movement. Rejecting the low density, neo-Georgian model of housing developed by Parker and Unwin, for their satellite town the students proposed that the inhabitants should live in a mixture of high flats and houses (terraced, detached and semi-detached). These would be prefabricated and erected on site, the flats by means of a travelling gantry,[72] and built at the (then) high densities of 52 per acre and 26 per acre respectively.[73]

Typologically and technologically such proposals went against all the GCTPA held dear. In its restatement of aims, issued in 1937, it had specifically noted that 'high flats and tenements … [provide] an environment entirely unsuited to family life'.[74] Despite their advocacy of the flat the students' plans did not ignore this widely held belief. One of the issues raised in the post mortem of the pre-thesis plan was the preponderance of flats over houses and the students sought, in the second scheme, to achieve a better balance between the two types of housing. They therefore proposed that most families with one or two young children should live in 12-storey blocks, each with a creche on its roof. A third of the families of three, two-thirds of the families of four and all large families would then live in the scheme's 3-storey terraced houses. Meanwhile, the town's single people would be accommodated in 15-storey blocks of bedsits and its childless couples in 8-storey blocks of small flats.[75]

The students' choice of housing was significant. In their combination of flats and houses, targeted at different communities, but sharing a social and physical environment, the students had assembled one of the earliest proposals, and rationales, for the use of mixed development in Britain. This technique, although widely used on the continent, was only just beginning to make its way into progressive housing theory in the mid-1930s.[76] It seems probable that the students' use of it derived from what were probably the first British proposals for its application to the problem of the modern city. Unveiled in 1936, Elizabeth Denby's scheme to re-house slum-dwellers within the urban context,[77] and Yorke and Breuer's 'A Garden City of the Future', both combined houses (terraced in Denby's case) and high flats with social amenities in contained neighbourhoods.[78] An early version of the MARS Plan did the same, again with houses and flats.[79]

The mixed development concept had much within it to attract the students. As good communists it gave them the political advantage of meeting popular demand for houses over flats and thereby bringing modernism to 'the people'. Hence it was another means to ensure the longevity of the movement.[80] Socially, its mixture of building types held the promise of a richer environment and, architecturally, one more challenging to design. Strategically, it also indicated that it was possible to bring together the GCTPA's preference for the house with the British movement's rhetorical device of the Modern Flat in one environment, thus rendering the prototype more appealing to a wider range of policy makers. Perhaps most importantly, the novelty of the technique, at the same time as it located the students in a continuum with the GCTPA and the MARS generation, also differentiated them from their predecessors. If the mixed development model were to prevail, they would be the generation who could give it form

Optimopolis

What form, then, did 'Town Plan' take? While the basic principles of plan and programme were carried from pre-thesis to thesis project, a real site required significant amendments to the scheme's layout. The students' first task, therefore, was to undertake research into the specifics of the site at Faringdon: geology, land use and so forth. While they were able to draw on a considerable amount of existing material to do so, to maintain, and indeed to surpass, their level of empirical engagement, two of the students hired a plane and conducted an aerial survey of the site.[81] From the two sets of material a set of survey drawings was then produced and from these a new plan created (Fig. 6.2).

Unit 15 placed the new town to the south of Faringdon. Its site was dominated by a crescent-shaped ridge and the students placed most of the town on its slope, the highest part given over to the civic 'centre' of the scheme. This contained a series of cruciform office blocks and a public square. Radiating west from this were the residential areas. First came the large slab blocks aligned approximately to the contours of the site and spaced to allow the passage of the gantries which assembled them. A

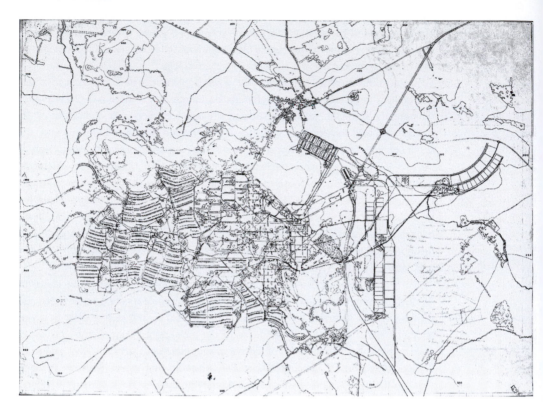

small number of houses were included in this area but the majority were placed still further west, clustered around the existing village of Great Coxwell which the students had elected to retain (Fig. 6.3).

Figure 6.2
Unit 15 of the
Architectural
Association, 'Town
Plan, Faringdon,
Berkshire', Unit 15
thesis project,

The civic and residential zones were separated from the industrial area by a green belt. This contained within it the main approach road to the town (which included 'an elaborate flyover') and the railway and bus station. The industrial zone was subdivided into three uses. 'Tenement factories', owned by the town, provided lettable space for small manufacturers while building sites, served by railway sidings, were available for lease. Finally, and a new addition to the programme, there was a further separate site for noxious industries. Together, these sites would provide employment for 80 per cent of the town's working population.

For their final submission of 'Town Plan', the students produced an impressive amount of material.[82] Drawings included town and regional plans, diagrams of the patterns of service and the sequence of building, and 'design drawings, working drawings, exterior and interior perspectives' of the different housing types. A number of models were also produced, one of the whole town and several to demonstrate the variety of flat blocks and the methods of constructions to be used for the houses.[83] When a jury assembled for a crit in spring 1938 it was deeply impressed. The town planner George Pepler's comment was typical, noting 'the high standard of work and

Figure 6.3
Model of 'Town
Plan' showing town
centre and housing
to south

particularly ... the thorough research made by the students preparatory to forming conclusions'.[84]

The jury's views were echoed by John Summerson in his review of the AA's end-of-year show.[85] It is worth quoting at some length from this, because it conveys so well the transformation which Rowse's method of teaching had effected since 1936; his approbation was given an added meaning if we remember that Rowse had been forced to resign only a few months before. Summerson began by commenting on the 'consistency of outlook' – modernism, in other words – reflected in the exhibition about the sort of architecture which was worth making. Where, he wondered, did this come from? In what was a carefully worded barb at Goodhart-Rendel he reasoned:

> To begin with, the outlook which the exhibition represents is that of a minority movement within the profession. On the face of it, it is strange that students should be irresistibly drawn to such a movement for it is one which does not by any means follow the peaks of material or academic success in the outside world. A few eccentric devotees would inevitably be claimed by any new stylistic departure, but this wholesale loyalty is a different thing altogether.

Summerson attributed its emergence and 'singular unanimity' to what he called the '*poetic appeal* ... of the Ruskin of our age – Le Corbusier'. He wondered, however, whether it was evidence merely of a superficial engagement with his ideas or the sign of something more profound? For Summerson it was the latter. He wrote:

> What I think everybody must agree about is that all this lovely French (or should I say Swiss?) poetry, so fully appreciated and so beautifully re-created in the Thesis and pre-Thesis designs, is all right, so long as there is behind it that spirit of curiosity and unflagging enquiry whose encourage-ment is the first and last duty of architectural education. So long as that spirit is there – and I believe there is ample evidence of it – I don't think anyone need worry about the condition of architectural education at the AA.

And it was surely proved, he concluded, by 'the impressive and extraordinarily beautiful town which Unit 15 has designed'.

The extent of approval given to 'Town Plan' can be imagined to have rein-forced in the minds of Unit 15 the rightness of the model of the future city they had created. Seasoned propagandists that they were, the students made sure they capitalized on this groundswell of support.[86] Their first move was to include the project in the first issue of *Focus*: its positioning a carefully choreographed interface between Le Corbusier's 'If I had to teach you architecture' and Anthony Cox's vituperative riposte to Goodhart-Rendel's first speech.[87] Equally strategic was the inclusion, in the spring of 1939, of the main model and plans of 'Town Plan' in the 'Future Development' section of the RIBA's Road Architecture Exhibition which explored the architect's role in urban and regional planning.[88] Reviewed by Ritchie Calder in the *Daily Herald* and christened 'Optimopolis', he described it as 'a city of ... clear vision' and noted that its design was based on the students' simple question, 'What have people a right to expect out of life?'[89] Their mentor Rowse, in turn, introduced the project to the GCTPA audience in an article in the *Journal of the Town Planning Institute*. In this he also noted that it was likely to be included in the 1939 New York World's Fair.[90]

In the process of its making and in its form 'Town Plan' is a project of immense significance. By early 1938 it had demonstrated, in microcosm, the efficacy of Rowse's principle of coordinated group work and the application of research to the reso-lution of an architectural problem.[91] Of equal, if not more, significance was the result of this group work. In its deployment of the principles of mixed development and the satellite town, Town Plan offered an early essay in the two of the planning forms which would domi-nate post-war reconstruction.[92] That they did so was largely to do with the ability of Unit 15 to forge a common ground from two opposing narratives: the GCTPA and the MARS generation of modernists. The satellite town, while a retreat from pro-urbanism, if devel-oped according to the principles of mixed development, offered a location rich in the social potential intrinsic to modernist-voluntarist housing praxis. It was also a site in which afford-able Modern Flats (as well as other forms of housing) could be built with the latest tech-nology. Likewise, mixed development allowed houses to remain the fundamental dwelling type in the new towns, while modernist principles of spatial and formal planning brought a welcome accommodation with the modern to the still pastoral GCTPA. Through this process of reconciliation – a classic English compromise - was created the ultimate progressive front in the fields of housing and planning. The oppositions no longer cancelled each other out, together they could take on the establishment and win.

The need to know

In its assimilation of narratives into 'Town Plan', Unit 15 had articulated the basic territory and techniques within and through which the modern architect should operate in
order to produce a living contemporary architecture. The decision to tackle a project as
large as a town, however, necessarily meant that some elements of design technique
were more developed than others, although, as we have seen, the students' attention to
detail was impressive. It would be a subsequent generation of pre-war AA students,
those trained almost entirely within the unit system, who would build on the foundations
laid by the propagators of the Yellow Book. To their beginnings these younger students
would bring an additional set of concerns, particularly in relation to housing design. In so
doing they further refined the architectural system which would be manifested in the
landscape of the post-war Welfare State.

The evolution of this method is demonstrated most thoroughly in the third-
year project, 'A Housing Scheme for Stepney', produced by Unit 11 in the academic
year 1938–9. Designed, with permission from the LCC, for the Ocean Street slum clearance area in Stepney, east London, it was developed under the leadership of tutor Max
Lock by a group of students which included Oliver Cox and David Medd. The project
offered an important expansion of the model of group work and research into design
which Unit 15 had developed for, at the heart of the design process, the students
placed the slum-dwellers of Stepney whose new homes they were creating. Through
the use of interview and social survey they made it their concern to discover what these
people wanted from the rehousing process. From this information they then sought to
create a model of housing which addressed the needs and desires of the rehoused
rather than those of the ostensible client, the LCC.

Such concerns may be traced to a number of influences which originated
from both within the AA, discussed below, and beyond it. Architecturally, some
members of the MARS generation had begun to move towards people-centred design
at this time in order to design better housing. Tecton, for example, would use the
surveys conducted by the Gas, Light and Coke Company into the technologies (gas,
electricity) and facilities (running water, a bathroom) available in working-class accommodation to inform the design of the high blocks of flats which would form part of the
Finsbury Plan. Most significantly, in preparing her proposal for mixed development, Elizabeth Denby had drawn directly on her visits to new housing schemes and interviews
with their inhabitants. Her design was an explicit attempt to formulate a model of
housing more in tune with their needs and it is known that Cox and his co-students were
in touch with her through Lock.[93]

A second context was that of contemporary (cultural) politics. Although it is
unclear precisely how radically oriented Oliver Cox and his fellows were, that they
inhabited a world permeated with left-wing sensibilities can be in little doubt. It therefore seems likely that developments within contemporary Left politics, particularly the
emergence of the strategy of the Popular Front, would, at least in part, have informed
their desire to develop new models of housing alongside workers; the formation of a
Popular Front was a deliberate attempt, in the wake of the Depression and the rise of
fascism, to bring together the working and middle classes – and different groups across
the Left – to fight against oppression however manifested.

In terms of culture, Popular Front politics had a singular influence on those in the avant-garde, demanding the evolution of forms of cultural expression closer to working-class taste. This was a challenge that painters and photographers would address sooner than architects and was manifested in the formation of the Artists' International Association (AIA) in 1933. Most of its members adopted various forms of realism – figurative painting, documentary photography – in place of the abstraction to which they had previously been committed.[94]

For architects, less able to control their subject matter, this was a more complex task. Its first manifestations were, perhaps, Tecton's application of the GLCC's research, Anthony Cox's casting of modern architecture as a social instrument and his and Llewellyn Davies's operation as a communist cell within the AA. For his younger brother, like Denby, this concern would be married to the development of an architectural form of Social Realism which, alongside a collaborative approach to design, gave rise to a preoccupation with the use of particularly English building types and materials.[95] The favouring of brick or timber over the unfamiliar surfaces of reinforced concrete, and the terraced house over the alien spaces of the *existenzminimum* flat, was then an overtly political statement.[96]

While such concerns were at the progressive end of the progressive spectrum, the knowledge of their existence, and their permutations, allow important correctives to be made to the traditional histories of architectural modernism in Britain. First, they point again to the central theme of this book that modernism emerged from a consensus – here between the working-class rehoused and middle-class architects – about the need for improved types of built form to accommodate new modes of life. Second, they are evidence of a bona fide concern among architects, which would only grow after the war, to assimilate working-class ways of living, both cultural and social, into the design of housing, rather than imposing new forms, unthinkingly, on an undifferentiated mass. The first evidence of a concerted effort to do so can be traced to 1938.

Strode Road

In August 1938, at the end of his first year at the AA, Oliver Cox, and four fellow students, undertook the measured drawing project which, despite the move to the unit system, was still a prerequisite of their course.[97] They would produce, however, no ordinary set of drawings. Under Cox's leadership, they instead undertook a survey of Strode Road, Fulham, in west London, a street of bye-law houses in multiple occupation by working-class and artisan tenants. This would result in a series of notebooks containing minute-by-minute observation of activity in the street and detailed drawings of each house, as well as inventories of their contents and records of discussions with their inhabitants (Fig. 6.4).[98] In both content and form they make a striking contrast to the drawings of the Petit Trianon at Versailles which Cox's future Unit colleagues David Medd and Bruce Martin had produced the previous year.[99]

No evidence survives to give a precise reason for Oliver Cox's decision to conduct such a survey. It may be partly explained by the general influences noted above, but should also be set against the context of the mid-'30s AA. Even had he not been Anthony Cox's younger brother, the nature of the survey's subject matter would

Figure 6.4
Unit 4 of the
Architectural
Association, cover
of Strode Road
survey notebook,
1938

have placed him firmly among the students who were campaigning most vociferously against the old values. Like Unit 15, at work on Town Plan throughout his first year at the AA, Oliver Cox understood that process and content were polemical tools. For him, however, content was, perhaps, paramount. Having entered the School in 1937, his cohort was the first to be educated solely under the unit system. Yet the fact that it still retained many of the old curriculum's *Beaux-Arts* impulses required students to remind tutors that modern life could also be measured, and with more useful results.

To elect to conduct a survey of a street of working-class dwellings reflected some more specific influences. Here Rowse's interest in behavioural patterns was important. While this is most often understood as having been manifested in a concern

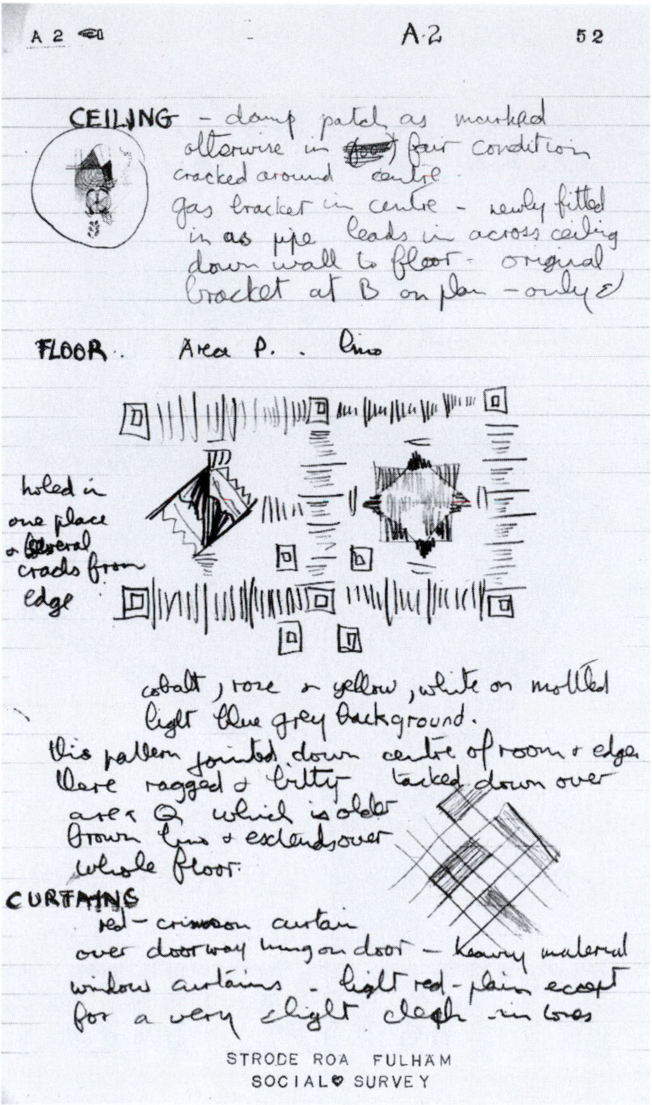

Figure 6.5
Unit 4 of the
Architectural
Association, Page
of drawings and
notes on the
interior of a house
in Strode Road

for anthropometric design,[100] it can also be seen as informing Cox's desire to engage with the everyday lives of working people. As he explained to one of the inhabitants of Strode Road, the concern was:

> To find out how this class of people live, consequently [the students] were trying to find out as much as possible about this street and the people who live there … the people's tastes and distastes: what kind of wallpaper they liked on their walls and so on … .we might never discover all the facts, but the impression gained – however limited – was bound to be very valuable to us.[101]

The minutiae of the detail into which Cox and his co-surveyors went, however, reflects a further, and complementary, influence on the project, that of Mass Observation (Fig. 6.5). This organization had been founded in January 1937 by the anthropologist Tom Harrisson, poet and journalist Charles Madge, and the photographer and film maker Humphrey Jennings, and was then pioneering ethnographic research into the values, mores and desires of ordinary Britons. Its emergence formed part of what its historian Tom Jeffery has characterized as a widespread 'need to know',[102] born from the realization of what the founders described as:

> How little we know of our next door neighbour and his habits. Of conditions of life and thought in another class or district our ignorance is complete. The anthropology of ourselves is still only a dream.[103]

Such ignorance, in their view, was a catastrophic obstacle to progress, but it might be remedied through investigations of the everyday lives of the ordinary man and woman. As Harrisson and Madge argued, 'a scientific knowledge of their own social environment, habits, behaviour, and those of forty or fifty million others is going to benefit most people'.[104]

The 'anthropology of ourselves' would be conducted through a number of techniques. Specially recruited 'observers' would act as barometers of public opinion through the keeping of a regular diary (on the 12th of each month) and the provision of responses to particular questions (directives). More elaborate surveys would also be conducted in which observers located themselves in a specific environment over a longer period of time, documenting everything which went on according to set criteria.

The survey of Strode Road conducted by Oliver Cox and his fellow students clearly conformed to the practices of Mass Observation, to the extent that Cox himself lived in the street during the week of the survey. Although the study was conducted independently of the organization, it does seem probable that it had some informal influence on what the students did.[105] Cox may have had access to its founders through his fellow student, John Madge, brother of Charles, and he recalled that he chose the Fulham site because it was Harrisson's London base. That the students' work in turn had an influence on Mass Observation is reflected in the fact that, the following spring, the organization would help them to develop a fully-blown questionnaire and survey when they embarked on a live project to design a scheme for workers' housing in Stepney.[106]

Ocean Street

The development of what became the project for the Ocean Street clearance area represented a meeting of minds between students and one of the younger and more progressive tutors who began to work at the AA after the instigation of the unit system. In Max Lock, who joined the School in August 1937, Oliver Cox and his fellows found someone who shared their interest in people-centred planning and who gave them the opportunity to apply it in as realistic a context as possible.

Lock came to this approach via a number of routes. A graduate of the AA, he had attended the School during its first phase of modernization under Robertson (1926–31). The latter's advocacy of Scandinavian modernism appears to have been a significant influence on the young Lock, particularly the social welfare of housing and planning practised there.[107] Such preferences may also be attributed to the cohort of students among whom he trained, many of whom were involved in the NHFO movement, not least the future leading modernist voluntarist, Judith Ledeboer. Lock would subsequently become a prominent member of the Housing Centre.

To such sympathies Lock brought the experience of life in practice – he had an office in his native Watford – and, more significantly, a direct engagement with the day-to-day politics of architecture. In 1935 Lock became an independent councillor in the town, representing one of its 'oldest and slummy wards',[108] standing on a platform which demanded that 'our town [be] planned with efficiency and imagination, laid out with beauty'.[109] From this time grew his interest in planning and he would later describe it as his 'best period' of training in the discipline. This was augmented by an interest in Geddes' insistence on people and place as the starting point for planning, although it is not clear where Lock first encountered his ideas. Such influences would ultimately coalesce into a distinctive praxis which he would implement in a series of wartime plans, notably at Hull and Middlesbrough,[110] and summarize thus:

> [For] too long we have treated urban problems as if they were merely skin deep, forgetting that the aesthetic superstructure of the building can only grow upon sound economic and social foundations. The regeneration of our obsolete and blighted towns, industrially overdeveloped, culturally stilted, requires a penetrating diagnosis of all aspects of town life. This can only be achieved by team work among the planners and the eager co-operation of the citizens – their clients.[111]

It was at the AA that Lock was first able to develop these ideas. Like the students, he disliked the individualistic hangovers from the *Beaux-Arts* days, approaching Rowse to argue for an alternative project for his Unit's members to work on. Lock recalled 'I went to Rowse [and said] look here, this competitive programme is hopeless. I think what we ought to do is pool our knowledge, and work on an already existing municipal problem as a multi-disciplinary team'.[112] In the students who had worked at Strode Road he had the beginnings of just such a team. With the addition of a few more sympathizers, including David Medd and John Madge, work could begin.[113]

In spring 1939, Lock approached the LCC for its permission for Unit 11 to conduct its own investigation and design of the 17-acre site at Ocean Street, Stepney, which the Council was proposing to develop as a flatted estate. This was granted and the students embarked on a design process which had much in common with the method Unit 15 had applied to the development of 'Town Plan'. A series of research groups was established to investigate and draw up design propositions for different aspects of the plan. These included siting and planting, traffic circulation, equipment, byelaws and Mass Observation.[114] The latter was a reference to the practice which differentiated Unit 11's approach most from Unit 15's: that of seeking out the opinions of those due to be rehoused in order 'to give them the houses they really need'.[115]

The chief technique to achieve this was the implementation of a survey. This time the students worked directly with Mass Observation and the organization would create a detailed questionnaire which, in combination with interviews, was given to inhabitants of all the houses due to be demolished (some 300). Presumably at Mass Observation's insistence, and to make the study more widely applicable,[116] the questionnaire was also given to tenants who had recently been rehoused at the Cable Street Estate in Stepney and to residents at the LCC's Pye Street estate in Westminster. Oliver Cox and his friends also used the survey in an extended study of Fulham.[117]

The five-page questionnaire asked questions which ranged from the general to the particular. Tenants were asked what their current rents were and how long they had lived in the area, for example, as well as more direct questions such as 'Would you prefer a terrace/flat on this site?' or 'Do you prefer a house and garden on an LCC estate?' Other topics included methods of heating, cooking and lighting, use of the garden and any structural alterations they might have made to their homes. Mass Observation also wanted to know about the taste in furnishings, wallpaper and architecture of the locals and the questionnaire included a series of photographs which they were asked to rate according to preference. Since the page of house and flat types included Kensal House ('alright for those that like that sort of thing'), as well as F. R. S. Yorke's recently completed workers' cottages for Flowers' Brewery in Stratford-upon-Avon ('puts me in mind of a big shed on a farm'), it seems likely the students had some hand in this part of the survey (Figs 6.6 and 6.7).

The key findings of the survey were that of all those interviewed, 45 per cent would prefer to be rehoused in a flat and 50 per cent in a house.[118] In Stepney specifically, 85 per cent were recorded as wanting a house in a row, many voicing 'the strongest objections to living in a flat'. In addition, 90 per cent wanted a separate garden in which they responded that they would sit (97 per cent), grow flowers (98 per cent) and vegetables (90 per cent); 100 per cent wanted a back garden not a front one. While at Cable Street, when tenants were asked what they liked least about their flats, three per cent 'hated everything'.

From such opinions, the students then proceeded to create their scheme. Reflecting the 'live-ness' of the project, the students elected to work within existing housing legislation which, they noted, prevented them from designing the scheme they would have liked since it would not have qualified for subsidy. So their preference for a mixed-development scheme of ten-storey flats and two-storey terraces gave way to one which combined six-storey blocks with three-storey maisonettes (a house plus flat on the top floor), at densities of 269 people per acre. Alongside this would be allotments, gardens and a community centre.[119]

Like 'Town Plan', the scheme for Ocean Street was well received. The AA's *Journal* reprinted a notice in the left-wing *New Statesman and Nation* whose author opened his review with 'I hope Mr Morrison and my other friends on the LCC are going to examine the housing-scheme prepared by the Architectural Association School under the guidance of Mr Max Lock'. He also noted that the final scheme was 'a skilful compromise' given prevailing legislation.[120] In his review of the AA's annual show, the RIBA's librarian, and modernist sympathizer, Bobby Carter, reiterated Summerson's message of the previous year, writing:

> The 1938–39 AA Exhibition is vastly different not merely because much of
> the work is as good and no more so than anywhere else, but because the
> exhibition shows sharply the symptoms of a vitality which can be detected

rising in powerful and irritating cells, in schools and in general architectural practice all over the country.

And he singled out Unit 11 for particular praise. He observed the students' reluctance 'to swallow LCC facts and figures' and their insistence that they

> must question the workers who will live in their houses, photograph their slum, balance up the varying obstructions of law and landownership to produce a result, showing maybe some but very little rawness of youthful enthusiasm or the demerits of six months' work done in eight weeks.

ILLUSTRATIONS OF BUILDINGS

Figure 6.6
Unit 11 of Architectural Association, Questionnaire for the Ocean Street Survey: photographic survey

Like the reporter from the *New Statesman*, Carter hoped too that the LCC would take note of the students' proposals, 'if they care to look'.[121]

The scheme for Ocean Street offered an important reinforcement of the model of planning developed by Unit 15 for Town Plan: here again was a mixed development scheme.[122] The fact that it was located in an urban environment making it the universally applied prototype for redevelopment it would become after 1945. But the project also embodied two further innovations. First was the students' insistence that attention to the opinions of those rehoused was central to the execution of a successful design, and their concomitant development of techniques and collaborations to achieve this. Second, was the nature of the ultimate client for whom the students were 'working'. In choosing to engage with a local authority, not the social enterprise Unit 15 had chosen, Lock had anticipated the ascendancy of the state over the voluntary and private sector which would prevail post-war. He therefore took the crucial step of connecting a

BUILDINGS.

Illustration.	Like.	Dislike.
1.	P1. – P2. Like the ones in Wigan. P3. More individual – private. S1. Like very much. T1. Like small windows & garden. U2. – V1. Nice inside – like garden. W4. Airy – nice bit of garden.	U1. Proper Council Houses.
2.	W.4 They look airy enough and built better. They each get their their share of light & air.	S1. Dont like it. U1. – V1. Dont like it– dont know why.
3.	Q1. Looks comfortable. S1. Very nice that. T1. Like the look of it – like the garden. U1. If had enough money. U2. – V1. Nice garden. Windows that openout. Likes doorway. W4. Looks nice and comfortable and sunny – there's something to look at there.	
4.	P3. Sun ahd air on balconies. U1. V1. Not bad. Nice outlook – wouldnt like th live there, no pets allowed I expect. W4. That's all right.	S1. Alright for those that like that sort of thing.
5.		Q1. Big blocks of flats are crowded, little room, noisy. Many people cannot keep it clean. V1. Wouldnt care to lime in it. W4. People leave their washing all across the yard.
6.	P3. Sun and air on balconies.	U1. Puts me in mind of a big shed on a farm. V1. Certainly looks like stables, windows like ventilators – too flat. W4. Too cold and bare.

Figure 6.7
Unit 11 of the Architectural Association, Questionnaire for the Ocean Street Survey: sample questions

model of housing, modernist-voluntarist to the core, with state patronage. This was a profound conceptual and tactical shift.

'Your Britain, Fight For It Now'

> In September 1939 all the blinds came down and civil building stopped dead. For six years the participants in the movement of the 'thirties were absorbed in this or that part of the war machine.[123]

As John Summerson wrote so poetically, the momentum the British modernists had generated by 1939 was cut cruelly short by the declaration of war on 3 September. Existing projects were hastily completed, the movement's leaders were called up – Fry to the Royal Engineers, Coates to the RAF – while its younger members awaited conscription into the army or war work. In the bleak days of the phoney war and as the Blitz began, it must have been hard to retain the hope that the optimistic vision of the late thirties, embodied in Kensal House, 'Town Plan' or Ocean Street, might ever reach fruition.

In August 1941, however, the first sign that things were changing, and changing for good, came when Churchill and Roosevelt signed the Atlantic Charter. This outlined the war aims for which the allies were fighting and laid down the principles which should underpin reconstruction once peace was achieved. They included 'freedom from fear and want' and 'securing for all improved labour standards, economic improvement and social security'; all concepts promoted by reformers in the thirties.[124] In the Charter's wake came a concerted move by the state towards planning for recon-struction in Britain.[125] Across the political spectrum there emerged a consensus that the chance to transform the country should not this time be lost, as it had been in the period after 1918. It was in this context that the progressives discussed in this book, who had worked so hard to make a space for themselves and their narratives of modernity in the thirties, were able to seize an unparalleled opportunity to create a modern Britain.

As members of government convened reconstruction committees or witnesses to them, modernists and voluntarists married their praxes with the will to re-form Britain. Perhaps the most typical example of this process is the Dudley Committee which was appointed in March 1942 'to make recommendations as to the design, planning, layout, standards of construction and equipment of dwellings for the people throughout the country' and which had Judith Ledeboer as its Secre-tary.[126] The list of witnesses reads like a roll call of modernist-voluntarist luminaries and included organizations such as the Gas, Light and Coke Company, the Housing Centre, the Kensington Housing Trust, Mass Observation, the National Smoke Abatement Society, the RIBA, Stepney Metropolitan Borough, and the Town and Country Planning Association (the renamed GCTPA), and individuals such as Eliza-beth Denby, Geoffrey Jellicoe and Henry Morris.[127] Its report would advocate, as already noted, new towns and mixed development as well as the adoption in new housing schemes of the array of amenities and facilities first promoted at NHFO.

Alongside such official work, the movement and its allies in the progressive front did not relent in their campaigning. The Housing Centre continued to hold exhibi-tions, regular talks and discussions throughout the war, while in March 1941 an RIBA now dominated by modernists formed its own reconstruction committee. This in turn set up a sub-committee on housing in June 1941, which was chaired first by Max Fry and subsequently by Jellicoe, and included Denby, Frederick Gibberd, Eugene Kent and Judith Ledeboer as committee members. It would give evidence to Dudley, and issue its own report in 1944.[128] The RIBA would also make a clear statement of its members' willingness to take their place in the reconstruction which lay ahead through the exhibition, 'Rebuilding Britain', which was held at the National Gallery in London in February 1943. Curated by the architect Jane Drew, and with a catalogue written by Anthony Cox, the intention was to present a profession 'intent on better building' and to demonstrate 'the working out of a lucid and satisfying replanning programme that must precede the rebuilding of Britain'.[129]

That the protagonists who have peopled the pages of *Re-forming Britain* might have expressed their views, and exhibited their prototypes, not with hope but in the knowledge that they had at last persuaded policy makers of their validity came in October 1942. In that month the Army Bureau of Current Affairs, which prepared educational and propaganda material for those serving in the British forces, released a set of posters which would be seen in barracks across the land. Depicting the new Britain for which each Tommy was fighting, their designer Abram Games had chosen three modernist buildings to depict the future of health (Finsbury Health Centre), education (Impington Village College) and housing provision (Kensal House).[130] Into an official narrative of modernity, modernism had finally made its way.

Figure 6.8
Abram Games,
'Your Britain, Fight
For It Now', poster
for the Army
Bureau of Current
Affairs, 1942

Notes

Introduction

1 Arts Council of Great Britain, *'45–55, Ten Years of British Architecture*, London: ACGB, 1956, 5.

2 See N. Bullock, *Building the Post-war World, Modern architecture and reconstruction in Britain*, London: Routledge, 2002 and A. Saint, *Towards a Social Architecture, The Role of School Building in Post-War England*, London and New Haven: Yale University Press, 1987. Their primary focus on the post-war era has, nevertheless, meant that their considerations of this process, although insightful, have not been in great detail.

3 Saint, *Towards a Social Architecture*, ix.

4 W. Curtis, *Modern Architecture since 1900*, London: Phaidon, 1990, 221.

5 K. Frampton, *Modern Architecture, a Critical History*, London: Thames & Hudson, 1987, 252.

6 For this story see, *inter alia*, ibid.; D. Dean, *Architecture of the 1930s, Recalling the Architectural Scene*, New York: Rizzoli, 1983; Curtis, *Modern Architecture since 1900*; D. Watkin, *A History of Western Architecture*, London: Laurence King, 1992, 559; J. Lubbock, *The Tyranny of Taste, The Politics of Architecture and Design in Britain, 1550–1900*, London and New Haven: Yale University Press, 1995, Part VI, 'Good Modern Design'; C. Benton, *A Different World, Emigré Architects in Britain, 1928–58*, London: RIBA Heinz Gallery, 1995. Honourable exceptions include Summerson's essay in *'45–55, Ten Years of British Architecture* and his subsequent essay in T. Dannatt, *Modern Architecture in Britain*, London: Batsford, 1959, and A. Jackson, *The Politics of Architecture*, London: Architectural Press, 1970, both of which look back to the 1920s with a serious appraising eye, although both are reluctant to accord what Summerson calls 'talk, travel and illustration' the same value as buildings, as this author does. More recently, the work of Bullock and Saint, and John Gold's monograph, *The Experience of Modernism, Modern Architects and the Future City, 1928–1953*, London: E. & F. Spon, 1997, have gone some way to complicating the history of British architectural modernism.

7 N. Pevsner, *Pioneers of the Modern Movement, from William Morris to Walter Gropius*, London: Faber & Faber, 1936, 29.

8 Ibid., 69.

9 H.-R. Hitchcock and P. Johnson, *The International Style, Architecture since 1922*, New York: W. W. Norton & Co., 1995 [1932], 37.

10 See S. Cantacuzino, *Wells Coates*, London: Gordon Frazer, 1978; J. Allan, *Berthold Lubetkin: Architecture and the Tradition of Social Progress*, London: RIBA Publications, 1992; A. Powers, *Serge Chermayeff, Designer Architect Teacher*, London: RIBA Publications, 2001.

11 Such an interpretation is long overdue in architectural history. It is already prevalent, for instance, in the fields of art history, geography, cultural history and manifested in studies such as D. P. Corbett *et al.* (eds), *The Geographies of Englishness: Landscape and the National Past, 1880–1940*, New Haven and London, Yale University Press, 2002, D. Matless, *Landscape and Englishness*, London: Reaktion, 1998 and M. Daunton and B. Rieger (eds), *Meanings of Modernity, Britain from the late-Victorian Era to World War II*, Oxford: Berg, 2001.

12 M. Berman, *All that is Solid Melts into Air: the Experience of Modernity*, London: Verso, 1983, 16.

13 M. Freeden, 'The Stranger at the Feast: Ideology and Public Policy in 20th Century Britain', *20th Century British History*, 1: 1(1990), 9–34.

14 That those who stayed, such as Peter Moro and Eugen Kauffman (Kent), ploughed a more useful furrow should not, of course, be denied. On them and the émigré phenomenon generally see Benton, *A Different World*, passim.

Part 1 Introduction

1 Anon, 'Tradition in Relation to Modern Architecture', *ABN*, 125 (1931), 352. The meeting had previously heard papers from Beresford Pite and Arthur Penty.

2 W. Coates, 'Materials for Architecture', *AJ*, 74 (1931), 589.

3 S. Chermayeff, 'A New Spirit and Idealism', ibid., 619.

Chapter 1 The conditions for an architecture for to-day

1 N. Carrington, *Industrial Design in Britain*, London: George Allen & Unwin, 1976, 87.

2 W. Coates, 'The conditions for an architecture for to-day', *AAJ*, 58 (1938), 447–57.

3 In subsequent chapters, more detailed discussions of specific aspects of Britain's modernization will be given.

4 J. Stevenson, *British Society 1914–45*, Harmondsworth: Penguin, 1984, 105. This is my principal source for the account of 1920s Britain given here.

5 Ibid., 107.

6 S. Bowden, 'The New Consumerism' in P. Johnson (ed.), *Twentieth Century Britain, Economic, Social and Cultural Change*, London: Longman, 1994 and Stevenson, *British Society 1914–45*, chapter 4.

7 Bowden, 'The New Consumerism', 242.

8 Stevenson, *British Society 1914–45*, 408.

9 M. Berman, *All that is Solid Melts into Air, The Experience of Modernity*, London: Verso, 1983, passim.

10 P. Addison, *The Road to 1945, British Politics and the Second World War* (revd edn), London: Pimlico, 1994, 14.

11 Ibid., 24.

12 M. Berman, *All that is Solid Melts into Air*, 135. I also draw here on Hilde Heynen's immensely insightful discussion. 'Architecture Facing Modernity', chapter 1 of her *Architecture and Modernity, a Critique*, Cambridge, Mass. and London: MIT Press, 1999.

13 J. Habermas, 'Modernity, an Incomplete Project' (1983) cited in Heynen, 'Architecture Facing Modernity', 11.

14 Only two accounts hint at the significance of the DIA. See L. Campbell, 'The MARS Group, 1933–1939', *RIBA Transactions*, 4: 2 (1985), 69–79 and J. Holder, 'Design in Everyday Things: Promoting Modernism in Britain, 1912–1944', in P. Greenhalgh (ed.), *Modernism in Design*, London: Reaktion Books, 1990, 122–43.

15 The DIA printed lists of new members in its journal, *DIA Quarterly Journal*. These also published the membership of the newly elected Council each year. Such information was not, however, recorded consistently, and it is not always possible to be precise about the dates when individual members joined or the constituency of Council.

16 See J. Pritchard, *View from a Long Chair, the Memoirs of Jack Pritchard*, London: Routledge & Kegan Paul, 1984, 80–1, 169–70 and M. Fry, *Autobiographical Sketches*, London: Paul Elek, 1975, 133, 137–8.

17 'Proposal for the Foundation of the Design and Industries Association', cited in R. Plummer, *Nothing Need be Ugly, The First Seventy Years of the Design and Industries Association*, London: DIA, 1985, 1. Founder and early members included: the architects Cecil Brewer, Charles Holden and W. R. Lethaby; retailers such as Ambrose Heal and Crofton Gane, manufacturers including

Harold Stabler, director of the pottery firm Carter Stabler and Adams, Frank Pick of the London Underground and Harry Peach of Dryad Cane Furniture; printer-publishers such as Francis Meynell of the Nonesuch Press and Joseph Thorp; and the industrialists W. J. Basset-Lowke and R. D. Best.

18 A full history of the DIA remains to be written and is much needed. To date, the main sources are Carrington's *Industrial Design in Britain*, F. MacCarthy, *British Design since 1880, a Visual History*, London: Lund Humphries, 1982 and Plummer, *Nothing Need be Ugly*, which draws heavily on Carrington's book. Only Michael Saler in his 1999 study, *The Avant-Garde in Interwar England, Medieval Modernism and the London Underground*, Oxford: OUP, has attempted to provide an intellectual history of the DIA, one which has gone a considerable way to establishing its significance in the inter-war decades. I, in turn, draw on all these for my account of the DIA's early history, as well as reconstructing some aspects of its work through analysis of some of its members' papers and its many publications. Further research – and the primary reason for the lack of a scholarly monograph on the DIA – is hampered by the inaccessibility of its archives. At the time of writing, these were awaiting conservation work at the Archive of Art and Design, Victoria and Albert Museum.

19 Fry, *Autobiographical Sketches*, 133.

20 Such practices conform to the idea of 'exhibitionary culture' as outlined by Tony Bennett. See T. Bennett, 'The Exhibitionary Complex', *New Formations*, no. 4 (1988), 73–102 and *The Birth of the Museum*, London: Routledge, 1995, chapter 2.

21 For a far more detailed discussion of the factors which informed the DIA's early visual prejudices, see chapter 4 of Saler's *The Avant-Garde in Interwar England*.

22 N. Carrington, '21 Years of DIA', *Trend in Design in Everyday Things*, no. 1 (1936), 42.

23 Carrington, *Industrial Design in Britain*, 79.

24 Terms of reference cited in Council for Art and Industry, *Education for the Consumer, Art in Elementary and Secondary School Education*, London: HMSO, 1935, 3.

25 Gloag (1896–1981) is an immensely interesting figure and would repay further work. A hugely prolific writer on design and active in many reformist organizations he scarcely warrants a mention in most histories. The information outlined here comes from his entry in *Who's Who*.

26 Information from obituaries contained in Carrington's Information File held in the National Art Library. Although his memoir does provide some insight into his life, Carrington (d.1989) is another fascinating and influential figure well worthy of further study. Neither he nor Gloag are included in the revised *Dictionary of National Biography* (2004).

27 Carrington, *Industrial Design in Britain*, 62.

28 Ibid., 77.

29 Ibid., 90.

30 J. Gloag, 'Introduction' in DIA, *Design in Everyday Things, the Yearbook of the DIA, 1926–1927*, London: Ernst Benn Ltd, 1927, ix.

31 Undated autobiographical manuscript by Fry among the Fry and Drew papers, BAL/V&A. I am grateful to Eleanor Gawne for allowing me access to these papers.

32 The months cited here correspond to the issue of the *DIA Quarterly Journal* in which the reports appeared.

33 'The Weissenhof Siedlung', *DIA Quarterly Journal*, 1:2 (1927), 8–9.

34 'Recent Developments in Germany', *DIA Quarterly Journal*, 1:6 (1928), 10. Given his feelings, it is telling that when Basset-Lowke commissioned a new home, intended as an essay in modernity, his architect, though German, was the older, more modern, and less modernist, Peter Behrens. 'New Ways' in Northampton, completed in 1926, though startlingly modern in its façade and its household technologies, exhibited none of the spatial innovation nor homogeneity of interior treatment intrinsic to modernist practice. For contemporary discussion of the house see *DIA Quarterly Journal*, 1:3 (1928), 6–7 which called it 'unique in England for its uncompromising modernity'. What might now be seen as a very English compromise was also exhibited in the commission by another DIA modern, W. Crittall, for the workers' estate at Silver End in Essex. Designed by a British firm, Burnet, Tait and Lorne, here some, though by no means all, of the houses were similarly flat-roofed, whitewashed

and, of course, metal-windowed, and at the same time had plans which adhered to English housing traditions rather than the *existenz-minimum* terraces of Frankfurt. On Silver End see 'Modern Domestic Architecture, Some Houses at Silver End Garden Village, Essex', *Country Life*, 64 (1928), 601–2 and on both schemes L. Campbell, 'Patrons of the Modern House', *20th Century Society Journal* (The Modern House Revisited), 2 (1996), 41–50.

35 *DIA Quarterly Journal*, 1:2 (1927), 13.

36 *DIA Quarterly Journal*, 1:11 (1930), 18.

37 This effort would result in the publication of the DIA's *Cautionary Guides*. These would demonstrate through a series of photographic plates of chosen case study areas – Oxford, St Albans among others – 'how the amenities of town and country are being destroyed by lack of organized control and design', (*DIA Quarterly Journal*, 1: 11 (1930), 1). In addition, a special yearbook was published in 1930, edited by Carrington and Harry Peach under the title, *The Face of the Land*, London: George Allen & Unwin.

38 Carrington, *Industrial Design in Britain*, 100.

39 The exception is the collaboration between the MARS Group and the Housing Centre (the collective body which represented housing associations nationally, discussed in Chapter 4) on the exhibition 'New Homes for Old' held in 1934. This is considered by, *inter alia*, J. Gold, *The Experience of Modernism, Modern Architects and the Future City, 1928–1953*, London: E. & F. Spon, 1997, 120–4. This collaboration, as the discussion in this chapter and in Chapter 4 will show, in fact represented the culmination of a relationship between modernists and voluntarists which had its origins in the 1920s.

40 PEP Industries Group, *Housing England*, London: PEP, 1934, 43. PEP estimated that by 1932, two million dwellings had been built and thus a shortfall of approximately 300,000 remained. Paul Oliver gives a figure of 600,000 families without houses in 1918 but does not cite a source, see P. Oliver, 'Introduction' in P. Oliver, I. Davis and I .Bentley, *Dunroamin, the Suburban Semi and its Enemies*, London: Barrie & Jenkins, 1981, 16.

41 M. Swenarton, *Homes fit for Heroes*, London: Heinemann, 1981, especially chapter 4.

42 The emergence of this sentiment is discussed more thoroughly in Chapter 2, 'A New Landscape of Health'.

43 This is a necessarily brief overview of what was a very complex shift in welfare theory and practice. Some aspects of it will be amplified more fully in Part 2, but more thoroughgoing analyses may be found in M. Cahill and T. Jowitt, 'The New Philanthropy: The Emergence of Bradford City Guild of Help', *Journal of Social Policy*, 9 (1980), 359–82, M. Daunton (ed.), *Charity, Self Interest and Welfare in the English Past*, London: UCL Press, 1996, J. Harris, *Private Lives, Public Spirit: Britain 1870–1914*, Harmondsworth: Penguin, 1993, M. J. M. Moore, 'Social Work and Social Welfare, the Organisation of Philanthropic Resources in Britain, 1900–1914', *Journal of British Studies*, 16 (1977), 85–104,

44 E. Macadam, *The New Philanthropy, a Study of the Relations between the Statutory and Voluntary Services*, London: Allen & Unwin, 1934, 32.

45 See J. Tarn, *Five Percent Philanthropy, an Account of Housing in Urban Areas between 1840 and 1914*, Cambridge: Cambridge University Press, 1973 and A. Ravetz, *Council Housing and Culture, the History of a Social Experiment*, London: Routledge, 2001.

46 As Swenarton has noted. The degree of control was significant. All local authorities worked from Ministry of Health *Housing Manuals* which laid down the main criteria to which social housing had to adhere. They were also required to submit all plans to the Minister for authorization.

47 See Swenarton, *Homes fit for Heroes* and Burnett, *A Social History of Housing, 1815–1985*, London: Routledge, 1986, chapter 8 for a detailed discussion of such estates.

48 PEP Industries Group, *Housing England*, 43.

49 PEP, ibid., quoting figures from 1929 generated by the National Housing and Town Planning Council, noted that one million houses were 'below a satisfactory standard' and two million (including many of the unfit houses) were 'seriously overcrowded'.

50 As noted in P. Garside, 'Central Government, Local Authorities and the Voluntary Housing Sector 1919–1939' in A. O'Day (ed.), *Government and Institutions in the post-1832 UK*, Lampeter: Edwin Mellen Press, 1995, 82–125. Between 1919 and 1930 approximately 11,000 dwellings were pulled down for state-sponsored slum clearance and replaced with blocks of flats, and this was under the terms of the 1890 Housing Act, S. Merret, *State Housing in Britain*, London: Routledge & Kegan Paul, 1979, 49.

51 The history of the inter-war voluntary housing sector remains to be written and the existing accounts have not, in this author's mind, accorded the sector the significance it warrants. See, for example, R. Best, 'Housing Associations: 1880–1990' in S. Lowe and D. Hughes (ed.), *A New Century of Social Housing*, Leicester: Leicester University Press, 1991, I. Emsley, *The Development of Housing Associations, with Special Reference to London*, London: Garland, 1986 and Garside, 'Central Government, Local Authorities and the Voluntary Housing Sector 1919–1939'. I have sought to address this oversight in my '"Enriching and enlarging the whole sphere of human activities": The Work of the Voluntary Sector in Housing Reform in inter-war Britain' in C. Lawrence and A.-K. Mayer (eds), *Regenerating England, Science, Medicine and Culture in inter-war Britain*, Amsterdam: Rodopi, 2000, 149–78 and in '"To induce humanitarian sentiments in prurient Londoners": the Propaganda Activities of London's Voluntary Housing Associations in the inter-war Period', *London Journal*, 27:1 (2002), 42–62.

52 Macadam, *The New Philanthropy*, 31–32. The DIA, another voluntary organization, might also be seen as an exemplar of the New Philanthropy.

53 Greater London Council, *The Survey of London: vol 37: Northern Kensington*, London: Athlone Press, 1971, 300. St Pancras Borough Council was also Municipal Reform. In 1934, H. Llewellyn Smith reported that the proportion of people living two or more to a room in north Kensington was 38 per cent compared to an average in London of 25 per cent. See idem, *The New Survey of London Life and Labour, vol VI: Survey of Social Conditions (a) the Western Area*, London: P. S. King Ltd, 427–8.

54 For a history of the SPHIS see I. Barclay, *People need Roots, the Story of the St Pancras Housing Association*, London: SPHA, 1976

55 See A. Tanner, *Bricks and Mortals, 75 Years of the Kensington Housing Trust*, London: Kensington Housing Trust, 2001 for a history of the Trust's work.

56 For an interpretation of the employment of paid workers as part of the voluntary sector's own modernization see my chapter, 'Enriching and enlarging the whole sphere of human activities'. On Denby in particular, see my, "The Star in the profession she invented for herself": a brief biography of Elizabeth Denby, housing consultant', *Planning Perspectives*, 20:3 (2005), 271–301.

57 In a decade's fundraising the SPHIS would have raised £315,000 which was enough to build 246 flats; figures from a chart on the Society's housing progress included in its magazine, *Housing Happenings* (1935).

58 See, for example, Westminster Survey Group, *Report on and Survey of Housing Conditions in the Victoria Ward, Westminster*, London: Westminster Survey Group, 1927.

59 For a discussion of the SPHIS' films and those of other London housing associations, see T. Haggith, 'Castles in the Air: British Films and the Reconstruction of the Built Environment, 1933–1951', Unpublished PhD thesis, University of Warwick, 1998. I am grateful to Dr Haggith for saving me a journey by lending me a copy of this thesis and for discussing the volunteers' films with me.

60 Barclay, *People need Roots*, 22.

61 A. Vincent and R. Plant, *Philosophy, Politics and Citizenship*, Oxford: Blackwell, 1984, 2. See also J. Harris, 'Political Thought and the Welfare State', *Past and Present*, 135 (1992), 116–41 and D. Heater, *Citizenship, the Civic Ideal in World History, Politics and Education*, London: Longman, 1990.

62 Vincent and Plant, *Philosophy, Politics and Citizenship*, 26. The two approaches to welfare theory which would emerge from the Idealists' innovations would be associated, on the one hand with the more state-ist and economic approach of Beatrice and Sydney Webb and the more purely Idealist ones which are the focus of discussion in this chapter. This theme will be developed further in Part 2

where two concepts of citizenship, one of 'responsibility' and one of 'entitlement' will be proposed as having informed the development of different modes of modernist practice in the 1930s. For the background to these twin practices see J. Harris, 'The Webbs, the COS and the Ratan Tata Foundation', in M. Bulmer *et al.* (eds), *The Goals of Social Policy*, London: Athlone Press, 1989.

63 Harris, 'The Webbs', 33.

64 Vincent and R. Plant, *Philosophy, Politics and Citizenship*, 133.

65 On settlements see, S. Meacham, *Toynbee Hall and Social Reform*, New Haven and London: Yale University Press, 1987 and D. Weiner, *Architecture and Social Reform in late-Victorian London*, Manchester: Manchester University Press, 1994.

66 Anon, 'London Public Utility Societies', *Garden Cities and Town Planning*, 18 (1928), 162.

67 Under Forty Club, *Youth and Housing*, 1928 (pamphlet), 8.

68 A. E. Chaplin, 'Youth and Housing', in K. England (ed.), *Housing, a Citizen's Guide to the Problem*, London: Chatto & Windus, 1931, 104.

69 Ibid., 100.

70 *Daily Mail* Ideal Home Exhibition, *Catalogue*, London: *Daily Mail*, (1930), 139.

71 E. Pepler, 'The Evolution of the Housing Centre', *Housing Review*, 33 (1984), 158.

72 Letter from Forbes to Wells Coates, 8 December 1931, Wells Coates Archive (WCA), Fond 30, Box 12/D, Canadian Centre for Architecture. This episode will be discussed further in Chapter 4.

73 M. Pentland, 'The New Homes for Old Exhibition', *The Phoenix*, 3 (1932), 7.

74 Reviews of NHFO 1931 may be found in 'Westminster Housing Exhibition', *AJ*, 74 (1931), 793 and F. Yeats Brown, 'New Homes for Old', *The Spectator*, 5 December 1931, 761.

75 During 1932, for example, the KHT was working in collaboration with the RIBA on its own 'Plan for Kensington' which linked the provision of new housing with the creation of a new road network. The leaflet 'chaos or planning', produced to publicize this venture, declared, 'Town Planning is not a luxury; it is an urgent necessity if future generations are to avoid a recurrence of our problems'. See KHT archive, mss 18025/46, Royal Borough of Kensington and Chelsea Local Studies Library. The plan is also discussed in E. Denby, 'Overcrowded Kensington', *AR*, 73 (1933), 115–18 and J. Fletcher, 'Kensington builds for the poor', *AR*, 75 (1934), 82–86. I also discuss the scheme in my article, 'To induce humanitarian sentiments'.

76 Anon, 'New Homes for Old', *ABN*, 131 (1932), 397.

77 J. Cornforth, 'Continuity and Progress, Christopher Hussey and Modern Architecture I', *Country Life*, 22 October 1981, 1366–8 and 'Qualities of Generalship, Christopher Hussey and Modern Architecture II', *Country Life*, 29 October 1981, 1468–70. See also his *The Search for a Style, Country Life and Architecture, 1897–1935*, London: André Deutsch, 1988. I draw on all these here.

78 See M. Hall, 'Country Life and New Country Houses between the Wars' in M. Airs (ed.), *The Twentieth Century Great House*, Oxford: Oxford University Department of Continuing Education, 2002, 57–74 and A. Powers, *The Twentieth Century House in Britain from the Archives of Country Life*, London: Aurum Press, 2004, 7–10.

79 Articles cited in Cornforth, 'Qualities of Generalship'.

80 The exact chronology and nature of this group is very unclear. Carrington, in *Industrial Design in Britain*, 136, dates the group to 1923 and mentions 'a few other writers' as members. Cornforth, in 'Continuity and Progress', 1366, cites Carrington calling the club the '63 Club'. Alan Powers in his study, *Serge Chermayeff, Designer Architect Teacher*, London: RIBA Publications, 2001, 39, mentions the 'Vers' Club, 'mooted' by Etchells in 1924.

81 Cornforth, 'Continuity and Progress', 1368.

82 In partnership with Hugh MacDonald from 1924, Etchells' practice was mostly traditional in style. The exception came with the commission for an office for the advertising firm, Crawfords, on High Holborn, London, of 1929–30 (see W. Crawford, 'Number 233 High Holborn', *AJ*, 72 (1930), 652–6). His client, William Crawford was a member of the DIA and wanted a modern building; but it was rare in Etchells' oeuvre. Like many of those who were influential in the 1920s, Etchells' undogmatic commitment to the modern meant he withdrew in the 1930s, ultimately becoming a specialist in

church restoration. He is, however, a figure of immense interest and would repay further study. I draw here on N. Bullock, 'Etchells, Frederick, 1886–1973' in *Oxford Dictionary of National Biography*, Oxford: Oxford University Press, 2004.

83 This was commissioned by the avant-garde publisher John Rodker some time in 1923–4. Rodker, like Etchells, and several others discussed in this chapter, shared a background in the Lewis side of the contemporary British artistic avant-garde. Etchells' translation, entitled *Towards a New Architecture*, would be published in 1927. On Rodker see J. Dunnett, 'Words of Wisdom', *Building Design*, 29 May 1987, 20–1.

84 For a useful discussion of Hussey's move to the picturesque, and the general context of architectural writing in this period see D. Watkin, 'Architectural Writing in the Thirties', *AD Profile* 24 (Britain in the Thirties), 84–9.

85 A history of the Architectural Press remains to be written but a useful overview of its activities can be found in the centenary issue of the *AR*, 199 (May 1996), on which I draw here.

86 Hastings (1984) cited in S. Lasdun, 'H de C Reviewed', *AR*, 200 (1996), 69.

87 D. A. C. A. Boyne, 'Hubert de Cronin Hastings (1902–1986)' in *Oxford Dictionary of National Biography*.

88 Summerson quoted in Lasdun, 'H de C Reviewed', 69.

89 It was Christian Barman (1893–1980) who introduced Fry to the DIA. Barman left the *AR* in 1935 to become the publicity officer of the London Passenger Transport Board (source *Who Was Who* volume 7). The new editor would be J. M. Richards who, as we shall see in Chapter 2, would do much to promulgate a movement which, by that date, was fully launched.

90 Shand (1888–1960) is a figure of exceptional interest but has been little studied. My main source here is J. Betjeman, 'P. Morton Shand', *AR*, 128 (1960), 325–8.

91 Gloag, quoted in Lasdun, 'H de C Reviewed', 69.

92 Ibid.

93 Robertson was then Principal of the Architectural Association (of which a great deal more in Chapter 6) and Yerbury the School's Secretary. Robertson was also Shand's cousin. On their work for the *ABN* see AA, *Travels in Modern Architecture, 1925–33, Howard Robertson and F. R. Yerbury*, London: the AA, 1989.

94 A small instance of this synonymy may be found in the content of the *AJ* special issue on the 'New Materials' referred to in the Introduction to Part 1. The choice of subject matter was, in the first place, significant, then there was the matter of its contributors: Wells Coates and Frederick Etchells. Finally, the inclusion of the report on Serge Chermayeff's speech in which, a further example of synonymy was given under the auspices of the DIA, can, at the least, be interpreted as a happy coincidence.

95 M. Freeden, 'The Stranger at the Feast: Ideology and Public Policy in 20th Century Britain', *Twentieth Century British History*, 1:1 (1990), 9–34.

96 Fry, *Autobiographical Sketches*, 134.

97 It is difficult to be precise about the early years of Fry's early career. Little archival material survives from his first years of practice and the only published account of his life is his sometimes unreliable memoir, *Autobiographical Sketches*. As *Re-forming Britain* seeks to show, Fry was a central figure in the establishment and development of the British movement and a serious study of his life and work is long overdue.

98 It would take Fry nearly ten years before he was able to design as a modernist. In the meantime, he worked first for Adams and Thompson, then for the Southern Railway before returning to his first employer as a partner in 1930. Fry's first modernist commission, and the circumstances in which it was achieved, are discussed in Chapter 2.

99 For the account of Coates' life at this point I draw on a series of autobiographical writings among his papers. Chief among these are his 'letter to Marion' (Marion Groves would become his wife in 1927) of March 1926, WCA, Box 35/A and the letter to Marguerite Broad, September 1927–January 1928, WCA, Box 35/B. Broad seems to have been a close woman friend of Coates.

100 'Biographical Outline: Dr Wells Wintemute Coates', 1955, WCA Box 4/D. Coates' life is much better documented than Fry's, see, *inter alia*, S. Cantacuzino, *Wells Coates, a Monograph*, London: Gordon Fraser, 1978 and L. Cohn, *The Door to a Secret Room, A Portrait of Wells Coates*, Aldershot: Scolar Press, 1999.

101 Letter to Marguerite Broad.

102 Fry, *Autobiographical Sketches*, 135. Although Coates would later claim he met Le Corbusier at this time (see, for example, 'Biographical Outline: Dr Wells Wintemute Coates'), there is no evidence to support this. Nor is it something he mentions in his autobiographical letters to Grove or Broad which date only two or three years after this trip. His friendship with Le Corbusier most likely dates from their mutual involvement in CIAM in the 1930s.

103 Letter to Marguerite Broad. I have edited some of the references but this is substantially the list the letter contains. How much Coates actually read of this is impossible to ascertain at this distance and youthful boasting to a woman friend cannot be discounted. Nevertheless, the utmost seriousness with which Coates conducted all of his activities suggests to this author that he probably read most of it.

104 For an eminently insightful account of the modernism performed in the Woolf half of Bloomsbury see C.Reed, *Bloomsbury Rooms, Modernism, Subculture and Domesticity*, New Haven and London: Yale University Press, 2004.

105 D. Goldring, *The Nineteen Twenties, A General Survey and some Personal Memories*, London: Nicholson & Watson, 1945, 145.

106 Marion Groves, 'About Wells', typescript memoir, February 1970, WCA Box 35/C.

107 This is discussed in Saler, *The Avant-Garde in Interwar England*, chapter 4.

108 E. Lanchester, *Charles Laughton and I*, London: Faber & Faber, 1938, 51.

109 Hale, 1994, cited in V. Nicholson, *Among the Bohemians, Experiments in Living 1900–1919*, Harmondsworth: Penguin, 2003, 101.

110 'Marion on Wells Coates', 1968, WCA Box 35/C. A gift of £100 from Groves' grandmother paid for this first venture into design.

111 Ibid.

112 Lanchester, *Charles Laughton and I*, 191.

113 For the account of McGrath (1903–76), given here, I draw on B. Hanson, 'Rhapsody in Black Glass, Raymond McGrath interviewed by Brian Hanson', *AR*, 162 (1977), 58–64, A. Powers, 'Simple-Intime, the Work of Raymond McGrath', *30s Society Journal*, no. 2 (1982), 2–11 and D. O'Donovan, *God's Architect, a Life of Raymond McGrath*, County Wicklow: Kilbride Books, 1995.

114 On Forbes (1889–1936), see R. McGrath, 'Mansfield D. Forbes, An Intimate Appreciation', *AR*, 79 (1936), 173–6 and H. Carey, *Mansfield Forbes and his Cambridge*, Cambridge: Cambridge University Press, 1984.

115 McGrath in Hanson, 'Rhapsody in Black Glass', 60.

116 R. McGrath, 'Recalling the 20s and 30s', typescript of lecture to the Architectural Association of Ireland, Dublin, 1972, held in the National Art Library.

117 Strathdon, 'The Transformation of a Victorian House', *Country Life*, 22 March 1930, 439. This article was written by Forbes under a pseudonym and offers a wonderfully camp description of his and McGrath's masterpiece. McGrath also discusses the house in his book, *Twentieth Century Houses*, London: Faber & Faber, 1934, 19 and 85–7.

118 Visitors taken from Hanson, 'Rhapsody in Black Glass' and O'Donovan, *God's Architect* and correspondence between Forbes and Pritchard, Jack Pritchard Archive (JPA), University of East Anglia, PP/34/1/A/1.

119 On one glorious occasion this collective impulse would also be manifest on a grand architectural scale when, under McGrath's direction, he, Coates and Chermayeff collaborated on the interior design of the new Broadcasting House for the BBC, completed in 1932. This commission had been generated by Finella herself: the Corporation's Deputy Controller having visited the house on the recommendation of a friend of Forbes who thought its architect might be able to achieve the

differing mises-en-scène the new building required. Ever loyal, the *AR* devoted the whole of its August 1932 (volume 72) issue to what it called 'The New Tower of London'.

120 There is very little detailed archival material for this period of activity. I have pieced together the account given here from material in the Pritchard and Coates archives, as well as from the publications of the DIA. How systematic their efforts were is ultimately a matter for conjecture, nevertheless the view taken here, and one borne out by the gravitas with which the organization of MARS was conducted, was that Coates and Fry were determined to establish a British movement of equivalent weight and authority to those on the continent.

121 Letter from Forbes to Pritchard, 28 July 1930, JPA, PP/34/1/A/25. Forbes' desire to form a company may well have been informed by the fact that the costs of Finella had driven him some £7,000 into debt.

122 Recap of founding aims included in Twentieth Century Group (TCG), 'Agenda for meeting at Arts Club, Dover Street, 26.2.31', WCA Box 12/D.

123 Letter from Pritchard to Forbes, 29 July 1930, JPA, PP/34/1/A/26. No evidence has been discovered to date to explain what this 'similar organisation' was.

124 See, for example, confidential memorandum from Forbes to Pritchard, 22 October 1930, JPA PP/34/1/A/28 in which Forbes quoted Pritchard's notion that he believed 'very strongly that the original group of people should maintain as much control as possible'.

125 Forbes to Coates, 21 February 1932, WCA Box 12/D.

126 Report included in *DIA Quarterly Journal*, 1:11 (1930), 1.

127 Although Coates would join the DIA and contribute to this campaign, he seems to have taken a lesser role on this occasion. This probably reflects a discussion of February 1931 in which he wrote to Pritchard suggesting one of them opted to go on the TCG's exhibition committee while the other stood for DIA Council. Letter of 23 February 1931, JPA PP//23/1/3.

128 The machinations of Fry, Pritchard *et al.* within the DIA are partially documented in JPA, series 28 and discussed in Pritchard's *View from a Long Chair* and Carrington's *Industrial Design in Britain*.

129 N.Carrington, 'Design: A Necessity', *DIA Quarterly Journal*, 1:15 (1931), 13.

130 'The National Crisis and the DIA and A Plan for the DIA', *DIA Quarterly Journal*, 1:16 (1931), 6–9.

131 Fry, *Autobiographical Sketches*, 135.

132 Only two issues of *Design in Industry* were published. No. 1 in spring 1932 and no. 2, guest edited by Mr and Mrs W. F. Crittall and devoted to the kitchen, in the autumn. It would be superseded by *Design for Today* from the beginning of 1933.

133 M. Fry, 'The Management of Space Organization, a Word to the Architect', *Design In Industry*, no. 1 (1932), 5.

134 M. Fry, 'The Modern Office, What Is It', *Design In Industry*, no. 1 (1932), 2.

135 Ibid.

136 I draw here on chapter 11 of Carrington's *Industrial Design in Britain*.

137 Coates served on the Display and Design, and Kitchen committees, Gloag on Furniture and Equipment, source *Catalogue of the Exhibition of Industrial Art in Relation to the Home*, London: John Murray, 1933.

138 This particular episode, and the design of the Lawn Road scheme, are discussed in detail in Chapter 3.

139 For an account of the exhibition see 'The Exhibition of British Industrial Art in Relation to the Home', *Country Life*, 1 July 1933, 708–13.

140 Giedion's letter to Coates cited in A. Jackson, *The Politics of Architecture*, London: Architectural Press, 1970, 34. Eric Mumford in his book *The CIAM Discourse on Urbanism, 1928–1960*, Cambridge, Mass: MIT Press, 2002, 91, dates the correspondence to the autumn.

141 Mumford, *The CIAM Discourse*, ibid.

142 Coates would, however, have a reserve plan in hand through his participation in Unit One whose foundation, under the leadership of Paul Nash, would be formally announced in June 1933. Its primary preoccupation with painting and sculpture suggests, however, that it was only ever a back up. Nevertheless, its exhibition and publication provided useful exposure for Coates, see H. Read (ed.), *Unit One, the Modern Movement in England, Architecture, Painting and Sculpture*, London: Cassell, 1934.

143 'Confidential memorandum, 28 February 1933, The INTERNATIONAL CONGRESS OF MODERN ARCHITECTURE' [sic], WCA, Box 12/A. The name MARS would be agreed by May 1933 after a brief flirtation with G.B.M.A. (the Group of British Modern Architects) was rejected (this was first mooted in the Memorandum of 1 March 1933, from Coates, WCA, Box 12/A).

144 'Confidential memorandum, 28 February 1933'.

145 The first addition to the inner circle was the architect F. R. S. Yorke, whom Coates proposed as Secretary in the Memorandum of 1 March 1933. It seems probable that Yorke was known to the founders of MARS through his association with the Architectural Press for whom he edited its technical notebooks. Within a few months the members of Tecton and Connell, Ward and Lucas would all join up. All members had to be proposed and seconded by an existing member.

146 'Memorandum of 1 March 1933'.

147 'Confidential memorandum, 28 February 1933'.

148 M. Fry, 'How Modern Architecture came to England', tape/slide set, London: Pidgeon audio-visual, c.1975.

149 'Confidential memorandum, 28 February 1933'.

Part 2 Introduction

1 Rare and notable exceptions to the more commonly architect-focused accounts are S.Bayley, 'Patrons of the Modern Movement', *AD Profile* 24, (Britain in the Thirties), 90–5 and L.Campbell, 'Patrons of the Modern House', *Twentieth Century Architecture* 2 (The Modern House Revisited), (1996), 41–50.

Chapter 2 A new landscape of health

1 Chesterton (1905) cited in G. R. Searle, *The Quest for National Efficiency*, Oxford: Basil Blackwell, 1971, 61.

2 J. Stevenson, *British Society 1914–45*, Harmondsworth: Penguin, 1984, 104–9.

3 Charles Booth, *Life and Labour of the People in London, (1889–1903)* cited in A. Davin, *Growing Up Poor, Home, School and Street in London 1870–1914*, London: Rivers Oram Press, 1996, 21.

4 A. Davin, 'Imperialism and Motherhood', *History Workshop Journal*, 5–6 (1978), 15.

5 Report summarized in J. Harris, *Private Lives, Public Spirit: Britain 1870–1914*, Harmondsworth: Penguin, 1994, 206.

6 Searle, *The Quest for National Efficiency*, 2–13.

7 The efforts of the DIA to reform British industry can usefully be understood as part of this drive to National Efficiency; an alliance signalled most evidently in their motto 'fitness for purpose'.

8 This period also saw some of the earliest eugenic legislation designed to segregate what were seen as 'undesirables' from the rest of the population. This included the 1905 Aliens Act, which allowed the refusal of entry into Britain of diseased, pauper or criminal aliens, and the 1913 Mental Deficiency Act which created the category of the feeble-minded, as against lunatic, people and provided powers for their compulsory detention. On this period of legislation see Harris, *Private Lives, Public Spirit*, chapter 7, 'Society and the State', passim.

9 This discussion offers further evidence of the shifting sensibilities about the nature and purpose of state intervention which was initiated in Chapter 1.

10 R. A. Solloway, *Birth Control and the Population Question in England, 1877–1930*, London: University of Carolina Press, 1982, 160.

11 Searle, *The Quest for National Efficiency*, 260.

12 *Survey of the Social Structure of England and Wales* (1937) cited in Stevenson, *British Society 1914–45*, 204–5.

13 Here I return to the themes outlined in Part 1 and paraphrase M. Berman, *All That is Solid Melts into Air, The Experience of Modernity*, New York: Verso, 1983, 169.

14 For a contemporary analysis of these differences see F. Singleton, 'Health Centres: Two Styles', *The Spectator*, 28 October 1938, 708–9. For a much more recent interpretation see P. Gruffudd,

'"Science and the Stuff of Life", Modernist Health Centres in 1930s London', *Journal of Historical Geography*, 27 (2001), 395–416. My analysis of the work at Peckham and Finsbury shares much with Gruffudd's; however, mine differs in its concern to emphasize the equal, if not increased, modernity of the Peckham model and to locate its organizational principles within the tradition of British Idealist theory as it had developed by the inter-war decades.

15   Innes Pearse (1898–1979) qualified at the Royal Free Hospital, London, in 1916 and was the first woman medical registrar at the London Hospital. In the 1920s she worked as an assistant to George Scott Williamson and practised at an ante-natal clinic in Stepney. Williamson (1885–1953) trained at Edinburgh and between 1920 and 1926 worked as Director of Pathological Studies at the Royal Free. See A. Stallibrass, *Being Me and Also Us: Lessons from the Peckham Experiment*, Edinburgh: Scottish Academic Press, 1989, 9–12.

16   'Pioneer Health Centre Pilot Scheme', recollections of Mrs Ewen Montagu, 1998, Wellcome Institute for the History of Medicine, Contemporary Medical Archives Centre (WIHM/CMAC), Pioneer Health Centre (PHC) papers, SA/PHC Box 4, B1.1. Mrs Montagu singled out Dorrit Schlesinger, daughter of Henry van den Bergh, the wealthy manufacturer of Stork margarine, as the initiator of the scheme.

17   Ultimately the Experiment would go through three phases: 1926–30; 1935–9 and 1945–51 when it finally closed. For an insightful overview of the Experiment, see J. Lewis and B. Brookes, 'A Reassessment of the work of the Peckham Health Centre, 1926–1951', *Millbank Memorial Fund Quarterly*, 61 (1983), 207–380.

18   I. Pearse and G. Scott Williamson, *Biologists in Search of Material, an interim report of the Pioneer Health Centre*, London: Faber & Faber, 1938, 10.

19   I. Pearse and G. Scott Williamson, *The Case for Action, a survey of everyday life under modern industrial conditions with special reference to the question of health*, London: Faber & Faber, 1931, 1.

20   The doctors cited in G. Godwin,'The Peckham Experiment', *Fortnightly Review*, 135 (1934), 189.

21   D. Porter, 'Changing Disciplines: John Ryle and the making of Social Medicine in Britain in the 1940s', *History of Science*, 30 (1992), 137–64.

22   I use the term ideological field as outlined by M. Freeden, 'Eugenics and Ideology', *Historical Journal*, 26 (1983), 959–62. This defines ideologies as clusters of ideas, some core, some peripheral, rather than discrete discourses, and it allows the historian to account for the overlapping of people and ideas outlined here. Hence although eugenics may traditionally be presented as right wing and conservative, in the 1930s many of its ideas overlapped sufficiently with those of other social welfare ideologies to allow their practitioners to work together and reform to be enacted.

23   On eugenics and its context see G. Jones, *Social Hygiene in Twentieth Century Britain*, London: Croom Helm, 1986.

24   Huxley is listed as a member of the Centre's Scientific Advisory Council from 1931 onwards. See also, J. Huxley, *Scientific Research and Social Needs*, London: Watts & Co, 1934, 101–3 for his approving account of the doctors' work.

25   J. Huxley, 'Eugenics and Society', *Eugenics Review*, 28 (1936), 11–31. All quotations are from this until signalled otherwise.

26   Pearse and Williamson, *The Case for Action*, 5.

27   A. D. Lindsay, Master of Balliol College, University of Oxford, ibid., viii.

28   PHC, *Annual Report*, 1926, SA/PHC.

29   Pearse and Williamson, *The Case for Action*, 63–4.

30   In fact, the original motivation for the founding of the Centre had been the recognition by Dorrit Schlesinger that birth control was unavailable to working-class women and she had initially sought to establish a birth control clinic to meet this need. Following a meeting with first Pearse then Williamson, and under their influence, her project became the Peckham Experiment though it did not lose sight of her original aim. The only treatment the Centre provided throughout its existence was birth control and it was officially recognized by the local borough council of Camberwell in this capacity. Source: Recollections of Mrs Ewen Montagu SA/PHC.

31   See Pearse and Williamson, *The Case for Action*, passim, for an outline of this argument.

32 If disease were found, members were referred for treatment elsewhere. The doctors discuss their prescriptions in *The Case for Action* and *Biologists in Search of Material* and I. Pearse and L. Crocker, *The Peckham Experiment, a study of the living structure of society*, London: George Allen and Unwin, 1943.

33 Pearse and Williamson, *The Case for Action*, 5.

34 PHC, *Annual Report*, 1926, 4.

35 Pearse and Williamson, *The Case for Action*, 39.

36 Ibid.

37 The average size of the Centre families was 4.5 people; incomes ranged from £2 10 shillings to £3 15 shillings a week and average accommodation was in 2.5 rooms. Fathers' occupations included a clerk, fireman, porter, busman, mechanic and some who were on the dole, ibid., 155.

38 Pearse and Crocker, *The Peckham Experiment*, 12.

39 Pearse and Williamson, *The Case for Action*, 132.

40 PHC, *Annual Report*, 1927, 5, notes that 'a fine and suitable site' had been found and purchased with 'the generosity of a few faithful friends'. This purchase seems to have been some sort of option on the site and it would not be until 1933 that it came into the full ownership of the Centre.

41 Pearse and Williamson, *The Case for Action*, 132.

42 Ibid., 146.

43 Ibid., 10.

44 The PHC's *Annual Report* for 1926, 5, mentions the yellow and blue colour scheme of the clubroom and flowered cretonne upholstery, while the 1927 *Report*, 4, notes that a hut had been built in the garden to accommodate the Centre's nursery.

45 PHC, *Annual Report*, 1929, n.p.

46 Ibid. No evidence survives to explain the choice of architect. E. B. Musman (1888–1972) was subsequently to become well known for designing public houses. See D. Dean, *The Thirties, Recalling the Architectural Scene*, New York: Rizzoli, 1983, 121–2.

47 PHC, *Annual Report*, 1933–4, 3.

48 Richards describes this encounter in his *Memoirs of an Unjust Fella*, London: Weidenfeld & Nicholson, 1980, 88–9. Shortly afterwards he was appointed assistant editor of *The Architects' Journal*.

49 PHC Executive Committee minutes, 15 October to 11 November 1933, SA/PHC.

50 PHC, *Annual Report*, 1936, 8, SA/PHC.

51 PHC Executive Committee minutes, 15 October to 11 November 1933, SA/PHC. The other architects were Messrs Elcock and Sutcliffe, Cecil Masey, and a Mr Spenceley.

52 Coates' estimate did not include fees. Unfortunately, neither his nor any of the other applicants' designs have survived, nor is it clear how this shortlist was arrived at.

53 PHC Executive Committee minutes, 11 November 1933, SA/PHC.

54 Richards, *Memoirs of an Unjust Fella*, 89.

55 *Annual Report* of the PHC, 1936, 8, SA/PHC.

56 Pearse and Crocker, *The Peckham Experiment*, 69.

57 On Nicholson's designs see G. Summer, 'Plywood Furniture at the Pioneer Health Centre', *Design for Today*, 3 (1935), 219–20.

58 Pearse and Crocker, *The Peckham Experiment*, 74–6.

59 In 1935 the Centre acquired a Home Farm at Bromley Common, Kent. This was farmed organically and supplied fresh milk, vegetables and fruit to the member-families.

60 Although this is not shown separately on the plan, it is referred to in documents produced for the opening ceremony. The room was paid for by subscriptions in memory of Mrs C. S. (Dorothy) Peel the well-known writer on labour-saving design (whose ideas will be discussed further in Chapters 3 and 5). See, 'Synopsis of Remarks by Sir Owen Williams at the private views', SA/PHC Box 5, B.3/1.

61 Pearse and Crocker, *The Peckham Experiment*, 68.

62 As Jane Lewis and Barbara Brookes have shown in their 'A Reassessment of the work of the Peckham Health Centre', there is little evidence that the member-families shared, or were even

aware of, the doctors' beliefs or ambitions for them. In interviews, most reported that they attended for the excellent primary health care and the availability of birth control.

63 PHC *Annual Report*, 1926, 4, SA/PHC.

64 I. Pearse, 'The Peckham Experiment', *Eugenics Review*, 37 (1945), 48–55. This was a retrospective account of the Centre's work in the 1930s.

65 This coincided with the financial crisis and the doctors and their committee did contemplate having to accept such offers. Before doing so they sought reassurance from Camberwell Borough Council that it wished the Centre to remain; the fact it stayed suggests this was forthcoming. Such acceptance was evidence for both the doctors and for A. D. Lindsay writing in *The Case for Action*, viii, of 'the fruitfulness of the co-operation between the State and voluntary sector' which is so characteristic of the mixed economy of welfare which prevailed in this period (see Chapter 1). This upheaval is recorded in the PHC *Annual Report*, 1932–33, 4–5, SA/PHC.

66 Minutes of the Executive Committee of the PHC, 26 October 1933, SA/PHC.

67 On her life, see S. Jackson, *The Sassoons*, London: Heinemann, 1968. Sassoon's charitable interests hitherto had been primarily medical and there is no evidence to show her interest in the Experiment until 1933. The PHC's *Annual Report* for 1926, 18–19, lists a Mrs Dulcie Sassoon as a donor but Mozelle Sassoon only became a regular donor after 1933. In the early 1930s, perhaps through an acquaintance with the Prince of Wales who was a close friend of her cousin Phillip Sassoon, she began to donate to charities for the unemployed and became interested in social housing.

68 I discuss this collaboration among Sassoon, Denby and Fry in detail in my 'Denby versus Fry? A Matter of Attribution', in B. Martin and P. Sparke (eds), *Women's Places: Architecture and Design 1860–1960*, London: Routledge, 2003, 149–70.

69 Kensington Housing Trust Management Committee minutes, 14 June 1933 to 2 October 1933, archive held at the Royal Borough of Kensington and Chelsea Local Studies Library. The failure of the Trust to provide a site led Denby to resign her post and devote herself full-time to independent practice as a consultant.

70 The doctors' secretary recalled that they and Denby were good friends and shared 'an interest in the environmental influences on health.' Correspondence with Mary Langman, November 1996.

71 A more thorough elaboration of this modernist-voluntarist approach to housing will be given in Chapters 4 and 5.

72 PHC Executive Committee minutes, 26 October 1933, SA/PHC. The site was occupied by seven houses, numbers 1–13 St Mary's Road. Mrs Sassoon was given the site of number 13. It, and all the other houses were demolished, except for number 9 which became the PHC's staff accommodation.

73 Ibid., 2 November 1933. Jack Donaldson would become one of the leading figures in the Centre's work. It was his donation of £10,000 in 1933 which enabled its construction to go ahead. Donaldson is also noteworthy as one of Gropius' English clients. He and his wife commissioned The Wood House at Shipbourne, Kent. See F. Donaldson, *Child of the Twenties*, London: Rupert Hart Davies, 1959, chapter 14.

74 Pioneer Housing Trust, *Articles of Association*, 1934, 1.

75 Anon, 'R. E. Sassoon House, Peckham', *ABN*, 140 (1934), 241–4, 253.

76 See S. Henderson, ' A Revolution in the Woman's Sphere: Grete Lihotzky and the Frankfurt Kitchen' in D. Coleman *et al.*, *Feminism and Architecture*, Princeton: Princeton Architectural Press, 1996, 221–53, for a discussion of the *existenz-minimum* dwelling in the European context.

77 M. Fry, *Autobiographical Sketches*, London: Paul Elek, 1975, 142.

78 Anon, 'Five Hundred Apply for Model Flats', *South London Press*, 20 November 1934.

79 According to Donaldson, in correspondence with the author in February 1995, Sassoon House 'was largely occupied by Peckham members'. A comparison of the names listed in the 1936 rates book for the flats with names of member-families gathered from *Annual Reports* and other material has found few such correlations. However, the doctors' secretary, Mary Langman, recalled one example. David Chapman was an unemployed Welsh miner who had walked to London in search of a job. Once he had found work he was joined by his pregnant wife and young son but they could only afford to live in

tenement housing which soon had an impact on Mrs Chapman's health. The family's plight was discovered by a social worker who arranged for them to move to Sassoon House and join the Centre. Langman observed, 'This was a case where the combination of decent housing with the unusual opportunities offered by the family club, made a dramatic difference to a whole family'; Langman correspondence, November 1996.The rate book confirms that the Chapmans lived at 2 Sassoon House.

80 PHC *Annual Report,* 1934–35, 3, SA/PHC.

81 Pearse and Crocker, *The Peckham Experiment,* 93.

82 Albums of press cuttings are held in the Centre's archives.

83 The albums do include some cuttings from the local papers when the scheme was first announced which document protests about the fact that several large houses would have to be demolished to make way for the Centre, for example the *South London Press,* 25 March 1933.

84 'Pioneer Work at Peckham', *AJ,* 77 (1935), 514–15, 520; 'The Pioneer Health Centre', *AR,* 76 (1935), 203–16; 'Designing for Health', *Country Life,* 77 (1935), 382–3.

85 See, 'The Pioneer Health Centre', *ABN,* 141 (1935), 400–5.

86 (J. M. Richards), 'Pioneer Work at Peckham', 514.

87 (J. M. Richards), 'The Pioneer Health Centre', 203. All quotations are from this source until signalled otherwise.

88 Junius, ibid., 222.

89 The BBC programme was reported as 'Health at a Shilling a Week', *The Listener,* 13 January 1937, 51–4. See also, Singleton, 'Health Centres: Two Styles'.

90 On this report, see A. Beach, 'Potential for Participation: Health Centres and the Idea of Citizenship *c.*1920–1940' in C. Lawrence and A.-K. Mayer (eds), *Regenerating England: Science, Medicine and Culture in Inter-War Britain,* Amsterdam: Rodopi, 2000, 207.

91 Singleton, 'Health Centres: Two Styles', 709.

92 Ibid., 708.

93 Berthold Lubetkin papers, BAL/V&A, LuB/1/21/6(xvi), 'Survey of Finsbury made for the Gas, Light and Coke Company' 1937–8. The tenancy rate of the borough was 100 per cent. The survey was used in the research Tecton undertook in preparation for the design of housing in the borough.

94 Finsbury's Medical Officer of Health reports cited in Gruffudd, 'Science and the Stuff of Life', 406.

95 Singleton, 'Health Centres: Two Styles', 709.

96 Although by the time Finsbury was being designed Lubetkin and Tecton had distanced themselves somewhat from the more mainstream modernist position represented by Fry, I want to suggest here that the opportunity which both schemes offered to promote modernism as the only conceivable architecture for the age over-rode any differences of opinion about its form and orientation that its practitioners might have had.

97 See Beach, 'Potential for Participation', 203–5 and her and Richard Weight's 'Introduction' to their edited volume, *The Right to Belong, Citizenship and National Identity in Britain, 1930–1960,* London: I. B. Tauris, 1998.

98 Finsbury Health Centre Opening Day Commemorative Brochure, 21 October 1938. Lubetkin papers, BAL/V&A, LuB/1/15/1.

99 This crucial observation is made in Beach, 'Potential for Participation', 212.

100 J. Allan, *Berthold Lubetkin, Architecture and the Tradition of Progress,* London: RIBA Publications, 1992, 331.

101 P. Coe and M. Reading, *Lubetkin and Tecton, Architecture and Social Commitment,* London: Arts Council of Great Britain, 1981, 141.

102 This is according to Allan. Coe and Reading, however, state that Katial saw the plans at the Hospitals Exhibition at the Building Centre in early 1933.

103 Allan, *Berthold Lubetkin,* 332.

104 These were Anthony Chitty, Michael Dugdale, Lindsay Drake, Valentine Harding, Godfrey Samuel and Francis Skinner.

105 Allan's magisterial biography remains the central source on Lubetkin's work and life but it is usefully complemented by Coe and Reading's *Lubetkin and Tecton*. I draw on both here for my account of the early Tecton years and the events surrounding the commissioning of Finsbury Health Centre.

106 In the absence of evidence of how other modernist practices worked at this time, it is hard to know how unusual Tecton was. What is clear is that it was Lubetkin's skills as a publicist that ensured the practice's reputation for its difference and for his ubiquity in accounts of English modernism. Though he is of undoubted significance, this book ventures to suggest that many of his contemporaries were equally, if not more, influential on the development of the British movement and the modernisms it would practise.

107 Katial's foreword in Finsbury Health Centre Opening Day Commemorative Brochure, Lubetkin papers, BAL/V&A.

108 The *AAJ*, 54 (1939), 197, for example, reports a visit by AA students to Finsbury.

109 See, for example, 'Finsbury Health Centre', *ABN*, 158 (1939), 65–74.

110 'Finsbury makes a Programme', *AR*, 85 (1939), 5–22 (three more pages than awarded to the Pioneer Health Centre).

111 This also reflects the common practice of *The Review*'s, and other journals' editors, of collaborating with architects on coverage of their work, a practice of mutual benefit, especially to the modernist project, which will be discussed in more detail in Chapter 3.

112 Singleton, 'Health Centres: Two Styles', 709.

113 Reilly in the *News Chronicle*, 19 October 1938, cited in Allan, *Berthold Lubetkin*, 332.

114 Here it is useful to remember the name of Tecton's exhibition for the Centre's users, 'Getting it across to the Layman'.

115 A similarly didactic approach to health can be found in another socialist borough, Bermondsey. Throughout the 1920s and 1930s it pursued a relentless campaign to teach its working-class citizens about personal hygiene. This included the device of a mobile cinema which drove into slum areas and showed public health films in the streets. For a discussion of this work see, E. Lebas, '"When Every Street became a Cinema": The Film Work of Bermondsey Borough Council's Public Health Department', *History Workshop Journal*, 39 (1995), 42–66.

116 Tecton spent two years working on the design of a series of new estates on Rosebery Ave and near Pentonville Road in Finsbury. The Lubetkin papers, BAL/V&A, LuB/1/17 and 18 contain the extensive research undertaken in preparation and document the proposals for seven-storey, north–south oriented blocks at Busaco Street (what became the Priory Green Estate post-war). See Allan, *Berthold Lubetkin*, 350, for a reconstruction of the Plan.

117 See Tecton, *Planned A.R.P.*, London: The Architectural Press, 1939, for Tecton's scheme for Finsbury.

Chapter 3 Modern Dwellings for Modern Needs

1 On the space standards and general design of the housing built under the Housing Acts of the 1920s see M. Swenarton, *Homes fit for Heroes, The Politics and Architecture of Early State Housing in Britain*, London: Heinemann, 1981, especially chapters 7, 'The Ministry and the Housing Campaign', and 8, 'House-building in London and York'.

2 The emergence of the market for owner occupation will be discussed in more detail later in this chapter.

3 The exact figures are local authorities, 1,136,457 dwellings and private enterprise, 2,969,050, taken from J. B. Cullingworth, *Housing and Local Government*, London: George Allen and Unwin Ltd, 1966, 20.

4 P. Oliver, 'Introduction' in P. Oliver, I. Davis and I. Bentley, *Dunroamin, the Suburban Semi and its Enemies*, London: Barrie & Jenkins, 1981, 14–16.

5 The Housing Manuals on which local authorities based their designs for council housing drew heavily on the recommendations of the Tudor Walters Report of 1918. This had formed part of the investigations which preceded the passage of the 1919 Housing Act, and was written under the aegis of Raymond Unwin.

6   On the GCTPA's inter-war activities see D. Hardy, *From Garden Cities to New Towns, Campaigning for Town and Country Planning, 1899–1946*, London: E. & F. Spon, 1991, especially chapter 4, 'The Long Campaign'.

7   See D. Matless, *Landscape and Englishness*, London: Reaktion Books, 1998, chapter 1, 'Ordering England' for an insightful account of this activity.

8   M. Fry, 'The Small House of Today', *AR*, 76 (1934), 20.

9   F. R. S. Yorke and F. Gibberd, *The Modern Flat*, London: The Architectural Press, 1937.

10 'Dr Rosemary Pritchard's Speech' at the opening of Lawn Road Flats, July 1934, PP/16/2/23/3/1, Jack Pritchard Archive (JPA), University of East Anglia.

11 This observation should be qualified here by an acknowledgement that this distinction can be made less clearly in the case of the garden city model of housing which was, of course, founded upon a particular notion of the creation of new forms of community. At this date, however, the suggestion is that it was more important for modernists to distinguish themselves from all planning orthodoxies than to seek common ground. Later, as I will suggest in Chapter 6, their shared desire for new modes of communal life would allow an assimilation of modernist forms with the garden city.

12 J. Pritchard, *View from a Long Chair, the Memoirs of Jack Pritchard*, London: Routledge & Kegan Paul, 1984, 79.

13 Presumably the second house was a speculative venture. See C. G. Holme and S. B. Wainwright (eds), *Decorative Art 1930, The Studio Year Book*, London: The Studio, 1930, 58.

14 Pritchard, *View from a Long Chair*, 79.

15 A comment on Cooke and Harrison's output by Pritchard in July 1930 sheds further light on the problems of their work. In a letter to Coates, Jack wrote 'I went to see a house by Cook [sic] and Harrison this afternoon … Christ! Dead as stagnant water but quite clean and without any reflexion whatsoever'. Pritchard–Coates, 26 July 1930, Wells Coates Archive (WCA) Box 25, Fond 30, Canadian Centre for Architecture.

16 The birth years of others of this generation who feature prominently in this account were 1894 (Elizabeth Denby); 1897 (Max Fry); 1898 (Innes Pearse); 1900 (Serge Chermayeff); 1901 (Berthold Lubetkin) and 1906 (F. R. S. Yorke).

17 See the 'Introduction' in M. Daunton and B. Rieger (eds), *Meanings of Modernity, Britain from the Late-Victorian Era to World War II*, Oxford: Berg, 2001, for a discussion of British modernity around the turn of the century.

18 N. Carrington, *Industrial Design in Britain*, London: George Allen & Unwin, 1976, 77.

19 My discussion of the Pritchards' early lives is drawn mainly from Pritchard, *View from a Long Chair*.

20 Jack Pritchard lecture on 'Isokon', 1973, JPA, PP/14/4/2.

21 The friendship with Sargant Florence also led Pritchard to become a founder member of Political and Economic Planning (PEP) in 1931, alongside Gerald Barry, Basil Blackett, Leonard Elmhirst, Julian Huxley, Kenneth Lindsay and Max Nicholson. PEP was an early think tank, which sought to act as 'a bridge between research on the one hand and policy making on the other, whether in government, the social services or industry … its aim [was] a practical one, to find out the facts, to present them impartially, to suggest ways in which the knowledge could be applied'. See J. Pinder (ed.), *Fifty Years of Political and Economic Planning*, London: Heinemann, 1981, 9–10. Elizabeth Denby, Max Fry and Innes Pearse would all become involved in PEP.

22 Untitled speech by Pritchard, JPA, PP/14/4/1, n.d. [1970s]. It was their friendship that led to the commission for the Village College at Impington being awarded to Walter Gropius and Max Fry.

23 D. Russell, *The Tamarisk Tree, Vol 2, My School and the Years of War*, London: Virago, 1980, 11–12. See also 59–60 for a description of her friendship with the Pritchards.

24 Venesta was formed in 1897 to import plywood boards from the Estonian manufacturer Luterma. See J. Kermick, *The Luther Factory, Plywood and Furniture, 1877–1940*, Tallinn: Museum for Estonian Architecture, 2004.

25 This was Robert Spicer, a future PEP colleague and member of the Isokon Board of Directors, Pritchard, *View from a Long Chair*, 55. The interest in statistics may also have come from Sargant

Florence whose particular specialism was the statistical analysis of industrial problems, see A. Silberston, 'Sargant Florence, Philip', *Oxford Dictionary of National Biography*, Oxford: Oxford University Press, 2004.

26 Kermick, *The Luther Factory*, 101.

27 Pritchard, 'Isokon'.

28 Ibid.

29 Venesta Ltd–Coates, 14 March 1929. 'We understand that you did an interesting job for Messrs Crysede Ltd, in which you used Venesta birch [plywood] stained, we think by Drytone Ltd. The Writer would be very interested to see this job as we are trying to make a collection of photographs where Venesta Plywood has been used in various ways'. JPA, PP/23/2/2.

30 Coates–Pritchard, 17 January 1930. WCA Box 23. This is also underlined by their initial agreement that Coates would not work to the professional scale for the design but that beyond a nominal fee and expenses his 'remuneration would largely take the form of credit accruing from … publicity value'. Coates–Pritchard, 14 February 1930, JPA, PP/23/1/3.

31 Coates' diary entries for 30 January 1930 and 2 February 1930, WCA Box 5/F.

32 On Cresta see, *AR*, 67 (1931), 43–6; on the interiors at Broadcasting House, see *AR*, 72 (1932), passim.

33 Coates–Pritchard, 13 July 1930, PP/23/1/26, JPA.

34 The evidence suggests that in the initial phases of the project Coates and Jack Pritchard were the primary forces. Nevertheless, Coates' diary notes frequent meetings with Molly. Coates' diary entries for February–June 1930, WCA Box 5/F.

35 For the account of the evolution of Isokon presented here, I have drawn on papers in Series 23, JPA and Box 25, WCA. Coates' debates with Jack Pritchard are much better documented than those with Molly, which comprise simple references to a time of meeting or the sending of a letter.

36 Pritchard, *View from a Long Chair*, 60–1. At the time that he and Coates were exchanging ideas about the house, Pritchard was in the process of recruiting Perriand and Jeanneret to design the Venesta stand for the forthcoming Building Trades Exhibition in September 1930. It was this collaboration which brought Perriand to England and thence to Cambridge to visit Finella.

37 Coates–Pritchard, 18 February 1930, WCA, Box 25.

38 Coates–Pritchard, 14 February 1930, JPA, PP/23/1/3.

39 Pritchard–Coates, 19 March 1930, WCA, Box 25.

40 This was probably a market research trip for Venesta, see Kermik, *The Luther Factory*, 101 and Pritchard, 'Isokon'. Coates' diary outlines the trip. Between 16 April and 25 April 1930 they visited Strasbourg, Karlsruhe, Stuttgart, Heidelberg, Cologne, Dusseldorf, Brussels and Paris, Wells Coates' diary for April 1930, WCA Box 5/F. A year later, Pritchard, Coates and Serge Chermayeff would return to Germany, this time to visit Berlin, where they met Erich Mendelsohn, and to Dessau.

41 Coates' diary also mentions that on one occasion he stayed up until 1.30 am reading Bruno Taut; diary entry for 28 March 1930, WCA Box 5/F. The book was probably Taut's *Modern Architecture* which had recently been published in English by *The Studio*.

42 It is not clear why or when this decision was made. Both schemes are illustrated in D. Dean, *Architecture of the 1930s, Recalling the English Scene,* New York: Rizzoli, 1983, 48.

43 Jack Pritchard–Coates, 11 July 1930, WCA Box 25.

44 This is covered well in, *inter alia*, S. Cantacuzino, *Wells Coates, A Monograph*, London: Gordon Frazer, 1978, C. Buckley, *Isokon Exhibition*, Newcastle: University of Newcastle, 1980, and A. Grieve, *Isokon*, London: Isokon Plus, 2004.

45 The first attempt to facilitate this new ambition was through the formation of Wells Coates and Partners Ltd, Architects, Engineers, Constructors in September 1930 (see Memorandum and Articles of Association, Wells Coates and Partners Ltd, 30 September 1930, JPA, PP/15/1/2/3). In the first months of its existence Coates worked to re-conceptualize the linked houses as prototypes – 'Exhibition Houses' – for what he would call 'our mass-production scheme' (Memoranda from Coates–Pritchard of 15 December 1930, WCA Box 25). Meanwhile, Pritchard took on the role of entrepreneur and there are various references to his attempts to interest speculative builders in their

work, for amongst the Company's aims was to develop land. These include reference to a link to Bovis via their DIA colleague, Joseph Thorp, and Jack's lunch with 'an intelligent young speculative builder' (Memoranda from Coates–Pritchard of 15 and 16 December 1930, WCA Box 25).

46 Pritchard–Coates, 1 July 1932, JPA, PP/23/2/106.

47 Correspondence between Isokon's solicitor [Graham Maw] and the Board of Trade, 31 December 1931 and 8 January 1932. JPA, PP/15/3/1/ and PP/15/3/1/4.

48 Isokon was formed in December 1931 (a process documented in ibid). Coates was appointed Consultant Architect and contracted 'to produce plans and specifications for four types of houses … [which] shall include some provision for inbuilt furniture and accessory equipment varying according to the cost of the type'. The Company also agreed to erect one of the houses and the contract noted that Coates retained copyright of the plans; draft agreement between Coates and Isokon, c. February 1932, WCA, Box 25. The origin of the name Isokon has been much debated. A memo between Coates and Jack Pritchard in Wells Coates' papers appears to solve the mystery. It reads '[Pritchard] I like the Russian type of name but we must consider popular prejudice what do you think? [Coates] Why not ISOMETRIC Constructions Ltd ….ISOCON??? [sic]. This is FGM's [Graham Maw] idea'. 'Name of Company', memorandum from Pritchard, n.d., WCA Box 25.

49 Memorandum of March 1932, cited in Buckley, *Isokon Exhibition*, 2.

50 Oliver, 'Introduction', 13. It should also be noted that under the terms of the 1923 Housing Act, passed by a Conservative Government, speculative builders could apply for subsidies from government. The intention was to facilitate the (rightful, in Conservative minds) re-entry of private enterprise into the housing market.

51 As Ian Bentley has shown, it was the peculiar circumstances of the economic boom after the end of war in 1918 that had created this growth in speculative house building. Initially, the future had looked bleak for the speculators as increased construction costs, high interest rates and the continuation of the wartime policy of rent control had combined to squeeze them from their traditional role as supplier of housing for rental. The advent of central government into the housing market through the Homes fit for Heroes programme further sidelined the speculators from their market. From the early 1920s onwards, however, investors continued to pour money into the building societies which funded the builders, a situation which would lead to a profound shift in the inter-war housing market. For the speculators and the societies realized that the only option if both were to survive was to start to build not for rental but for owner occupation: suburbia was born. See I. Bentley, 'Arcadia becomes Dunroamin', ibid., 71.

52 Coates would subsequently take the Isotype scheme to the speculative builders Berg, a decision precipitated by the very poor relationship he had with the Pritchards by the end of the Isokon flats project. He was able to do this because he retained copyright of the design. These would eventually become the Sunspan houses, some of which, much amended, would be built in suburbia. On Sunspan see L. Cohn (ed.), *Wells Coates, Architect and Designer*, 1895–1958, Oxford: Oxford Polytechnic Press, 1979, 36–7.

53 On Isokon furniture see Grieve, *Isokon*, passim.

54 Coates and Pritchard were not alone in their enthusiasm for high technologies of construction. As Jeremy Melvin has documented, their contemporary F. R. S. Yorke was likewise working to promote the merits of prefabrication and mass-produced parts in architecture. See J. Melvin, *FRS Yorke and the Evolution of English Modernism,* Chichester: Wiley-Academy, 2003, chapter 2.

55 Letter of 11 August 1931 cited by Buckley, *Isokon Exhibition*, 9.

56 Pritchard–Coates, 25 February 1932, WCA Box 25.

57 The Pritchards' fairly frequent revision of demands of Coates reflects their inexperience as clients and business people. They failed to realize, as an exasperated Coates would point out, that every time they asked him to change or add something to the programme, that this could entail a complete revision of the whole scheme and consequently a complete set of new drawings.

58 Jack Pritchard–Fleetwood Pritchard, 24 March 1932, JPA, PP/16//1/18. Their intention was to find another site on which they could build one or more of the Isotype houses and to begin 'the

experiment in selling unit furniture'. Coates would spend most of 1932 working on plans for both the flats and the Isotype houses.

59 F. R. S.Yorke, *The Modern House*, London: The Architectural Press, 1934 (the quotations taken here are from the 2nd edition of 1935). See Melvin, *FRS Yorke*, chapter 1, for a brief history of the genesis of this book.

60 All quotations until signalled otherwise are taken from the Introduction to *The Modern House*.

61 Indeed, as will become apparent in the discussion of plans for cities in Chapter 6, modernists of a slightly later generation, or with a less dogmatic attachment to the flat, would recognize this by the mid-1930s.

62 Yorke and Gibberd, *The Modern Flat*, 8.

63 Ibid., 10.

64 As Jack Pritchard himself pointed out in *View from a Long Chair*, 79, this was asserted in A. Jackson, *The Politics of Architecture*, London: The Architectural Press, 1970, 58; it is also repeated in Cantacuzino, *Wells Coates*, 57 and in Cohn, *Wells Coates, Architect and Designer*, 40.

65 Pritchard, *View from a Long Chair*, 79.

66 Molly Pritchard–Coates, 25 January 1935, WCA Box 25/4.

67 This is also reinforced by the fact that most of the detailed correspondence about the flats' design is between Molly and Coates whereas in the case of the Isotypes and its predecessors it was between Jack and Coates. These discussions can be traced in WCA Boxes 25–8 and JPA series 16.

68 Pritchard–Coates, 6 September 1933, WCA Box 27/4.

69 Memorandum from Molly Pritchard to Coates, 7 September 1930, WCA Box 25. Grieve, *Isokon*, 45 n.7 describes two briefs from April and May 1932.

70 Undated draft advertisement for Lawn Road Flats, probably winter 1932, PP/16/1/1/33, JPA.

71 A definitive history of the inter-war speculatively-built flat remains to be written and is much needed for it is against this context that the Isokon scheme can be best understood.

72 This observation is made in D. Beddoe, *Back to Home and Duty, Women between the Wars 1918–1939*, London: Pandora, 1989, 92; see also her chapter 3 for a discussion of the shifts in working-class female employment between the wars.

73 Mrs C. S. Peel, *The Labour-Saving House*, London: John Lane, the Bodley Head, 1917, 38, 53.

74 The basic principles of Taylorism may be discovered in F. W. Taylor, *The Principles of Scientific Management*, New York: Harper & Bros Publishers, 1911. It was north American household engineers who first domesticated his principles, most significantly Christine Frederick in a series of articles which were then published as C. Frederick, *Household Engineering: Scientific Management in the Home*, Chicago: American School of Home Economics, 1919. The British history of this movement remains largely unwritten; however the work of American scholars offers valuable insights into its adoption, see R. Schwartz Cowan, *More Work for Mother, the Ironies of Household Technology from the Open Hearth to the Microwave*, New York: Basic Books, 1983 and E. Lupton and J. Abbot Miller, *The Bathroom, the Kitchen and the Aesthetics of Waste*, New York: Kiosk, 1992. Contemporaries to Peel in England include R. Binnie and J. Boxall, *Housecraft, Principles and Practice*, London: Sir Isaac Pitman & Sons Ltd, 1929.

75 Peel had been Editor of the magazines *House and Home* and *Woman* and Managing Director of Beeton & Company before the war, and served as Director of Women's Services in the Ministry of Food between 1917 and 1918. In the 1920s she resumed her role as a writer, working for the *Daily Mail* and as the Domestic Expert of *The Lady*. A second book of household advice was published after her death in 1934, as *The Art of Modern Housekeeping*, London: Frederick Warne & Co Ltd., 1935. Much of this activity is recalled in Mrs C. S. Peel, *Life's Enchanted Cup, An Autobiography*, London: John Lane, the Bodley Head, 1933.

76 Peel's advocacy for electricity was somewhat optimistic since the National Grid would not be initiated until 1926 and by 1938 a good quarter of homes in England and Wales remained unconnected to it. See S. Bowden and A. Offner, 'The Technological Revolution that never was: Gender, Class and the Diffusion of Household Appliances in inter-war England' in V. de Grazia (ed.),

The Sex of Things, Gender and Consumption in Historical Perspective, Berkeley: University of California Press, 1996, 251–2.

77 Peel, *The Labour-Saving House*, 42

78 Ibid., 46.

79 Ibid., 10.

80 Undated draft advertisement for Lawn Road Flats. The author's use of the term 'labour-making' is interesting given its use by Mrs Peel.

81 From about 1935, the MARS Group moved away from its initial focus on research to a preoccupation with the principles of modernism; this culminated in the New Architecture Exhibition of early 1938, discussed in Chapters 5 and 6.

82 Coates' earliest substantial articles were published in November 1931: 'Inspiration from Japan' and 'Materials for Architecture' both in *AJ*, 74 (1931), 586–9.

83 The following discussion draws on two texts contemporary to work on Lawn Road: 'Furniture today – Furniture Tomorrow – Leaves from a Meta-Technical Notebook', *AR*, 73 (1932), 29–38 and the transcript of his radio discussion with the critic Geoffrey Boumphrey from the BBC series 'Design in Modern Life', 'Modern Dwellings for Modern Needs', *The Listener*, 24 May 1933, 819–22.

84 Chief among these were the interiors for the Russell Strausses at 1 Kensington Palace Gardens and Elsa Lanchester and Charles Laughton at Gordon Square. There were also a number of other smaller projects.

85 Coates, 'Furniture Today', 32.

86 Ibid., 31.

87 Ibid., 32. Compare this with Yorke and Gibberd's observations in *The Modern Flat*, 20: 'The amount of time spent in the home has in recent years been much reduced through such innovations as the cinema, cheap travel, playing and watching games, careers for women, creches, and so on'.

88 Coates and Boumphrey, 'Modern Dwellings for Modern Needs', 819.

89 Coates, 'Furniture Today', 34.

90 Coates and Boumphrey, 'Modern Dwellings for Modern Needs', 821.

91 Correspondence between Coates and Graham Maw, 11, 21 and 22 April 1933, Box 27/1, WCA.

92 Coates, 'Furniture Today', 34.

93 Pritchard–Coates, 1 July 1932, JPA PP/23/2/106. At this point it was agreed not to exhibit the flat.

94 There is some suggestion in the correspondence between Pritchard and Coates that the latter may have gone ahead without Isokon's sponsorship. See letters, January–March 1933, WCA Box 27/1.

95 Correspondence between Coates and Jack Pritchard, July–September 1933, WCA Box 27/2–4. The final cost was £14,850, Grieve, *Isokon*, 10.

96 George Barker (the builder)–Coates, 13 April 1934, WCA Box 28/1. Although the block was handed over on 26 June, much work remained to be done: the Pritchards' own flat was not finished and subsequent files in the archive point to endless problems with, for example, the roof surface, ill-fitting doors and leaks.

97 'Dr Rosemary Pritchard's Speech', JPA.

98 Although the authorship of the idea of the Isokon flats will remain debatable, there can be no doubt that their formal and spatial design, though predicated on the highly specific brief, was the sole work of Coates.

99 Coates and the Pritchards were rather vague about the 'finer society' and type of living which their reforms would produce. They certainly did not conform to the materialist notion that environmental reform was an end in itself. They had most in common with the British Idealist notions of the combination of material and social reform insofar as what they imply they envisaged was a more communally-oriented society populated by people like them: earnest, engaged, intellectual, progressive emotionally, socially and politically and prepared to devote their energies to improving the lives of themselves and others. In this respect it is worth noting that they advertised the block in the *New Statesman*.

100 Coates and Boumphrey, 'Modern Dwellings for Modern Needs', 820.

101 This worked out at £2 (40 shillings) a week, compared with the rents of 18 shillings or 13 shillings and 6 pence a week tenants paid at Kent House and 9 shillings and 6 pence and 11 shillings and 6 pence a week paid at Kensal House. Lawn Road was aimed at people earning between £250 and £500 a year; working-class tenants in Ladbroke Grove or Chalk Farm would have had incomes of no more than £200 a year and probably considerably less.

102 Coates, 'Furniture Today', 34.

103 Ibid.

104 William Curtis notes that the level of articulation given to the balconies can also be seen as metaphor for the communal nature of flat life; a communality which would eventually be fostered through the conversion of the staff quarters into the Isobar restaurant and club in 1937 to designs by Marcel Breuer. See W. Curtis, *English Architecture of the 1930s*, Milton Keynes: The Open University Press, 1975, 57.

105 The Coates and Pritchard papers contain some material which documents this process, but it presumably operated on an informal level as well for which no evidence has survived. See WCA Box 29/1 and 3; JPA series 16/2.

106 P. Nash, 'Unit One', *The Listener*, 5 July 1933, 14–16; W. Coates, 'Unit One' [letter], *The Listener*, 12 July 1933, 68. It was typical of Coates to deploy what was then a new form of rendering to further signify the modernity of the scheme.

107 Postgate to Coates, 13 April 1934, WCA Box 29/1.

108 Correspondence between Coates and Hastings, 15 and 18 June 1934, WCA Box 29/3.

109 Phone Message Slip with annotation by Coates, 20 June 1934, WCA Box 26/2.

110 Hastings to Coates, 15 June 1934, WCA Box 29/3; see *AR* August 1934, 77–82 (following further amendments by Coates) and *AJ*, 78 (1934), pp 409–12, 415–16, 469–72 (see also WCA Box 26, for correspondence between Coates and J. M. Richards about this coverage).

111 Coates to Bertram, 4 September 1934, WCA Box 26.

112 'Dr Rosemary Pritchard's Speech', JPA.

113 See JPA series 16/2 for the promotional activities outlined here.

114 Isokon to Hilton Young, n.d., JPA, PP/16/2/23/1. As Minister of Health, Young was responsible for the enactment of the slum clearance programme first initiated under the 1930 Housing Act. He had also overseen the passing of the 1932 Town and Country Planning Act.

115 Silkin's Secretary to Isokon, 2 May 1934, JPA, PP/16/2/23/4/26. This response should be compared with his comments on Kent House considered in the next chapter.

116 *News Chronicle*, 12 July 1934, clipping in JPA, PP/16/2/23/4/4.

117 It is not surprising that it was featured by Yorke and Gibberd in the introduction of *The Modern Flat*, 13. More recently it has been illustrated in Dean, *Architecture of the 1930s*, 49–51.

118 See JPA series 11 and 25, for documentation of their efforts.

119 These schemes include Tecton's Highpoint I and II in north London of 1935 and 1938; Gibberd's later blocks Park Court, south London of 1936 and Ellington Court, north London of 1937 and Coates' Embassy Court in Brighton of 1936.

Chapter 4   New Homes for Old

1 A. Ravetz, *Council Housing and Culture*, London: Routledge, 2001, 87–8.

2 See ibid., 88–9 and also A. Ravetz, *The Government of Space, Town Planning in Modern Society*, London: Faber & Faber, 1986, 28–30.

3 'Report on a Project for an Exhibition', dated Armistice Day 1931, Jack Pritchard Archive (JPA), University of East Anglia, PP/23/2/13. Its front cover is annotated in pencil by Pritchard 'Exhibition for Planned Industrial Construction, EPIC'. All quotations come from this document until signalled otherwise.

4 It was certainly ambitious in cost. Fry and Coates gave a figure of £4,625 (including 300 guineas each as fees) as their estimate.

5 There were, nevertheless, some positive outcomes from the EPIC project. In the short term, Fry was able to realize some of the proposals about a better-planned factory in the first issue of the new DIA

journal, *Design in Industry* published in spring 1932, which was devoted to the office (EPIC would have included a full-size mock-up of an office). Indeed, given Pritchard's involvement, and the emphasis on planning, the EPIC project as a whole is perhaps best understood as part of the trio's efforts to render the DIA modernist (on which see Chapter 1).

6   There are no references in the Coates papers to this venture nor in the Fry papers (such as survive). The only correspondence to survive is one letter and two memoranda dated mid-November 1931 in the Pritchard papers.

7   'Report on a Project for an Exhibition', JPA. The moving exhibition would display – it is unspecified how – the stagnation attained by 'Unplanning'.

8   D. Dean, *The Architect as Stand Designer, Building Exhibitions 1895–1983*, London: Scolar Press, 1985, 13.

9   It is worth noting that in 1930 the CPRE had exhibited at the BTE, ibid., 55.

10 'Report on a Project for an Exhibition'.

11 Ibid. The outline budget lists the figure of £50 for a floral tribute to Unwin in recognition of his anticipated co-operation. Since this was twice the cost of the *Entr'acte* section it is evidence either of the over-ambition of the proposal or is a rather significant typographical error.

12 Unwin was also due to become President of the BTE in 1932, Dean, *The Architect as Stand Designer*, 55.

13 'Report on a Project for an Exhibition'.

14 By the time this proposal had been written, Coates and Pritchard had twice visited Germany, as discussed in Chapter 3.

15 It would be some time before the British movement would again attempt a full-scale exhibition. In 1935 the first preparations were made for what became the MARS 'New Architecture' exhibition of 1938 (for a partial discussion of which see Chapter 5). The suggestion here is that EPIC should be understood as the ultimate starting point for this exhibition. It likewise used the device of chaos before order, and sought, not entirely successfully, sponsorship from manufacturers to meet its considerable budget.

16 Hilton-Young cited in *The Phoenix* (journal of the Fulham Housing Association), spring/summer 1933, 5. The introduction of the Act reflected a consensus that sufficient houses had been built to meet the shortage and that private enterprise could now be relied upon to meet any remaining need. The economic exigencies of the Depression meant that it was seen as inappropriate for government to subsidize housing for any but the worst-off.

17 See M. Fry, *Autobiographical Sketches*, London: Paul Elek, 1975, 134.

18 See, for example, the 'Planning' issue of the *AR* published in March 1933 and its 'Special Issue on Electricity and Planning' of November 1933.

19 'Planning Issue', *AJ*, 74, 11 January 1933 and 'Special Issue on Slums', *AJ*, 74, 22 June 1933.

20 M. Fry, 'De-Slumming', *AJ*, 74 (1933), 366.

21 The evolution of the Isokon project from a house to a block of flats may also be considered a further influence.

22 M. Fry, 'The Architect's Problem'. *AJ*, 77 (1933), 844.

23 This was subsequently published as G. C. M. M'Gonigle and J. Kirby, *Poverty and Public Health*, London: Gollancz, 1936.

24 Fry, 'The Architect's Problem', 844.

25 Lutyens' designs were for seven blocks occupying a large site between Vincent Street and Horseferry Road, Pimlico. Their street facades were notable for being constructed in a checked pattern of grey and white bricks. On the estate see C. Hussey, 'The Grosvenor Estate, Millbank', *Country Life*, 68 (1930), 49–50.

26 Fry, 'The Architect's Problem', 845.

27 Ibid., 846.

28 Memorandum re BTEP [Building Trades Exhibition Proposal], undated, c. November 1931, JPA, PP/ 23/2/74. Interestingly, Coates would annotate the memo 'but re housing only' next to Pritchard's reference to the similarities between the projects.

29 Letter from Mansfield Forbes–Wells Coates, 8 December 1931; 'I have been at the "NHFO" Exhibition nearly half to-day. … Miss Denby … told me you were there this morning'. Wells Coates Papers, Fond 30, CCA, Box 12/D.

30 See Fry, *Autobiographical Sketches*, 133–5. His chronology is very skewed and largely informed by the desire to place himself at the forefront of the British movement and, in particular, to assert his primary authorship of Sassoon House and Kensal House. Devonshire House was re-built by Carrere and Hastings, with Fry's old tutor Charles Reilly as Consultant between 1924 and 1926 at which time Fry was certainly in London. He does not seem to have joined the DIA until 1927–8. It seems most likely that the interest in concrete and social housing dates to the latter time.

31 London Housing Societies, *New Homes for Old*, London: London Housing Societies, 1932, 15. The catalogue was produced by Lady Pentland of the Saint Pancras House Improvement Society (SPHIS) of whom more later in this chapter.

32 Fry, 'The Architect's Problem', 845.

33 London Housing Societies, *New Homes for Old*, 15.

34 See P. Garside, 'Central Government, Local Authorities and the Voluntary Housing Sector 1919–1939', in A. O'Day (ed.), *Government and Institutions in the post-1832 UK*, Lampeter: Edwin Mellen Press, 1995, 82–125.

35 Ministry of Health, *Report of the Departmental Committee on Housing*, London: HMSO, 1933 (The Moyne Report). The recommendations were ultimately not enacted.

36 Although a thoroughgoing slum clearance programme would not commence until after 1930, some local authorities had carried out small programmes of clearance and rebuilding under the provisions of earlier housing acts, particularly after 1928.

37 LCC, *Housing 1928–30*, London: LCC, 1931, 68–9.

38 Lady Frances Stewart's speech to the 1935 SPHIS AGM, 30 January 1935, reported in minutes of the SPHIS AGM, Saint Pancras Housing Association (SPHA) archive, now housed at Camden Local Studies Library. I am grateful to Ingrid Khedun for allowing me access to the Society's papers while they were still housed at the SPHA's head office.

39 The process was initiated after NHFO 1931 and may be partially traced through papers which survive in the Housing Centre Trust (HCT) archive. These include position papers by Elizabeth Denby and C. M. Wynne. The process also led to the foundation of the National Federation of Housing Societies which focused its attention on the constructional aspects of the sector's work. The HCT archive is now housed with the Harry Simpson Memorial Library in premises at the University of Westminster. I am grateful to Marjorie Cleaver for giving me access to the papers at the Housing Centre Trust's premises.

40 File c/5 in HCT archive.

41 A history of the Housing Centre remains to be written but a valuable account of its activities since its foundation may be found in a special issue of *Housing Review*, 35:5 (1984) celebrating its Diamond Jubilee.

42 The founding of the Centre saw the dissolution of the NHFO group and the organization of subsequent exhibitions became one of its functions.

43 The first documentation of the invitation is in the minutes of a MARS Group meeting held 11 March 1934 which notes that the Group had been offered 'one of the bays allotted to them at the Building Trades Exhibition for the display of MARS slum clearance programme' by Elizabeth Denby and Judith Ledeboer, Godfrey Samuel Papers (GSP), BAL/V&A, SaG/90/2.

44 'Slum Clearance: Short Term Programme', paper issued by the Executive Committee of the MARS Group, October 1933, BAL/V&A, SaG/90/2.

45 See E. Mumford, *The CIAM Discourse on Urbanism, 1928–1960*, London: MIT Press, 2000, 91–8 for a discussion of this activity.

46 The strategic catholicity of the Centre is reflected in the composition of its committees. The Executive Committee included stalwarts from the London voluntary housing scene such as its founding Chairman Reginald Rowe, long active in North Kensington, Anne Lupton of the Fulham House

Improvement Society, and Lady Pentland of the SPHIS as well as Judith Ledeboer. The Centre's Director of Research was Eugen Kaufmann who had formerly worked with Ernst May at Frankfurt, while its Technical Consultants included Wells Coates, Elizabeth Denby, Max Fry and Walter Gropius. See, The Housing Centre, *Annual Report*, 1938–9.

47 Minutes of a special meeting of the MARS Group, 11 March 1934, GSP, BAL/V&A, SaG/90/2.

48 Anon, 'New Homes for Old', *Town and Country Planning*, 2 (1934), 143.

49 The Housing Centre, *New Homes for Old*, London: The Housing Centre, 1934 (catalogue), 5.

50 Ibid.

51 J. Ledeboer, 'New Homes for Old', *Design for Today*, 2 (1934), 407–8.

52 Housing Centre, *New Homes for Old*, 7.

53 Minutes of a meeting of the MARS Group, 6 June 1934 record the decision to accept Fry's proposal. Ove Arup papers, BAL/V&A, ArO/1/2/4.

54 On Abercrombie and his method of planning see M. Dehaene, 'Urban Lessons for the Modern Planner, Patrick Abercrombie and the Study of Urban Development', *Town Planning Review*, 75 (2004), 30.

55 The device of chaos before planning had, of course, first been deployed in the EPIC proposal and would resurface as the opening device of the 'New Architecture' Exhibition in 1938.

56 Housing Centre, *New Homes for Old*, 8–9.

57 Both *Design for Today* and the *AJ* devoted several pages to reproductions of the panels and MARS' analysis of Bethnal Green. See Ledeboer,' New Homes for Old' and F. R. S. Yorke and R. Townsend. 'MARS Exhibit at Olympia', *Design for Today*, 2 (1934), 407–10 and 411–14 respectively, and Anon, 'The New Homes for Old Housing Exhibition, the MARS Contribution', *AJ*, 75 (1934), 425–7.

58 Housing Centre, *New Homes for Old*, 8. The emphasis on anonymity echoed Lubetkin's decision to give his practice a collective name rather than the more usual amalgamation of partners' surnames.

59 J. Ledeboer, 'Jocelyn Adburgham [Abram], obituary', *Housing Review*, 28:3 (1979), 71. Abram served on the Housing Centre's Council from 1937–74.

60 Housing Centre, *New Homes for Old*, 10.

61 In late 1933 Denby had been awarded a Leverhulme Research Fellowship to study social housing on the continent and the lessons it might hold for the British programme. Her findings were published in her 1938 book *Europe Rehoused*, London: George Allen & Unwin.

62 Ibid., 12. The balcony was designed by Janet Pott and Alison Shepherd.

63 See M. Allen and M. Nicholson, *Memoirs of an Uneducated Lady, Lady Allen of Hurtwood*. London: Allen & Unwin, 1975.

64 Housing Centre, *New Homes for Old*, 14.

65 *The Times*, 13 September 1934; clipping in the HCT archive.

66 N. Scott, *Challenge, Slum Clearance, the Faith in Action, 1833–1933*, London: SPHIS, 1933, 11.

67 I. Barclay, *People need Roots, the Story of St Pancras Housing Association*, London: Bedford Square Press, 1976, 22.

68 The account of the NSPG's activities given here is assembled from the minute books of the SPHIS Executive Committee and the NSPG's Executive Committee.

69 Barclay, *People need Roots*, 29. The fact that so many volunteers like Shaw or Day saw their work as what they would have called 'personal social service' has tended to mean they have left little documentation of their lives which is immensely frustrating to the historian. It is therefore impossible to say much more about them than can be discerned from Barclay's memoir and the record of their activities in the minutes of the SPHIS.

70 In her history of the SPHIS Irene Barclay, ibid., contrasts the more Conservative but inter-denominational politics of the NSPG, with the more Liberal and High Church politics of the parent body, but insists that when it came to the Society's work, all were apolitical. Its proselytizing was, however, heavily inflected by High Anglicanism.

71 The Countess' interest in urban reform is discussed in H. Meller, 'Gender, Citizenship and the Making of the Modern Environment', in E. Darling and L. Whitworth (eds), *Women and the Making of Built Space in England, 1870–1950*, London: Ashgate, forthcoming (2007).

72 The Pentlands settled in a house in Hampstead which, in a further sign of his modernity, the now retired Sinclair insisted be run by electricity because 'it was the coming power'. His advocacy of electricity was manifested in his son, also called John, who became an electrical engineer. He would briefly work with Coates and Pritchard as a Director of Wells Coates and Partners Ltd. On the Pentlands see Lady Pentland, *The Rt. Hon John Sinclair, Lord Pentland, a Memoir*, London: Methuen, 1928.

73 M. Baker, 'The Housing Centre Trust: The Beginning, Aims and Activities', *Housing Review*, 33:5 (1984), 160.

74 Ian Hamilton (d.1971) was a graduate of Magdalen College, Oxford, which had set up the mission in St Pancras from which the SPHIS ultimately derived. He qualified as ARIBA in 1920 and, on the recommendation of the President of Magdalen, went to work with the SPHIS from its foundation. See his obituary in *Builder*, 220 (1971), 19, 84.

75 See *Housing Happenings* (the SPHIS magazine), 16 (1933), 29 for an account of Athlone House. The funds for this had been raised, £10,000 by Christmas 1932, through a series of garden parties and 'at homes', two of which were hosted by J. B. Priestley and his wife Jane who would serve on the NSPG committee from February 1933. Priestley would later comment approvingly that 'Instead of spoiling the country, the Society was helping to rebuild London', *Housing Happenings*, 24 (1937).

76 See minute books of the NSPG for September–December 1933.

77 NSPG minutes record that the Society's usual architect Hamilton was happy to stand aside and allow the scheme to be designed by another practice.

78 In none of the surviving minutes is there any documentation of a discussion of whom the Society might commission to design the experimental block.

79 Lucas appears to have played no part in the design of Kent House. In all the references to the practice in SPHIS minutes it is invariably Connell who is mentioned with very occasional references to Ward.

80 B. Ward, 'Connell, Ward and Lucas' in D. Sharp (ed.), *Planning and Architecture*, London: Barrie & Rockliff, 1967, 73.

81 For an insightful analysis of the practice's work see D. Thistlewood and E. Heeley, 'Connell, Ward and Lucas, Towards a Complex Critique', *Journal of Architecture*, 2 (1997), 83–101; the discussion here complements their contention of the practice's conflation of the English Free Style and modernist principles in its linking of modernist and voluntarist ideals.

82 Minutes of the Executive Committee of the NSPG, May 1934.

83 'Working-Class Flats for St Pancras', *AJ*, 79 (1934), 885. This shows two blocks, one face-on to Ferdinand Street and linked to a second, rear, block by a walkway at fourth-storey level.

84 The first plans were actually submitted in July 1934 but the LCC did not consider them until the following October. Minutes of the LCC's Housing and Public Health Committee, October 1934 and May 1935, London Metropolitan Archive, LCC/MIN/7293–1934 and 7294–1935.

85 *Housing Happenings*, no. 20 (1934), 43. Jellicoe had died that year.

86 *Housing Problems*, (1935), production company, the British Commercial Gas Association (BCGA), produced by Arthur Elton and Edgar Anstey; directed by Arthur Elton and Edgar Anstey. All quotations are taken from this until signalled otherwise. Similar testimonies can be found in *Housing Happenings* and other publications produced by the voluntary housing sector in this period.

87 Scott, *Challenge*, 1–22. All quotations are taken from this text until signalled otherwise.

88 F. R. S. Yorke and F. Gibberd, *The Modern Flat*, London: The Architectural Press, 1937, 129.

89 C. Sweett, 'Kent House, Ferdinand Street, Cost Analysis', *AJ*, 82 (1935), 912–14.

90 Yorke and Gibberd, *The Modern Flat*, 103, 155.

91 Fry, 'The Architect's Problem', passim.

92 This tendency will be explored in more detail in the discussion of Kensal House in Chapter 5.

93 Wyndham Deedes (1883–1956) was Chair of the National Council of Social Service, an umbrella organization which sought to coordinate the work of local voluntary welfare groups.

94 'The North and South-West Groups', *Housing Happenings*, no. 21 (1935), 39. This article also reported a visit by the Duke of Kent, for whom the flats were named, later that month and that it was filmed by Leonard Day. The footage was incorporated into a film, no longer extant, called 'Castles in Chalk Farm'.

95 Ibid., 40.

96 See 'Kent House, Chalk Farm', *ABN*, 144 (1935), 349–52; Sweett, 'Kent House, Ferdinand Street, Cost Analysis', and 'Flats in Ferdinand Street', *Building*, 151 (1936), 21.

97 Yorke and Gibberd, *The Modern Flat*, 128–9.

98 Anon, 'The Contemporary House', *Design for Today*, 4 (1936), 3–4.

99 Minutes of the SPHIS Executive, 18 February 1935 and minutes of the Building Sub-Committee of the NSPG 5 March 1935.

100 Connell, Ward and Lucas' relationship with the MARS Group was difficult. Despite their early membership they constituted a rather separate grouping within the organization. Their urbanist efforts in St Pancras might be further understood as an attempt to demonstrate their commitment to MARS' principles but it was doomed. A year later they were effectively dismissed from MARS following their submission of a neo-classical style entry in the competition for Newport Civic Centre; on this see Sharp, *Connell, Ward and Lucas*, 11, 23.

101 See Mumford, *The CIAM Discourse on Urbanism*, 91–104.

102 For example, *Westminster Survey Group, Report on and Survey of Housing Conditions in the Victoria Ward, Westminster*, London, 1937.

103 'Chaos or Planning', Kensington Housing Trust leaflet, KHT archive, Royal Borough of Kensington and Chelsea Local Studies Library, no. 18025/46. See also, E. Denby, 'Overcrowded Kensington', *AR*, 73 (1933), 115–18 and J. Fletcher, 'Kensington builds for the Poor', *AR*, 75 (1934), 82–86.

104 Lewis Silkin himself would observe how valuable the work of the volunteers could be to municipal authorities (although he would not have countenanced their sole charge of housing provision). In a speech given when he presided over the opening of Athlone House – itself a sign of his approval – he referred to the fact that groups such as the SPHIS were able to experiment, an option not available to public bodies like the LCC. He noted 'Every mistake we make is multiplied manifold at a great cost to the people of London. We are watching the experiments of Public Utility Societies with great interest and are prepared to accept such as turn out to be successful'. 'North and South-West Groups', *Housing Happenings*, no. 19 (1934), 28.

105 This was established on 2 April 1935 at a meeting of the SPHIS Executive. It also agreed that should the survey result in a published report then it would be entitled 'Report on a Survey of the Borough of St P, prep by Messrs CWL in conjunction with (here would follow the names of the person consulted, an advisory committee or panel)'.

106 The organization of the survey was outlined in a memorandum by Connell of June 1935, minutes of the Survey Committee.

107 Only the minutes of the main Survey Committee survive and these stop, suddenly, in November 1937. Nor is there any further reference to the work in SPHIS Executive Committee minutes after this date.

108 Memorandum on Redevelopment in St Pancras under the Overcrowding Act of 1935, Letter 18 May 1936.

109 D. Sharp (ed.), *Connell, Ward, Lucas*, London: Book Art, 1994, 12 includes a photograph of a model of workers' flats, eight storeys high, which perhaps formed part of this scheme. The practice had also submitted a design to the 1935 Cement Marketing Company's competition for working-class flats on which they might have drawn.

110 Under the 1935 Act, areas which had more than 950 overcrowded dwellings qualified for clearance and redevelopment. Connell and Ward identified two such areas, one around Litcham Street, near to where Athlone House was sited, and the other from the no longer extant Seymour Street to St Pancras Station.

Chapter 5 The Modern Flat

1 A. Bertram, 'Housing the Workers', *The Listener*, 18 (1937), 1007–9. This series was subsequently produced as a Pelican Special, in collaboration with the DIA. See A. Bertram, *Design*, Harmondsworth: Penguin, 1938.

2 For example, he spent some time discussing the use of technology at the Quarry Hill Estate in Leeds and noted the 'noble' work of Liverpool City Council.

3   The other 'contender' for this title is the Quarry Hill estate designed for Leeds City Council by R. H. Livett and opened in 1938. Like Kensal House, it represented an attempt to apply new materials and technology to housing reform as well as incorporating social amenities into its planning (though not all of these were realized) and thus may be considered as its municipal equal. On balance, however, Kensal House remains the more progressive block. Its design was far more sophisticated, especially in the interior planning of the flats, while its emphasis on tenant-led management as well as the provision of social amenities from the start, point to a much broader conception of how housing might function than that which operated in municipal Leeds. The definitive work on Quarry Hill remains A. Ravetz, *Model Estate, Planned Housing at Quarry Hill, Leeds*, London: Croom Helm, 1974.

4   M. Fry, 'Kensal House' in Ascot Gas Water Heaters Ltd, *Flats, Municipal and Private Enterprise*, London: Ascot Gas Water Heaters Ltd, 1937, 56.

5   E. Denby, 'Kensal House, an Urban Village', in ibid., 60.

6   This account of the early history of the GLCC is drawn largely from S. Everard, *The History of the Gas, Light and Coke Company 1812–1949*, London: Ernest Benn Ltd, 1949.

7   This led to a prolonged period of lobbying parliament to secure legislation which required gas piping to be laid in all municipal schemes; it was finally achieved in 1934.

8   Everard, *The History of the Gas, Light and Coke Company*, 344.

9   'Report of the Proceedings of the Ordinary General Meeting of the GLCC, 5 February 1937', 8, held in the archive of the GLCC in the National Gas Archive (NGA), NT:GAL/A/R/9.

10 The phrase is Jack Pritchard's. It is worth noting that the GLCC's concern to adopt modern methods of office organization is akin to the sort of methods Pritchard sought to introduce at Venesta in the late 1920s.

11 Goodenough was Controller of Gas Sales between 1903 and 1931; his work at the GLCC is outlined in F. Goodall, 'Goodenough, Sir Francis William (1872–1940)', *Oxford Dictionary of National Biography*, Oxford: Oxford University Press, 2004.

12 'Report of the Proceedings of the Ordinary General Meeting of the GLCC, 8 February 1935', 4, NGA: NT:GAL/A/R/9.

13 Goodenough was also instrumental in the creation of the British Commercial Gas Association in 1912.

14 Minutes of the Directors' Court of the GLCC, meeting held 3 November 1933, papers held at the London Metropolitan Archive (LMA), B/GLCC/54. The archival material which relates to the GLCC and Kensal House is very limited. Though it is evident that the project was extensively documented, this material has not survived. The scheme's genesis can only be traced through the minutes of the Directors' Court held at the LMA which contain short summaries of the building's progress and through the sundry papers held in the GLCC papers at the NGA. Fry's papers contain no material pertaining to Kensal House and Denby's papers include only some blueprints of the plans.

15 S. C. Leslie (1898–1980) would become head of the GLCC's Publicity Department in 1936 and was responsible for much of the promotional work for Kensal House. An absolute 'modern', in the thirties he combined his work in Public Relations with membership of PEP and would later become the first Director of the Council of Industrial Design in 1944. I am grateful to Lesley Whitworth for sharing her work on this overlooked figure with me.

16 The architects were recruited on the recommendation of the RIBA, see J. Allan, 'The Unknown Warriors, Architecture in Britain in the inter-war Period', unpublished BA Thesis, University of Sheffield, 1969. Fry was then inveigling his way into the Institute as part of MARS' campaign to convert the profession. I am grateful to John Allan for allowing me to consult this dissertation.

17 Wornum's design for the RIBA Headquarters was nearing completion at this date while Atkinson had recently completed the entrance hall at the *Daily Express* building in London, and James, with Rowland Pierce, had won the commission for Norwich Town Hall (completed 1938).

18 The inclusion of a woman on a committee which dealt with the design of domestic services would not have been unusual at this date. The GLCC had already employed the kitchen expert Dorothy Braddell to write promotional leaflets for it in the 1920s and had a team of women advisers to

popularize gas cooking through demonstrations in shops. A lack of evidence prevents a definitive explanation for the choice of Denby as the 'other'. Fry claimed that he had persuaded the Company to let her join him on the Committee (see M. Fry, *Autobiographical Sketches*, London: Paul Elek, 1975, 143) but she was a member of the Committee from its inception. It seems more likely that she was already known to the Company through her work for Kensington Housing Trust. The GLCC was a local employer. In the 1920s it had provided exhibition space in its showrooms for the Trust's propaganda work for which Denby was responsible.

19 Minutes of the Court of Directors, 17 November 1933, 12 January and 9 February 1934, LMA: B/GLCC/54.

20 National Archive (NA): HLG/49/60 and LMA: GLC/AR/BR/17/075406.

21 The original proposal was to construct three blocks, two of which ran parallel to Ladbroke Grove, one following the curve of the, now demolished, gas holder site, with a third block at right angles to the Grove. In all these would contain 72 flats. The social club would replace four of these flats and was marked as an amendment on the first set of plans. The playground, occupying the site of the former gas holder, was added by March 1935 (GLCC Memorandum to the Minister of Health, 5 March 1935) and the nursery school in May (NA: HLG/49/60 Directors' Court minutes, 3 May 1935, LMA: B/GLCC/56).

22 'All-Gas Flats', *The Times*, 16 March 1937, 13.

23 Denby and Fry were about to commence work at Sassoon House when they were appointed to the GLCC Committee.

24 Leslie quoted in T. Haggith, 'Castles in the Air: British Film and the Reconstruction of the Built Environment', unpublished PhD Thesis, University of Warwick, 1998.

25 This was at the suggestion of the surveyor the GLCC had appointed to estimate the cost of redevelopment and building at Kensal Green; meeting on 5 October 1934, LMA: B/GLCC/55. It is possible that it was this recommendation which precipitated the reconceptualization of the scheme.

26 The local council agreed to provide a rate subsidy of £3 15 shillings per flat. This was on the condition that the GLCC formed a housing association and allowed the council to nominate tenants for the new flats from its waiting list; Minutes of the Royal Borough of Kensington (RBK) Housing Committee, 11 and 30 October 1934, held at Royal Borough of Kensington and Chelsea Local Studies Library (RBKCLSL). The Ministry of Health (MOH) subsidy was £3 10 shillings per person rehoused; NA: HLG/49/60.

27 The final permission was secured in November 1935 when the nursery school was approved. Minutes of RBK Council meeting, 7 November 1935.

28 This consensus would, of course, be codified by the publication of *The Modern Flat* in November 1937.

29 No figures for the costing of Kensal House appear to exist other than for the modern gas system. Given its structural similarity with Sassoon House, and the lowness of its rents (in part achieved through subsidy) it can be conjectured that its cost was comparable to the Peckham block. Balance sheets included in the *Annual Reports* of the Capitol Housing Association suggest the scheme remained in the black; NGA: GAL/ZCH/A/M/1.

30 Fry, 'Kensal House', 56.

31 In *The Modern Flat*, 27, Yorke and Gibberd argue that the use of direct access to a pair of flats, as at Kensal House, was a good one, allowing cross-ventilation and, on open sites, such as Ladbroke Grove, allowing orientation north-south which allowed west light for living rooms and east light to bedrooms.

32 This discrepancy has been explored in the author's, 'What the Tenants think of Kensal House: Experts' Assumptions versus Tenants' Realities in the Modern Home', *Journal of Architectural Education*, 53:3 (2000), 167–77.

33 The 1984 documentary film, 'Twelve Views of Kensal House', Capital Films for the Arts Council of Great Britain, producer/director Peter Wyeth, includes interviews with some of the original tenants which support this notion.

34 At ground-floor level the flats had two bedrooms in order to release space in the entrance halls for pram and bicycle sheds; on the upper floors there were three bedrooms.

35 It is noteworthy that located near Kensal House was the North Kensington Birth Control Clinic. Founded in 1924 by a committee which included Margery Spring Rice and Margaret Lloyd (a close friend of Denby) this was among the earliest such clinics in Britain. Like the Pioneer Health Centre, it was concerned to enable working-class women to plan their pregnancies and thus produce healthier babies. See *Annual Reports* of the clinic held among the papers of the Family Planning Association at the Wellcome Institute for the History of Medicine, Contemporary Medical Archives Centre and the small collection held at the RBKCLSL.

36 Fry, 'Kensal House', 57.

37 Marjory Allen, 'New Houses, New Schools, New Citizens', speech to a conference on the Pre-School Child held under the auspices of the National Council for Maternity and Child Welfare, 1 November 1934. Allen papers, Modern Records Centre, University of Warwick, MSS.121/NS/3/1/1.

38 E. Denby, 'Kensal House, an Urban Village', *The Phoenix*, June (1937), 12. It is telling that the primary purchase by the new tenants was beds. The provision of separate sleeping spaces at Kensal House was one of the most dramatic transitions for those who came to the estate from slum accommodation in which a bed was most likely shared by several family members.

39 N. Scott, 'A New Venture', *Housing Happenings*, no. 21 (1936), 16.

40 Anon, 'House Furnishing Ltd', *ABN*, 335 (1936), 62. The SPHIS Executive Committee agreed to the founding of a shop at its meeting on 21 October 1935 (SPHA Archive). The war brought the scheme to an early end and it closed in May 1941.

41 The HFL directors agreed to the sum of 5 per cent on top of the retail price as the hire-purchase rate; the more usual increase was 100 per cent. HFL minute book, meeting 20 April 1936, SPHA Archive.

42 Denby was present at the first meeting of the committee which ran HFL on 17 December 1935. Her fellow directors were Edith Neville, Stanley Shaw and Dudley Ryder. The shop occupied premises at 60 Seymour Street; now part of Eversholt Street, just by Euston Station.

43 HFL Executive Committee minutes, 2 February and 25 March 1936.

44 W. Coates, 'Furniture Today, Furniture Tomorrow – Leaves from a Meta-Technical Notebook', *AR*, 73 (1932), 34.

45 Scott, 'A New Venture', 16.

46 The rugs cost 1 shilling, curtain fabric between 1 shilling and 6 pence and 2 shillings and 3 pence and the embroidered cushions 2 shillings and 3 pence. See, Hydrangea, 'A Brave New Effort', *London Week*, 7 May 1936, clipping in SPHA Archive. Mention might also be made here of an advert for HFL which mentions 'polished birch chairs from Finland', suggesting that the shop was an early stockist of Finmar, see *Housing Happenings*, no. 23 (1937), 34.

47 This was two months after the SPHIS had decided to establish HFL. Pick reported this intention in a letter to Kingsley Wood, Minister of Health, 17 December 1935, NA: BT/57/A191/35.

48 As might be expected, given Pick's presidency of the DIA, the sub-committee was filled with DIA members and DIA sympathizers. They were: Denby, Cycill Tomrley, DIA activist, A. E. Barnes, of the High Wycombe and District Furniture Manufacturers' Federation, J. T. Davis of the Cooperative Wholesale Society, the kitchen designer Dorothy Braddell, and Francis Yerbury of the Building Centre. Press Release issued 20 May, 1936, NA: BT/57/A191/35.

49 Denby's hope was that with the backing of a state body, she would be able to encourage manufacturers and designers to develop new products which she could then sell in the shop. See letter from Tomrley–G. L. Watkinson (secretary of the CAI), 12 December 1935 and ongoing series of memoranda in NA: BT/57/A191/35.

50 Minutes of the Committee on Furnishing the Working Class Dwelling, 9 June 1936, NA: BT/57/A191/35.

51 Council for Art and Industry, *The Working Class Home, Its Furnishing and Equipment*, London: HMSO, 1937. There is not space to discuss the report in detail here, see, instead, my doctoral thesis. 'Elizabeth Denby, Housing Consultant, Social Reform and Cultural Politics in the inter-war period', Unpublished PhD thesis, University of London, 2000, especially chapters 7 and 8.

52 Council for Art and Industry, *The Working Class Home*, 42–3.

53 Ibid., 29.

54 M. R., 'Minimum Standard, Furnishing Design and Economics for the Mass Market', *Art and Industry*, 23 (1937), 66. The chair also featured in a later paean to good design Sadie Speight and Leslie Martin's, *The Flat Book*, London: Heinemann, 1939, plate 243 (the Russell chest and dressing table are plates 383 and 384 respectively).

55 Both this set and the Russell range were on sale at HFL.

56 This was sold under the name Denbigh, suggesting the guiding hand of Denby in its making. Indeed, workbooks in the Russell archive list it as the Denby range; correspondence with the archivist, January 1998.

57 Margery Spring Rice, *Working Class Wives, their Health and Conditions*, Harmondsworth: Pelican, 1939, 15.

58 S. C. Leslie, *Kensal House, the Case for Gas is Proved*, London: BCGA publications, 1937, 4.

59 It is worth contrasting this vision of a modern working-class domesticity with the vision of middle-class domestic modernity promoted at Lawn Road. In the latter, similar devices served primarily to liberate the single professional, man or woman, from domestic responsibility in order that they might enjoy, in Coates' words, 'a new exciting freedom'. Furthermore, while the family as a cohesive social unit was seen to be intrinsic to working-class progress, at Lawn Road the Pritchards' roof-top flat, though large enough to house the family, accommodated their two sons in a self-contained cabin.

60 Mrs C. S. Peel, *The Labour-Saving House*, London: John Lane, the Bodley Head, 1917, 46.

61 Information about the estate's colour scheme from an interview by the author with Kensal House tenants, 1999.

62 As John Allan has noted in his thesis 'The Unknown Warriors', this unit was the subject of immense research and study. A full-size mock-up was erected by the GLCC and tested for workability before it was approved.

63 The film will be discussed in more detail later in this chapter.

64 Bertram, 'Housing the Workers', 1009.

65 See Ravetz, *Quarry Hill*, 62–5.

66 Leslie, *Kensal House, the Case for Gas is Proved*, passim. The rents were at the cheaper end of contemporary rates. The Kent House three-bedroom flats were 13 shillings and 6 pence a week, at Quarry Hill approximately 14 shillings (two-room) and 16 shillings (three). No precise figures for the incomes of Kensal House tenants survive. In Denby, 'Kensal House, an Urban Village', 64, she notes that many were 'poor, many of them really poor – that is to say that they have about 3s 6d to 6s a head for food and clothing after they have paid their rent and outgoings'. The *Annual Reports* of the North Kensington Birth Control Clinic in the 1920s documented the average local workers' wage as £2 10 shillings a week, while Mr Norwood, featured in *Housing Problems*, was paying 10 shillings a week for two rooms.

67 Leslie, *Kensal House, the Case for Gas is Proved*, 11.

68 See, *inter alia*, B. Ehrenreich and D. English, *For Her Own Good, 150 Years of Experts' Advice to Women*, London: Pluto Press, 1979; S. Henderson, 'A Revolution in the Woman's Sphere: Grete Lihotzky and the Frankfurt Kitchen', in D. Coleman *et al.*, (eds), *Architecture and Feminism*, New York: Princeton Architectural Press, 1996, 221–53 and U. Maasberg and R. Prinz (eds), *Die Neue kommen! Weibliche Avantgarde in der Architektur der zwanziger Jahre*, Hamburg: Junius, 2004.

69 The Congress was organized by a committee that included the Director of the GLCC, David Milne Watson, and lasted two days. In addition to the 'Domestic' strand, the others were 'Manufacturing'; 'Agriculture and Distribution'; 'Educational and Training'; 'Distribution and Development'. There were also visits and keynote speeches. Full documentation of the Congress may be found in the two substantial volumes: Sixth International Congress for Scientific Management, *Papers*, London: P. S. King Ltd, 1935, and idem, *Proceedings*, London: P. S. King Ltd, 1935.

70 E. Denby, 'The Role of Organized Services outside the Home in relation to Scientific Management in the Home', in Sixth International Congress for Scientific Management, *Papers*, 154.

71 Ibid.

72 Shena Simon, Lady Simon of Wythenshaw (1883–1972), with her husband Sir Ernest Simon, was active in municipal politics in Manchester. In addition to her advocacy for women's citizenship, evidenced in her founding of the Women Citizens Association as a branch of the National Women Citizens Association, she also campaigned for better housing and for free secondary education.

73 S. Simon, 'Report', in Sixth International Congress for Scientific Management, *Proceedings*, 155.

74 We might say that it was also a North American concern since Christine Frederick took a similar view of the benefits of the rationalization of the dwelling. In her book *Scientific Management in the Home*, she observed 'Women have wrongly permitted homemaking to be both *a vocation and an avocation*'. To remedy this confusion of roles she listed appropriate replacement avocations which included reading more; daily exercise; membership of a local civic club or consumer league and 'giving a short moment each day to abstract thinking, and cultivating a well thought out philosophy of life'. See C. Frederick, *Scientific Management in the Home*, London: George Routledge & Sons Ltd, 1920, 502.

75 On New Feminism see H. Jones, *Women in British Public Life, 1914–50, Gender, Power and Social Policy*, Harlow: Pearson Education Ltd, 2000.

76 S. Simon, 'Report'.

77 F. and G. Stephenson, *Community Centres*, London: The Housing Centre, 1942, 4. This report reviewed the main centres which had been built under the 1925 legislation including those at the LCC estates Downham and Watling.

78 See, for example, National Council of Social Service, *New Housing Estates and their Social Problems*, London: National Council of Social Service, 1938 and the SPHIS's memo to St Pancras Borough Council cited in Chapter 4.

79 The Housing Centre, *New Homes for Old*, London: The Housing Centre, 1934, 14.

80 Anon, 'Opening of Kensal House', *Co-partners Magazine*, April (1937), 181–2.

81 For an exploration of how this process had an impact on one tenant in particular see the author's chapter, 'A Citizen as well as a Housewife: New Spaces of Domesticity in 1930s London', in H. Heynen and G. Baydar (eds), *Negotiating Domesticity, Spatial Productions of Gender in Modern Architecture*, London: Routledge, 2005, 49–64.

82 Leslie, *Kensal House, the Case for Gas is Proved*, 3.

83 Denby discussed the correct planning of communal facilities in her article, 'Housing', *Design for Today*, 2 (1934), 270–1.

84 E. Denby, 'First Report of the Council for Research into Housing Construction', *AJ* (Housing Supplement 4), 30 (1934), 942.

85 See N. Whitbread, *The Evolution of the Nursery-Infant School, a History of Infant and Nursery Education in Britain, 1800–1970*, London: Routledge Kegan Paul, 1972.

86 E. Bradburn, *Margaret McMillan, Portrait of a Pioneer*, London: Routledge, 1989, 140–4.

87 H. Myles-Wright and R. Gardner-Medwin, *The Design of Nursery and Elementary Schools*, London: The Architectural Press, 1938, 14. The 1918 Maternal and Child Welfare Act legislated only for children up to the age of two.

88 McMillan quoted in P. Cusden, *The English Nursery School*, London: Kegan Paul, 1938, 9. Cusden was the first Organizing Secretary of the NSA.

89 Myles-Wright and Gardner-Medwin, *The Design of Nursery and Elementary Schools*, 15. The Association's ultimate ambition was to convince government to establish nursery schools as an integral part of primary education.

90 Cusden, *The English Nursery School*, 15.

91 Ibid., 18–19.

92 Fry, *Autobiographical Sketches*, 144, refers to the 'indefatigably solicitous Lady Allen of Hurtwood' in his description of the production of Kensal House.

93 Denby, 'Kensal House, an Urban Village', 62.

94 Meeting of the Court of Directors, 3 May 1935, LMA: B/GLCC/56.

95   Children had a glass of milk on arrival, at noon and another with a sandwich before they went home. A typical lunch was minced meat, mashed potato and greens, milk pudding and baked apple for pudding, and a piece of apple and toasted bread. See, Capitol Housing Association, *Kensal House, a Contribution to the New London*, London: GLCC, 1937, 14–15.

96   E. Hubback and E. D. Simon, *Education for Citizenship*, London, 1934, (no publisher given), 12. The four principles were: a sense of social responsibility; a love of truth and freedom; the power of clear thinking in everyday life; and a knowledge of the broad political and economic facts of the modern world (achieved, perhaps, by listening to the wireless in each flat).

97   Cusden, *The English Nursery School*, 32–3.

98   Capitol Housing Association, *Kensal House*, 16. Both parents were expected to take an interest in their child's development, a practice which echoed the emphasis on joint responsibility for parenthood at the Pioneer Health Centre.

99   Denby, 'Kensal House, an Urban Village', 62.

100   Interview with tenants, 1999.

101   See plate 14 of Spring Rice, *Working Class Wives*, and scenes of club life in the Kensal House film.

102   Capitol Housing Association, *Kensal House*, 19.

103   Denby, 'Kensal House, an Urban Village', (*The Phoenix*), 12. The total population of Kensal House was 380, of whom 244 were children.

104   Capitol Housing Association, *Kensal House*, 18–19. Such a hope again reflects the influence of the Pioneer Health Centre on the estate's social programme.

105   No history of the FCA exists. The account given here is assembled from surviving minute-books held by the Association at its offices in Marylebone, London, from *Annual Reports* held in the RBKCLSL, interviews with the architect Janet Pott (1995) and Lady Angela Laycock, daughter of the club's president Freda Dudley Ward, (1997). There are also some references in the biographies of the Duke of Windsor (see, *inter alia*, F. Donaldson, *Edward VIII*, London: Weidenfeld & Nicholson, 1974). From the late 1920s, the Prince had interested himself in social matters, becoming a patron of the National Council of Social Service in 1928 and recruiting Denby, some time in the early 1930s, as an adviser on housing. The formation of the FCA was a response to his intimation that he would like to see his circle of friends make some form of direct contribution to the improvement of the conditions of the urban poor, something he could not do directly himself. Under the leadership of his then girlfriend, Dudley Ward, and the guidance of Denby, the decision was taken to raise funds to establish social clubs for the families of the unemployed. The first club was opened in Kensal Road, north Kensington in 1933, to the designs of Janet Pott and Alison Shepherd. Three more followed in Notting Hill (designed by Wells Coates and David Pleydell Bouverie), Chelsea and Marylebone. The club at Kensal House was the first to be designed as an integral part of an estate and replaced the first at Kensal Road.

106   Motto of the FCA on its *Annual Reports*, 1934 onwards.

107   FCA *Annual Report*, 1937–38, v.

108   This discussion also allows a more precise attribution of the design of Kensal House. The contemporary press invariably stated that it was the Architects' Committee, with Fry as executant architect and Denby as housing consultant, who were responsible for its design (see, for example, Anon, 'Kensal House', *AJ*, 85 (1937), 453). The evidence suggests that the attribution to the GLCC's official Committee had more to do with the project's rhetorical nature. The idea that its in-house team of experts had designed the flats fitted in with the progressive image the Company was trying to project. In reality, however, it was Denby and Fry who were its chief authors, and rather than work with the existing Committee they recruited their own team of experts to assist them.

109   Denby, 'Kensal House, an Urban Village', 60.

110   In 1935 only 17 local authorities in England and Wales had a housing manager in post; see M. Brion and A. Tinker, *Women in Housing, Access and Influence*, London: Housing Centre Trust, 1980, 72.

111   Denby, 'Kensal House, an Urban Village' (*The Phoenix*), 15.

112   Ibid., 64.

113 M. Fry, 'Deslumming', *AJ*, 74 (1933), 366.

114 Tenant quoted in M. Bruce Allen, 'What the tenants think of Kensal House', unpublished survey conducted for the GLCC, 1942, among the papers of the Improved Tenement Association, RBKCLSL. The GLCC was, in turn, contributing to the research which formed part of the preparation of what would become the main wartime report on the future of social housing, *Design of Dwellings*, London: HMSO, 1944 (*The Dudley Report*).

115 See, 'Kensal House, special issue', *Gas Bulletin*, 26 (April 1937), 'Kensal House, an all-gas contribution to the new London', *Gas Journal*, 217 (1927), 716–17 and 'Application of Gas to Social Needs', *Gas World*, March (1937), 284–6.

116 'All-gas Flats', *The Times*, 16 March 1937, 13, 20, 'Model Flats opened in North Kensington', *Kensington News and West London Times*, 19 March 1937, 6.

117 Leslie, *Kensal House, the Case for Gas is Proved*, n.p. Two versions of this were published. The first as a reprint of a lecture by Leslie given to the BCGA's annual conference, 26–9 September 1937, and then as a booklet proper in early 1938, with a cover depicting the rear block of Kensal House.

118 This was the same survey used by Tecton in its research for the housing in Finsbury, see Chapter 2.

119 Capitol Housing Association, *Kensal House*, 1.

120 Leslie, *Kensal House, the Case for Gas is Proved*, 19.

121 Advert for a *Daily Telegraph* and *Morning Post* supplement on the National Fitness Campaign reproduced in 'Gas Advertising Review', *Gas Bulletin*, 27 (February 1938), 23.

122 Advert in *The Phoenix*, June 1937.

123 Ascot Gas Water Heaters Ltd, *Flats, Municipal and Private Enterprise*, London: Ascot Gas Water Heaters Ltd, 1938.

124 B. Friedman, 'Foreword' in ibid., 5.

125 See J. Gold and S. V. Ward, 'Of Plans and Planners: Documentary Film and the Challenge of the Urban Future 1935–1952' in D. B. Clarke (ed.), *The Cinematic City*, London: Routledge, 1997, 59–82 for an overview of documentary film making in inter-war Britain.

126 Leslie quoted in Haggith, 'Castles in the Air'.

127 *Children at School* (GB) 1937 and *The Smoke Menace* (GB) 1937, both directed by Basil Wright and produced by the Realist Film Centre and John Grierson. They are reviewed, alongside Kensal House, in T. Baird, 'The World we live in', *Sight and Sound*, 6 (1937), 145.

128 Such films were not intended for general release but were shown to audiences ranging from the gas industry itself to film societies and voluntary organizations. They would also have been shown at exhibitions such as the Building Trades Exhibition.

129 Cusden, *The English Nursery School*, 192. See plates facing 80, 204 (two), 213 and plan of nursery school, 193.

130 Spring Rice, *Working Class Wives*, 16.

131 'Kensal House', *The Phoenix*, no. 12 (1937), 1.

132 National Smoke Abatement Society, *Britain's Burning Shame*, London: National Smoke Abatement Society, 1937. I am grateful to Tim Boon for drawing this pamphlet to my attention.

133 'Events and Comments', *ABN*, 149 (1937), 347 and 'Kensal House, Ladbroke Grove', 380–4; 'Opened Last Monday, Kensal House', *AJ*, 85 (1937), 453, 466–8; 'Flats and Nursery School, Ladbroke Grove, *AR*, 81 (1937), 207–10; 'Kensal House', *Builder*, 152 (1937), 687–92; R. Vaughan, 'Kensal House: An Analysis', *Design and Construction*, 7 (1937), 238–9.

134 'Kensal House', *JRIBA*, 44 (1937), 499–505.

135 'How to use Gas in Slum Clearance', *Architectural Record*, 82 (1937), 27.

136 'Kensal House, Ladbroke Grove', *ABN*, 149 (1937), 380.

137 'Events and Comments', *ABN*, 149 (1937), 347.

138 The schemes are Brinkmann and Van der Vlugt's *Bergpolder* Flats at Rotterdam, Gibberd's Pullman Court, south London and Gropius, Forbat and Scharoun's *Siemensstadt*, Berlin: Yorke & Gibberd, *The Modern Flat*, 41–63.

139 Ibid., 128–9, 102–3 and 98–101 respectively.

140   MARS Group, *New Architecture*, London, 1938 (no publisher given), 23. Other members, notably the group around Lubetkin, would have preferred a more politically oriented exhibition, on which see J. Gold, 'Commodities, Firmenes and Delight': modernism, the MARS Group's "New Architecture" exhibition (1938) and imagery of the urban future', *Planning Perspectives*, 8 (1993), 360.

141   MARS Group, *New Architecture*, all quotations are taken from this catalogue until signalled otherwise.

142   'The MARS Group Exhibition', *AR*, 83 (1938), 116. This issue of March 1938 includes an extensive set of photographs of the exhibition.

143   Ibid.

Part 3   Introduction: Towards a new Britain

1   E. M. Fry, 'Review of the Exhibition', *AR*, 83 (1938), 121.

Chapter 6   A living contemporary architecture

1   G. Stamp, 'Conversations with Erno Goldfinger', *Thirties Society Journal*, no. 2 (1980), 23.

2   Anon, 'Editorial', *Focus*, 1 (1938), 1.

3   Unit 15, 'The MARS Exhibition, reviewed by Students in Unit 15 of the AA School', *AAJ*, 53 (1938), 386–8.

4   Ibid., 386. All quotations are taken from this article, with page numbers noted in the main text, until signalled otherwise.

5   The reference to Daks was a calculated sideswipe. It was a brand of clothing sold at the clothing store Simpsons whose displays and advertising were designed by Laszlo Moholy Nagy who was also responsible for the overall design of the MARS Exhibition.

6   M. Fry, 'How Modern Architecture came to England', London: Pidgeon Audio-Visual, *c.*1975 (tape and slide set).

7   Anon, 'Editorial', 1.

8   That the MARS Group always intended to address the matter of education is evident in the fact that an Education group was to be one of its first sub-committees, with John Summerson and Christopher Nicholson pencilled in as potential appointees to it (Memorandum, n.d., *c.* April 1933, and Circular Letter, 31 October 1933, Godfrey Samuel Papers, BAL/V&A, SaG/90/2). This group appears to have achieved little. A renewed attempt to instigate 'propaganda work in schools' was made in October 1935 but again, nothing concrete arose from this decision (Draft Report on Policy and Programme, 6 February 1936, ibid.). The lack of action can be attributed less to inertia on MARS' part and more to the difficulty its members found in combining private practice with the commitments the Group had to CIAM and NHFO.

9   For this necessarily abbreviated account of the professionalization of British architectural practice I draw on J. Wilton Ely, 'The Professional Architect in England' in S. Kostof (ed.), *The Architect: Chapters in the History of a Profession*, Oxford: OUP, 1977, 180–208 and M. Crinson and J. Lubbock, *Architecture – Art or Profession*, Manchester, Manchester University Press, 1994.

10   Crinson and Lubbock, *Architecture – Art or Profession*, 89.

11   It is worth noting here the hybrid nature of training experienced by the rhetorical modernists in contrast to the school-based training of the *Focus* generation. Fry (Liverpool), Goldfinger (École des Beaux Arts), Lubetkin (Vkhutemas in Moscow and Svomas in Petrograd), Lucas (University of Cambridge) and Yorke (Birmingham School of Art) had received an entirely academic training while Connell and Ward combined articled pupillage in their native New Zealand with diplomas at the Bartlett School of the University of London. Others had no formal architectural training at all: Chermayeff (professional ballroom dancer then Director of Modern Art Studio at Waring and Gillow, his wife's family's firm) and Coates (background in engineering and a PhD on the diesel engine).

12   The activities of AA students were paralleled by a wave of activism at other schools, most notably Liverpool and Hull. The agitation at the AA is, however, comparatively better documented (although the archival material is somewhat contingent). It is for this reason that the discussion here is

necessarily metropolitan in its focus. The ultimate transformation of architectural education was, of course, due to the combined efforts of these modernist revolutionaries. A full history of this vibrant phase in British architectural history remains to be written.

13 On the first 100 years of the AA see J. Summerson, *The Architectural Association, 1847–1947*, London: Pleiades Books, 1947.

14 Howard Robertson (1888–1963) had trained at the AA before taking the Diploma at the École des Beaux Arts in 1913. His series of autobiographical sketches are the most useful source on his career, see 'Obbligato to Architecture', *The Builder*, 202 (April–June 1962).

15 As Crinson and Lubbock note in their study, *Architecture – Art or Profession*, 100. Further, as Anthony Jackson has noted, although Robertson and Yerbury's survey of European work included high modernist work such as the Weissenhof Siedlung, Robertson's preferences were for the more conservative modernism of the Dutch and the Swedes. At the same time, his work in private practice, such as the Royal Horticultural Society Hall, London 1928 (with J. Murray Easton), though structurally bold, adhered stylistically to the traditions of the neo-Georgian. See A. Jackson, *The Politics of Architecture*, London: The Architectural Press, 1970, 16–17.

16 Illustrations of student work in the AA *Prospectus* for 1931–2 (held in the AA Collection in the AA Library, London) demonstrate the evolution of this influence. It includes, for example, Justin Blanco White's exquisite first-year rendering of the Greek Doric order then, a few pages later, her third year project for a small sports club which has strong echoes of Dudok's work at Hilversum.

17 AA *Prospectus*, 1931–2, 4–5.

18 Interview between Andrew Saint and Anthony Cox, July 1984, National Sound Archive, British Library (NSA/BL).

19 Recollections of Gardner-Medwin recorded in M. Pattrick, 'Architectural Aspirations', *AAJ*, 73 (1958), 158.

20 'Assistant Director of the AA School', *AAJ*, 69 (1933–4), 169. Rowse (b.1896) remains a rather obscure figure. A brief discussion of his life may be found in K. Watts, *Outwards from Home: a Planner's Odyssey*, Sussex: The Book Guild Ltd, 1997, 54–6.

21 The archives of the AA are extremely limited and to date no copies of Council minutes have been discovered. For this account I rely on the papers of some of those involved, interviews and contemporary reports. I have also drawn on discussions of Rowse by Crinson and Lubbock, *Architecture – Art or Profession*, 100–1 and A. Saint, *Towards a Social Architecture, The Role of School Building in Post-war England*, London: Yale University Press, 1987, 2–3.

22 Watts, *Outwards from Home*, 3.

23 In a valedictory note on the occasion of Rowse's retirement, 'H. P.' stated that Rowse was 'solely responsible for the idea of the school', see H. P., 'A Personal Note', *AAJ*, 53 (1938), 523.

24 AA, *School of Planning and Research for National Development*, London: the AA, c.1935, 14.

25 Anon, 'The School of Planning and Research for National Development', *AAJ*, 50 (1935), 302.

26 AA, *School of Planning and Research for National Development*, 18–21.

27 Ibid., 22.

28 As Alan Powers has observed, see his comments in his *Look Stranger at this Island Now, English Architectural Drawings of the 1930s*, London: AA, 1983, 33.

29 A further reason for the watchfulness of the AA Council was that since early 1935 the government's Board of Education (BOE), which supported the AA with a grant, had been expressing concern about the School's constitution. The origins of the AA meant that it was organized not on an academic basis but as an association run by and for its members. So when they joined the School, each student was elected a member of the AA, thereby acquiring the right to vote at general and other meetings. In theory, therefore, and this was what worried the Board, they could affect the running, and hence the educational policy, of the School. If the AA were to continue to receive state funding then the BOE required it to take action against this potential threat to academic authority. The Council believed that it had resolved the problem when in July 1935 it introduced a new system of voting at meetings – a postal ballot would replace the previous (and

more manipulable) show of hands. This angered the students, while it mollified the BOE, but only briefly. In the longer term, the problem would resurface and with added urgency, for by this time the students were not simply rebelling against the attack on the vote but against the School itself. The papers of Godfrey Samuel at the BAL include a series of memoranda from the AA Council which document the ongoing debate with the Board of Education, see in particular 'Memorandum from the AA Council' n.d. (*c.* July 1938) in SaG/89/3. For existing accounts of this period in the AA's history see, M. O. Ashton, 'Tomorrow Town: Patrick Geddes, Walter Gropius, and Le Corbusier' in V. M. Welter and J. Lawson (eds), *The City after Patrick Geddes*, Bern: Peter Lang, 2000; Crinson and Lubbock, *Architecture – Art or Profession*, 100–10; Pattrick, 'Architectural Aspirations', 147–59; Saint, *Towards a Social Architecture*; and Summerson, *The Architectural Association 1847–1947*. See also the author's, 'Into the world of conscious expression: Modernist Revolutionaries at the AA, 1933–1939', in I. Boyd Whyte (ed.), *The Manmade Future, Planning, Education and Design in Mid-20th Century Britain*, London: Routledge, 2006.

30 Crinson and Lubbock, *Architecture – Art or Profession*, 100.

31 Ibid.

32 Anon, 'The AA Story 1936–1939', *Focus*, 3 (1939), 83.

33 Ibid.

34 Saint and Cox interview.

35 Cox reported in Anon, 'Quo Vadis, AA', *AAJ*, 67 (1952), 207.

36 Bruce Martin would recall that within two months of Tim Bennett bringing a copy of Le Corbusier's *Oeuvre Complet* into the school 'he had converted our year, our unit'. Interview between Andrew Saint and Bruce Martin, March 1984, NSA/BL.

37 Saint and Cox interview.

38 Saint and Martin interview.

39 Saint and Cox interview. This approach to communist politics reflects the policy of the CPGB at this time. In a shift from its previously proletarian focused line, it now sought to encourage activism among intellectuals which would target middle-class institutions. This is discussed in S. Parsons, 'Communism in the Professions: The Organisation of the British Communist Party Among Professional Workers, 1933–1965', unpublished PhD thesis, University of Warwick, 1991, I am grateful to Louise Campbell for this reference.

40 Saint and Cox interview.

41 The speech is transcribed in the *AAJ*, 52 (1937), 381–4.

42 Ibid., 381–2.

43 Ibid., 383.

44 Anon, 'The AA Story 1936–1939', 86 (this includes a reprint of the Yellow Book). The author was almost certainly Anthony Cox.

45 The lack of evidence underpinning the AA story makes it difficult to know who, precisely, were the authors of the Yellow Book. Cox and Llewellyn Davies are obvious candidates but who else remains uncertain. All questions taken from the book are signalled by page numbers in the main text.

46 Saint, *Towards a Social Architecture*, 3.

47 Anon, 'The AA Story 1936–1939', 97.

48 Ibid., 98.

49 For the whole text, and that of the ensuing discussion, see 'The Training of an Architect', *AAJ*, 53 (1938), 403–16.

50 Ibid., 403.

51 Ibid., 405–7.

52 Interview between Andrew Saint and Oliver Cox, March 1984, NSA/BL.

53 Transcript of Llewellyn Davies' response in 'The Training of an Architect', 412–13.

54 'Mr E. A. A. Rowse', *AAJ*, 53 (1938), 523.

55 Again, the dramatic nature of events owed something to the BOE's complaint about the School's constitution. The Board had made an inspection of the School the previous May and in February

wrote again to the Council to express its concern about this matter, adding that if the vote remained, then it would have to withhold its financial support. This threat was almost certainly the reason for Rowse's departure.

56 Editorial in *Focus*, 1 (1938), 1.

57 Saint and Cox interview.

58 My account of the *Focus* story comes from the Saint and Cox interview and also correspondence between Cox and Fry, July 1980 and Cox and Jane Drew, September 1987 which forms part of the Anthony Cox papers now in the BAL/V&A archives. I am indebted to Eleanor Gawne for enabling me to use these papers prior to their final cataloguing.

59 In the interview with Saint, Cox states that it was his idea for the name. He wanted something that sounded like Leavis' *Scrutiny*, from which he also borrowed the small quarto format.

60 Cox to Lock, 9 December 1940, Max Lock Papers, box 11.7: Hull, University of Westminster archives.

61 The retention of the unit system may have been a 'reward' for the loss of the student vote. Following the BOE's decision to suspend the School's grant in May 1938, the Council embarked on a series of votes which, in early 1939, resulted in the establishment of a probationary class of membership for students which did not include the vote.

62 Jellicoe's address of 15 February 1939 is reprinted as part of 'The AA Story', *Focus* 3, 107–11.

63 Interview between Andrew Saint and Elizabeth Chesterton, 15 February 1984, NSA/BL. See also, Rowse–Chesterton, 4 May 1939: 'most certainly I shall never call it "Tomorrow Town" again'. Cox papers (BAL/V&A).

64 'Tomorrow Town', typescript by P. L. Cocke, January 1973, Cox papers, BAL/V&A. See also Ashton, 'Tomorrow Town: Patrick Geddes, Walter Gropius, and Le Corbusier', *passim*, for a discussion of Rowse's influence on the two schemes.

65 For the programme and other details of the two phases of Town Plan I draw on Cocke's recollections of 1973 and his 'A New Town', typescript for an AA Students' Forum, May 1951, as well as surviving pages from the original report for the second scheme which are also among the Cox papers.

66 The group comprised a town planning team: Elizabeth Chesterton, P. L. Cocke, R. V. Crowe, D. Duncan, A. Pott, P. M. Thornton, J. Wheeler and a housing team: A. J. Brandt, R. L. Davies, D. S. Gladstone, J. C. de H. Henderson, A. W. Nicol, P. Saxl and F. L. Sturrock. TS, 'Tomorrow Town' by P. L. Cocke, 1973 among the Cox papers.

67 Cox, for example, designed the post-primary school as his pre-thesis project and a hotel as his thesis project. Elizabeth Chesterton designed a canning factory and Leo de Syllas the local shopping centre. List of projects in ibid.

68 Rowse's notes survive among Cox's papers.

69 It is likely that the students would have been aware of the development of the MARS Plan for London which was worked on from 1936 onwards. In its first incarnation, primarily the work of William Tatton Brown, the proposal was for a series of linear strips projecting into the countryside around London containing individual neighbourhood units, on this see J. Gold, *The Experience of Modernism, Modern Architects and the Future City, 1928–1953*, London: E. & F. N. Spon, 1997, 146–51.

70 See D. Hardy, *From Garden Cities to New Towns, Campaigning for town and country planning, 1899–1946*, London: E. & F. N. Spon, 1991, especially chapter 4. Hardy notes, 205–6, that the appointment of F. J. Osborn as the Association's new Honorary Secretary in 1937 galvanized the organization and prompted the publication of a new statement of policy which included the goal 'to fix in the public mind, as the pattern for future urban development the Garden City or Satellite Town – by which is meant a planned town, limited in size but large enough to provide a modern economic, social and civic life, designed both to live and work in, and surrounded by a permanent country belt'.

71 An early discussion of this planning concept may be found in E. Kaufmann, 'Neighbourhood Units as New Elements of Town Planning', *JRIBA*, 44 (1936), 165–75.

72 A photograph of a model of the prefabrication system for the terraced houses is included in 'AA School, Co-operative Thesis, Unit 15', *AAJ*, 54 (1938), 98.

73 Cocke, 'A New Town'.

74 Osborn's 1937 aims cited in Hardy, *From Garden Cities to New Towns*, 206.

75 Cocke, 'A New Town'.

76 See E. Denby, *Europe Rehoused*, London: Allen & Unwin, 1944 [1938], 77–9 and 236–8 for a discussion of mixed development schemes in Stockholm (Kungsholmen Estate) and France (Drancy-La Muette). It should be noted here that the advocacy of mixed development has customarily been dated by historians to the war years (see, for example, N. Bullock, 'Plans for post-war housing in the UK: the case for mixed development and the flat', *Planning Perspectives*, 2 (1987), 71–98). The existence of the three schemes discussed here allows us to push this date back and offers another example of the embedding of a wide, and complex, range of modernist prototypes well before thoughts turned to reconstruction.

77 Denby announced her proposal in a much publicized and highly controversial speech given to the RIBA in November 1936, entitled 'Rehousing from the Slumdwellers' Point of View'. She proposed what she described as 'a close urban development for working people, a mixed development which will bring in the strength of the better-off people to assist the more precariously placed working people, and proper provision for play, for recreation, for health, for fun'. Her design included terraced cottages for families at 40 per acre and flats for the childless or unmarried. Her speech and proposals are reprinted in *JRIBA*, 44 (1936), 61–80. This proposal was later re-worked as the All-Europe House and plan for a site in North London exhibited at the *Daily Mail* Ideal Home Exhibition of 1939, on which see Anon, 'The All-Europe House designed by Elizabeth Denby', *JRIBA*, 46 (1939), 813–19. I discuss both these projects and their context in my '"The Star in the Profession she invented for herself": a brief biography of Elizabeth Denby, housing consultant', *Planning Perspectives*, 20: 3 (2005), 271–300.

78 The scheme was produced for the Cement and Concrete Association in early 1936. Breuer would lecture about it to the students of the Regent Street Polytechnic in the December. A transcript of his talk, and related correspondence from August–December 1936, may be found in the Yorke Papers (BAL/V&A), YoF/2/3. The scheme was subsequently published in J. L. Martin, B. Nicholson and N. Gabo (eds), *Circle, International Survey of Constructive Art*, London: Faber & Faber, 1937, 181–3. In terms of aesthetics, this scheme was quite influential on Unit 15, socially, however, in Yorke and Breuer's proposal there is less integration of social services, flats and houses.

79 Gold, *The Experience of Modernism*, 148–9.

80 It is telling therefore, that the older generation could not quite divorce themselves from their rhetorical tendencies. The final version of the MARS Plan (published in 1942) comprised high flats only for, as Fry recalled, 'houses-with-gardens had no place then in our view of the future'. Fry cited in ibid., 151.

81 The students were David Gladstone, who flew the plane, and Michael Grice, who took the photographs. Source: Grice in discussion with the author, ACP evening held by the 20th Century Society, London, September 2005. The resulting photographs are among Cox's papers.

82 This is listed in a description of the project prepared by the students for the US Housing Authority, 'A Plan for a New Town near Faringdon', undated typescript among Cox papers.

83 A short outline of the project with illustrations of some of this copious material may be found in 'AA School Co-operative thesis', 89–98.

84 Typescripts of jury comments, spring term 1938, among Cox papers. Other critics included Thomas Wallis (of Wallis, Gilbert and Partners), E. D. Brandt of the Railway Research Station, Major Hardy Sims of the SPRND, E. C. Willats of the Land Utilisation Survey at the LSE, each chosen for their specific expertise. Basil Ward, the AA's External Examiner would also comment favourably on the work.

85 J.Summerson, 'Exhibition of Students' Work, session 1937–38', *AAJ*, 53 (1938), 68–72, all quotations are taken from this article until signalled otherwise.

86 The students had already ensured that the pre-thesis plan was publicized at the exhibition 'Satellite Towns' held at the Housing Centre in May 1937, see *AAJ*, 52 (1936–37), 475.

87 See *Focus* 1, 1938, 12–23. More specifically, 'Town Plan' began on the page facing Le Corbusier's valedictory aphorism: 'Architecture is organisation. YOU ARE AN ORGANISER, NOT A DRAWING-BOARD STYLIST' [sic].

88 See 'Road Architecture – the Need for a Plan', *JRIBA*, 46 (1939), 503, 505–9 (the latter being a transcript of the opening speech given by Herbert Morrison).

89 '"Optimopolis" is dream city of youth', undated clipping from the *Daily Herald* in the Cox papers.

90 E. A. A. Rowse, 'The Planning of a City', *Journal of the Town Planning Institute*, 25 (1939), 167–71.

91 For many of the students involved it led to the creation of the Architects' Co-operative Partnership (ACP). Formed by Kenneth Capon, Peter Cocke, Michael Cooke-Yarborough, Anthony Cox, Leo de Syllas, Michael Grice, Arthur Nichol, Anthony Pott, Greville Rhodes, Michael Powers and John Wheeler in early 1939, it sought to bring the methods developed at the AA into professional practice; their politics were reflected in the fact that it was organized as a co-operative. After the war ACP would make its name with the Brynmawr Rubber Factory, south Wales (completed 1951), one of the first large-scale modernist projects to be completed as reconstruction began. The firm would subsequently specialize in school and university architecture. On ACP see V. Perry, *Built for a Better Future: The Brynmawr Rubber Factory*, Oxford: White Cockade Publishing, 1994. Llewellyn Davies would go on to direct the Investigation into Function and Design of Hospitals under the auspices of the Nuffield Foundation from 1948–60 before becoming Professor of Architecture at the Bartlett School, University College London (see W. Dudley Hunt Jr, 'Llewellyn Davies, Richard', in A. Lee Morgan and C. Naylor (eds), *Contemporary Architects*, London: St James Press, 1987, 538–9). Elizabeth Chesterton would become a distinguished town planner (see E. Harwood, 'Dame Elizabeth Chesterton', *The Guardian*, 27 August 2003 (obituary)).

92 Both would be among the recommendations of the main wartime report on future housing policy, see Design of Dwellings Sub-committee of the Central Housing Advisory Committee, *Design of Dwellings*, London: HMSO, 1944 (also known as the Dudley Report). Of particular interest is its appendix, 'Site Planning and Layout in Relation to Housing', a report by a study group of the Ministry of Town and Country Planning. It argued for 'self-contained residential neighbourhoods of mixed types of housing' with 'amenities such as parks, playgrounds, recreational facilities, community buildings and shopping centres' (60–1).

93 Denby's influence is acknowledged in the interview between Andrew Saint and Oliver Cox, and in an interview between Saint and Max Lock and David Medd, August 1984, NSA/BL. In her speech in 1936 Denby would declare 'with all my heart I agree with the working man and woman that the choice for a town dweller between a flat at fifty and a cottage at twelve to the acre is a choice between two impractical and unnecessary extremes … it is safe to say that opinion is generally overwhelmingly in favour of some form of development which houses the people nearer to their work and nearer to the companionship of the centre of the town'. See Denby, 'Rehousing', 66.

94 On the AIA and the cultural politics of the Popular Front see L. Morris and R. Radford, *The Story of the Artists' International Association*, Oxford: Museum of Modern Art, 1983 and R. Radford, *Art for a Purpose, the Artists' International Association*, Winchester: Winchester School of Art, 1987. I draw on both for the account given here.

95 Alan Powers points towards the development of this concept in his essay, 'The Search for a New Reality' in J. Peto and D. Loveday (eds), *Modern Britain*, London: Design Museum, 1999, 28.

96 It is against this concern that we might also place the choice of furnishings deployed by the Council for Art and Industry and House Furnishing Ltd discussed in Chapter 5. A yet further, and related, narrative, and one there is not space to address sufficiently here, is that of the desire to produce a definably British modern culture. On this see, *inter alia*, D. Peters Corbett *et al.* (eds), *The Geographies of Englishness, Landscape and the National Past 1880–1940*, New Haven and London: Yale University Press, 2002.

97 The other students were Brian Field, David Goldhill, Timothy Grimm and G. Farjeon.

98 The notebooks survive, although some are incomplete, in the Mass-Observation Archive (M-OA) at the University of Sussex, see M-OA, TC Housing, 10/A, Strode Road, 1938 (Housing).

99 Saint and Cox interview.

100 Anthony Cox (in interview with Saint) would recall the significance of Rowse's idea of the 'action sequence': following the path which a person followed, for example, when they entered a room. ACP would apply this technique in their post-war work.

101 Folder for number 28 Strode Road, interview with tenant, M-OA, TC Housing, 10/C, Strode Road.

102 T. Jeffery, *Mass-Observation, A Short History*, Sussex: M-O Archive, 1999, 4, on which I rely for the account of Mass-Observation given here. Jeffery relates the organization back to the social surveys of the 1890s and to the contemporary emergence of market research in Britain; Gallup would open a British office in 1938.

103 Madge and Harrisson (1937) cited in ibid., 1.

104 Ibid., 21.

105 According to Cox in his interview with Saint.

106 Indeed, it may not be too far-fetched to contend that it was Cox and his friends' experiment in Strode Road which inspired Mass-Observation to consider housing as one of their subject areas in the first place.

107 Lock would visit Sweden and Finland in 1937. Max Lock Centre Exhibition Research Group, *Max Lock, 1909–1988, People and Planning*, London: University of Westminster, n.d. I rely on this short pamphlet for a general overview of Lock's life; to date there exists no substantial study of this significant figure.

108 Max Lock in interview with Saint.

109 Max Lock Centre Exhibition Research Group, *Max Lock, 1909–1988*.

110 See M. Lock, *Civic Diagnosis, a Blitzed City analysed*, Hull, 1943 (no publisher) and M. Lock, *The County Borough of Middlesbrough: Survey and Plan*, Middlesbrough: the Middlesbrough Corporation, 1946.

111 Lock quoted in B. Le Mare, 'Planning for the People, the Max Lock Survey and Planning Group', *Our Time*, 47 (1948), 248; offprint of article in the Max Lock Papers, 1: 24, University of Westminster Archives.

112 Lock, Medd and Saint interview.

113 Like Oliver Cox, both Medd and Madge would spend their professional careers pursuing the techniques first learned at the AA in the 30s. Cox and Medd would both work for the Hertfordshire County Council schools programme. Cox moved on in the early 1950s to work for the LCC Architects' Department, most notably at Alton East. Madge would later specialize in the application of sociology to architectural design and work for the Building Research Station after the war. On Madge, see his obituary by V. Hole, 'John Madge', *JRIBA*, 75 (1968), 479. The best sources on Cox and Medd to date are the interviews with Andrew Saint and his *Towards a Social Architecture*.

114 'Research Groups' manuscript dated 1 May 1939 in Box 11.7, Max Lock Papers.

115 Text from one of the ten diagrams outlining the final project, illustrated in 'Unit 11, Term's Subject' *AAJ*, 55 (1939), 68.

116 The questionnaire would ultimately contribute to the work conducted for a major wartime survey of public attitudes to housing that Mass-Observation conducted for the Advertising Service Guild. This was published as Mass-Observation, *People's Homes*, London: The Advertising Services Guild, 1943.

117 A copy of the questionnaire may be found in M-OA, TC Housing, 1/N Fulham Housing Survey and material from the final report TC Housing, 1/D Housing Studies, Stepney.

118 This statistic is not included in the archival material which survives but was widely cited in contemporary publications such as 'Unit 11, Term's Subject', 60. The other statistics mentioned here are taken from O.S.A. Report in M-OA, TC Housing, 1/D Housing Studies, Stepney.

119 The only illustrations which survive of the Ocean Street scheme are the two panels depicted in the *AAJ* article of August 1939, neither of which, unfortunately, given any indication of the materials or precise forms of the housing proposed.

120 'Unit 11, Term's Subject', 60.

121 B. Carter. 'Review of Exhibition', *AAJ*, 55 (1939), 53–5.

122 Had not war broken out, the scheme would have been accorded the publicity given to 'Town Plan' and been included in *Focus* 5. There it would have taken its place among articles by Gropius on 'Elementary Education' and reports on the Royal Commission on Industrial Population and on education at the Hull School of Architecture. Draft list of contents among Anthony Cox's papers, BAL/V&A.

123 J. Summerson, 'Introduction' in T. Dannatt, *Modern Architecture in Britain*, London: Batsford, 1959, 18.

124 Atlantic Charter cited in A. Calder, *The People's War, Britain 1939–45*, London: Pimlico, 1992 [1969], 264.

125 For a detailed discussion of the process of reconstruction see P. Addison, *The Road to 1945, British Politics and the Second World War*, London: Pimlico, 1994 (revised edition).

126 *Design of Dwellings*, 8.

127 Ibid., 53–4.

128 RIBA, *Housing, a report by the Royal Institute of British Architects*, London: RIBA, 1944.

129 Correspondence in the Fry papers makes it clear that Drew and Cox were responsible though no author is given to the catalogue. Two catalogues were published, RIBA, *Rebuilding Britain*, London: Lund Humphries, 1943, from which the quotation taken here is on p. 5. A compact edition was issued as RIBA, *Towards a New Britain*, London: The Architectural Press, 1943.

130 For contemporary responses to the posters see 'ABCA Posters', *AJ*, 97 (1943), 283 and the special issue of *Art and Industry*, 34 (July 1943). For more recent analysis see N. Games, C. Moriarty and J. Rose, *Abram Games, Graphic Designer, Maximum Meaning Minimum Means*, London: Lund Humphries, 2003.

Bibliography

Archival Sources

Architectural Association Library
AA Collection: lists of students; prospectuses

British Architectural Library, Royal Institute of British Architects
Ove Arup papers
Wells Coates drawing
Anthony Cox papers
Jane Drew and Maxwell Fry papers
Berthold Lubetkin papers
MARS papers
E. B. Musman drawings
Christopher Nicholson drawings
Harry Peach papers (Design and Industries Association)
Godfrey Samuel papers
F. R. S. Yorke papers

Canadian Centre for Architecture
Wells Coates papers

Design Archives, University of Brighton
Material relating to the Design and Industries Association

The Feathers Club Association, Marylebone
Minute books and Annual Reports of the Feathers Club Association

Harry Simpson Memorial Library
Elizabeth Denby papers (previously Building Research Establishment Library, Garston)
Documents relating to the New Homes for Old Group and founding of the Housing Centre

London Borough of Camden Local Studies Library
(Previously at Saint Pancras Housing Association Headquarters, London)
Saint Pancras House Improvement Society archive

London Borough of Hammersmith and Fulham Local History Library

Material relating to the Feathers Club Association

London Borough of Southwark, District Surveyors Department

Files on R.E.Sassoon House

London Borough of Southwark Local Studies Library

Material relating to the Pioneer Health Centre
Minutes of the Metropolitan Borough of Camberwell

London Metropolitan Archives

Directors' Court Minutes of the Gas, Light and Coke Company
Minutes of the London County Council Housing and Public Health Committee

Modern Records Centre, University of Warwick

Marjory Allen papers

The National Archives of the UK, Public Record Office, Kew

Papers of the Departmental Committee of Housing (Moyne Committee), HLG 49 & 50
Papers of the Council for Art & Industry, BT 57
Papers relating to construction of Kensal House, HLG 49
Papers relating to Central Housing Advisory Committee Sub-Committee on the Design of Flats (Dudley
    Committee) HLG 37

National Gas Archive

Gas, Light and Coke Company papers

National Sound Archive, British Library

Interviews with Elizabeth Chesterton, Anthony Cox, Oliver Cox, Max Lock and David Medd, Bruce Martin

Royal Borough of Kensington and Chelsea Local Studies Library

Records of the Kensington Housing Trust (including the Kensington Housing Association)
North Kensington Women's Welfare Centre: reports
The Feathers Club: reports
Minutes of Borough Council meetings, 1933–1938
Minutes of the Borough Council Housing Committee, 1933–1938

University of East Anglia

Jack Pritchard archive

University of Sussex Library

Mass-Observation Archive

University of Westminster Archives

Max Lock papers

Wellcome Institute for the History of Medicine Contemporary Medical Archives Centre
Pioneer Health Centre archive
Marjory Spring Rice papers
Family Planning Association archive

Newspapers and periodicals
The Architect and Building News
The Architects' Journal
Architectural Association Journal
The Architectural Review
The Builder
Co-partners Magazine
Country Life
Design and Construction
Design for Today
Design in Industry
DIA Quarterly Journal
DIA Yearbook
Eugenics Review
Focus
Garden Cities & Town Planning
Gas Journal
Housing Happenings
Journal of the Royal Institute of British Architects
Journal of the Town Planning Institute
The Listener
The Manchester Guardian
New Statesman & Nation
The Phoenix
The Spectator
The Times (London)
Trend in Design in Everyday Things

Unpublished sources
Allan, J., 'The Unknown Warriors, Architecture in Britain in the inter-war Period', unpublished BA Thesis, University of Sheffield, 1969
Darling, E., 'Elizabeth Denby, Housing Consultant: Social Reform and Cultural Politics in the Inter-War period', unpublished PhD Thesis, University College London, 2000
Haggith, T., 'Castles in the Air: British Films and the Reconstruction of the Built Environment, 1933–1951', unpublished PhD thesis, University of Warwick, 1998
McGrath, R., 'Recalling the 20s and 30s', typescript of lecture to the Architectural Association of Ireland, Dublin, 1972 (National Art Library)
Parsons, S., 'Communism in the Professions: The Organisation of the British Communist Party Among Professional Workers, 1933–1965', unpublished PhD thesis, University of Warwick, 1991

Published sources (contemporary)
AA, *School of Planning and Research for National Development*, London: the AA, *c.*1935
'The All-Europe House designed by Elizabeth Denby', *JRIBA*, 46 (1939), 813–19
Ascot Gas Water Heaters Ltd, *Flats, Municipal and Private Enterprise*, London: Ascot Gas Water Heaters Ltd, 1937

Bertram, A., *Design*, Harmondsworth: Penguin, 1938.

—— 'Housing the Workers', *The Listener*, 18 (1937), 1007–9

Binnie, R. and Boxall, J., *Housecraft, Principles and Practice*, London: Sir Isaac Pitman & Sons Ltd, 1929

Capitol Housing Association, *Kensal House, a Contribution to the New London*, London: GLCC, 1937

Carrington, N., '21 Years of DIA', *Trend in Design in Everyday Things*, no. 1 (1936), 39–42

Catalogue of the Exhibition of Industrial Art in Relation to the Home, London: John Murray, 1933

Chaplin, A. E., 'Youth and Housing', in England, K. (ed.), *Housing, a Citizen's Guide to the Problem*, London: Chatto & Windus, 1931, 97–102

Chermayeff, S., 'A New Spirit and Idealism', *AJ*, 74 (1931), 619–20

Coates, W., 'The Conditions for an Architecture for To-day', *AAJ*, 58 (1938), 447–57

—— 'Furniture today – Furniture Tomorrow – Leaves from a Meta-Technical Notebook', *AR*, 73 (1932), 29–38

—— 'Materials for Architecture', *AJ*, 74 (1931), 588–9

—— 'Inspiration from Japan', *AJ*, 74 (1931), 586–7

Coates, W. and Boumphrey, G., 'Modern Dwellings for Modern Needs', *The Listener*, 24 May 1933, 819–22

Council for Art and Industry, *The Working Class Home, Its Furnishing and Equipment*, London: HMSO, 1937

—— *Education for the Consumer, Art in Elementary and Secondary School Education*, London: HMSO, 1935

Cusden, P., *The English Nursery School*, London: Kegan Paul, 1938

Daily Mail Ideal Home Exhibition, *Catalogue*, London: *Daily Mail*, 1930

Denby, E., *Europe Rehoused*, London: Allen & Unwin, 1938

—— 'Rehousing from the Slumdwellers' Point of View', *JRIBA*, 44 (1936), 61–80

Design of Dwellings Sub-committee of the Central Housing Advisory Committee, *Design of Dwellings*, London: HMSO, 1944

'Designing for Health', *Country Life*, 77 (1935), 382–3

'The Exhibition of British Industrial Art in Relation to the Home', *Country Life*, 1 July 1933, 708–13

'Finsbury Health Centre', *ABN*, 158 (1939), 65–74

'Finsbury makes a Programme', *AR*, 85 (1939), 5–22

'Flats and Nursery School, Ladbroke Grove', *AR*, 81 (1937), 207–10

Frederick, C., *Scientific Management in the Home*, London: George Routledge & Sons Ltd, 1920

—— *Household Engineering: Scientific Management in the Home*, Chicago: American School of Home Economics, 1919

Fry, M., 'The Small House of Today', *AR*, 76 (1934), 20

—— 'The Architect's Problem', *AJ*, 77 (1933), 844–6

—— 'De-Slumming', *AJ*, 74 (1933), 366

Godwin, G., 'The Peckham Experiment', *Fortnightly Review*, 135 (1934), 189

'Health at a Shilling a Week', *The Listener*, 13 January 1937, 51–4.

Hitchcock, H.-R. and Johnson, P., *The International Style, Architecture since 1922*, New York: W. W. Norton & Co., 1995 [1932]

Holme, C. G. and Wainwright, S. B. (eds), *Decorative Art 1930, The Studio Year Book*, London: The Studio, 1930

The Housing Centre, *New Homes for Old*, London: The Housing Centre, 1934

Hubback, E. and Simon, E. D., *Education for Citizenship*, London, [no publisher], 1934

Hussey, C., 'The Grosvenor Estate, Millbank', *Country Life*, 68 (1930), 49–50

Huxley, J., 'Eugenics and Society', *Eugenics Review*, 28 (1936), 11–31

—— *Scientific Research and Social Needs*, London: Watts & Co, 1934

Kaufmann, E., 'Neighbourhood Units as New Elements of Town Planning', *JRIBA*, 44 (1936), 165–75

'Kensal House, Ladbroke Grove', *ABN*, 149 (1937), 380–4

'Kensal House', *JRIBA*, 44 (1937), 499–505

'Kent House, Chalk Farm', *ABN*, 144 (1935), 349–52

Lanchester, E., *Charles Laughton and I*, London: Faber & Faber, 1938

LCC, *Housing 1928–30*, London: LCC, 1931

Ledeboer, J., 'New Homes for Old', *Design for Today*, 2 (1934), 407–8

Leslie, S. C., *Kensal House, the Case for Gas is Proved*, London: BCGA publications, 1937

Llewellyn Smith, H., *The New Survey of London Life and Labour, vol VI: Survey of Social Conditions (a) the Western Area*, London: P. S. King Ltd, 1934

Lock, M., *Civic Diagnosis, a Blitzed City analysed*, Hull, [no publisher], 1943

London Housing Societies, *New Homes for Old*, London: London Housing Societies, 1932

'London Public Utility Societies', *Garden Cities & Town Planning*, 18 (1928), 162

Macadam, E., *The New Philanthropy, a Study of the Relations between the Statutory and Voluntary Services*, London: Allen & Unwin, 1934

McGrath, R., 'Mansfield D Forbes, An Intimate Appreciation', *AR*, 79 (1936), 173–6

M'Gonigle, G. C. M and Kirby, J., *Poverty and Public Health*, London: Gollancz, 1936

MARS Group, *New Architecture*, London, [no publisher], 1938

'The MARS Group Exhibition', *AR*, 83 (1938), 109–16

Martin, J. L., Nicholson, B., and Gabo N. (eds), *Circle, International Survey of Constructive Art*, London: Faber & Faber, 1937

Mass-Observation, *People's Homes*, London: The Advertising Services Guild, 1943

Ministry of Health, *Report of the Departmental Committee on Housing*, London: HMSO, 1933

'Modern Domestic Architecture, Some Houses at Silver End Garden Village, Essex', *Country Life*, 64 (1928), 601–2

Myles-Wright, H. and Gardner-Medwin, R., *The Design of Nursery and Elementary Schools*, London: The Architectural Press, 1938

National Council of Social Service, *New Housing Estates and their Social Problems*, London: National Council of Social Service, 1938

Pearse, I. and Crocker, L., *The Peckham Experiment, a study of the living structure of society*, London: George Allen and Unwin, 1943

Pearse, I. and Scott Williamson, G., *Biologists in Search of Material, an interim report of the Pioneer Health Centre*, London: Faber & Faber, 1938

—— *The Case for Action, a survey of everyday life under modern industrial conditions with special reference to the question of health*, London: Faber & Faber, 1931

Peel, Mrs C. S., *The Art of Modern Housekeeping*, London: Frederick Warne & Co Ltd., 1935

—— *Life's Enchanted Cup, An Autobiography*, London: John Lane, the Bodley Head, 1933

—— *The Labour-Saving House*, London: John Lane, the Bodley Head, 1917

Pentland, M., *The Rt. Hon John Sinclair, Lord Pentland, a Memoir*, London: Methuen, 1928

PEP Industries Group, *Housing England*, London: PEP, 1934

Pevsner, N., *Pioneers of the Modern Movement, from William Morris to Walter Gropius*, London: Faber & Faber, 1936

Read, H. (ed.), *Unit One, the Modern Movement in England, Architecture, Painting and Sculpture*, London: Cassell, 1934

'R. E. Sassoon House, Peckham', *ABN*, 140 (1934), 241–4, 253

RIBA, *Housing, a report by the Royal Institute of British Architects*, London: RIBA, 1944

—— *Towards a New Britain*, London: The Architectural Press, 1943

—— *Rebuilding Britain*, London: Lund Humphries, 1943

Richards, J. M., 'Pioneer Work at Peckham', *AJ*, 77 (1935), 514–15, 520

—— 'The Pioneer Health Centre', *AR*, 76 (1935), 203–21

Rowse, E. A. A., 'The Planning of a City', *Journal of the Town Planning Institute*, 25 (1939), 167–71

Scott, N., *Challenge, Slum Clearance, the Faith in Action, 1833–1933*, London: SPHIS, 1933

Singleton, F., 'Health Centres: Two Styles', *The Spectator*, 28 October 1938, 708–9

Sixth International Congress for Scientific Management, *Papers*, London: P. S. King Ltd, 1935,

—— *Proceedings*, London: P. S. King Ltd, 1935

Speight, S. and Martin, L., *The Flat Book*, London: Heinemann, 1939

Spring Rice, M., *Working Class Wives, their Health and Conditions*, Harmondsworth: Pelican, 1939

Stephenson, F. and G., *Community Centres*, London: The Housing Centre, 1942

Strathdon, 'The Transformation of a Victorian House', *Country Life*, 22 March 1930, 437–40

Summer, G., 'Plywood Furniture at the Pioneer Health Centre', *Design for Today*, 3 (1935), 219–20

Summerson, J., 'Exhibition of Students' Work, session 1937–38', *AAJ*, 53 (1938), 68–72

Sweett, C., 'Kent House, Ferdinand Street, Cost Analysis', *AJ*, 82 (1935), 912–14

Taylor, F. W., *The Principles of Scientific Management*, New York: Harper & Bros Publishers, 1911

Tecton, *Planned A. R. P.*, London: The Architectural Press, 1939

'Tradition in Relation to Modern Architecture', *ABN*, 125 (1931), 352

Under Forty Club, *Youth and Housing*, London: [no publisher], 1928

Unit 15, 'The MARS Exhibition, reviewed by Students in Unit 15 of the AA School', *AAJ*, 53 (1938), 386–8

Vaughan, R., 'Kensal House: An Analysis', *Design & Construction*, 7 (1937), 238–9

Westminster Survey Group, *Report on and Survey of Housing Conditions in the Victoria Ward, Westminster*, London: Westminster Survey Group, 1927

Yorke, F. R. S., *The Modern House*, London: The Architectural Press, 1934

Yorke, F. R. S. and Gibberd, F., *The Modern Flat*, London: The Architectural Press, 1937

Yorke, F .R. S. and Townsend, R.,'MARS Exhibit at Olympia', *Design for Today*, 2 (1934), 411–14

Published sources (post-1945)

AA, *Travels in Modern Architecture, 1925–33, Howard Robertson and F. R.Yerbury*, London: the AA, 1989

Addison, P., *The Road to 1945, British Politics and the Second World War* (revd edn), London: Pimlico, 1994

Allan, J., *Berthold Lubetkin: Architecture and the Tradition of Social Progress*, London: RIBA Publications, 1992

Allen, M. and Nicholson, M., *Memoirs of an Uneducated Lady, Lady Allen of Hurtwood*. London: Allen & Unwin, 1975

Arts Council of Great Britain, *'45-'55 Ten Years of British Architecture*, London: ACGB, 1956

Ashton, M. O., 'Tomorrow Town: Patrick Geddes, Walter Gropius, and Le Corbusier' in Welter, V.M. and Lawson, J. (eds), *The City after Patrick Geddes*, Bern: Peter Lang, 2000, 191–209

Baker, M., 'The Housing Centre Trust: The Beginning, Aims and Activities', *Housing Review*, 33:5 (1984), 160

Barclay, I., *People need Roots, the Story of the St Pancras Housing Association*, London: SPHA, 1976

Bayley, S., 'Patrons of the Modern Movement', *AD Profile* 24, (Britain in the Thirties), 90–5

Beach, A., 'Potential for Participation: Health Centres and the Idea of Citizenship *c.*1920–1940' in Lawrence, C. and Mayer, A.-K. (eds), *Regenerating England: Science, Medicine and Culture in Inter-War Britain*, Amsterdam: Rodopi, 2000, 203–30

Beddoe, D., *Back to Home and Duty, Women between the Wars 1918–1939*, London: Pandora, 1989

Bennett, T., *'The Birth of the Museum*, London: Routledge, 1995

—— 'The Exhibitionary Complex', *New Formations*, no. 4 (1988), 73–102

Benton, C., *A Different World, Emigré Architects in Britain, 1928–58*, London: RIBA Heinz Gallery, 1995

Berman, M., *All that is Solid melts into Air: the Experience of Modernity*, London: Verso, 1983

Best, R., 'Housing Associations: 1880–1990' in Lowe, S. and Hughes, D. (eds), *A New Century of Social Housing*, Leicester: Leicester University Press, 1991

Betjeman, J., 'P. Morton Shand', *AR*, 128 (1960), 325–8

Bowden, S. and Offner, A., 'The Technological Revolution that never was: Gender, Class and the Diffusion of Household Appliances in inter-war England' in de Grazia, V. (ed.), *The Sex of Things, Gender and Consumption in Historical Perspective*, Berkeley: University of California Press, 1996, 244–74

Bibliography

Bradburn, E., *Margaret McMillan, Portrait of a Pioneer*, London: Routledge, 1989

Brion, M. and Tinker, A., *Women in Housing, Access and Influence*, London: Housing Centre Trust, 1980

Buckley, C., *Isokon Exhibition*, Newcastle: University of Newcastle, 1980

Bullock, N., *Building the Post-war World, Modern architecture and reconstruction in Britain*, London: Routledge, 2002

—— 'Plans for post-war housing in the UK: the case for mixed development and the flat', *Planning Perspectives*, 2 (1987), 71–98.

Burnett, J., *A Social History of Housing, 1815–1985*, London: Routledge, 1986

Cahill, M. and Jowitt, T., 'The New Philanthropy: The Emergence of Bradford City Guild of Help', *Journal of Social Policy*, 9 (1980), 359–82

Calder, A., *The People's War, Britain 1939–45*, London: Pimlico, 1992 [1969],

Campbell, L., 'The MARS Group, 1933–1939', *RIBA Transactions*, 4: 2 (1985), 69–79

—— 'Patrons of the Modern House', *20th Century Society Journal* (The Modern House Revisited), 2 (1996), 41–50.

Cantacuzino, S., *Wells Coates*, London: Gordon Frazer, 1978

Carey, H., *Mansfield Forbes and his Cambridge*, Cambridge: Cambridge University Press, 1984

Carrington, N., *Industrial Design in Britain*, London: George Allen & Unwin, 1976

Coe, P. and Reading, M., *Lubetkin and Tecton, Architecture and Social Commitment*, London: Arts Council of Great Britain, 1981

Cohn, L., *The Door to a Secret Room, A Portrait of Wells Coates*, Aldershot: Scolar Press, 1999

—— *Wells Coates, Architect and Designer, 1895–1958*, Oxford: Oxford Polytechnic Press, 1979

Corbett, D. P. *et al.* (eds), *The Geographies of Englishness: Landscape and the National Past, 1880– 1940*, New Haven and London, Yale University Press, 2002

Cornforth,, J., *The Search for a Style, Country Life and Architecture, 1897–1935*, London: André Deutsch, 1988

—— 'Continuity and Progress, Christopher Hussey and Modern Architecture I', *Country Life*, 22 October 1981, 1366–8

—— 'Qualities of Generalship, Christopher Hussey and Modern Architecture II', *Country Life*, 29 October 1981, 1468–70

Crinson, M. and Lubbock, J., *Architecture – Art or Profession*, Manchester: Manchester University Press, 1994

Cullingworth, J. B., *Housing and Local Government*, London: George Allen and Unwin Ltd, 1966

Curtis, W., *Modern Architecture since 1900*, London: Phaidon, 1990

—— *English Architecture of the 1930s*, Milton Keynes: The Open University Press, 1975

Dannatt, T., *Modern Architecture in Britain*, London: Batsford, 1959

Darling, E., 'Into the world of conscious expression: Modernist Revolutionaries at the AA, 1933–1939', in Boyd Whyte, I. (ed.), *The Manmade Future, Planning, Education and Design in Mid-20th Century Britain*, London: Routledge, forthcoming

—— '"The Star in the profession she invented for herself": a brief biography of Elizabeth Denby, housing consultant', *Planning Perspectives*, 20:3 (2005), 271–301

—— 'A Citizen as well as a Housewife: New Spaces of Domesticity in 1930s London', in Heynen, H. and Baydar, G. (eds), *Negotiating Domesticity, Spatial Productions of Gender in Modern Architecture*, London: Routledge, 2005, 49–64

—— 'Denby versus Fry? A Matter of Attribution', in Martin, B. and Sparke, P. (eds), *Women's Places: Architecture and Design 1860–1960*, London: Routledge, 2003, 149–70.

—— '"To induce humanitarian sentiments in prurient Londoners": the Propaganda Activities of London's Voluntary Housing Associations in the inter-war Period', *London Journal*, 27:1 (2002), 42–62

—— '"Enriching and enlarging the whole sphere of human activities": the Work of the Voluntary Sector in Housing Reform in inter-war Britain' in Lawrence, C. and Mayer, A.-K., (eds), *Regenerating England, Science, Medicine and Culture in inter-war Britain*, Amsterdam: Rodopi, 2000, 149–78

—— 'What the Tenants think of Kensal House: Experts' Assumptions versus Tenants' Realities in the Modern Home', *Journal of Architectural Education*, 53:3 (2000), 167–77

Darling, E. and Whitworth, L. (eds), *Women and the Making of Built Space in England, 1870–1950*, Aldershot: Ashgate, (forthcoming)

Daunton, M. (ed.), *Charity, Self Interest and Welfare in the English Past*, London: UCL Press, 1996

Daunton, M. and Rieger, B. (eds), *Meanings of Modernity, Britain from the late-Victorian Era to World War II*, Oxford: Berg, 2001.

Davin, A., *Growing Up Poor, Home, School and Street in London 1870–1914*, London: Rivers Oram Press, 1996

Dean, D., *The Architect as Stand Designer, Building Exhibitions 1895–1983*, London: Scolar Press, 1985

—— *Architecture of the 1930s, Recalling the Architectural Scene*, New York: Rizzoli, 1983

Dehaene, M., 'Urban Lessons for the Modern Planner, Patrick Abercrombie and the Study of Urban Development', *Town Planning Review*, 75 (2004), 1–30

Donaldson, F., *Child of the Twenties*, London: Rupert Hart Davies, 1959

Ehrenreich, B. and English, D., *For Her Own Good, 150 Years of Experts' Advice to Women*, London: Pluto Press, 1979

Emsley, I., *The Development of Housing Associations, with Special Reference to London*, London: Garland, 1986

Everard, S., *The History of the Gas, Light and Coke Company 1812–1949*, London: Ernest Benn Ltd, 1949

Frampton, K., *Modern Architecture, a Critical History*, London: Thames & Hudson, 1987

Freeden, M., 'The Stranger at the Feast: Ideology and Public Policy in 20th Century Britain', *20th Century British History*, 1: 1(1990), 9–34

—— 'Eugenics and Ideology', *Historical Journal*, 26 (1983), 959–962

Fry M., *Autobiographical Sketches*, London: Paul Elek, 1975

—— 'How Modern Architecture came to England', London: Pidgeon Audio-Visual, *c.*1975 (tape and slide set)

Games, N., Moriarty, C. and Rose, J., *Abram Games, Graphic Designer, Maximum Meaning Minimum Means*, London: Lund Humphries, 2003

Garside, P., 'Central Government, Local Authorities and the Voluntary Housing Sector 1919–1939' in O'Day, A. (ed.), *Government and Institutions in the post-1832 UK*, Lampeter: Edwin Mellen Press, 1995, 82–102

Glendinning, M. and Muthesius, S., *Tower Block, Modern Public Housing in England, Scotland, Wales and Northern Ireland*, New Haven & London: Yale University Press, 1994

Gold, J., *The Experience of Modernism, Modern Architects and the Future City, 1928–1953*, London: E & F Spon, 1997

—— 'Commoditie, Firmenes and Delight': modernism, the MARS Group's "New Architecture" exhibition (1938) and imagery of the urban future', *Planning Perspectives*, 8 (1993), 357

Gold, J. and Ward, S. V., 'Of Plans and Planners: Documentary Film and the Challenge of the Urban Future 1935–1952' in Clarke, D. B. (ed.), *The Cinematic City*, London: Routledge, 1997, 59–82

Goldring, D., *The Nineteen Twenties, A General Survey and some Personal Memories*, London: Nicholson & Watson, 1945

Greater London Council, *The Survey of London: vol 37: Northern Kensington*, London: Athlone Press, 1971

Grieve, A., *Isokon*, London: Isokon Plus, 2004

Gruffudd, P., '"Science and the Stuff of Life" Modernist Health Centres in 1930s London', *Journal of Historical Geography*, 27 (2001), 395–416

Hall, M., 'Country Life and New Country Houses between the Wars' in Airs, M. (ed.), *The Twentieth Century Great House*, Oxford: Oxford University Department of Continuing Education, 2002, 57–74

Hanson, B., 'Rhapsody in Black Glass, Raymond McGrath interviewed by Brian Hanson', *AR*, 162 (1977), 58–64

Hardy, D., *From Garden Cities to New Towns, Campaigning for Town and Country Planning, 1899–1946*, London: E & F Spon, 1991

Harris, J., *Private Lives, Public Spirit: Britain 1870–1914*, Harmondsworth: Penguin, 1993

—— 'Political Thought and the Welfare State', *Past and Present*, 135 (1992), 116–41

—— 'The Webbs, the COS and the Ratan Tata Foundation', in Bulmer, M. *et al.* (eds), *The Goals of Social Policy*, London: Athlone Press, 1989, 27–63

Heater, D., *Citizenship, the Civic Ideal in World History, Politics and Education*, London: Longman, 1990

Henderson S., 'A Revolution in the Woman's Sphere: Grete Lihotzky and the Frankfurt Kitchen' in Coleman, D. *et al.*, *Feminism and Architecture*, Princeton: Princeton Architectural Press, 1996, 221–53

Heynen, H., *Architecture and Modernity, a Critique*, Cambridge, Mass. and London: MIT Press, 1999

Holder, J., 'Design in Everyday Things: Promoting Modernism in Britain, 1912–1944', in Greenhalgh, P. (ed.), *Modernism in Design*, London: Reaktion Books, 1990, 123–44

Jackson, A., *The Politics of Architecture*, London: Architectural Press, 1970

Jackson, S., *The Sassoons*, London: Heinemann, 1968

Jeffery, T., *Mass-Observation, A Short History*, Sussex: M-O Archive, 1999

Johnson, P. (ed.), *Twentieth Century Britain, Economic, Social and Cultural Change*, London: Longman, 1994

Jones, G., *Social Hygiene in Twentieth Century Britain*, London: Croom Helm, 1986

Jones, H., *Women in British Public Life, 1914–50, Gender, Power and Social Policy*, Harlow: Pearson Education Ltd, 2000

Kermick, J., *The Luther Factory, Plywood and Furniture, 1877–1940*, Tallinn: Museum for Estonian Architecture, 2004

Lasdun, S., 'H de C Reviewed', *AR*, 200 (1996), 69

Lebas, E., '"When Every Street became a Cinema": The Film Work of Bermondsey Borough Council's Public Health Department', *History Workshop Journal*, 39 (1995), 42–66

Le Mare, B., 'Planning for the People, the Max Lock Survey and Planning Group', *Our Time*, 47 (1948), 248

Lewis, J. and Brookes, B., 'A Reassessment of the work of the Peckham Health Centre, 1926–1951', *Millbank Memorial Fund Quarterly*, 61 (1983), 207–380

Lock, M., *The County Borough of Middlesbrough: Survey and Plan*, Middlesbrough: the Middlesbrough Corporation, 1946

Lubbock, J., *The Tyranny of Taste, The Politics of Architecture and Design in Britain, 1550–1900*, New Haven and London: Yale University Press, 1995

Lupton, E. and Abbot Miller, J., *The Bathroom, the Kitchen and the Aesthetics of Waste*, New York: Kiosk, 1992

Maasberg, U. and Prinz, R. (eds), *Die Neue kommen! Weibliche Avantgarde in der Architektur der zwanziger Jahre*, Hamburg: Junius, 2004

MacCarthy, F., *British Design since 1880, a Visual History*, London: Lund Humphries, 1982

Matless, D., *Landscape and Englishness*, London: Reaktion, 1998

Max Lock Centre Exhibition Research Group, *Max Lock, 1909–1988, People and Planning*, London: University of Westminster, n.d.

Meacham, S., *Toynbee Hall and Social Reform*, New Haven and London: Yale University Press, 1987

Melvin, J., *F. R. S. Yorke and the Evolution of English Modernism*, Chichester: Wiley-Academy, 2003

Merret, S., *State Housing in Britain*, London: Routledge & Kegan Paul, 1979

Moore, M. J. M., 'Social Work and Social Welfare, the Organisation of Philanthropic Resources in Britain, 1900–1914', *Journal of British Studies*, 16 (1977), 85–104

Morris, L. and Radford, R., *The Story of the Artists' International Association*, Oxford: Museum of Modern Art, 1983

Mumford, E., *The CIAM Discourse on Urbanism, 1928–1960*, Cambridge, Mass: MIT Press, 2000

Nicholson, V., *Among the Bohemians, Experiments in Living 1900–1919*, Harmondsworth: Penguin, 2003

O'Donovan, D., *God's Architect, a Life of Raymond McGrath*, County Wicklow: Kilbride Books, 1995

Oliver, P., Davis, I. and Bentley, I., *Dunroamin, the Suburban Semi and its Enemies*, London: Barrie & Jenkins, 1981

Pearse, I., 'The Peckham Experiment', *Eugenics Review*, 37 (1945), 48–55

Pepler, E., 'The Evolution of the Housing Centre', *Housing Review*, 33 (1984), 158–9

Perry, V., *Built for a Better Future: The Brynmawr Rubber Factory*, Oxford: White Cockade Publishing, 1994

Peto, J. and Loveday, D. (eds), *Modern Britain*, London: Design Museum, 1999

Pinder, J. (ed.), *Fifty Years of Political and Economic Planning*, London: Heinemann, 1981,

Plummer, R., *Nothing Need be Ugly, The First Seventy Years of the Design and Industries Association*, London: DIA, 1985

Porter, D., 'Changing Disciplines: John Ryle and the making of Social Medicine in Britain in the 1940s', *History of Science*, 30 (1992), 137–64

Powers, A., *The Twentieth Century House in Britain from the Archives of Country Life*, London: Aurum Press, 2004

—— *Serge Chermayeff, Designer Architect Teacher*, London: RIBA Publications, 2001

—— *Look Stranger at this Island now, English Architectural Drawings of the 1930s*, London, the AA, 1983

—— 'Simple-Intime, the Work of Raymond McGrath', *30s Society Journal*, no. 2 (1982), 2–11

Pritchard, J., *View from a Long Chair, the Memoirs of Jack Pritchard*, London: Routledge & Kegan Paul, 1984

Radford, R., *Art for a Purpose, the Artists' International Association,* Winchester: Winchester School of Art, 1987

Ravetz, A., *Council Housing and Culture, the History of a Social Experiment*, London: Routledge, 2001

—— *The Government of Space, Town Planning in Modern Society*, London: Faber & Faber, 1986

—— *Model Estate, Planned Housing at Quarry Hill, Leeds*, London: Croom Helm, 1974

Reed, C., *Bloomsbury Rooms, Modernism, Subculture and Domesticity*, New Haven and London: Yale University Press, 2004

Richards, J. M., *Memoirs of an Unjust Fella*, London: Weidenfeld & Nicholson, 1980

Robertson, H., 'Obbligato to Architecture', *The Builder*, 202 (April–June 1962)

Russell, D., *The Tamarisk Tree, Vol 2, My School and the Years of War*, London: Virago, 1980

Saint, A., *Towards a Social Architecture, The Role of School Building in Post-War England*, London and New Haven: Yale University Press, 1987

Saler, M., *The Avant-Garde in Interwar England, Medieval Modernism and the London Underground*, Oxford: OUP, 1999

Schwartz Cowan, R., *More Work for Mother, the Ironies of Household Technology from the Open Hearth to the Microwave*, New York: Basic Books, 1983

Searle, G.R., *The Quest for National Efficiency*, Oxford: Basil Blackwell, 1971

Sharp, D. (ed.), *Connell, Ward, Lucas,* London: Book Art, 1994

—— *Planning and Architecture*, London: Barrie & Rockliff, 1967

Solloway, R., *Birth Control and the Population Question in England, 1877–1930*, London: University of Carolina Press, 1982

Stallibrass, A., *Being Me and Also Us: Lessons from the Peckham Experiment*, Edinburgh: Scottish Academic Press, 1989

Stamp, G., 'Conversations with Erno Goldfinger', *Thirties Society Journal*, no. 2 (1980), 19–24

Stevenson, J., *British Society 1914–45*, Harmondsworth: Penguin, 1984

Summerson, J., *The Architectural Association, 1847–1947*, London: Pleiades Books, 1947.

Swenarton, M., *Homes fit for Heroes*, London: Heinemann, 1981

Tanner, A., *Bricks and Mortals, 75 Years of the Kensington Housing Trust*, London: Kensington Housing Trust, 2001

Tarn, J., *Five Percent Philanthropy, an Account of Housing in Urban Areas between 1840 and 1914*, Cambridge: Cambridge University Press, 1973

Thistlewood, D. and Heeley, E., 'Connell, Ward and Lucas, Towards a Complex Critique', *Journal of Architecture*, 2 (1997), 83–101

Vincent, A. and Plant, R., *Philosophy, Politics and Citizenship*, Oxford: Blackwell, 1984

Watkin, D., *A History of Western Architecture*, London: Laurence King, 1992

—— 'Architectural Writing in the Thirties', *AD Profile* 24 (Britain in the Thirties), 84–9

Watts, K., *Outwards from Home: a Planner's Odyssey*, Sussex: The Book Guild Ltd, 1997

Weight, R. and Beach, A., *The Right to Belong, Citizenship and National Identity in Britain, 1930–1960*, London: I. B. Tauris, 1998

Weiner, D., *Architecture and Social Reform in late-Victorian London*, Manchester: Manchester University Press, 1994

Whitbread, N., *The Evolution of the Nursery-Infant School, a History of Infant and Nursery Education in Britain, 1800–1970*, London: Routledge Kegan Paul, 1972

Wilton, Ely J., 'The Professional Architect in England' in Kostof, S. (ed.), *The Architect: Chapters in the History of a Profession*, Oxford: OUP, 1977, 180–208

Index

Illustrations are indicated in bold.

eBooks